A YEAR ACCORDING
TO ISHMAEL

A YEAR
ACCORDING TO
ISHMAEL
365 DAILY READINGS

ISHMAEL

Applying God's Word
to everyday life and relationships

Introduction

I have tried not to exaggerate any of the stories in this book, but I am afraid that they are only as accurate as my memory allows them to be. If any of you think that a story is about you or your church, I am sure it's not, but there again, it might be! My prayer is that God will speak to you each day, and as you read this book it will, in a small way, draw you even closer to Jesus.

Acknowledgments

Many thanks to the following for helping to jog my memory: Irene, Joseph, Daniel, Suzy, Mum, Heather, Tim, Andy, Tom, Lyn, Graham, Steve, Rod, Duggie, Belinda, Pat, Reg, Rob and Anthony.

Special thanks to the following for personal encouragement and help in my ongoing spiritual journey. In alphabetical order: Dean Peter Atkinson, Bishop Graham Cray, Bishop John Ford, Dean Nicholas Frayling, Bishop John Hind, Canon Peter Kefford, Rachel Moriarty, Canon David Nason, Canon Tim Schofield, Canon Derek Tansill, Deacon Brenda Waters, Deacon Moira Wickens.

To find out more:
www.ishmaeldirect.com

Foreword

When the old chap phoned me up to ask me to write this introduction, my first thought was one of fear – that he was calling about another computer problem. To say this is a regular occurrence would be something of an understatement and, according to my records, at least 98 per cent of these problems are 'human error'.

I am sure that some of the stories in this book will make you laugh, cry or both and you may even find yourself wondering if they are really true. In the cases of the 'golf ball injury' and the infamous 'chicken nuggets yarn', I can confirm they are both genuine as I was present at the time, either laughing or feeling a bit ill. In fact, I was recalling the latter tale to my flatmate yesterday, who responded with, 'That's strange, I always thought your dad was an intelligent guy!'

To me, Ish is a dad, a fellow Blackburn Rovers supporter, a golfing partner, a wise old man, a computer bozo, a Bible teacher, a cheesy action movie fan, an endless supply of drinks and curries, a storyteller (who is not afraid to laugh at himself or his own jokes!) and a friend. I hope you enjoy spending the next 365 days with him and perhaps, after you have finished the book, you can spare a thought for those of us who have had over 10,000 days of his crazy capers!

Happy reading,

Joseph

....

Dad has taught me a few valuable lessons over the years, some of the more important ones are:

Don't share a bedroom with him – after four years or so of touring on the road with him, I discovered that his snoring is louder than his singing.

Don't play golf with him – after numerous games I've discovered that he would rather spend time in the lakes and bushes searching for golf balls than actually playing the game.

Don't discuss movies with him – he rarely remembers the title, let alone the film. One of the most embarrassing occasions was when he was discussing with a group of us his thoughts on Kubrick's classic war film. The trouble was, he kept referring to it as *Full Leather Jacket*!

Don't watch a movie with him – watching any film with him usually requires someone having to explain what's happening every five minutes.

To be fair, he's a caring dad and he's been a great support to me. We have had some good laughs and fun times together over the years, as you will gather from this book.

Finally, the highlight of the year is the father–sons bonding weekend when we take our annual trip up to Blackburn for the Blackburn v Arsenal game – which is great, although, sadly, being the only Arsenal fan in the family, I am made to sit in the Blackburn end.

Thanks for fun times, Dad, love you loads, and mine's a pint of Guinness, please.

Daniel

....

What can I say about my dad that hasn't already been said or written? Well, he is very protective of me. When I was much younger and I had my first date with a nice Christian boy, he insisted on going to the funfair with us. The problem was, he never left us alone for one minute and even joined us on every ride! Then I recall the time when I was twenty and I booked a holiday abroad with my friends. Dad also decided to book a holiday at the same time in the same place!

A lot of people say that Dad and I are very similar, not just in personality, but also in looks. Apparently, I have the same-shaped head as my dad … BIG! I don't really know how to respond to that, except to say that as long as I haven't got the beard, I don't mind!

There has been many a funny story growing up with my dad, as I am sure you will read in this book. I have had some embarrassing times with him, but also some very special times, like when he gave me away on my wedding day and also conducted the service. Today, I still love our daddy-daughter times when we go for a drink or meal together and he gives me advice and we both put the world to rights.

It has to be said that when I tell my friends my dad is a reverend, they don't get it. Instead of seeing the normal clergyman in a collar quietly saying his prayers, they see someone who loves getting up on stage, preaching, dancing, making a lot of noise, socialising, going to the pub and ending the day with a curry. And, yes, he might do all those things in moderation, but underneath that fun exterior, Dad is a person who simply loves God. He has dedicated his life to being a Christian and helping other people. No doubt you will experience some of this in the stories in this book, and I hope you can laugh as much as we have through the years.

Enjoy the book,

Suzy

....

Ish asked me to write the Foreword for his first book back in 1988. By then we had been married for sixteen years. Now it's another twenty years on, and we have been together for over thirty-five incredible years. I would like to echo all those things I said about him originally and much more. As you might gather after reading this book, Ish is the first person I turn to when my car breaks down and the last when I need some domestic repairs carried out in our home. He is the first person I turn to when I need spiritual guidance and the last when map reading.

But joking aside, he has faithfully supported all five of our little family through thick and thin. He has worked tirelessly throughout his ministry and also in his role as a husband and father. He has kept a roof over our heads, he has fed us with endless curries and taken us on numerous holidays whether we wanted to go or not. He is good for us because he keeps us humble, but he's always the first to support our individual gifts and ministries. His natural warmth, openness and integrity has drawn an abundance of friends both inside and outside of the Church. He makes us laugh but he also makes himself vulnerable. He has been hurt and damaged, but has never become bitter. He is annoyingly positive and embarrassingly talkative. He is kind and generous and considers other people's needs before his own. Over the years we have travelled thousands of miles together. We have laughed and cried together. I am so grateful for the privilege of sharing this amazing journey with him as his wife and companion. In doing so my life has been impacted and transformed through our encounters with fascinating characters, numerous friends, and differing cultures. I have learned so much from Ish's astute and sometimes humorous insight into life, humanity and the Church.

As he enters into a new era of ministry as Deacon/Evangelist Missioner licensed to Chichester Cathedral, I know that the last thirty-five years have equipped him well for this responsible task. This is the culmination of all that has gone before throughout his eventful life. We are told that the ministry of the deacon is to herald Christ's kingdom by proclaiming the gospel in word and deed; to be an agent of God's purposes of love by seeking out the weak, the sick, the lonely and those who are oppressed and powerless; to make Christ known through a life of visible self-giving; to wash the feet of people including those we find difficult to like, let alone love; to shine as a light in dark places, and to reach into the forgotten corners of the world. This is a responsibility I know Ish has not entered into lightly. I look forward to seeing him not only join the procession that symbolically carries the gospel into Chichester Cathedral, but also to support him as he continually seeks to take the gospel out from there into a world that desperately needs to be touched by the compassion and love of God.

What more can I say? Ish, you are my best friend, my mentor, and I love you to pieces. I am so proud of you. What an incredible journey, what an amazing life, and the best is yet to come! Thank you.

Irene

01
JAN

'But the Lord stood at my side and gave me strength …' 2 Timothy 4:17

KEY WORDS 'at my side'

IT WAS SATURDAY, 1 January 1994. Three articulated lorries and a crane pulled up outside my front door. It was the Year of the Family and the BBC had decided to film their Sunday service around my family and me. It was chaos. The road was closed and electric cables were unravelled from all the vehicles and dragged through our front door. During the day we did some pre-filming at Arundel Castle and on the beach. This was fun because, as my talk was about the wise and foolish man, they decided to throw a bucket of water over me. Remember, it was January and freezing; fortunately, they did it in one take. Then came the Sunday when the live filming would take place in my lounge. Those present were my family, my mum and dad, and a few of the younger ones from the church. I am pleased to say that it went brilliantly, and although we were all very nervous of being filmed live on national television, it went without a hitch. There was only one very sad note: Dad's cancer was causing him great discomfort; yet, although he was in extreme pain, he wanted to be there. He would never want to let his son down, he wanted to be at my side until the end. This was one of the last times that Dad went out of the house; in less than two months he had died. Although I have a copy of that programme on video, still, all these years later, I have not been able to watch it. In today's reading, Paul was feeling alone and deserted. He had come under a lot of opposition and even some of his friends had left him. But Paul was sure of one thing; even though he was going through very difficult times, the Lord stood by his side and gave him all the strength that he needed.

THE POINT I am so grateful for my dad being at my side for this very important filming but I know that he was, like Paul, even more grateful that the Lord was standing by his side all through those final months of pain and suffering.

 PRAYER *Today, Lord, I realise that, whatever hardships I may go through, You are at my side.*

'The LORD said, "I will surely return to you about this time next year, and Sarah your wife will have a son." ' Genesis 18:10

'highly unlikely'

HAVING SPENT 35 years either leading or worshipping in the most extreme charismatic churches, I needed a change. It's not that the meetings were bad; the problem lay with me. I was bored with singing the same songs over and over again each week. I was bored by the preaching and prophecies, which seemed to have little or no content. To put it bluntly, I was as stale as old boots! I knew if I didn't change I would become a cynical, critical, miserable, discontented old man. I didn't want to end up like that, but was I too old for change? I was surprised when Irene suggested that we try a service at the cathedral. I though she must be joking. She knows that I am 'Ish the radical', the one who is totally anti-tradition; I'd even preached and written against archaic ritual! The cathedral could not possibly be God's plan for me – or could it? It would be highly unlikely for me to find God amongst old hymns, choirs, liturgy, smells and bells. But the highly unlikely did happen, after my very first early morning communion. Sitting in the vast cathedral with six other people, a dean and three cathedral canons, I met God in a brand-new way. One of the canons even told me afterwards that it was God's timing that I was there. Humble pie time, because he was right. Unlike most who go from the old to the new, I had to go from the new to the old to find a fresh walk with God.

Three heavenly messengers visited Abraham. After feeding them they suddenly came out with this amazing news: in one year, he and Sarah would have a baby boy. Abraham was surprised by their words. He must have thought this was highly unlikely to happen as both he and Sarah were far too old to become parents, but he knew that when God said something, even though it sounded impossible, God would do it.

THE POINT **God still speaks today, so keep listening and do not be surprised if what He is says sounds highly unlikely or even impossible.**

PRAYER *Lord, help me to listen to You today and to act upon whatever You say.*

03 JAN 'Shall I come to you with a whip, or in love and with a gentle spirit?' 1 Corinthians 4:21

KEY WORD 'whip'

I ONCE TOURED with a friend called Pete Gilbert. Pete was an evangelist who used tricks and escapology to communicate the Christian message. We called the tour The Great Escape. During the show Pete used a trick with a banana to explain the Trinity. To everyone's amazement, as he peeled the banana it came out in three equal sections. At his next performance in Swindon, I mischievously swapped his banana during a prayer time before the show. Of course I ruined his Trinitarian trick and Pete could not understand why the banana came out whole and not in three sections. He put it down to the heat of the spotlights welding the three pieces of banana back together, but when I confessed I had swapped it I was forced to do a great escape! Later, a company wanted to film Pete's escapes at an open-air festival in front of a live audience. I was invited to be part of the film, dressed as a ringmaster with top hat, red jacket and whip in hand. My job was to introduce his escapes. It was fun to watch him wriggle out of a straightjacket and even more exciting watching him escape from a locked oil drum full of water while handcuffed. It all went very smoothly, probably due to the fact that he would not allow me anywhere near his props. I also suspect that Pete kept his eyes open and fixed on me during any prayer time!

Although the film was supposed to represent a circus act, I never liked the circus much. I always felt that somewhere down the line, someone was cruel to these poor animals in order to make them do tricks that were not in their nature. I was sure that it was the fear of being whipped, not the joy of entertaining, that made them perform in front of an audience.

THE POINT **Paul brought correction to those who needed it by being loving and gentle, not through fear or intimidation. Today, if we need to bring correction to a member of our family or church, we must do the same, so that they love us, but never fear us.**

PRAYER *Lord, if I need to correct anyone today, help me to do it with love and gentleness.*

04 JAN 'The least of you will become a thousand, the smallest a mighty nation.' Isaiah 60:22

 KEY WORD 'growth'

I WAS BORN in Bristol into a small family. In our house lived my mum and dad, my older sister Heather, and a cat called Lucky. Little brother Tim followed twelve years later. Of course I had other relatives but they didn't live with us. When my parents began to be true followers of Jesus, we moved house to Sussex to become part of a Christian community. I was seven years old, and had no idea what this actually meant, but one thing that I did notice was that my family appeared to multiply overnight! There was Uncle Allan and Auntie Margaret, who were my real uncle and aunt, but then there was also Uncle John, Auntie Jean, Uncle Brian, Uncle Derek, Uncle Philip, Auntie Hilary and Uncle Tom Cobley and all! The number of my new 'uncles' and 'aunties' kept growing each week as more people joined the community. Although at times it was like being surrounded by dozens of parents, as every 'uncle' and 'auntie' felt that they had the right to discipline and correct me, the advantages far outweighed the disadvantages. This new extended family seemed closer to me than my blood family back in Bristol. The best thing was that being a lively seven-year-old who enjoyed kicking a football around, there was always some 'uncle' nearby who would be more than happy to stop what he was doing and join me for a game.

Although today's verse probably means that, with God's help, a small family can become a tribe and a tribe can become a mighty nation, it also reminds me of something else. When Jesus walked on the earth, there were only 11 of His 12 disciples plus a very small number of friends who proved to be true followers, and they were all living in Israel. From this tiny group, however, over 2,000 years later, there are now millions of followers of Jesus worshipping in every country in the world.

 THE POINT A little baby once born in a manger now has the greatest following the world has ever known.

 PRAYER *Lord, today I pray that Your Church will continue to grow in number and in godliness as more people give their lives to You.*

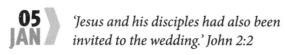

05 JAN 〉 *'Jesus and his disciples had also been invited to the wedding.' John 2:2*

KEY WORD 〉 'wedding'

IN ABOUT 1979, with a group of friends I formed a band called Ishmael United. We visited Holland on many occasions thanks to a crazy organiser called Frank. On one visit 'Crazy Frank' arranged for us to play at a wedding. We agreed to it for the cash more than anything, as this certainly was not an appropriate event for our style of music. But other odd things happened at this wedding. An offering was taken – literally *taken*, because Crazy Frank, for some strange reason, grabbed the offering bag full of money and started racing around the church building with it, leaping over pews and being hotly pursued by the ushers. The bride and groom and the rest of us just watched in amazement. But things got worse. After the service everyone was invited to go to the hall below to join in the reception. Crazy Frank beat everyone downstairs and picked up a plate full of chocolate éclairs and then hid. He then leapt out of hiding and proceeded to push a gooey éclair into each of the guests' faces as they walked into the reception area. I wasn't sure whether this was a Dutch wedding custom, or whether it was just Crazy Frank being Crazy Frank but, either way, to this day, I have never laughed so much at a wedding.

I don't imagine that Crazy Frank would have ever got on to the guest list of the wedding in today's verse. One of the things that thrills me about the Lord Jesus is that, while being God, He was also so human. He did not just attend church services and prayer meetings, He took time out to have fun and to be with His friends at weddings, parties and meals. He really was a friend of sinners. I sometimes meet Christians who have no idea how to enjoy themselves and mix with people. They are so serious and miserable that no one would ever want to put them on their party invitation list.

THE POINT 〉 **While on earth, Jesus was totally holy, yet He was someone people wanted to be with. I wonder how like Jesus we really are?**

PRAYER *Lord, throughout today, help me to be a holy yet fun person who can be friends with both believers and unbelievers.*

06 JAN

'People were bringing little children to Jesus to have him touch them, but the disciples rebuked them.' Mark 10:13

'time for children'

I ONCE VISITED a church and found the main pastor really hard to get on with. Now for me, this is a very unusual occurrence; I usually get on with everyone. This pastor seemed quite a hard man. He seemed good with adults but had no time for children. He really did not see them as significant and I imagine he thought they were only of value to Jesus when they reached teenage years. A while later I learned that this pastor had moved to start a new church in another town. The children's leader of this new church invited me over to minister to both adults and children there. I was a bit hesitant about going when I heard who the main church pastor was, especially when I remembered my past experience with him. I then reminded myself that I was doing it for the children and the children's leaders not for him. I led the first meeting and, to my relief, the pastor wasn't there, but as I was about to begin the second, he came and sat next to me. Immediately I noticed that there had been a major transformation in his life. He started telling me how important children were in this church and how the children's ministry was the fastest-growing part of the church. I was amazed and afterwards questioned some of the children's leaders and they readily acknowledged that the children's ministry had taken off and a lot of that was mainly due to their pastor.

So, let's not judge the disciples too harshly for thinking that Jesus only had time for adults since, I guess, many Christians still think this today. In most churches the adults are given more respect and treated as more important. Very often they have the superior venues, musicians, equipment, teachers, and, of course, a bigger budget. Even some parents consider their little ones a 'distraction' to their personal worship and, like the disciples, are relieved when their children disappear into another room so that they can spend time with Jesus without them.

THE POINT **Jesus had time for children. Let us try and emulate His attitude to children rather than that of the disciples.**

PRAYER *Lord, today I pray for the children I know. Please give me more of Your pure love for them.*

07 JAN

'The wicked man flees though no-one pursues, but the righteous are as bold as a lion.' Proverbs 28:1

 KEY WORD 'lion'

THE SUBURB OF Bristol where we lived during my childhood was called Horfield. The name Horfield derives from the Anglo-Saxon meaning 'filthy open land'. In the old days it had a reputation for being a lawless place full of thieves and vagrants. But in my early years, while Horfield was hardly the roughest area of the city, neither was it the most up-market. My grandparents lived in one of the nicest parts of Bristol in Clifton. They were located opposite Clifton Downs and close to Brunel's amazing suspension bridge. When my parents visited my grandparents, they would often let me go to the nearby Bristol Zoo. As a boy I would wander around, fascinated by the animals. The Monkey Temple would keep me amused for hours being full of hyperactive little monkeys chasing each other and climbing all over the concrete temple. I sometimes looked at the bears but found them a bit boring, as they just seemed to sleep most of the time. The only time they were exciting was when they plunged into the pool, drenching the watching crowd as they did so. But the scariest place by far was the lion enclosure. If I stayed just outside and watched them from a distance I was not afraid, but if I went inside the enclosure, as I always did, I was petrified. On entering, the pungent smell of ammonia almost burst my nostrils and then, just a few feet away from me, was a prowling lion with only a set of metal bars stopping it from eating me. When it roared I inevitably jumped and shivered!

Before Jacob died he said special words over his sons. He called Judah a lion's cub – this resembled royalty, strength and courage. Years later the Lord Jesus was born into the family of Judah, and in Revelation He is called the Lion of Judah.

 THE POINT As Christians we, too, should be like lions. We are children of the King of kings, so we are royalty, and we are bold because we have the power of the Holy Spirit filling us. The wicked may run away, but because we belong to God, we have nothing to fear.

 PRAYER *Lord, help me today to fear nothing and to be as bold as a lion.*

08 JAN

'Praise and glory and wisdom and thanks and honour and power and strength be to our God for ever and ever.' Revelation 7:12

 KEY WORDS 'true worship'

I WAS BOOKED to minister in a large church building in Southampton. I decided to take quite a few musicians with me as the organisers wanted me to play for quite a long period of time. The building was old with tiered seating, not too dissimilar to a small Roman amphitheatre. The strangest part of the building was the stage. This was certainly not built with rock bands in mind. It was so narrow that the only way that we could all fit on to it was literally to stand in a straight line. The meeting soon filled with people of all ages and all went well until we reached the third song. I suddenly felt the presence of God with such force that I could not stop myself falling to the floor straight on top of my guitar. I can assure you, this was not part of the stage act! It was then that the bass player hit the ground, followed by the keyboard player, and after a very short drum solo, the drummer slid off his stool and joined us. Many times I tried to climb up the microphone stand to continue, but each time it was as if God pushed me down again. On reflection, I think that God must have wanted us to fall down before Him that night rather than play our music to Him. This was a one-off; it never happened before, and it has never happened since – yet!

The verse before today's verse tells us that the angels fell down on their faces before the throne and worshipped; then said the words in our verse. I do not think anyone gave them instruction to do this – 'Let's all stand, now let's all fall down on our faces on the floor' – this was a spontaneous act of worship. I think when we really do enter His presence, like the angels we will not be able to stop ourselves from falling down before our holy God.

 THE POINT **Although God is all around us, I look forward to the day when we really experience what it is like to worship in the presence of Jesus.**

 PRAYER *Lord, today I want to enter into Your presence and truly worship You.*

'The sleep of a labourer is sweet …' Ecclesiastes 5:12

KEY WORDS 'a labourer's sleep'

ALTHOUGH I REALLY enjoy writing songs and recording them, things rarely go as smoothly as people imagine. I usually write my songs very quickly, it's arranging and crafting them that can take a little more time. When I was writing my eighth album, *The Power and the Glories*, I spent many weeks working on the songs for quite a few reasons, the main one being that the original *Glories* recording, *Land of Hope and Glories*, had been so well received that it would be a challenge to make the sequel as good; sequels rarely match up to the originals. I also had to do quite a bit of biblical research because, although the theological content was to be simple, it had to be accurate, as the theme was the Holy Spirit. I also had to make sure all the songs were in the right sequence to fit in with the little story and this involved writing a narrative to use between songs to link them together. Once all this was done, I then rehearsed with the session musicians, and I entered the unreal world of the studio, which was to be my home for many days as each song was recorded. Once the recording was completed, I listened to it over and over again to ensure that I was happy with it before it went to press. An album like this always takes its toll on my sleep. Every night when I put my head on the pillow one of these songs would keep going through my brain. I had deliberately written them to be catchy, but after endless listening, my own songs were driving me insane! One night, I became slightly delirious, and started laughing uncontrollably. My wife Irene was getting worried and began to think that I was starting to crack up, and it was only when she threatened to get the elders round to pray for me that I actually fell asleep!

THE POINT Life is busy for all of us. At the end of a day we need to ask the Lord to clear our minds of everything except Him; then our sleep will be sweet.

PRAYER *Lord, please help me to have a good night's sleep tonight.*

10
JAN *'Be merciful to those who doubt …' Jude 22*

KEY WORDS 'those who doubt'

IRENE OFTEN RELATES stories about her crazy husband and I know there will be those who doubt their authenticity. While on holiday with my cousins Graham and Lyn in Tenerife, we decided to go to a water park. We spent most of the day just lying by the pools but there was one feature I was determined to try out. I hate heights, but this looked fun. It involved climbing a ladder to a platform high in the air, then taking hold of a rope which was tied to a pulley. You had to jump off the platform and the pulley would hurl you over to the centre of the pool where, dangling in mid-air, you would let go and plunge about 20 feet into deep water. The family doubted that I'd do it, but I was determined to prove them wrong. My cousin even got his video camera ready to record this momentous occasion. Well, the ladder was fine, the platform was fine, hanging on to the rope on the pulley was fine, but the drop nearly killed me! Somehow I succeeded in letting go of the rope just at the wrong time, and instead of landing in the water feet first, it was my ample belly that broke my 20-foot fall. I was in agony as I swam to the side of the pool but I then remembered the filming, so I just about managed to force a weak smile for the camera. I didn't need to sunbathe much after that as my front stayed bright red for the rest of the holiday. If you are one who doubts the authenticity of Irene's stories, pop round to our house and I'll show you the video!

Some time after Jesus had died on the cross, some of His friends told Thomas that they had seen Jesus alive. Poor Thomas was full of doubts. 'Unless I touch him myself, I will never believe,' he said. Then Jesus appeared to him. Thomas didn't need to actually touch Jesus, once he saw Him; it was enough to take all his doubts away.

THE POINT **Doubting Thomas was still a best friend of Jesus. With all our doubts, we, too, are still friends of Jesus and, if we ask Him, He can help take those doubts away.**

PRAYER *Lord, today please help me not to doubt things You want me to believe.*

11 JAN *'Isaac ... loved Esau, but Rebekah loved Jacob.' Genesis 25:28*

 KEY WORD 'favourites'

I LOVE TO sit quietly in the corner of our local pub and watch people. As I do so, I see that there are quite a few similarities between the pub crowd and the church congregation. To start with, both pub and church have their 'regulars'. These are the loyal ones who always turn up whatever the weather. Not all of the regulars are necessarily nice; some are quite rude, abusive and some just plain nasty, but their regular giving, whether to the pumps or to the pastor, nevertheless helps to keep things ticking over. Then there are the boring ones. The person who tries to mix in and always pushes into other people's conversations. This person often just wants to bring the subject of the conversation round to himself or herself. Sadly, when they manage this they usually end up saying something of very little interest to anyone listening. Then there are the smelly ones. Wherever they stand or sit, everyone discreetly moves away. Nobody wants to be near them because either their breath smells or their body odour is unbearable. Finally, there are the 'favourites'. The people who are interesting, clean-smelling, who are very likeable, and who would never want to upset anyone. Both pub and church warmly welcome these. However, there is a major difference between the pub crowd and the church congregation. The pub is a crowd and allowed to have favourites, the church is a *family*, and is not. Jesus wants His Church to show a similar love to everyone and that includes the nasty, the boring and the smelly.

Isaac and Rebekah may have loved God but they were not so good at loving their children. Both Jacob and Esau would have known that they were loved by one parent more than the other and that must have brought about all sorts of upsets in the home. The sad thing is Jacob never learned from his parents' mistakes and made favourites of two of his own sons, Joseph and Benjamin.

 THE POINT In both family and church life there must be no favourites. Every person is different, but every person needs to know that they are equally loved.

PRAYER *Lord, today please help me to show an equal love to both my own family and to those who belong to the church family.*

'These people say, "The time has not yet come for the Lord's house to be built." ' Haggai 1:2

KEY WORDS 'Lord's house'

ALTHOUGH I DON'T believe that a church building is the 'Lord's house', I always feel that a nice, bright, clean building does encourage people to attend services, while dark, dirty ones can put people off. During my pastoral days in Lancashire a couple called Tom and Delia became followers of Jesus, and both became our very close friends. Our church building was in a very bad state and Tom made it his mission in life to renovate the whole building. After a lot of hard work it began to look good and smell clean. There was just the ceiling left to do. Tom knew that I was totally useless at DIY but I was always keen to make suggestions. He hired scaffolding to paint the high ceiling and thought it would be a good idea to clean the fluorescent lighting while he was up there. I decided to climb the shaky scaffolding and advise him not to bother with the lights. Once I joined him up in the dizzy heights, we had a bit of a debate about it. There was not much room at the top of the scaffolding and in the middle of our debate I accidentally kicked his paint pot. We both watched in horror as a very large tin of white paint soared through the air and splattered all over the lovely floor below. Tom did not seem to require my assistance after that, for some reason preferring to work alone!

In today's verse God's house did not need redecorating, it needed rebuilding; God's people were living in luxury and making excuses why it was not the right time to start doing it. Haggai's job was to tell them to get building if they wanted to please God. We are often like them. There are things that God wants us to do, but we tell Him that we will do them later, and make all sorts of excuses as to why we can't do them now.

THE POINT When God says He wants something done, He wants it done right now, not when we feel like doing it.

PRAYER *Lord, today when You tell me to do something I realise that I must do it when You say so, and not when I want to do it.*

13 JAN *'Set a guard over my mouth, O LORD …' Psalm 141:3*

KEY WORD 'mouth'

MY MOUTH HAS always been a large part of my ministry. God, however, for some reason known only to Him, gifted me more in shouting than singing. But even shouting can take its toll on the voice. When ministering with a band, I always shout much louder than is necessary, because I worry that people won't hear my words above the sound of the instruments. After these concerts, I can hardly speak for the next day or two, which comes as no small relief to some close family members!

After one concert I had damaged my voice big time and the following night I had another concert to perform. Of course the advice I was given was to cancel and to rest my voice because, if I continued to use it, it might cause long-term damage to my vocal chords. Throughout the years, and through all the many hundreds, if not thousands, of bookings I have fulfilled, I cannot remember cancelling any concerts through illness, and certainly none because of a stupid lost voice – and I was not going to start now.

It was a strange booking that night because my voice was so bad all I was able to do was to whisper each song, but I'm so grateful to God that He still used a whispering Ishmael. After the concert I continued whispering to a member of the audience, apologising that my voice had been so bad and that the singing must have sounded dreadful. Oddly enough, this person looked quite surprised by my apology and replied, 'Really? I didn't think it sounded any different to usual!'

The voice can be a very powerful tool. Some things we say, God can use, but other things we say can hurt and destroy people. I have to be on my guard because I may always be loud but I never want to be destructive with my speech.

 THE POINT **We need to try and think before we open our mouths. We don't want to hurt people, even unintentionally, by what we say. We must ask the Lord to help us to guard our mouths; we want to bless people when we talk to them, not destroy them by foolish and potentially dangerous words.**

 PRAYER *Lord, today help me to put my brain into gear before I put my mouth into action!*

14 JAN

'In the spring, at the time when kings go off to war, David sent Joab out with the king's men and the whole Israelite army.' 2 Samuel 11:1

'wrong place'

GOD HAS A daily plan for me but I often feel that reading correspondence is not part of that plan. I even skip read booking contracts, which can lead to embarrassing situations if I have missed something in them. I was once invited to a church in South Wales and I thought that I would find it easily as I had visited the same church fairly recently. It was quite a long drive but when I arrived I was pretty pleased with myself as I had found it all from memory, without even having to bother to look at a map or the directions that had been sent to me.

I walked up the driveway and stepped inside the relatively new building but could not find anyone. I shouted 'Hello, I'm here', but still no welcoming committee came to greet me. Eventually I met a cleaning lady and when I said, 'I am here', she replied that she could see that, but who was I? How embarrassing, they book me, and don't even know what I look like! I explained I was Ishmael and that I had come to do a concert that evening. She still looked blank; what on earth was going on? Eventually, she picked up a phone and rang one of the church leaders who told her that he knew nothing about it. It was not until I got back into the car and checked my booking form that I realised that I was in the right town but had come to the wrong church. This has happened to me quite a few times – I must learn to read the booking forms more closely!

King David could not blame his 'skip reading'. He should have led his men to battle, but he planned to be in the wrong place at the wrong time.

God has a daily plan for us and this means that there are specific places where He wants us to be and specific times when He wants us to be there. Let us live our lives by His timetable, and not just hope that He will fit into ours.

Lord, throughout today, help me to be in the right place at the right time.

15 JAN *'He lifted me out of the slimy pit, out of the mud and mire …' Psalm 40:2*

 KEY WORD 'mud'

FOR THE PAST thirty years we have ministered at Spring Harvest, which is held at a very large holiday camp. It is always held around Easter time when England usually experiences a large amount of rainfall, and consequently the ground is turned to mud. But not all God's creatures find this a problem. Sharing the site are dozens of ducks, and the muddier the ground the happier the ducks. Irene, our friend Steve Legg and I had just arrived at our allotted chalet and were unloading our luggage ready for our three-week stay. It was a long walk from the car to the chalet. Our drummer Davy also arrived, with only one bag to unload, so he agreed to leave his bag in the chalet and start setting up our venue. While unloading our car we saw Davy drift off towards our venue while eating a sandwich that he must have made in the chalet kitchen. Then it happened. As we entered the lounge we saw a large, dirty, muddy duck in the kitchen; it must have followed our drummer in unnoticed. Steve screamed, ran into his bedroom and locked the door, and I dived behind the sofa. Unfortunately, his scream scared the bird even more and the duck now tried to take flight in our lounge, covering everything in more than just mud! Eventually it found the door and flew out but what a mess it left behind. Two questions remain in my mind. Why did our Davy not see the duck and why did Steve lock himself away and leave me alone at the mercy of the demented bird?!

When I was young and worked on a farm, I would get up very early and wade through deep mud to collect the cows for milking. Sometimes my boots would get stuck in the mud and it was really hard to lift them out. Before I began to follow Jesus, it was as though I was 'spiritually' stuck in a slimy pit and deep mud.

 THE POINT Let's remember that Jesus has lifted us out of the slimy pit and put our feet on solid rock; our job now is to show others the way out of the mud and mire.

 PRAYER *Lord, today I pray for all my friends who do not yet know You.*

'Be careful not to do your "acts of righteousness" before men, to be seen by them.' Matthew 6:1

'giving secretly'

I MUST CONFESS that I have never been very tolerant of people begging on the streets, although I realise that some may be genuinely in need. I will never forget the 'orange man' in Tunisia, who offered me a slice of orange, which I assumed was a gift of generosity. He then proceeded to chase me down the road demanding some ridiculous payment for the one segment that he had pushed into my hand! Then there was the shoe cleaner in Spain who insisted on polishing my trainers. As I walked away he held out his hand for money and when I refused to give him any and explained that trainers did not need polishing, he put up his fists ready for a fight. Thankfully, he was smaller than I was so when I put mine up he didn't pursue it. Then there are the beggars in this country. How can some afford to keep such big dogs, be chain-smokers and get drunk? I don't mean to sound heartless, I know that there are some very genuine people who, for one reason or other, have hit hard times and feel forced to beg.

A short while ago I saw someone who I assumed was homeless, sitting by the side of the road in our shopping precinct. It was only a couple of days until Christmas and freezing cold and I felt really sorry for the person. I had coins in one pocket and a crisp £20 note in the other. I knew I should give the note so I walked over and as discreetly as I could, handed the money to the person, who was very appreciative. Soon afterwards came the temptation to tell someone about what I had just done so they could know what a nice, generous person I am. The only reason I am telling you this now is simply to put a point across.

THE POINT It's always good to do acts of kindness, but not good to let others know about them. It's good to give needy people food but by giving some people money, we can be actually hindering, not helping them.

PRAYER *Lord, help me today to be secretly generous to those in genuine need.*

17 JAN

'Have nothing to do with godless myths and old wives' tales; rather, train yourself to be godly.' 1 Timothy 4:7

KEY WORDS 'godless myths'

WHEN I WAS a young believer I was keen to listen to older Christians, and because I was lacking in knowledge of Scripture myself, I would swallow almost everything I was told. Nowadays, I cringe with shame and embarrassment at certain things I believed in the past. I'm sure that some of what was taught had some truth to it but other things were wrong and godless myths. In those days I was taught that Roman Catholics and even Anglo-Catholics could not be Christians. How could they be 'born again' believers while worshipping in buildings that displayed candles, crucifixes, icons and the odd picture or statue of the Virgin Mary? There was a town nearby which had a Roman Catholic cathedral, and people had convinced me that this town was Satan's stronghold for the area. I was instructed that it was full of religious spirits that were affecting everything that God wanted to do for miles around. I used to prayer-walk around this town, even round the outside of the cathedral, binding up the 'spirits of religion'. I was advised never to enter the cathedral in case I got tainted. Recently a friend of mine was getting confirmed and the Church of England bishop decided to use this very same Roman Catholic cathedral for the confirmation service. Reminiscent of my prayer-walk days I entered the building wondering what to expect. It was a lovely building, bright and light and yes, I could really sense the presence of God there. The bishop then preached the good news of Jesus to a packed congregation. I can't say I sensed any evil 'religious spirits' present, but there again, who knows, maybe I had chased them all off thirty years earlier?! In the Early Church, a lot of myths and untrue stories were taught based on ancient history and this was confusing people.

THE POINT **Of course, we need spiritual discernment and we must also be aware of the enemy at work, but let's not become superstitious Christians who just condemn and judge things that we don't understand or maybe just don't like.**

PRAYER *Lord, today help me to discern through Your Holy Spirit and not merely with my feelings and prejudices.*

18 JAN *'You have wearied the LORD with your words.' Malachi 2:17*

KEY WORDS 'wearied with your words'

I LOVE TALKING. So does my mother, so does my sister and, yes, so does my daughter. I can chat about any subject to any person. Even if I know nothing about a subject, I can still join in a conversation and chat about it. Some people like chatterboxes, but I can understand why others don't.

Years ago I found that being in a rock band gave me the opportunity to make lots of friends in other bands and I enjoyed listening to their music almost as much as playing myself. If I had a free night, I would sometimes scrounge a lift with them and go along to one of their gigs to cheer them on.

On one occasion I had made good friends with a very heavy and very theatrical rock band from Manchester. Being a large band they toured in a very large Mercedes truck so there was always room for the odd hanger-on like me to join them. One night I accompanied them on a midweek gig. Most of the members in the band had day jobs so they were quietly dozing off. I was not. I was wide awake and feeling very excited. The trouble is, the more excited I feel the more I talk, and if a silent gap occurs because nobody else is talking, I feel that gap needs to be filled, and I am always very happy to fill it. After a long while of just my voice resonating around the van, the very patient driver, who was also the only one awake apart from me, shouted in a loud voice, 'Will you shut up, your talking is driving me crazy!' Well, words to that effect anyway. I guess he must have grown weary of my words! After his outburst I did manage to stop talking – for at least five minutes!

THE POINT I wonder if the Lord ever gets fed up and weary with our words, especially when we do not mean what we are saying to Him. There is a time to speak and a time when our talk becomes tiresome to both God and others; we must know when to stop.

PRAYER *Lord, help me today to know when to stop talking and to start listening.*

19 JAN

'And they cried out in a loud voice: "Salvation belongs to our God, who sits on the throne, and to the Lamb."' Revelation 7:10

'salvation'

DURING THE ISHMAEL and Andy days I wrote a song which my sons describe as one of the most depressing songs they have ever heard. I called the song *Caroline Robbins*, and it is based on a true story of a girl whom we met on our travels, although, of course, her name was not Caroline Robbins. We first met her at one of our concerts. She stood out in the crowd for a couple of reasons. The first was that she had a very pretty face, but the main thing that struck me about her appearance was that her pretty face had a strange grey complexion and was extremely sad. After the concert Andy and I sat and talked to her for a long time. Although she was only young her story was heartbreaking. She had tried to find love and affection and in doing so had been used and abused by all around her. She had thought that drink and drugs might take away the pain, which they did, but only temporarily. She finally decided that peace and happiness could never be found on earth so she had tried to commit suicide, but even that failed. We explained to her about Jesus, how He really did love her and had died to save and help people in her position, and how He was the only one who could help her get her life back together again. My boys were right. It is a depressing song, because after spending all that time with her, she just could not believe that Jesus, or anyone else, could really love a person like her. She walked out into the night, the same sad person she'd been when she'd arrived. The last line of the song goes 'Caroline Robbins, your life is such a mess, and Jesus keeps calling your name but you won't listen.'

Salvation belongs to our God but we cannot force anyone to believe it.

THE POINT Let's remember that none of us deserves salvation but Jesus wants to save everyone even – no, especially – the 'Caroline Robbins' of this world. We still need to let them know this even if they won't listen.

PRAYER *Lord, today give me the opportunity to share the news of Your salvation with those whom I meet.*

20 JAN *'So, if you think you are standing firm, be careful that you don't fall!' 1 Corinthians 10:12*

'falling'

WHEN OUR CHILDREN were young and we visited an adventure park I was as excited as they were. Once inside the park it was Dad who led the way to try out the scariest rides. While visiting a theme park in Cornwall and wearing a very fashionable leather coat – well, I thought it was fashionable – I saw a sign pointing to the 'death slide'. That sounded like the ultimate in scary and really exciting and, although Irene and Suzy flatly refused to give it a go, Joseph and Daniel agreed to join their dad. We climbed a lot of steps and then, once at the top, we were looking down the 'death slide'. It was a sheer vertical drop! I am not good with heights and was having second thoughts about going through with it. What made things worse was that I had an annoying wasp buzzing around me, obviously attracted by my magnetic personality! The boys went down first and then it was my turn. I had to do it. I closed my eyes, leapt out, and fell. It seemed like ages that I was just falling through the air but eventually I hit the slide with a bump and slid very inelegantly the rest of the way with the family watching me. As I came to a halt I felt pain. It was then I discovered that not only had my lovely leather coat burned my skin on descent, but also that miserable wasp had got inside my coat and stung me as it joined me on what happened to be its real death slide!

There are times when I have felt really close to God; I am convinced that nothing could make me sin and do wrong things again. It's when I am feeling this good, that I am tempted with different sins, maybe pride, or maybe bad thoughts, and, sure enough, I often give in to them and, instead of standing firm, I fall.

THE POINT **Let's try and stand firm in God, but let's also be aware that when we do so, it is the most likely time that the evil one will come around to try and make us fall.**

PRAYER *Lord, please help me to stand firm today, and not to fall when temptation comes my way.*

21
JAN

'A fool finds no pleasure in understanding but delights in airing his own opinions.' Proverbs 18:2

KEY WORD '**opinions**'

DURING MY BIBLE college years, I found the lecturers fascinating. Some were young and really fired up. Using rhetoric, they delivered their specialist subject and rattled off points like a machine gun. Others seemed timid and nervous. They had a real knowledge of their subject but seemed a little unsure in the course of their delivery in case someone might question them and they might not have a suitable answer. At this college, however, the majority of lecturers were senior men. Many had led churches for most of their lives and experienced times of blessing, but also times of extreme hardship and even failure. They were not so much lecturers as pastors who believed that because of life's experience they had valuable things to pass on to young students.

I was a young Christian during these college days and felt rather unqualified to engage in some of the heated theological debates. Also, the arrogance of some of the young Christian students when questioning elderly lecturers made me sad. Some students seemed far sharper and, dare I say it, even more academic than some of the tutors, but what saddened me was that a few of the students seemed to believe their function in the college was to voice their opinion and try to belittle these men of God in front of the whole class. Even after the lecturer had tried to clarify a point, some young headstrong student would have none of it and continued to publicly humiliate the tutor. Some might argue that perhaps only scholarly academics should lecture at Bible college, but I found it a joy to listen to, and learn from, these senior men of God. They had stood the test of time, which is more than can be said for the students. Very few of those students are now in any form of Christian ministry and even less in the pastoral ministry for which they were trained.

THE POINT **Let us not be foolish or proud, people who like airing our own opinions but who refuse to listen and learn from those who have more experience of life than us.**

PRAYER *Lord, help me to listen to others today, especially older Christians who have more experience of life than myself.*

22 JAN ❯ *'He [King Nebuchadnezzar] said, "Look! I see four men walking around in the fire, unbound and unharmed …"' Daniel 3:25*

'fire'

I WAS ONE of a team leading a musicians' training course in a beautiful old Christian conference centre. While the delegates were in the main session with Graham Kendrick, I volunteered to sort out the lighting for a concert that evening. I knew nothing about lighting, but it seemed simple enough. I set up two tripods, one each side of the stage, screwed a few bulbs into the sockets, then extended the tripods to just below ceiling level. Easy! I then switched them on. Brilliant, all the lights shone brightly. It was then I had the fright of my life as the fire alarm suddenly started blaring. I assumed that some silly person had set it off by mistake, or maybe it was just a drill, I never dreamt that there could be a fire. We were all ushered out of the building and stood obediently in the dark at the fire assembly point. Conference staff were rushing everywhere – it was chaos. Soon a couple of fire engines raced up the driveway with lights flashing and sirens screaming. The firemen ran into the building hoping to find the fire quickly, thus saving this historic building from serious damage. After a little while a fire officer and the conference centre manager approached us all with a question. Who set up the lights in the concert hall? I owned up. They then suggested that in future I should not locate the lights right next to the fire alarm as the heat of the lights tends to set off the alarm. How embarrassing! I've never set up any lights since!

Shadrach, Meshach and Abednego worshipped God and refused to bow down to the idol that the king had made, so he threw them into a blazing fire. Being obedient to God meant that they were not only unharmed by the fire, but also that they were not left on their own, as a heavenly being also joined them.

If people try to encourage us to do things that we do not feel are right, we must say no. Whatever the consequence, God will be with us.

Lord, help me to stay obedient to You today, and not to be pressured into doing things that I feel are wrong.

23 JAN *'Dear friend, do not imitate what is evil but what is good.' 3 John 11*

 KEY WORD 'imitate'

I WAS PART of the Banquet Tour along with my good friends Gerald Coates and Noel Richards. Although it was tiring, it was fun. After the tour I felt like doing something a little crazy. Usually feeling like that I would dye my hair a different colour, but I was bored with doing this, having already tried every shade from blond to blue-black. Irene suggested that I get my ear pierced. This seemed like a good idea, it might even look rather trendy on an aging musician. Then I considered the pain but, being surrounded by kids who were covered in rings and who looked far less brave than I did, I thought it could not hurt that much. So I had it done. No Christians objected, although my 90-year-old grandfather thought it was the first step towards my turning into a woman. I only wore it on certain occasions and never to cause offence. To me, it was like wearing a tie; it was in no way necessary, but at certain events it seemed to add a little something.

A while later, after a concert, I heard a young boy arguing with his mum. He obviously wanted an earring but his mum was having none of it. Then I overheard his next statement: 'Mum, even Ishmael's got one, and they don't come more spiritual than him!' Encouraging words, but sadly the boy was slightly misguided on the spiritual bit! I did not wear my earring for long after that, not because I thought it was evil or that I was being a bad example and people might imitate me; I just couldn't be bothered to keep taking it in and out.

I used to love watching one of our leaders' children during the meetings. The little girl was a few years older than her brother and wherever she walked, he walked, whenever she danced he danced; he would copy everything that his older sister did. Oh yes, and whenever she did something naughty, little brother did likewise. We all imitate someone, even though we may not like to admit it.

 THE POINT People will imitate us, so let's try to be good role models.

PRAYER *Lord, help me today to be a godly role model and a good example to others.*

'The LORD *will be king over the whole earth.' Zechariah 14:9*

 'king over the whole earth'

NORTHERN IRELAND IS a great place with some really nice people, but I often wondered as I visited Belfast during the height of the troubled times if the Lord was the King there. How could people so hate each other yet still claim to follow King Jesus? As with many wars they claimed religious differences were the cause, yet I believe that Jesus is the King of love not hatred. It was strange not being able to park near the shops because of the fear of car bombs; it was strange to see all the police stations barricaded up and surrounded by high fences and barbed wire; it was strange to see soldiers fighting for Queen and country with loaded guns, standing outside Woolworths. One of the scariest times I experienced was when the band and I were innocently walking past a bar in central Belfast. Suddenly an army Land Rover screeched to a halt next to us, the soldiers in it jumped out, walked up to us, and whispered that it was OK for us to go on into the bar. We were not even planning to go in, but with an armed soldier suggesting that we did, we were not about to argue. They followed us into the packed bar, grabbed a man there, dragged him out with them to their Land Rover, and drove off. The amazing thing was that nobody took any notice; everyone just carried on chatting and drinking. For them, I guess, this must have been a common occurrence. The time will come when the Lord will be recognised as King over all the earth; then all fears, unrest and conflicts which are destroying people's lives around the world will cease.

The Roman Empire covered a lot of the world and the Caesars ruled as kings over this massive empire. The problem was that they never seemed to reign for long: in just over 80 years there were 11 Caesars.

 Some day soon the real King of the whole earth – Jesus – is going to return. This will be the end of Satan and everything bad, and the great news is that King Jesus will reign and rule forever.

 Lord, today I rejoice that You are King over all the earth. I pray for those who do not realise it.

25 JAN *'So I will always remind you of these things, even though you know them …' 2 Peter 1:12*

 ‘remind’

I ALWAYS NEED to be reminded of things, and that's not just due to the fact that I am getting old and my memory is fading, although, admittedly, that doesn't help. I was once about to begin a concert when a little girl came up and told me that it was her birthday and asked if I could sing happy birthday to her sometime during the evening. I told her that I would love to, but asked if she could ask her mummy to write it down on a note and put it on the stage to remind me. Sadly, I did not see the note and the whole event went through with this little girl waiting and me forgetting. Just as I finished and wished everyone goodbye, I saw the note. I felt so bad that I called everyone back into the hall and then we all sang happy birthday. On another occasion, when I was about to lead a church meeting, a couple came over to me and hugged me like they were old friends. Who on earth were they? Of course I did not want to let these lovely people think that I did not know who they were, so I played along with it for a while. Eventually, I managed to whisper into one of the leaders' ears to ask who this couple were, saying that I vaguely recognised them. He told me their names and then told me that I should recognise them, I married them!

As a pastor of a church, I often wondered how much of my Bible studies my listeners would remember. I did one study, then a short while later a friend of mine came and, strangely enough, gave practically the same talk to the same people. It amazed me to hear them tell him how wonderfully fresh his talk was, and that they could not remember ever hearing anything like that before.

THE POINT **We all need to be reminded of God's promises and truths time and time again. Even though we think we know them, we often forget to live them out.**

PRAYER *Lord, today as others remind me, help me to remind others of the wonderful truths written in Your Word.*

26 JAN *'When you ask, you do not receive, because you ask with wrong motives ...' James 4:3*

 KEY WORD 'wealth'

IN THE EARLY 1970s, Ishmael and Andy were invited to play at a concert in Lancaster University. Topping the bill was a young pop star called Cliff Richard who had recently publicly professed to being a 'born again' Christian. The concert turned into a riot when gay activist students stormed the hall, many dressed in drag. They thought that Cliff was also gay and objected to his claim to being a Christian. They stood in front of the stage and hurled abuse until the organisers were forced to bring the evening to a premature end. As our dressing room was next to Cliff's, I was very impressed to see that afterwards he invited some of those who had just ruined his concert backstage to talk with them about Jesus.

Years later I was invited to a party where Cliff was present. As I entered the party I knew that Cliff must now be hugely wealthy; how could he not be, with all those chart-topping records under his belt? Was he still the old Cliff Richard or was he now more of a 'Rich Clifford'? Would being a multi-millionaire have changed him from the hero I once saw at Lancaster University? I am pleased to say that it hadn't. He was very friendly, even though I'm sure he can't have remembered me from all those years ago. It was nice to meet someone whom God had blessed with wealth, but who had not let wealth change him.

I sometimes wish that I was as wealthy. All my worries would be over. I could perform concerts for free. I could give away my CDs instead of selling them. Then I could buy a nicer house, a better car, designer clothes, and have luxury holidays. Ah, that's probably the reason why I will never be that rich. God knows, that with all my wonderful intentions, I would probably end up wasting a lot of that money on myself.

 THE POINT We can ask God for anything, including wealth, but we must not be surprised when He does not give us everything that we ask for.

 PRAYER *Lord, thank You that today I can ask You for anything, but please help me to have the right motives.*

'But they will never follow a stranger …' John 10:5

KEY WORD 'stranger'

WHILE ON HOLIDAY in the Canary Islands with my cousins Graham and Lyn, we decided to hire a vehicle and tour the island. Now Gra and I both had video cameras and we were determined to get more footage of our holiday than Cecil B DeMille's epic *Ben Hur*! After driving some distance we discovered that we had consumed far too much coffee and, as there were no public conveniences for miles, a secluded spot was urgently needed. We were driving along a narrow road that was fenced on either side, and noticed that the fence was broken; through the gap we could see a large banana plantation. This seemed the perfect place to do what was necessary, so we got out of our vehicle and entered the plantation. Each found a suitable banana tree to hide behind. Then suddenly we heard it! Serious barking noises were rapidly heading in our direction. Two animals sensed that strangers had entered their territory! We raced back into the safety of the car just as two enormous German Shepherd dogs appeared and came bounding after us, ready for the kill! They started jumping up at the car, snarling with mouths foaming. We tried to calm them down, but they were not interested in obeying the voice of a stranger, besides, they probably only understood Spanish! We drove off very quickly, relieved, in more ways than one, but both shaken and very stirred, and we decided in future to cut down on the coffee before we went on our next excursion.

When I visit churches I am often invited into homes where there are large, vicious-looking dogs. The owners enter the house first shouting at the dog to stop barking then, as they hold the dog's collar, they invite me in, assuring me that their canine monster would not dream of hurting me. I am never convinced. Their dog may have recognised the voice of their master, but they certainly did not recognise the voice of me, a stranger.

Jesus said that His sheep would recognise His voice.

THE POINT **The more time we spend with Jesus, the Good Shepherd, the more we will recognise His voice and not be led astray by the voice of a stranger.**

PRAYER *Lord, help me today to recognise Your voice.*

'But God's word is not chained.' 2 Timothy 2:9

 'chains'

WE WERE INVITED to lead a family service at a church I had never visited before. Our family services tend to be very lively meetings, which keep the children well involved. If there are no pews, we encourage families to sit together on the floor and just put chairs around the edge for the elderly, the infirm and visitors. This particular morning there seemed to be great excitement as people entered the building, but the main leader told me that he had just heard that an important church member had died that night, and asked me when was the best time to announce it? There was never going to be a best time, so I suggested he do it at the very beginning. This he did, and I followed it up by telling some personal stories and explaining how death for the Christian is not the end. We then sang a song but now the people seemed very lethargic so, without thinking, I told them to wake up because they were singing like people who were half dead! Probably not the most tactful thing to say to a bereaved congregation. I quickly moved on and told the story of Peter being chained up in prison and how the angel led him out to freedom. Irene then encouraged the whole church to make a long paper chain that went right around the inside of the building. When it was complete, the people broke the chain into small pieces, signifying that neither Peter nor God's Word could be held in chains. After such a great interactive time, I think that, fortunately, everyone forgot my earlier accidental blunder.

As well as Peter, Paul also knew what it was like to suffer. Paul knew what it was like to be chained up just for teaching about Jesus. When he was chained up he couldn't go anywhere and sometimes people were not even allowed to visit him.

 God's Word can never be chained up or locked in a cell. It lives in millions of people's hearts and can never be silenced, even in countries that have made Christianity illegal. It's often in those countries, where persecution is being faced, that we find the most dedicated Christians.

 Lord, today I pray for Christians in countries where they do not have the freedom I have.

'I am not ashamed of the gospel ...' Romans 1:16

'ashamed'

THROUGHOUT OUR MARRIED life, Irene has often been embarrassed by my crazy behaviour. Soon after we were married we lived in a very small two-roomed flat comprising a bedroom and a kitchen/lounge. We even had to share the bathroom with others who lived in the building. Anyway, Irene felt that we should invite a couple of church friends around for the evening. Now these were nice people, but I felt they had two problems. The first was that I found them boring, and the second was that I knew that if they visited us, they would be there all night, as they never knew when to leave. But, as always, Irene was right. Christians should be hospitable so, sure enough, around they came. As I predicted, within a couple of hours, everything interesting had been said and there was no sign of them getting ready to go home. I waited and waited and waited some more, and dropped every hint under the sun that it was time for them to go, but to no avail. Eventually, my patience ran out. I asked them to forgive me but it was my bedtime. Of course there was nothing wrong with that, you might say, but as I said it, I brought out my pyjamas and proceeded to undress in front of them! You will be relieved to hear that I had only got down to removing my T-shirt before this couple made the quickest exit I had ever seen. I then had to face the wrath of Irene, who was staring at me and saying that she couldn't believe that I could have done such a thing.

I know it was naughty and Irene had every right to be embarrassed and ashamed of me, but since she didn't tell me off too much, I believe that deep down she, too, may have been relieved that I had got rid of them so quickly.

Jesus never did anything wrong and we should never be ashamed to tell people about Him. In fact, the opposite is true; we should be so proud that we have such a wonderful Friend and Saviour, that we should want to tell everyone about Him.

Lord, today I ask that I will never be ashamed of passing on Your good news to others.

30 JAN *'But Jonah ran away from the LORD and headed for Tarshish.' Jonah 1:3*

'disobedience'

SOME PEOPLE SEEM to think that church leaders have got their act all together, but this is rarely true; that's why we need to treat them with the love and care they deserve. Although many leaders are godly people, sometimes they feel they need to put on a performance for church members. Why? Well, how would you feel if your church leader arrived at a meeting looking thoroughly depressed and then told you that he or she often felt far from God and sometimes felt a total failure? Most congregations do not want to hear such honesty from those who lead them. When I was younger, one of the elders of my local church was very honest with me. He was a good church leader, he had a very steady and successful job, a lovely wife and family – in fact, on the face of it, everything seemed perfect for him. Then he confessed that many years earlier God had called him to missionary work overseas but he had never responded to God's call. He gave me many reasons why he hadn't obeyed God but he himself knew that each one of these was not reason enough, just an excuse. He then explained that although everyone thought of him as secure and successful, he believed that he was living in God's second best. What this sad godly man shared really spoke to me as a young follower of Jesus. It spurred me on even more to try and live in obedience to God. I would never want to run away from God and be content to live with His second best.

Jonah had reasons for not wanting to obey God or go to Tarshish but none of these was right. We all know the story well – into the boat, into the storm, into the sea, into the big fish, then on to the beach and finally on to Tarshish. A sort of scary, smelly, horrible, roundabout route to take really. It is impossible to run away from God.

THE POINT   When God tells us to do something let's never think that we know best and so disobey Him. There are still a lot of big fish out there, you know!

PRAYER   *Lord, if today I am running away from something that You had told me to do, please reveal it to me.*

31 JAN *'He who has the Son has life; he who does not have the Son of God does not have life.' 1 John 5:12*

 KEY WORD 'alive'

ALTHOUGH I HAVE conducted many funerals, I do not think that I would ever have the nerve to say what my friend Alan said at one he was taking. As he was unavailable, the senior pastor had asked Alan to lead a funeral for a very respected person in his city. The departed had also been a member of his church and a devout Christian. Many mourners gathered as the hearse arrived. Reverently the pallbearers slowly carried the coffin to the front of the building before placing it down gently. The music ceased, the introductory prayers were said, and everyone sat down very solemnly. The only sound that could be heard was that of gentle weeping from the close family. It was then in the hushed stillness that my friend Alan walked over to the coffin, tapped on the lid, and pronounced, 'He's not in there, you know.' Before he could explain that he meant the departed was now with Jesus, some members of the congregation gasped! Added to the sadness and tears suddenly there was also confusion. Un-churched mourners were left wondering whose body was inside the coffin, if it wasn't that of their friend! Of course, the point Alan was trying to make was that those who love Jesus cannot die, they just cease living on earth and move on to continue living with Jesus. However, I'm still not sure that this was the most diplomatic way to put this message across at a funeral.

We are surrounded by people who are breathing but who as yet have not started living. They laugh, cry, walk and run, sleep and wake, but, according to the Bible, they are not really alive. When we become followers of Jesus, He gives His life to us and that means that He breathes real life into every part of our being.

 THE POINT **There is no one on earth who can enjoy living as much as a Christian can. I hope those around us can see how much we appreciate being alive.**

 PRAYER *Lord, help those I meet today to see that Christians really are alive and are not just miserable sinners – they are happy saints!*

'Finally, brothers, pray for us …' 2 Thessalonians 3:1

 KEY WORD 'pray'

I WAS ONE of a number of speakers at a large conference for children's leaders in America and I was intrigued by what some of the other speakers told me. One said that often when the Holy Spirit was present, she smelt freshly baked bread. I had to confess that all I could smell was the perfume or body odour of those sitting near me. Another speaker said that he had to walk out of a restaurant because there was 'too much of the flesh in there'. Well, I wondered what he expected to find in a steak restaurant? Was I less spiritual than my American friends, or were they the odd ones? Perhaps a bit of both! It was late one night when a speaker approached me. He was heading for bed because he said he felt quite unwell. I thought about offering him Paul's simple advice to Timothy and that he should try a little wine, but decided as everyone apart from me at this conference appeared to be teetotal, this might not be a wise suggestion. We talked a little because he was such a nice guy. Just as he was leaving, I said the usual, 'Goodnight, I hope you sleep well and I will pray that you feel better in the morning.' Off he went to bed and soon after he had gone, I found myself talking with lots of other people. When eventually I got into bed I was so tired that I went straight to sleep, and so completely forgot about praying for my sick friend. The following morning he must have felt a lot better because he was up and teaching at his early morning seminar while I was eating my breakfast. Afterwards one of the delegates who had attended his seminar told me that the speaker had announced to everyone that a wonderful healing miracle had taken place thanks to Ishmael's prayer. Oh dear, I felt terrible, and was so grateful that God still does wonderful things even when I forget to ask for them.

 THE POINT **When we tell people that we will pray for them, we must remember to pray for them.**

 PRAYER *Lord, help me today to remember to pray for all those people for whom I promised I would pray.*

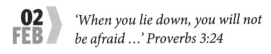

02 FEB *'When you lie down, you will not be afraid …' Proverbs 3:24*

KEY WORDS 'sleep without fear'

THE WEEK BEFORE Irene and I got married we had not found anywhere to live. But from our big day onwards God always miraculously provided a roof over our heads. When Irene was expecting our first child we had to move out of our flat. We were so grateful to our Christian friends who went on holiday that year. Several allowed us to 'house sit' for them for one or two weeks, which provided us with temporary accommodation. After our first son was born I was commuting daily to Bible college and we had no regular income. We were offered the chance to have our own small apartment in a large house in a seaside town, rent free. This was a real answer to prayer. But there was one condition: we had to act as house wardens, as it was sheltered accommodation. So we had to share the house with three young couples who were facing various domestic difficulties. Each couple had their own apartment and during the daytime we really got on well, but at night, the trouble started. Trying to get our new little baby to sleep, and then settle down ourselves while in the next apartment a couple were screaming and beating the living daylights out of each other was hard going. I sometimes intervened but soon learned in domestic situations a third party was not welcome. I also knew that if I had thumped on the next-door wall hoping to quieten things down, someone in an uncontrollable rage, often fuelled by drugs and alcohol, would most likely have come round and thumped me. These were nights when we were often afraid and sleep was not always forthcoming, but we always knew that God was looking after us.

THE POINT **For some of us there may be times when we lie down to sleep and feel frightened for all sorts of reasons. My advice is to pray when this happens, as I believe God wants all His children to sleep soundly.**

PRAYER *Lord, please help me not to be frightened tonight when I lie down and sleep. I also pray for a good night's sleep and for your protection on those who are afraid and who live in rough and dangerous conditions.*

03 FEB *'For where two or three come together in my name, there am I with them.' Matthew 18:20*

'church'

IT WAS A hot day in June and our family had joined up with my old singing partner Andy and his family for a caravan holiday in Dorset. The days were filled with fun and games and visits to various sights, but each morning we had a little service where the children would act out a Bible story after which we would pray. Of course, being Ishmael and Andy, we did have the odd disaster, such as when Andy tried to have a barbecue and burnt all the surrounding grass in the process, but that's what happens when you try and turn a musician into a cook! On the Sunday we all went for a walk up a nearby hill. It was a beautiful day and it was a steep climb, so once at the top we sat down and gazed at the bright blue sea on one side of us and the rolling green hills on the other. We unanimously decided that we could go no further until we had given thanks to God for His beautiful creation. We then had some Coca Cola and biscuits and, as adults and children, we had our own simple little thanksgiving service. We quietly praised God for Calvary, then we noisily praised God that Jesus rose again from the dead and is alive today. It was a very precious time, and we really felt the presence of Jesus with us. Let's always remember that church is not a building that Christians meet in, nor does anyone 'go' to church; church is not a meeting on Sunday. Church is often described as the Body of Jesus on earth. Another way to think of church is when two or three people who love Jesus meet together. One person cannot be church, although they can, of course, be part of the Church.

THE POINT **How important it is that we regularly meet up with other believers because, as our Scripture reading says, that is where we are going to find Jesus.**

PRAYER *Lord, thank You for allowing me to be a member of Your Church. Please help me today to see the need of being part of Your Body and to not try to live my life as a lone Christian.*

'From the roof he [David] saw a woman bathing.
She was very beautiful.' 2 Samuel 11:2

'temptation'

WE DECIDED TO take our little family with some friends on holiday to France. We bundled into two cars and drove hundreds of miles in convoy. The trouble was my friend had never heard of 'careful driving' and following him through a foreign country was an absolute nightmare. Many hours later we reached the seaside resort and soon recovered from the long-haul car chase. The next morning we were up early, packed a picnic and set off to the nearby beach. As we walked along the sand it didn't take us long to notice that this beach was slightly different from Bognor Regis. The main difference was that we were surrounded by naked women (and men) bathing, but very few were beautiful! We were on a nudist beach! The children were hungry so we sat down to eat our picnic while trying to ignore their giggling and comments. Personally I felt no sexual temptation whatsoever. I agree God makes every human being beautiful, but not all look particularly attractive. I did find it interesting to note that the children soon got bored of seeing people with no clothes on and just got on with playing in the sand. Once the picnic was over we packed everything up and quickly moved on. We didn't go back to that beach because I was frightened that one of the unclothed might recognise me and come over for a chat and I wouldn't know where to look!

Instead of being on a battlefield with his men David was on his roof watching a beautiful naked woman and he was sexually tempted. Of course he had not sinned by looking at the naked human body but, for David, the looking turned to lusting and the lusting turned to having sexual intercourse with someone else's wife. He was very wrong but David did so many other things that pleased God, it would be unfair only to remember him for his sins.

David's temptations and sins are recorded in the Bible so that we can learn from them and not fall into the same trap.

Lord, please help me today not to be tempted to do wrong by the things that my eyes see, whether on a screen or in real life.

05 FEB

'... the Pharisees and the teachers of the law began to oppose him fiercely, and to besiege him with questions ...' Luke 11:53–54

KEY WORD 'oppose'

WHEN I GET invited to teach children's leaders, I often have no idea what awaits me. Usually I am welcomed by lovely Christians who are excited about me coming and who are keen to hear the teaching that I bring – but not always. I knew the minute I arrived at a certain church that I was in for a hard time as I was welcomed with fierce stares and miserable faces. They had obviously heard of my reputation and did not approve of what they had heard; I felt like a lion entering a den of Daniels! There was no response as I spoke. As I finished, I didn't expect a standing ovation, but nevertheless I was surprised when the only reaction came from someone standing up and shouting at me angrily, saying that she disagreed with everything I had said. She then continued raging that she had been doing Sunday School work for fifty years and that there was no way that she was going to change the way she did things just because someone like me came in with new ideas. Then my seminar group all marched out en masse.

Strange as it may seem, some people do come along to my meetings simply to oppose me. They are not interested in learning from what I have to say; they are just waiting for me to say something that they can object to. These types of people are quite dangerous because even if what they are saying is right and what I am saying is wrong, they have become unteachable, totally set in their ways, and will not allow the Holy Spirit to bring in new things.

The Pharisees were like this with Jesus, except that there are two big differences in my case. The first is that I do say wrong things; Jesus never did. The second is that the people who oppose me are happy just to walk out, but the people who opposed Jesus wanted to find a reason to kill Him.

THE POINT

We must stay open to being taught new things and never just look for things we can disagree with when a Christian teacher is instructing us.

PRAYER

Lord, today help me to not be deliberately argumentative, opposing others without really listening to what they have to say.

KEY WORD 'sovereign'

ALTHOUGH I HAVE yet to meet a sovereign, I do have respect for people who have earned their title. Some bishops, deans, vicars and pastors are very worthy of their title, not only because of their academic qualifications, but also because they earn their title in everyday life. I do object to Christians, though, who think their role or gifting somehow makes them superior and that they deserve special treatment. I was in a changing room at a concert hall in Cheltenham when the star of the show, who shall remain nameless, ran in with a towel over his head, afraid that some adoring fan might recognise him, then mob him or ask him for an autograph. Who did he think he was? What made the situation even crazier was that there was no one around anyway! Confidentially, a wicked thought did enter my mind, which was that he looked better with the towel over his head! On another occasion, I was told that a brand-new luxury minibus was sent to pick up an African archbishop and his large entourage at an airport. When the archbishop saw it, he flatly refused to travel in it, saying that archbishops did not travel in minibuses, and he waited for a Mercedes to arrive. I would have been tempted to offer him a push-bike because I know, ironically, that most of the poor people from his country would have been thrilled at the opportunity to ride on anything! The greater our position in church life, the more humble servants we should be.

The word 'sovereign' is a very old word. It was first used in France in the thirteenth century, and because it contains the word 'reign', we tend to think of kings and queens who reign over us. Nowadays kings and queens have very little power and the most important people in most nations are the president or the prime minister. When the Lord is called sovereign we see the real meaning of the word.

THE POINT The Sovereign Lord in our reading refers to the One with supreme authority who, of course, is God alone. There is no other living person to whom the title Sovereign Lord could ever apply.

PRAYER *Lord, please help me to remain humble today before other people and to never forget that You are the Sovereign Lord.*

07 FEB

'Then his [Moses'] sister asked Pharaoh's daughter, "Shall I go and get one of the Hebrew women to nurse the baby for you?"' Exodus 2:7

 KEY WORDS 'quick thinking'

I WAS ONCE faced with a no-win situation. On a return visit to a church, I had been teaching the children that Jesus had set them free and that they shouldn't let people put 'chains' back on them. I was then shown their new church building and discovered the leaders had invented silly rules just because they had this new building. I could not be a hypocrite, so I had to tell the leaders that while those rules were being imposed on the children, I could not preach in the new building. It was a stalemate and I needed to do some quick thinking. I then asked if they still had their old building where I had ministered the previous year, and they said they had. I knew that old gymnasium was 'new-rule' free, so I suggested that we held the meeting there instead. They agreed. Rather than change their new petty rules, they moved all the technical and sound equipment back into the old building. We had the most wonderful time. I was so pleased I had done some (hopefully inspired) quick thinking. I did not really want to return home without preaching because they were such great people. And no, before you ask, I have never been invited back for a third visit!

Our Bible verse is part of a wonderful story that also required quick thinking from Moses' sister. Moses had been saved from death by his mother, but she could then so easily have lost her child for ever to Pharaoh's daughter. However, thanks to the quick thinking of her own daughter, she ended up being paid to raise her own child. We must also remember that the word 'nurse' is not just a child minder. Little Moses needed to be fed milk, and again it's great to see that it would be his mum who would be holding him close and feeding him through those very important early years.

 THE POINT Today we may be in a position where we need to do some quick thinking; let's pray that God inspires our thoughts.

 PRAYER *Lord, today I may need to think quickly; please put the right thoughts into my mind.*

08 FEB '*... I will pour out my Spirit on all people.*' Joel 2:28

 KEY WORDS 'Holy Spirit'

EARLY IN MY ministry I ministered with a guy who had just completed Bible college training. Today he is a well-known preacher. In those early days he was rather sceptical about young children being filled with the Holy Spirit – I blame his theological lecturers. He married, and he and his wife soon had a family. One evening they asked Irene and I to babysit as they both had been invited to speak at a meeting. We willingly agreed as they had such lovely children. After they had gone, his six-year-old daughter came downstairs to talk to us. This little girl was quite special and, thanks to her parents' upbringing, knew a lot about God. We talked about Jesus for a little while and then she asked me to pray for her. Of course I did so and as I did she was wonderfully filled with the Holy Spirit. She then went to bed a very excited little girl. When the parents returned, we explained what had happened and they were not convinced until they talked with their daughter the following morning. From that moment on that couple were 100 per cent sure that God wanted to pour out His Spirit on all people, and that meant little people as well. That little girl is now a young lady who is being mightily used by God.

Today's verse continues by saying that sons and daughters will prophesy, old men will dream dreams, and young men will see visions. In other words, all ages will be filled with the Holy Spirit and used by God. If people still think children cannot be Spirit-filled, I suggest that they read this scripture over and over again until it sinks in. By the way, I'm not sure that it's true that you can prove if you are young or old by whether you get either dreams or visions!

 THE POINT **Over the years I have had the privilege of praying for all ages to be filled with the Holy Spirit, so today please note that when our verse says ALL people, it actually means ALL people.**

PRAYER *Lord, please fill me today with more of Your Holy Spirit so that I in turn can pass on more of Your love and power to others.*

09 FEB

'After he said this he showed them his hands and side.' John 20:20

KEY WORD 'pain'

SOME FRIENDS OF ours invited us to spend a weekend ministering in France to some Christians who were refugees from Sri Lanka. We really did not know what to expect because we had not met any of them before. I was reasonably sure that they would need a bit of encouragement and some Bible teaching, so I packed quite a few talks that I hoped might be relevant. I was sure I had a lot that I could pass on to them. About fifty refugees welcomed us, and what 'warmer' welcome could there be than being told that every meal was going to be a delicious curry! When the first meeting began I sat at the front with my Bible in hand, waiting to do my bit. These people really knew how to worship, and as I watched them singing and dancing their praises to God, it made me feel like an absolute beginner. Then came the testimonies; every one of them without exception had been to hell and back. They had all been through the most dreadful persecution, some had been raped and abused. None of them knew what was happening to their loved ones back home but, with all the pain they had suffered, nothing was going to stop them praising God. I did not want to preach; these people had far more to give to me than I had to give to them. They forced me to preach in the end, but I know that after my time with them I would have learned more from their suffering and praising than they would from my preaching. During His Passion, the perfect Jesus suffered more than any man. He was whipped, beaten, tormented and then hung up like a criminal to die on a wooden cross. Even Father God seemed to turn away from His own Son that He loved so much, as Jesus took our sins into Himself to give us the chance to be made right with God.

THE POINT How important it is that we take communion both regularly and very seriously. We can never celebrate the living Jesus properly unless we keep remembering the price that the dying Jesus paid.

PRAYER *Lord, today I say thank You as I remember the pain You went through so that all my sins could be forgiven.*

10 FEB ‘ *"Don't be afraid," the prophet [Elisha] answered. "Those who are with us are more than those who are with them." ' 2 Kings 6:16*

KEY WORDS ‘don't be afraid’

ONCE I WAS touring in north Kent and booked to perform in some of the roughest places that I have ever been. Prisons were bad but nothing could be rougher than an army barracks bar. As I entered, it was complete mayhem and chaos. It was packed with soldiers shouting and swearing and, until this very day, I have never seen so many drunken people in one room at one time. There may, of course, have been a reason for this. I'm guessing that it was because the following day many of the young squaddies were going to be drafted to Northern Ireland. At this particular time it was at the height of its troubles and a place where many of the young soldiers dreaded being sent. Who knows?

I set up my gear on stage, trying to ignore the scary comments that were being hurled in my direction. The last thing these guys wanted to hear was a Christian singing songs accompanied by an acoustic guitar. But you know Christian organisers, they think it's a great witness to get Christian evangelists into wild places like this, so long as they don't have to be there themselves. Before I started to sing, I glanced around again and saw some faces looking back at me very aggressively, as if I was invading their space. Well, actually I was! I was extremely afraid and found myself in one of those situations where I had to believe what Elisha had taught his servant. God's angels were surrounding me, and were far stronger than the army of men I was facing. It ended up a very short set and appreciated by a very small minority. I was actually forced to finish abruptly and prematurely thanks to a drunken soldier who collapsed on to the stage. He just missed falling on me and left no room for me to get back to the microphone. Oh well, never mind!

THE POINT **Whatever situations God takes us into, don't be afraid. He has an army of angels ready to protect us.**

PRAYER *Lord, if today I get into any fearful situations where I feel unprotected, help me never to forget that Your angels are forever watching over me.*

11 FEB) *'The* LORD *is slow to anger and great in power …' Nahum 1:3*

'slow to anger'

TODAY MY VEHICLE is a people carrier. Unlike in the days of old with my band, I do not have to take a lot of equipment, but I do take boxes of CDs, DVDs and books, which I hope to sell. I also take my wife Irene, and I really appreciate her travelling with me and keeping me company; she even graciously endures endless hours of football chat coming from the radio! Up until very recently Irene has always been my trusty map reader. Confession time: I am very slow to anger but I have discovered that I have got an Achilles' Heel. One thing that would get me 'hot under the dog collar' was if Irene got us lost. She of course blamed the organisers' directions, saying that they were unclear, and in some cases they were, but I would take no excuses! I remember one time we were scouring the streets to find a church building. I pulled over and asked someone if they knew where the church was only to discover that we were in the wrong town. On another occasion, when we were totally lost and I knew that I was going to arrive late for the first meeting, I annoyed her so much that she threatened to throw the map out of the window, and if she'd had the chance, she'd probably have thrown me out with it. Still, the great news is that I never get angry about Irene's map reading any more because we now have a satellite navigator. This little machine has proved to be one of my greatest investments. I have a little lady, whom I have named Jane, who repeats the directions many times over and speaks very clearly. Jane never gets me angry and unlike my previous map reader, there is even a control where I can turn her volume down or silence her altogether!

Our verse tells us that the Lord does get angry, but even then it is a controlled anger and only over important issues.

We must try and stay self-controlled. If we get angry and lose it, we always live to regret it.

Lord, if I begin to feel angry today, please help me to control that anger, especially when I am feeling tired and frustrated.

12 FEB *'But the* Lord *provided a great fish to swallow Jonah …' Jonah 1:17*

KEY WORD 'fish'

I LOVE VISITING aquariums but have never been very successful as a keeper of fish. Once we had a disaster when one tank leaked overnight and we woke up to see our lovely beige living-room carpet covered in green slimy water. Irene was not amused! Another time while living in a flat in London I managed to get hold of a large but very ancient fish tank and I filled it with water, weed, rocks and fish. Upstairs lived a couple who bought a little modern tank and I thought theirs looked rather inferior compared to my old-fashioned absolute whopper of a tank. However, within a very short time mine was looking like the green hole of Calcutta, as it was covered in algae, while theirs was all things bright and beautiful. When we moved house I bought yet another tank, but this time I thought that I would try something different and add some unusual sea life into the water in the form of a couple of small crabs. They looked great in the shop and I thought I might have many happy hours watching these little chaps frolicking about. Not so. They were more intelligent than I had imagined. Somehow they managed to climb up the filter pipe and escape out of the tank to the freedom of the carpet but, sadly for them, not for long. Early next morning my son Joseph decided to come down for breakfast barefoot, and had the shock of his life when he accidentally trod on them. Good night, crabs! That was my final attempt as an aquarium keeper.

I guess as Jonah was thrown overboard into the rough sea, he must have thought this is the end, things can't get worse, I'm going to drown. Then he must have seen this monstrous fish with its mouth wide open heading towards him, and I guess he thought perhaps things can get worse after all. He would never have guessed that the big fish was sent by God to prevent him from drowning and to be his transportation back to dry land.

THE POINT **If we think things can't get worse, they probably can. But that may also be God's route to take us to better times.**

 PRAYER *Lord, today please help me to see that bad times can often lead to better times.*

13 FEB

*'Joshua told the people, "Consecrate yourselves, for tomorrow the L*ORD *will do amazing things among you." ' Joshua 3:5*

'consecrate'

WHEN IRENE AND I first started attending cathedral services they did many things that we did not understand. After 35 years of going along to charismatic Free Church meetings we had never experienced such ritual and symbolism. We quickly befriended one of the cathedral canons and told him of our predicament and he immediately invited us to his house on a monthly basis so that he could answer some of our questions. On one visit we were discussing communion. In the churches where I had previously been a member, the communion service was held sporadically, only when we thought it was right. At the cathedral there is daily communion, and it is sometimes celebrated two or three times in one day. I had always felt that the bread and wine should not be taken too often; in fact, when I was a Pentecostal pastor, I even thought that maybe once a week was too frequent. The canon explained, 'Jesus said as often as you do this you remember me.' You can never break bread too often, but you must always be sincere when you do it. I knew that he would take communion at least once each day so I asked him if familiarity ever bred contempt. In other words, did he sometimes do it without thinking about it? He looked me straight in the eyes and said a very emphatic 'Never!' He really meant it. From that moment on I knew I was in the company of a consecrated godly man who was a lot of fun but who really loved Jesus.

'Consecrate' means to make holy or, in today's verse, it means the people needed to get things sorted out with God. When this was done God was going to supernaturally dry up the river Jordan so they could cross the river on dry land and then of course miraculously provide a way for them to conquer the fortress of Jericho.

One of the reasons that we may not be seeing wonderful miracles today could be because we fail to consecrate ourselves, and to keep things right between us and almighty God.

Lord, today I, too, need to be consecrated; please help me to be more holy, and please continue to do amazing things amongst us.

14 FEB ‘ *"I will go," she [Rebekah] said.' Genesis 24:58*

 KEY WORD ‘proposal’

IT WAS ON this very day, Valentine's Day in 1972, when I was a mere 23 years old, that I had my first date with a young Scottish lass called Irene. A short while later I knew I was so in love with her that I wanted her to be my wife. In those days, I like to think that I was a reasonable man of faith. I had trusted the Lord to provide all my needs, which he had done. I had prayed in money, musical equipment, even vehicles, but now I was about to enter a new level of faith. I was going to propose to Irene and it was hard to believe that she would say yes. As we sat in the car my faith died and my pathetic proposal went as follows: 'Irene, what would you say if I asked you to marry me?' I thought by saying this, if she said no I would just laugh it off and say that I wasn't going to ask her anyway. Fortunately, I didn't need to use plan B because she said yes. I was so pleased because with what little faith that I did have, I had already booked to see the minister that afternoon to organise the wedding! We got married on 24 June and have been happily married ever since.

In Abraham's day marriage proposals were different to today; even so, it is great to see God's hand guiding all the way in finding Isaac his wife. Do read the story to remind yourself of it. However, I still think it was great that Rebekah chose to go for herself and was not forced to. She was to meet and marry a man she had never seen; all she knew about him was what the servant had told her, but she still felt it right to go and marry Isaac. Because this was God's will, when she met her man they married instantly, and Isaac loved her very much.

 THE POINT **God can guide us today in our relationships including a marriage partner, but only if we let Him. We need to be careful that we have not already made up our own mind without involving Him.**

 PRAYER *Lord, today I thank You that You want to be involved in my relationships and marriage.*

15 FEB *'The LORD has taken away your punishment ...' Zephaniah 3:15*

KEY WORD 'punishment'

I WAS NEVER a bad boy at school but back then you didn't have to do anything too bad to be severely punished. In my primary school I will never forget a sadistic teacher who may have been good at teaching, but who also took great pleasure in humiliating young children and in beating them. Many a time some small boy, who had not really committed any serious crime, would be sent to him. He would put two desks together, make the child lean over them, and then, after a short run-up, he would hit them as hard as he could on their backside with a slipper. All the class just watched as the suffering child cried, usually before he had received his first stroke.

When I was 11 years old, I attended a senior school. Here the pupils were far more rebellious and many, without a doubt, certainly deserved punishment. I was not a bad boy but I still suffered during one lesson in the art class. The art teacher, Mr Williams, was a large but mild-tempered man who was normally firm but fair and quite rightly would not take any abuse from any undisciplined pupil. In one of his lessons I was sitting on a bench enjoying drawing and he must have seen me whispering to a friend sitting next to me. For some reason or other the teacher snapped and completely lost it. He ran over to me as if I had just committed the unforgivable sin and smacked me with his huge hand as hard as he could around the head. As I said, he was a large, powerful man, and the blow knocked me clean off the bench and left me lying on the floor. To be fair he was very apologetic afterwards as he realised that my whispering did not deserve the punishment he dealt out, but all I remember was the headache that I had for some time afterwards.

THE POINT **Although we all deserve to be punished for the sinful lives we have led, the perfect Jesus was punished in our place by dying for us on a cross. We can never be thankful enough.**

PRAYER *Today I thank You, Lord, for Your wonderful grace and mercy. All I deserve is Your punishment but You have chosen to shower upon me Your precious love.*

16 FEB *'Do not be like the horse or the mule, which have no understanding ...' Psalm 32:9*

KEY WORD 'horse'

WHEN I WAS a child living in a Christian community, I used to love horse riding. I was only given a very small amount of pocket money, so I could not afford to go riding on a regular basis. I was then introduced to Pauline, the owner of the stables, and she offered me a Saturday morning job. She offered me a deal: if I was prepared to help out with the chores, instead of payment, I would get to ride the horses for free. It sounded a great deal to me. So this was how I spent my Saturday mornings. My first job would always be to clean out the stables, but I had to be careful when doing this because although I liked all the horses, not all the horses seemed to like me, especially a silver-coloured mare called Calypso. I remember on one occasion clearing up the mess at the rear end of this horse in a very confined stall and failing to see her ears going back. Smack. Out kicked her rear right hoof, sending me flying. I actually ended up sitting in a bucket, which gave everyone around me a good laugh! But the odd kick was worth it, because once all the chores were completed, we were off into the countryside for a long ride. But even then some of the horses showed their contempt for me. I often seemed to find myself sitting on an arrogant horse that didn't seem to have any understanding that I was its master. These horses were far stronger than a ten-year-old boy, and they proved this to me time and time again. I tried to counteract their rebellion by pulling hard on the reins and, sometimes, I won and I managed to steer them to where I wanted them to go; at other times I lost and fell off the horse!

THE POINT **God does not want to control us like horses. He will not use reins and a bridle to force us in the right direction, He wants us to choose to be obedient and to follow Him.**

PRAYER *Lord, thank You for not forcing me to do things, but for allowing me choice. Today I am going to try to choose to do what pleases You.*

'Dear friends, let us love one another, for love comes from God.' 1 John 4:7

 KEY WORDS '**love comes from God**'

I WAS INVITED to give an evangelistic talk at an adult meeting in a small town. I knew very little about the church, but I never turn down the chance to share the good news of Jesus with people. On arrival the leaders were very friendly and they thrust a nice cup of tea in my hand, which always makes me feel welcome. We had a prayer time together while the audience arrived. I decided that in my talk I would go straight for the jugular and share with them how Jesus suffered while dying for us upon the cross and how that affects us today. As usual, the meeting started with lots of singing, far too much, in my opinion, bearing in mind that the evening was supposed to be for the un-churched who, of course, didn't know any of the songs. Eventually I got up and began my talk. All was going well until I started talking about Calvary. At that point a man leapt from his seat, ran to the front of the meeting, put his hands around my throat, and began to strangle me. I don't mind response or even critical reaction at my meetings, but I was not prepared for strangulation. The leaders of the church ran forward and started grappling with the man, trying frantically to release his grip on my windpipe. Eventually they managed to overpower him and dragged him away. I managed to finish my talk, albeit with a slightly gruffer voice than when I had started. It's a shame, because I never saw my attacker again. I felt no hard feelings and even felt a strange love for him that must have come from God. I would have enjoyed the opportunity of finding out why he responded as he did. Something I'd said had caused him to react, and for once it was not my singing or my song lyrics!

 THE POINT **We must show love to everyone, even to people who have said and done hurtful things to us because love comes from God, and we belong to Him.**

 PRAYER *Lord, because love comes from You, I must love others. I do find it hard to love everyone and today I will need Your help to be able to do this.*

18 FEB › *'... so faith without deeds is dead.' James 2:26*

 KEY WORDS 'faith without deeds'

ISHMAEL UNITED WAS a loud rock band which often struggled with personnel relationships but, to be fair, some of the organisers didn't make our lives any easier. We had a booking at a large parish church in Eastbourne. As usual we loaded all the heavy equipment into our Ford transit van and set off. The organiser, his wife and daughter were there to greet us when we arrived, and we set about the lengthy task of unloading all the gear, setting it all up and then sound checking. The concert was booked for 8.00pm and we expected a good turnout as it was a local gig and we were reasonably popular around that area. When 7.30pm came, to our surprise there wasn't a queue outside the door – in fact, there was no one around at all; 8.00pm approached and still there was no one to be seen. At 8.15pm, the organiser approached us and asked us when we were going to start playing, to which I replied 'To whom?' His answer was to him and his family. I asked him how widely had he advertised the event. Had he put posters up, put an advert in the local paper? His answer shocked all of us in the band. He told us he hadn't done any advertising at all; he'd expected God to send in the right people, those who should be there. As we packed all the gear back into the van, having not played a note, I really didn't know what to think. Either this guy was a man of great faith and God had answered his prayer by not sending anyone along, or else he was a complete nutcase who made us load up, drive all this way, unload, and then load up again for nothing. Perhaps this will help you to understand just a little bit of the strain Ishmael United were under.

 THE POINT **We must have faith and even believe in God doing the impossible, but God doesn't just expect us to sit back and let Him do it all; He wants us to be active and to be part of what He is doing. Let's believe, but let's also act!**

PRAYER *Lord, today I realise I need to have faith, but it's a faith that will require me doing something.*

19 FEB 'You should not look down on your brother in the day of his misfortune ... ' Obadiah 1:12

KEY WORDS 'days of misfortune'

A FRIEND OF mine got romantically involved with a pretty girl who was a lot younger than he was. Both were Christians, but after that any similarity personality-wise between them was hard to see. The relationship became more and more serious until the engagement was announced and the wedding day set. I still had serious reservations about their compatibility and told him so, but at the end of the day, love is a strange thing and advice given to the mind is rarely received by someone who is being ruled by their heart. The wedding day came and, just as expected, the bride looked wonderful, and the groom didn't look too bad either! Not so long after returning from the honeymoon it was easy to see cracks appearing in the relationship. The arguments became more frequent and they started putting each other down in public. She was still young and wanted to go out and do exciting things in the evening, while he was happy to sit at home and watch the television. Sadly, after a few years and a few children, they separated, then divorced. It was a heartbreaking time for all involved. It would have been so easy for me to look down on my friend in the day of his misfortune and to remind him that I had told him this would happen, but that would be very wrong. This was just the time that he needed my support and encouragement to pick up his life and get on with what God had called him to do.

We have all heard the expression about kicking a man when he is down, and some people seem to get a weird pleasure and satisfaction by doing this. Why would any Christian, when they see someone going through a difficult time, want to have a go at them and hope to make them feel worse than they are already feeling? I can't understand that.

THE POINT **When someone is going through 'a day of misfortune' let's not look down on them, let's try and lift them up, and then, maybe, they will do the same for us when we next reach a low spot in our lives.**

PRAYER *Lord, when I meet someone today who is feeling low, help me to be an encouragement to them.*

'When Jesus came into Peter's house, he saw Peter's mother-in-law lying in bed with a fever.' Matthew 8:14

'mother-in-law'

I HAVE TO admit that I had a wonderful mother-in-law. Irene's mum, Marion, was unique; I don't think I have ever met anyone who was so full of fun. I didn't meet her until the day of our wedding, so neither of us knew what to expect. Coming from a non-religious background, I think she must have wondered how she would get on with a 'man of the cloth' as a son-in-law. It was hilarious because every time we met she felt that she should bring some biblical movie into the conversation at some point to prove to me that she, too, knew something about religion. As we got to know each other better she knew that she could just be herself, and from that time on I could expect a very rude birthday card from her each year. What Marion loved doing most was getting all her family together, and whenever there was a birthday or special occasion she would insist that we would all be there. Each Christmas Marion would join us for lunch where she was always the life and soul of the party. She would arrive dancing up our driveway carrying a ghetto blaster with music blaring out. We took her on holiday with my parents to Tunisia and in no time she was chatting to the locals as if she had known them all her life; she had no fear. It was in the airport departure lounge, waiting for our return flight, that we discovered how seriously ill she really was. She had collapsed in the duty free shop, of all places, which of course she made a joke about later on. She had cancer and was in remission when we planned the holiday for her. Shortly after we got back she deteriorated and, although in great pain, she never wanted people to see her miserable. To the end Marion was great company. Christmas has never been the same without her.

THE POINT Peter's mother-in-law had a fever. The first thing that Jesus did when He entered the house was to see her and heal her. Jesus' priority was the sick mother-in-law, not talking with the healthy Peter. Is our priority caring for the sick or talking with the healthy?

 Lord, today I thank You for happy memories of loved ones.

KEY WORD 'seek'

I HAVE A reputation for losing things. I often lose my wallet, but usually find it in a coat somewhere. Then I lose my coat and find it's in a cupboard somewhere. I even sometimes lose my wife, and find she's in a shop somewhere! But the biggest thing I have ever lost is my car. I had a booking in Wales but, thanks to clear roads, I had time to spare so I pulled into Gloucester to grab a coffee. It was late in the afternoon and a dull day with spitting rain, so I was glad to enter the bright lights and warmth of the shops. Five-thirty came and I decided it was time to go back to the car and move on. That was when the trouble began. I couldn't remember where I had parked my car. I went down every street, north, south, east and west, but no street looked familiar. However, by the time I had done this many times, every street looked familiar. I started to panic as it was now dark and I had sought everywhere and still not found my car. Then I had an idea. I knew it would be an expensive idea, but I had no choice. I got into a taxi and when the driver asked where I wanted to go, I told him 'To find my car'. I think he thought me a bit mad, but since I was paying he went along with it. I got him to drive me outside of the city to the road that many hours previously I had travelled in on. I then got him to retrace my steps into the city and sure enough there was my car exactly where I had left it. An expensive couple of hours' shopping, especially as I didn't actually buy anything! Whether we have a reputation for losing things or not all the best things have to be sought after.

THE POINT The Bible is full of hidden treasures but we have to search to find them. Life, too, is full of excitement but we have to keep seeking the Lord Jesus if we want to experience that excitement.

PRAYER *Lord, today I am going to take some time out to pray and seek You. I know that the more I seek You, the more real life I will find.*

22 FEB *'... knock and the door will be opened to you.' Matthew 7:7*

KEY WORD

'knock'

ALTHOUGH I LIVED in a large Christian community situated in 11 acres of grounds which were populated with cows, chickens, geese and Christians, at times I still got bored in the evenings. The adults had their meetings but there was not too much for a young boy to do. The village we lived in was very small; it had one street, one sweet shop, and one post box, to be precise. The only nightlife for my age group was to attend the Thursday evening choir practice in the village school hall. Sometimes I would attend the practices, but for two reasons only: the first was that all those who attended were given a sweet at the end, and the second reason was that it happened to be the only place to find pretty girls in the evening. However, even the sweet and pretty girls did not compensate for the boring time of singing hymns and psalms.

As happens in most communities, a little gang of bored lads soon began gathering; we used to assemble outside the school hall on Thursday nights. While waiting for the choirgirls to come out, we would make a nuisance of ourselves. To help pass the time we would throw the odd dustbin lid on the school roof; it would make a lot of noise but never cause much damage. It was fun to see the girls giggling and the choirmaster come running out, shouting, as we all hid. Another remedy for boredom was to knock on people's doors and then run away when they opened them. Of course the angrier the residents' response, the more we would knock on their doors. I guess I didn't quite deserve an 'ASBO', but this was not the thing a normal child from a Christian community would do – or maybe it was! There will be a lot of doors in our lives that we should keep knocking on, but let's keep on knocking until they open and let's not run away.

THE POINT On life's journey we will find Jesus opening doors for us, and inside those doors are all sorts of wonderful things which He has in store for those who follow him. Never give up knocking.

PRAYER *Lord, today please direct me to new doors which, when they open, will lead me on to new adventures with You.*

23 FEB *'And he said, "Who told you that you were naked?"' Genesis 3:11*

KEY WORD 'naked'

BY AN AMAZING coincidence two of our best friends had booked a holiday in Majorca on the same date as us. As they were in a different town we arranged to meet on a nearby beach. When we met, the sun was hot, the sand was golden, the sea was turquoise, and the beach was packed with holidaymakers. But that was not going to spoil our fun. After eating pizza we hunted down a free bit of beach and laid our towels out. It was then I noticed that my friend, who is a well-known preacher, was wearing white shorts instead of swimming gear. I suggested we take two bats and a ball down to the water's edge and have some fun; he agreed. Because of the crowds we had to go out quite deep in the sea before we could play our game. We had a very happy hour of mindless fun splashing around in the warm water. Then I thought I'd have some fun. As I looked at my friend, I pointed out that the water had made his white shorts see-through. Panicking, he quickly dived underwater and told me to get his wife to bring a towel down to cover up his nakedness. Still feeling mischievous, I just stood on the shore and yelled to his wife to bring a towel down because her husband's shorts were see-through. Most of the beach heard and were now staring at my friend, waiting for him to emerge from the water. Eventually he waded out with a towel discreetly around his waist and a very red face. Later I told him that I was only joking and that his shorts were not really see-through. I won't say what he said, but I can't imagine him ever using those words in a sermon!

 THE POINT Adam suddenly feared God seeing him naked. This was a strange fear since God had only recently created the body he was trying to cover up. It was not just his body he was trying to cover up, it was his disobedience. The one thing God told him not to do, he had done. The world would never be the same again.

 PRAYER *Today, Lord, I know that it is useless to try and hide anything from You.*

24 FEB

'for all have sinned and fall short of the glory of God.' Romans 3:23

KEY WORD 'target'

WHILE LIVING ON the farm I was amazed at what the farmer kept in his kitchen. Leaning up against the kitchen cabinet were three rifles. One was a rather smart .410 shotgun which looked like something straight out of a Clint Eastwood movie; the second was a twelve-bore double-barrelled rifle which the farmer would use when he accompanied the Lord of the Manor on his pheasant shoots; and the third was an air rifle. Now I have always fancied myself as 'the man with no name', so I asked the farmer if I could borrow a rifle and get a bit of shooting practice. He didn't trust me with the 'big guns' but handed me the air rifle and some pellets, and told me that if I wanted a target I should go and shoot some sparrows as they plagued the farm and were eating up his freshly planted seeds. I went out into the field and was shooting away, but my pellet never seemed to reach my target; then I saw a sparrow within range quietly perched on a gatepost. I took aim, fired, and got it; my first kill! I walked over to look at my trophy and nearly burst into tears, I had shot a robin by mistake. I picked up the poor little bird and carefully went and buried it. I then took the rifle back to the kitchen and stood it back in its place next to the kitchen cabinet and the other guns. That was the end of my shooting days.

One of the meanings of the word sin is falling short of the mark. It was sometimes used of an archer when he shot his arrow at a target; if it didn't reach that target it had sinned, fallen short of the mark.

THE POINT God's target for the man that He created in His image was not to do wrong things but to be like him. In the beginning Adam and Eve sinned, and today you and I sin. We have all fallen short of God's perfect target. When we sin, let's be sure to say sorry to God.

PRAYER *Lord, today, when I think, say or do wrong things, help me to be quick to confess them so that I can stay close to You.*

25 FEB *'... without faith it is impossible to please God ...' Hebrews 11:6*

KEY WORD 'faith'

AFTER SERVING AS a pastor in Lancashire, I believed that God wanted me to pick up where Ishmael and Andy had left off, and to go back on the road as an itinerant preacher-musician. Now this sounds great but as my diary was almost empty, I knew it really was going to be a step of faith for us. However, what was going to require even more faith was buying a house for our family to live in. We saw a lovely little house for sale and both Irene and I were convinced that it was where God wanted us to live. Irene has always looked after our finances and we knew that we would need a mortgage to buy this house. Irene examined our accounts and was unsure that a visit to the building society would achieve anything. Neither of us had a 'proper job' or any savings. We prayed about it and I decided to try because I believed that if God really wanted us to have this house, no one could stop us getting it. I put on my suit and set off. As I entered his office the manager was sitting behind a big desk looking over the top of his glasses at me. I was told to sit down, which I did, feeling slightly intimidated. I then explained how much we wanted to borrow. He enquired about my work and savings and this presented me with the opportunity to give him my testimony. I explained that God had always supplied our needs and I was very confident that He would also supply our repayments. He stared at me in disbelief; obviously he had never been approached with such a proposal before. Then he stood up, shook me by the hand, and told me that we could have the full amount that we had applied for. Yes, I had a bit of faith, but I was so pleased that God had visited the manager before I had!

THE POINT **Faith is hearing God's plans, then believing they will come to pass before they actually do. Today God still does both the impossible and the improbable. Let's ask God for more faith to believe that.**

PRAYER *Lord, today please give me more faith to step out and believe that You still do humanly impossible things.*

'They mourned and wept and fasted till evening for Saul and his son Jonathan ...' 2 Samuel 1:12

 'mourning'

IN MY PASTORAL days in Lancashire I decided to make some door-to-door visits to tell people about Jesus. This town was ideal for house visits because many of the two-up, two-down terraced houses had a front door opening directly onto the street. At one house I visited a middle-aged couple called Tom and Delia. I invited them along to one of our church services, explaining that it would be easy for them to find our building as it was situated just down the end of their road. They began coming and very soon both committed their lives to Jesus and were baptised. From the first time we met our friendship began. I went to watch football with them on Saturdays, they babysat our children in the evenings, and we even went on camping holidays together to the West Country. When we moved on from the church our friendship remained as strong as ever, and if I was passing through Lancashire I would always stay with them. A while ago Delia died. We were all heartbroken, especially her husband Tom, who had relied upon her so much. He rang me very soon after she had passed away and I must admit I was worried about how he would manage without her.

Time has since passed and although the initial mourning is over and Tom is coping really well, I know that the sadness and sense of loss will never leave him.

In today's reading the king and prince were both dead; David was heartbroken. Sooner or later we will all know how David felt as loved ones that we are close to, die.

 When Christians die, we believe that although their human body may die, there is a part of them that cannot die and will continue living for ever with Jesus. It is right for those left on earth to have a time of mourning and weeping. It is also biblical, as some of God's best friends mourned when a loved one died, even though they believed that one day they would see their loved ones again.

 Lord, today help me to mourn with those who are mourning, and to weep with those who are weeping.

27 FEB *'But Martha was distracted by all the preparations that had to be made.' Luke 10:40*

 KEY WORD 'distracted'

IRENE AND I were invited out to some friends for a meal. I didn't particularly want to go because, deep down, I thought we were only being invited as they had also invited another couple whom I knew our hosts found difficult to talk to. Irene told me not to be so cynical! I never have enjoyed going to dinner parties anyway, so maybe she was right. When we arrived we were warmly welcomed by the hosts and introduced to their friends and then invited to sit in the lounge. We were asked if we would care for a pre-dinner drink. We all said yes and then our hosts disappeared to sort out the drinks. We chatted with their friends but really had little in common with them. The hosts reappeared and invited us all to move to the dining room and we were instructed where to sit. I noticed that we were sitting next to the other two guests while the hosts were down the other end of the table. Then as we ate the starter our hosts disappeared again. They were in and out of the kitchen to check on the main course. We continued to try and communicate with their friends, and by this stage had found that we had even less in common than we originally thought. Then the main course was served and as we began to eat, again our hosts disappeared. This time they were in and out of the kitchen checking on the dessert. Meanwhile, we were running out of things to say and by now found out that we had absolutely nothing in common with the other couple. We finished the dessert and were served coffee, then our hosts disappeared again to wash up. This was my cue. Just as they disappeared, I said to Irene that it was time we also disappeared, realising that we had hardly said a word to our distracted hosts all evening and had nothing left to say to their other guests.

 THE POINT I don't think that Jesus was too worried about what Martha was going to cook, He just wanted to talk to her without her being distracted. Food is nice, but let's always remember that fellowship is far more important.

 PRAYER *Lord, help me today not to be distracted and never to put preparation before people.*

28 FEB *'Marriage should be honoured by all ...' Hebrews 13:4*

KEY WORD › 'marriage'

AFTER MANY YEARS of marriage and three children, I still have fantastic memories of our wedding day. Each year Irene kindly reminds me of our anniversary date and we try and arrange something a little special for that day. On our thirtieth wedding anniversary we flew off for a week's holiday on one of the Balearic Islands. We couldn't afford to be extravagant so we chose a self-catering apartment, which in the brochure looked fine but, as it was only 3-star, there were no guarantees. As we had never been to these apartments before I was really praying that they would be a bit special for this very special occasion. We arrived at the airport in time, the flight was not delayed, and the sun was shining as we reached our destination airport. Everything so far looked great, but as we boarded the courtesy coach which was to take us to our resort, the unthinkable happened. The coach was full when the holiday rep asked if Mr and Mrs Smale were on board. We signalled to her and she came over and explained that they had double-booked; we could no longer go to the resort and apartment of our choice and would have to go elsewhere. She kept apologising and said that we would receive some money to compensate for the inconvenience. My heart sank, but then we arrived at our new destination. It was the most beautiful luxury hotel, a much nicer resort, and, of course, we also had the extra compensation money to spend. It was a wonderful wedding anniversary and we were so grateful to God both for each other and for answering our prayers in such a special way. Nowadays many people think that marriage is not important and that it's fine just living together and bringing up a family. The Bible says that marriage is very special.

THE POINT › **Marriage is not just a church service, signing a form, or exchanging rings, it is something that God wants loving couples to enter into and to take very seriously.**

PRAYER *Lord, today I pray for those I know who may be experiencing difficulties in their marriage, and also for those I know who have chosen to just live together and who do not think that marriage is necessary.*

01 MAR *'In the spring, at the time when kings go off to war ...' 1 Chronicles 20:1*

'spring'

WHEN I THINK of spring, I don't think of going off to war, I think of the past thirty years of preparing and going off to minister at Spring Harvest. Just to remind you, Spring Harvest is a very large Christian holiday that began way back in 1979 with a couple of thousand people meeting in a Pontins holiday camp in Prestatyn. In 1980, Ishmael United were invited to perform at a late-night concert. I remember that our concert really worried the organisers both because of the aggressive style of punk music that we were playing, and also the response of the young Christian audience. The organisers were not used to seeing Christians pogo-ing on the dance floor; they were sure that this only happened at secular concerts. They were quite pleased when we finished because they were very anxious that these young Christians might get out of control. However, there was one person who showed no such fear. He was an evangelist from Argentina and his name was Luis Palau. As soon as we left the stage we were expecting a mixed response from the leadership team. Luis came running up to us, thrilled by what he had seen and heard, and prayed over us. Spring Harvest provided just the encouragement we needed as we embarked on this new ministry that was going to prove highly controversial in future.

Around the time when King David was alive, spring was the time when the battles began. I would imagine that it was not a season that the wives, children or even the soldiers would look forward to too much. Today, of course, it's different. Personally, I love spring. I love to see evenings get lighter, and to feel the weather getting warmer. I also enjoy seeing the flowers begin to blossom and grow and the leaves forming on the trees. It's a time of year signifying the beginnings of new life.

THE POINT Springtime also incorporates Easter, a great reminder of Jesus dying and rising again from the dead, and giving you and me the opportunity to start a real new life, living for Him.

PRAYER *Lord, today I thank You for spring, and thank You for the new life that You have given to me.*

'The king's heart is in the hand of the LORD …' Proverbs 21:1

 KEY WORD 'authority'

WHEN I ARRIVED in Lancashire to pastor my first church I knew it would be a challenge.

The church had a small congregation and was in debt. It could not afford to pay a full-time pastor but I believed that God wanted me to be there, so finance was not my priority. I have always believed that if I am in the right place, then God will supply all my needs. I felt very young and inexperienced to be leading a church, as I realised it would be my responsibility to make important decisions. The church had deacons, who were lovely, godly people but not as strong in character as myself. For the first time I was in a position of authority and whatever I instructed would be carried out. This was a potentially dangerous position for someone of my age. Thanks to the grace of God the church grew, and it seemed many of the decisions I made were the right ones. But I knew my 'one-man' ministry would have to change, a team ministry was needed. I encouraged the congregation to stop calling me 'pastor' and to call me by my Christian name. I wanted to lead them as their friend and not as a hierarchical figure. I began to expand the leadership team and encouraged them to start to make decisions for themselves. True, the more confident they became, the more I was challenged, but this was a far healthier position to be in. Ever since then I have worked in leadership teams where each is accountable to the other.

In Solomon's day, a king was a mighty ruler, who often had the ultimate say in everything. However, although the king's heart may have been in the hands of the Lord, sadly many rulers never consulted God before making a decision. Nowadays many senior people in world government do not even believe in the existence of God, so it's not surprising that our world is in such a terrible state.

 THE POINT Let's remember our government and let's pray that they listen to God and godly people before they make decisions on behalf of the people they govern.

 PRAYER *Lord, today I pray that those who are leading our country listen to You.*

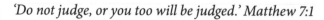
'Do not judge, or you too will be judged.' Matthew 7:1

KEY WORD 'judge'

MY SISTER HEATHER and I have always been very close, but I can remember one time when we were not. I would probably have been about six years old and she about nine at the time. We had been given a lovely little guinea pig as a pet, and although it was to live its life behind bars in a cage, it did seem reasonably happy. One day Heather went round to her friend's house, and by some strange coincidence she too had a pet guinea pig. I guess there must have been a guinea pig birth explosion at this time in pet shops, as these little creatures seemed to be the trendy thing to own! Anyway, my sister was amazed when her friend proudly opened the cage door and her little guinea pig, which must have been quite tame, didn't even attempt to run away; it just scampered around happily in front of the two admiring girls. Now this gave Heather ideas. When she came home she decided to try the same with our guinea pig. She opened the cage door and out hopped our little furry animal but instead of merrily scampering around in front of us it raced towards the open back door and leapt for freedom. The last thing we ever saw of our beloved pet was it crawling under the concrete coal bunker. Even at six years old I was furious with my sister. I not only judged her, I pronounced her guilty and sentenced her. She was a guinea pig murderer!

Nowadays I am learning never to judge others. As a child in Sunday school I was taught that if I pointed my finger at someone, there were always three fingers pointing back at me! How true that is; I wish I had remembered that all through my life.

THE POINT **We are all sinners and it is only the grace and mercy of God that allows us forgiveness when we confess those wrong things. We have no right to judge other people's faults because we have so many faults of our own.**

PRAYER *Lord, please help me today not to judge other people, as I realise that I am not in the position to do so.*

04 MAR

'But when you pray, go into your room, close the door and pray to your Father ...' Matthew 6:6

 KEY WORDS 'loud and quiet prayer'

DURING THE 1990s, a wonderful, fresh outpouring of the Holy Spirit was experienced by many people in many different countries. I had been to a meeting where this was taking place and returned home so full of the power of God I thought I was going to burst. I immediately rang all my leadership team and invited them round that night as I wanted to try and pass on to them some of what I had received. One of the first people that I prayed for was an older, warm, but rather reserved gentleman. As I prayed for more power of God in his life he just fell to the floor and started rolling around laughing. His wife was rather concerned, as she had never seen him like this before. By the time I had finished praying, God had touched everyone in the room in different ways. We spent a long time together that night, not only because no one wanted to leave, but also because one person was praising God while lying on the carpet and blocking the door, so nobody could get out! I enjoy the loud prayer times but I also enjoy the silent times that I spend with God. Sometimes I sit alone and pray in our vast cathedral reflecting on the fact that for a thousand years many Christian brothers and sisters have done the very same thing. Other times just animals and birds accompany me as I walk and pray in the quiet of a park or even the golf course.

In biblical times some people enjoyed making a great performance out of praying to impress those around them, and to make their audience think that they were very spiritual. Nowadays in our meetings let's never feel that we need to try and impress people with our prayers or by making an exhibition of ourselves while pretending to praise.

 THE POINT It's good to pray loud prayers with others, but if we really want to follow Jesus' example, we also need to spend time praying by ourselves in a quiet place.

 PRAYER *Lord, help me to find time today in this very busy, noisy world to spend quality quiet time with You.*

05 MAR *'His father Isaac asked him, "Who are you?" "I am your son," he answered, "your firstborn, Esau." ' Genesis 27:32*

 **'truth'**

I HAVE ALWAYS had a very vivid imagination. At times, this has proved useful – especially when I have allowed God to inspire me in writing a book or a song. When writing my first novel *Children of the Voice*, a kind friend had allowed me to use his fantastic house overlooking the sea. I would arrive early each morning, write a chapter, then, at lunchtime, Irene would bring me down a sandwich and we would have lunch together. After she had left I would write another chapter in the afternoon, then some more into the evening. I really felt that God was inspiring my writing because the whole book took about a week to write. Even writing it was exciting, as I had no idea what was going to happen to my hero until I actually wrote the next chapter. It proved to be a bestseller and was enjoyed by many thousands of children, and although it was fiction, it contained much truth. However, my vivid imagination is not always good. When I was very young I had imaginary friends. These were Manquin and Judy Hoo, Africa and Apricot! Now I can't remember much about Africa and Apricot, but I can remember that Judy Hoo was good but Manquin was very bad. When I did something wrong and my parents corrected me I would really believe that it wasn't me who was responsible, but Manquin. Poor Manquin got the blame for every bad deed I did. It's strange, but even a child can believe something to be true yet tell an outright lie.

In Isaac and Esau's time, a dying man's blessing was very important; he was passing on something special to his sons. Esau arrived back from hunting and, having prepared his father's supper, he discovered that Jacob had not told the truth and had stolen the blessing that was meant for him. Both old Isaac and Esau were devastated.

 THE POINT Let's remember that the truth always comes out in the end and when people discover it, usually someone feels very hurt and the deceiver should feel very guilty.

 PRAYER *Lord, please help me today to tell the truth, and nothing but the truth.*

06 MAR

'If you belonged to the world, it would love you as its own.' John 15:19

 KEY WORDS 'belonging to this world'

DURING A MUSIC tour in New Zealand my band and I found we had an evening free. The pastor with whom we were staying decided that we could have a 'boys' night out' at his local Indian restaurant which he guaranteed served some of the best curry in New Zealand. We loved the idea as we all loved Indian food. We arrived at the large restaurant, and found a secluded table hidden around a corner. This was an ideal place for us to eat, drink, chat and share fellowship together without being disturbed. All was well until a large, noisy party arrived, but even they didn't disturb us as they sat at a table a long way away; they were around a corner and so were out of sight, out of mind, and nearly out of earshot. Our food arrived and it was delicious. Later, as a member of our band went to the toilet, we heard some familiar music being played. On returning, he informed us that the loud party around the corner had hired a striptease act. It was then that we remembered what the tune was. From that moment on none of us dared to look up from our food or even visit the toilet. I am not saying that one or two may not have been tempted, but all temptation was definitely resisted at the cost of being put off our food! On returning to the pastor's home we sat in the lounge and heard a rather heated argument taking place in the kitchen. The pastor had obviously mentioned to his wife about the striptease act and she was furious at him for not instantly walking out of the restaurant. We stayed quiet and were just very grateful for the wonderful curry that we had just eaten! I guess the party around the corner firmly belonged to this world and understandably had different standards and enjoyed different pursuits than we Christians enjoy.

 THE POINT As Christians, we should have different standards from the unbelievers around us, but this doesn't make us superior. We are all sinners saved by grace, but as Christians we will never really belong to this world we live in.

 PRAYER *Lord, today please help me to be in this world but not belong to it.*

'Do not be overawed when a man grows rich, when the splendour of his house increases.' Psalm 49:16

 'house'

WHEN MY DAUGHTER Suzy got married to a fantastic guy called Adam, they could only afford a small semi-detached house. Like most young couples they wanted to decorate their new house and, fortunately, our in-laws Des and Sue were not only brilliant at DIY, but they also loved the challenge of doing it. I watched with interest as the lounge was soon transformed into what looked like a show house. The old kitchen had been restyled to look hi-tech and upstairs the bathroom and bedrooms were completely renovated. Eventually, the hours, days and months of hard work had paid off; once finished, the house looked fantastic. A beautiful house personally designed by Adam and Suzy and lovingly redecorated by Des and Sue. I thought after all that hard work they would live happily there for years to come. How wrong I was. Adam and Suzy sold it within a year and with the profit were able to invest in another house which was far more run down. Soon all the hard work started all over again and now the new house looks brilliant, but will they live in it for many years? Somehow I doubt it! I am just so glad that Suzy married someone who had such skilful and talented parents; if they had had to rely upon my DIY skills they would have ended up perhaps merely getting the walls painted with most of the paint ending up on the floor.

All around us are people who are earning or borrowing a lot of money to invest in property. Some are buying large homes that they do not really need, while others are spending thousands improving houses that do not really need improvement. It seems that if we have money, we must spend it, and homes are the obvious thing to spend it on. The next verse in our reading reminds us that we cannot take our property with us when we die.

 For some, it's right to invest money in a home; for others, it will be right to invest in ways that will benefit others. The main thing is that we invest our money where God wants us to invest it.

 Lord, please teach me today how I should spend my money.

08 MAR

'Therefore keep watch, because you do not know the day or the hour.' Matthew 25:13

 KEY WORDS 'keep watch'

MY JOB IS unusual. Unlike many Christians, my whole life is spent either with Christians, or with those who have an interest in Christianity. This being the case, I have always felt the need to balance this out, just as Jesus did, and to regularly spend time in places where I can talk to and befriend those with no church background or even any Christian interest. That is why I decided to join our local village 'Sports and Social Club'. I signed in as 'Rev', so everyone knew there was something 'religious' about me. The close-knit members were suspicious of me for a long time but eventually I befriended nearly everyone. I say nearly everyone because there was one guy who was hard to reach. This guy was loud, wild, and seemed to be the local hero. He could both swear and drink more than anyone else. He always ignored me, but one night I saw him sitting by himself, so I went and sat next to him. He explained that he had just had a big row with his wife and had nowhere to sleep that night, so I offered him our sofa. Irene had already gone to bed when we returned so I settled him down in the lounge and met Irene on the stairs who had been woken by the voices. She rightly quizzed me. Who was he? Was he safe to have in the house with three small children? I didn't have a clue. He was drunk and was certainly stronger than me. Unsure, I kept watch on the stairs for most of the night to protect our little family. As it happened there were no problems and he left early the following morning. To my knowledge he never chose the Christian life, but at least he had tasted a bit of Christian care and hospitality.

 THE POINT Keep watching because Jesus is going to return to earth and none of us knows when. Let's make sure that every day we are living a life that pleases Him, then when He does return, we will not be too surprised and will be ready to welcome Him.

 PRAYER *Lord, today and every day help me to keep watch and be prepared for the wonderful day when You will return.*

09 MAR *'May your father and mother be glad; may she who gave you birth rejoice!' Proverbs 23:25*

 KEY WORDS 'father and mother'

ALTHOUGH MY FATHER has passed away I often wonder how he and my mother would sum up my life so far. Perhaps as follows:

From 0–15: Our son has been brought up in the ways of God. He has been christened and confirmed. We think he has all the potential to be a strong Christian.

From 15–19: Our son is wildly out of control and doing everything that we as Christian parents taught him not to do. He is far away from God and we pray for him regularly.

From 20 until today: Our son is far from perfect but, over the years, he has proved to be a committed follower of Jesus.

Nearly every week I have the joy of visiting my widowed mother. First I have a cup of tea at her house and we update each other with any news. Then I take her out to a garden centre or café, where we drink either coffee or hot chocolate. However, I know that the highlight of my visit for her is when we discuss and debate the Bible together. Although her body is getting frail with age, her mind is as sharp as it ever was. When people get older they can often get set in their ways but not my mother; I am amazed that with all her years of charismatic evangelicalism, she can still come out with the most radical ideas and opinions. After more than 80 long years she is still a lady with an open mind and is always willing to learn new things. She keeps me constantly on my toes and, having known me longer than any other living person, will never stop influencing my life. It's not my place to say whether or not she rejoices over me like today's verse says – although I hope she does – but I can honestly say that I rejoice over her and I would not be the person I am today if it was not for her influence in my life.

 THE POINT We must always put God first, but our parents should have a special place in our lives.

 PRAYER *Lord, help me today to live a life that would make my father and mother glad that they brought me into this world.*

10 MAR

'Away from me, you evildoers, that I may keep the commands of my God!' Psalm 119:115

KEY WORD 'evildoers'

WHEN I WAS at primary school I became very close friends with a policeman's son who lived just around the corner from our Christian community. We would enjoy doing things together that a lot of nine-year-old boys enjoyed doing in the late 1950s. Things like rock-pooling on the beach and trying to find crabs and eels; kicking a football around the large green opposite his house. We also spent many hours rolling marbles and playing the most popular game of the day that involved flicking cigarette and tea cards. But as young as he was my little friend had a dark side. One evening after school we went into our local sweet shop; he didn't buy anything, but I bought a bag of my favourite pear drops. Once outside I saw him looking very pleased with himself and when I asked him why he was looking so pleased he put his hand into his pocket and brought out some bars of chocolate he had stolen. I couldn't believe it; a policeman's son shoplifting. I demanded that he take them back into the shop and return them. He flatly refused so I grabbed the bars out of his hand, walked back into the shop and laid the chocolate bars on the counter explaining to the shopkeeper that I believe these belonged to him. His face was a picture and he did not know what to say. He obviously had never had someone return stolen goods before and I was just relieved that he had not thought that I was the one who had originally taken them.

Needless to say, my little evil-doing friend, the policeman's thieving son, was not my best friend from that day onwards. Hanging about with him might eventually get me into serious trouble with his dad!

THE POINT As Christians we will always be tempted to do wrong things by some of those around us. Sometimes we need to part from these so-called friends if their evildoing is proving too persuasive and is encouraging us to break the commands of God.

PRAYER *Lord, today help me to keep away from people who may be intent on dragging me down and leading me away from You.*

'worthless things'

WHEN I WAS about six years old, I lived in a terraced house in Bristol and I really wanted a goldfish. In those days we had regular visits from the rag and bone men. These men were junk dealers who travelled around the streets on a horse and cart collecting rags, which would be converted to fibre or paper, bones that would be converted to glue, and small pieces of scrap iron. I guess they were the original 'recyclers'. They heralded their arrival by a distinctive yell that was supposed to be rag and bones, but it never sounded like that to me. Whenever I heard them coming I would rush out into the street to watch them. That is when I set eyes on the goldfish. If neighbours gave them something they found useful, in return they would hand over a goldfish. At last I thought I saw my chance! The next week I was ready for them. Immediately I heard their familiar howl I ran into the kitchen and pulled out a large bag from the cupboard which contained all my mother's best dusters. I then ran out into the road to exchange these treasured cloths for a real live goldfish swimming in a plastic bag! I am afraid I cannot remember the reaction from my mother over losing her precious dusters or what happened to my precious fish, or maybe I just don't want to remember. I wonder why we put such great value on relatively worthless things? Houses are important since we all need somewhere to live, but does God really want us to spend a lot of time, money and effort on four walls and a roof which will eventually crumble to dust? Most of us need cars, but why do some Christians show more excitement when hearing about a new car than they do when hearing about someone finding faith in Christ? A car is just metal and rubber that will eventually rust and perish.

THE POINT   **People are far more valuable than anything we can buy; let's enjoy the things we possess but, as our verse reminds us, let's ask God to turn our eyes away from worthless things.**

PRAYER   *Lord, please help me realise today that people should always be far more important than the things I possess.*

12 MAR *'Therefore encourage one another and build each other up ...' 1 Thessalonians 5:11*

 KEY WORD '**encourage**'

THE MAJORITY OF places I visit require me to perform at concerts, but as well as being involved in music I also speak and lecture at seminars on various subjects. Obviously most people want to hear me speak on subjects relating to children or families as that is where most of my experience lies, but other times people give me a completely different subject. Whatever the subject, I always add a bit of teaching based on Scripture that I feel may be relevant and a help to those delegates present that day. One thing I always try to impress on people is the value of honouring one another, because nowadays 'put down' talk seems to be in vogue. I remember at one specific seminar, where I had laboured the 'honouring' subject a great deal, a surprising thing happened. Straight after my seminar I decided to join Irene at the bookstall. Then I could not believe my ears; I heard a shout from the far end of our table. A person who was looking straight at me yelled in a loud voice, 'Oi, fatty, pass us a book!' I looked around in bewilderment and realised he was shouting at me! It was unbelievable! After all I had taught about honouring people this person insults me in front of a crowd of people! Of course I laugh about it now, but I do wonder why people like this attend my seminars if they are obviously not interested in listening to a word I say. That reaction, however, I am glad to say is rare. More often I get people telling me wonderful stories of how in the past God had used me to bless them or their families. Usually feeling embarrassed they start by saying apologetically 'you must hear this all the time' and then tell their story thinking I may not be interested. I am always interested and like everyone else I, too, need to hear encouraging words. I am too old to get big-headed about what they say; I am just so thrilled that God has used me in the past and hopefully is still using me today.

 THE POINT **We need to build each other up regularly by encouraging words.**

 PRAYER *Lord, help me today to be encouraging to all I meet.*

13 MAR ' "This is a remote place," they [the disciples] said, "and it's already very late. Send the people away …" ' *Mark 6:35*

 KEY WORDS 'remote place'

IRENE AND I love to take a winter break in the Canary Islands. The resorts are less crowded as are the shops and bars, and even the beaches are reasonably quiet. On one such holiday I decided we would explore the island, so I hired a small car and we headed towards a remote beach. Once we were miles from habitation I decided to be even more adventurous and go 'off road' to explore a really isolated area. After a short distance the road changed into a track and then the track seemed to disappear, leaving our little vehicle to bounce along on solid volcanic rock. Irene suggested we turned back as the sun was going down and it was getting late, but there was nowhere to turn around and I certainly couldn't reverse all the way back. I realised that we were lost in a very remote place and was praying like mad that we would not get a puncture! Eventually we did reach a track and then, O bliss, rejoined a road. I have never praised God for tarmac before! It was great to get back to our resort; it was even great to get back to our beach where we would spend the rest of our holiday in safety with the rest of civilisation!

Imagine over 5,000 people stuck in a remote place. They were keen to listen to Jesus but seemed to have lost all track of time. The disciples suggested that the most sensible thing to do would be to dismiss the crowd before it got too late, after all, everyone was getting hungry, and they had no food. Jesus decided the sensible thing to do was to let them stay, and then to feed them all by using five loaves and a couple of fish.

 THE POINT I wonder if some of the 'sensible' people realised that they were in a remote place and wandered off early and missed one of the greatest miracles that have ever taken place. Next time you go to a church meeting beware of leaving early to check the roast dinner; you just may miss out on something very special.

PRAYER *Lord, today I need to be sensible but not too sensible, in case I miss out on seeing the supernatural.*

'But you were washed …' 1 Corinthians 6:11

 ## 'washed'

DURING MY TIME as a Bible college student I was assigned a church in central London to gain some practical experience on how to be a pastor. The senior pastor, who still remains a good friend, was convinced nothing could shock him, but then, he had never worked with me before. A baptismal service was scheduled and it was going to be my first experience of baptising by immersion. In this denomination, going under the water symbolised death to the old life and coming up out of the water, resurrection to the new life as a follower Jesus, having been washed clean. When I asked the pastor what I should wear he told me I could wear what I liked. The big day came and the first shock I gave the pastor was to get changed into Bermuda shorts. The second, which was even more outrageous, was that I put on an old T-shirt advertising a brand of beer and the clergy in this particular denomination had taken an oath of abstinence from alcohol. Of course I changed into more appropriate clothing and the service proceeded. The pastor, who I'm sure was determined to get his revenge, told me that I was to baptise the first person, and that he would baptise the second, and so on. Now I didn't know the first person, who happened to be an elderly lady. I became very nervous when I saw how old she was. Suppose I drop her or, worse, drown her, she'd never forgive me. Things got worse; she sat down by the baptismal tank, pulled up her skirt, and proceeded to remove her false leg. 'I have to take this off, love,' she shouted over to me, 'I'm not allowed to get it wet.' By now I was standing in the water petrified and, without thinking what I was saying, announced into the microphone, 'Hop in!' Fortunately everything went smoothly and I managed to totally submerge her and miraculously get her back on to her one leg.

 THE POINT **We all need washing. Having a bath or shower washes our skin clean but the Bible tells us that sin makes us unclean inside. Jesus died on the cross to take away all our wrongdoing and by confession, we can be washed clean inside.**

 PRAYER *Lord, today I ask that You wash me clean inside.*

15 MAR *'They are shepherds who lack understanding; they all turn to their own way ...' Isaiah 56:11*

'shepherd'

I BELIEVE IT'S a mistake to exchange biblical titles for more fashionable ones. A classic example is to change the name pastor to facilitator. A facilitator tries to instruct and release others to look after the sheep. Sadly, many who instruct don't have the heart, patience or calling of a true pastor or shepherd. As Christians we should look after one another but every church needs real shepherds who will give their time, if not their lives, for the sheep. I met one pastor who lived 20 miles away from his church building because he didn't want to live anywhere near his congregation. I met another pastor who told me he would have a great church if it were not for the people who attended it. But these are a couple of bad exceptions; I have met hundreds of pastors who are true and good shepherds. Of course sometimes the sheep can abuse the shepherd. A friend of mine is a very good pastor who would do anything for anyone, but some of the congregation think that because they pay his wages this makes him their paid slave and they can call him out any time, day or night, for any reason. I tried my best to be a pastor, but my calling was really as an evangelist. On many a pastoral visit I made people would inevitably leave their television on and after a few minutes of listening to their tale of woe I found myself totally distracted by the television instead of listening to them. In one house I visited, I thought the lady there asked me if I would like a coffee, to which I replied yes please, with milk and two sugars. She walked off and returned pushing a small paper bag under my nose quite aggressively. 'I said would you like a toffee?' she hissed with no sign of a smile on her face. I burst out laughing the minute I left her house.

Isaiah was very annoyed with the shepherds who were supposed to be looking after the people of Israel but who were only looking after themselves.

Every church needs true shepherds, but let's make sure that we take care of our shepherds as they take care of the sheep.

Lord, today I thank You for those who pastor me.

16 MAR *'No-one can serve two masters … You cannot serve both God and Money.' Matthew 6:24*

 **KEY WORD** 'money'

IN MY EARLY days when living in our Christian community, I knew that sometimes money was non-existent, but this was for a purpose. With no money or savings to dip into it would be a case of everyone having to trust the Lord to supply all of our needs. This helped to raise everyone's faith, even the children's. One day when we were at school my mother realised that we only had potatoes left in the cupboard and some fish that had been assigned for the cat. Deciding that our need was greater than the cat's, she mixed the fish with the potatoes and made some very tasty fish cakes. She did, however, feel sorry for the cat. After all, it was our personal pet, which had travelled all the way down with us from Bristol when we first joined the community. The cat was called Lucky but today it didn't look like it was going to live up to its name. God had provided for the humans, was He going to provide also for an animal? Later, my cousin Lyn returned home from school with a packet. Entering the kitchen she asked my mother to guess what was wrapped up in the packet and Mother replied, 'A fish?!' Sure enough, that very day her class had been dissecting a herring and she had asked if she could take the remains of the fish home for the cat. So even with no money God still provided for all of us, including the cat. I could say the cat really was lucky that day but thankfully 'God's provision' has nothing to do with luck or good fortune, just His promise. Throughout a normal day I wonder if we spend as much time thinking and talking about God as we do thinking and talking about money. I have been in some church meetings where the introduction to the offering has been as long as the sermon. Our verse tells us that money is not just a coin or a note; it can be a master that we serve.

 THE POINT **Christians beware; if we are living for money, we cannot be living for God as well.**

 PRAYER *Lord, help me today to realise that with You as my Master, I do not need to worry about money.*

17 MAR *'Much dreaming and many words are meaningless. Therefore stand in awe of God.' Ecclesiastes 5:7*

'much dreaming'

I AM AT present going through a Church History course, a Theology course, and having practical tuition on the role of a Church of England deacon. Three very qualified and experienced mentors are guiding me through these courses. At times it's quite hard to get my brain working, as it feels as if it's been lying dormant for years. I also have to read what seems like half a library of books. The reason for this intense study is that by the time this book is published, I will be ordained into the Church of England. This is obviously playing on my mind, as I seem to do 'much dreaming' about the cathedral and ordination. Recently, I had the strangest dream: I think it was a mixture of my past and my present. I dreamt it was the day of my ordination and a bishop was instructing me as to what was expected of me at the service. As usual, I had a lot of questions but he silenced me. He said, 'Don't say anything, just follow me and do exactly what I do.' He then proceeded to dance around the cathedral. I, of course, followed him as instructed. Fortunately, it was just a dream. A few years ago I would have thought that dancing with the bishop at my ordination service would be a dream come true, but nowadays I really believe there is a time and a place for everything, and this isn't the time for dancing! When I am being ordained, I just want the bishop to lay his hands on me, pray over me, and then I want to kneel down and worship God in silence as I enter a new dimension of my ministry! It's strange how some people never dream, yet I've always dreamt a lot. Most of my dreams over the years have proved to be irrelevant rubbish and probably the result of a late cheese supper, but occasionally God speaks to me in a dream, and those dreams I tend to remember.

The Lord does still speak to us through dreams, but before we act upon any dream, we must spiritually discern that it is from Him.

Lord, tonight, if I dream, help me to know if that dream contains a message from You.

18 MAR *'How great is the love the Father has lavished on us, that we should be called children of God!' 1 John 3:1*

 KEY WORDS 'children of God'

WE WERE IN America on what promised to be a very special historic occasion. It was the worldwide March For Jesus day when Christians from many countries and from every denomination were going to take to the streets as a sign of unity and as 'God's children' to pray for the nations. We arrived early in the city square where thousands had turned out. What a sight! Every colour and creed marched together singing songs of praise as they did so. After the short march everyone congregated in the hot sunshine to hear some church leaders give a short speech on the importance of unity. We had managed to get near the front because I was keen to film this historic occasion with my camcorder. I need to explain here that we were in an American state which had suffered terrible racial conflict as a result of white people's dreadful treatment of black people. Then the most emotional thing happened. Spontaneously, or so I thought, a white pastor, from the largest white church in the city, took the microphone and spoke face to face with a black pastor from the largest black church in the city. In front of the many thousands he apologised for the way that the white people had treated black people over the years. Then they both embraced, both in tears. They were not the only ones in tears; there was not a dry eye in the crowd, including mine! The crowd dispersed and I wandered on to the stage and mentioned to one of the organisers what an amazing moment I thought that was. He replied that it should be, considering the amount of rehearsals the two pastors had beforehand to try and get it right! Ah!

Historically, it was only the Jewish nation who were known as the Children of God, but since Jesus died and rose again, all believers, whatever their nationality, are known as God's children. Racism is a terrible thing and, as Christians, we should be actively trying to stamp it out.

 THE POINT **Christians must never be racist. Whatever the colour of our skin we are all God's children, so that makes us all brothers and sisters belonging to the same family.**

 PRAYER *Lord, today I pray for an end to racism.*

19 MAR

'Away with the noise of your songs! I will not listen to the music of your harps.' Amos 5:23

KEY WORD 'songs'

I WAS INVITED to preach at a large church in Wales. At this service they had some very talented musicians playing. Welsh people are known for their love of singing so the musicians led us in a wonderful, melodic, joyful noise of praise. In my opinion, the singing seemed to go on forever, but eventually it was my turn to preach. As I spoke, I felt God move powerfully, and people really seemed to be listening intently. I closed with a personal challenge and felt God saying that He did not want any more singing, He just wanted quiet so people could reflect on what had been said. I told the congregation that there would be no more songs, and that we should just pray quietly, then go and get a coffee and share fellowship together. I waited a few minutes but nobody moved. I repeated what I had just said but still nobody moved. By now the musicians were itching to start playing again but I said no. I suddenly realised that nobody was going to leave the service until they had sung a final song because the pastor, musicians and congregation all believed that every meeting had to end with a song. We did not sing another song and they finally got up from their seats but I knew that they were not happy with me at all for changing the routine. Needless to say, I was never invited back again! I wonder how much time in our services is taken up with music? For some, perhaps a quarter; for others, maybe half, or perhaps even more. Singing songs and playing musical instruments do nothing for God unless the people who are singing and playing are doing it to the glory of God, not just because they enjoy a good 'sing song' or 'jam session'. I think we should sometimes hold services without songs to make sure that we have not become reliant on music.

THE POINT Worshipping God is not about songs and music, but about the kind of life we are living and how we are treating others.

PRAYER *Lord, today help me to realise that it's more important to live for You than to sing songs to You.*

20 MAR *'Jesus did many other things as well.' John 21:25*

KEY WORDS 'did many other things'

MOST WEEKS I lead a Bible study group in our home and our small group consists mainly of young musicians. Before I give the study everyone has the chance to share how their week has been and to say if they would like prayer for anything specific. On one occasion my son Joseph attended. Now Joseph is known for his skill with computers. Having attained a computer science degree he worked in a highly paid job for a short time but then felt that he should work freelance in a Christian environment so that he could also concentrate on writing specialist music. For years he has worked for me maintaining my website and also created some great cartoon karaoke DVDs which have been enjoyed by many. At the study, I asked all the musicians about their music and then asked Joseph about his computer work, but nothing relating to music. Afterwards, we went for a walk and he told me that he did many other things as well as computer work. I knew he was referring to his music but I had thought his music was just a bit of fun. He then went on to tell me that he now had four of his songs recorded by different people and some released on albums. I was amazed; why had he kept so quiet about this? The truth was that he had not kept quiet about it but I had selfishly only wanted to hear about his computer work because it was the thing he did which affected me most.

The next sentence that follows today's Bible verse says, 'If every one of them were written down, I suppose that even the whole world would not have room for the books that would be written.' This is incredible. We have got just four books in the Bible telling us about the life of Jesus, but those pages only contain a tiny fragment of the things that Jesus did in His 33 years on earth.

THE POINT Imagine the conversations Jesus had, the healings He did, the miracles He performed that we know nothing about. Imagine what those disciples must have witnessed in three short years.

PRAYER *Lord, today I realise that I know so little about You. I pray that as I read Your Word You will reveal more of Yourself to me.*

21 MAR *'If your enemy is hungry, give him food to eat …' Proverbs 25:21*

'give him'

I ARRIVED AT a large, cold conference centre on a miserable dark, wet winter's day. Once settled in my bedroom I went to see who else had arrived. It was at that point one of my close friends came bursting through the door looking very annoyed. He walked over to me and started laying in to me with some extremely harsh words that were just not true. I tried to calm him down but he wouldn't listen and continued to repeat the harsh words over and over, his voice getting louder all the time. Soon it had reached such volume that others standing around stopped their conversation and were looking in our direction. Eventually he walked away, leaving me feeling very shaken. How should I react? A friend had now made me his enemy. Should I ignore him for the whole conference, or just wait until he calmed down? Perhaps, given time, he would see that what he had said to me was out of order; he might come and find me and apologise, wanting to try and rebuild our broken friendship. He was due onstage that night and I decided that I should take the initiative. I saw him standing alone looking very miserable so I decided to go up to him and give him a hug. He hugged me back and apologised, explaining that he had just had a dreadful day and needed to take it out on someone. We prayed together and instantly our friendship was renewed and today we are closer than we ever had been.

Today's verse was written at a time when getting revenge was OK by God. An eye for and eye and a tooth for a tooth was the Old Testament way of doing things. But this little proverb is a taster of what Jesus was going to teach in the New Testament.

THE POINT **Instead of retaliating against someone, give that person kindness and love. Hopefully, by doing this, the person who has done wrong may feel guilty and want to put things right. If they don't, we who have been wronged must still continue to show love to them.**

PRAYER *Lord, today please help me to continue to love those who do wrong against me.*

22 MAR *'All of them were filled with the Holy Spirit and began to speak in other tongues as the Spirit enabled them.' Acts 2:4*

 KEY WORDS

'speak in other tongues'

I WAS INVITED to speak at a weekend youth retreat. There seemed nothing unusual about this, as I had done many similar retreats in the past, but when the youth leader told me his plans for the weekend, I could see that this was going to be very different. His church was not known to be what we refer to as 'charismatic', so I was surprised when he asked if I would teach his youth about the Holy Spirit. He believed that throughout the weekend God wanted to fill both him and his youth group with the Holy Spirit and he was not concerned about what the rest of his church thought.

I do not usually like going against what local church leaders are teaching, but when young people ask for me to pray for them to receive more power from on high, I can never refuse. The weekend went brilliantly. On the Saturday night nearly everyone was filled with the Holy Spirit and, just like in our Bible verse, were speaking in other tongues – or perhaps I should say praising God in a new language. When I say nearly all, the only one who wasn't was the poor old youth leader who was accompanying me on guitar and getting more and more miserable by the minute. I stopped the meeting and took him into a separate room. He was so disappointed that he hadn't received the power that everyone else had received from God. He was also desperate to pray in other tongues but just couldn't seem to be able to let God release this gift in him. I prayed over him and told him to try and praise God in the new language that God had given him: again, nothing seemed to happen. Then, in desperation, I told him to stop trying to speak in tongues and to praise God in English. The minute I said that he started praising God in other tongues!

 THE POINT **Speaking in tongues is a gift from God, and all His gifts are important and available for Spirit-filled Christians of all ages.**

 PRAYER *Lord, today please fill me with Your Holy Spirit and help me to speak out and praise You in other tongues.*

23 MAR ⟩ *'When his parents saw him, they were astonished.'* Luke 2:48

'astonished'

MANY ASTONISHING THINGS happened in my early years while living in a Christian community, and what I am going to tell you is a true story. One year, my parents kindly gave my sister and me a pet rabbit to share. We didn't have a rabbit hutch but discovered that our new pet soon made friends with the chickens and was happy to live alongside them in the chicken run. My father was in charge of the farm and he soon became very attached to our rabbit. Then disaster happened. Early one morning when he went to collect the eggs my father discovered that our rabbit had gone. The run was very close to a large wood which was home to its fair share of foxes. Had our rabbit escaped, or had a fox got it? None of us knew. We were all very sad and none more so than my father. Every morning he would look out for our rabbit hoping that a miracle had happened and that it had somehow returned to the chicken run. Around that time my father was praying about something specific and he wanted a sign from God to know if it was something he should pursue. He then prayed a very strange prayer. He asked God for a sign. He prayed that if our lost rabbit returned, he would be sure that it was God's will that he should pursue that particular thing. The following morning as he walked towards the chicken run the little rabbit ran straight out of the woods and even jumped right into his arms. So my father received his confirmation from God, and we all got our rabbit back!

Mary and Joseph frantically searched for the young Jesus in Jerusalem. Eventually they found Him and when they did, they were astonished. I wonder why? Was it because Jesus didn't tell them where He was going, or was it because they found Him sitting with the highest level of religious leaders of the day? We may never know.

THE POINT It's important to notice that Jesus was not teaching the religious leaders. He, like you and me, needed to learn from others before He began to teach.

PRAYER *Lord, today I've lots to learn. Help me always to be willing to learn from others, even from those who are a lot younger than I am.*

24 MAR

'Man looks at the outward appearance, but the LORD *looks at the heart.'* 1 Samuel 16:7

KEY WORDS 'outward appearance'

ALTHOUGH ISHMAEL UNITED played loud Christian punk songs with 'in your face' Christian lyrics, we did more than just play music at our concerts. Sometimes our rock concert turned into a variety show, thanks to Laurie our multi-talented bass player. One little game he played with the audience was 'guess the bass riff'. He would play some bass notes from a well-known song and the audience had to guess which song it was. Another skill he was perfecting was card tricks. Once, in a very dark hall, Dave our guitarist broke a string. While repairs were done, Laurie thought it was time to get out his cards. He asked for two volunteers from the audience to join him onstage. Halfway down the hall he saw two hands go up in the air, and he called the volunteers up. Something I forgot to mention was that not only was the hall dark, but also Laurie did not have the best eyesight. As he was looking at his cards all of us couldn't help noticing that the spotlights were shining on his two volunteers. They happened to be two very attractive young ladies, one of whom was wearing a rather transparent top. Some male members of the audience began to giggle, but our card-shuffling bass player still hadn't looked up and he assumed that everyone was giggling at him shuffling the cards. Still oblivious of the girls, he walked over to the microphone waving the cards proudly in his hand and announced in a very serious voice. 'Ladies and gentlemen, in a few moments all will be revealed!' The audience collapsed into laughter, and so did the rest of the band. Laurie just took a bow, amazed that he had such a great reaction from a such an average card trick!

THE POINT Although 'outward appearance' doesn't seem of importance to God, and He is certainly not against fashion, it is important that we as Christians dress sensibly. Wearing provocative clothing will send out the wrong signals to both the believer and the non-believer.

PRAYER *Lord, I know You are interested in my heart, not my clothes, but please help me to dress sensibly so as not to be a stumbling block to others.*

'They laughed at him [Jesus], knowing that she was dead.' Luke 8:53

KEY WORDS 'dead funny'?

ISHMAEL AND ANDY were on a mission in Norwich and we were staying with a really nice lady. One night we arrived at her house quite late to find her on the doorstep looking rather anxious. She was worried about an elderly lady who lived opposite whom she had not seen all day and whose house was in darkness. Andy and I crossed the road to investigate. We rang the doorbell a few times but there was no answer, yet through a gap in the lounge curtains we could see that the television was on. I noticed an upstairs window open so Andy helped me up on to the top of the porch and from there I was able to climb in the window. It was a bit frightening entering a house that I had never been in before, in the dark, and unsure of what I was going to find. I made my way downstairs and entered the lounge where the television was on. Then I had the fright of my life. Lying on the floor in the corner was this poor old lady, obviously dead. I ran to the front door to let in Andy and the neighbour we were staying with, feeling quite shaken. An ambulance arrived quickly and took her body away. I was surprised that the ambulance men seemed fairly jovial at such a sad sight. But they explained that they attended so many sad scenes that joking was the only way to keep their spirits up. I could understand that. It was a very different situation in today's verse: Jairus's young daughter had died. When Jesus arrived at the house and said she was not dead but only sleeping, the 'so called' mourners stopped weeping for the girl and started to laugh at Jesus. I would imagine their mockery soon stopped when a short while later the young girl walked out the door!

THE POINT It's a sobering thought, but some day we will all be dead – that is, if Jesus doesn't return first. I hope there's some laughter at my funeral, because I'll be having a great time in the presence of Jesus.

PRAYER *Lord, I thank You that when I am dead, I will really just continue living, but in a perfect place.*

‘a time to laugh’

AT ONE CHURCH we were attending, we were encouraged to join a cell group. A cell has nothing to do with prisons, although at some meetings I felt like I was in one! It involved about a dozen of us meeting up in each other's homes once a week and we followed a routine called 'the four Ws', which stood for welcome, worship, word and witness. Personally, it wasn't my thing at all. Sitting in a lounge staring at people, some with whom you had little in common, and struggling to make conversation was quite alien to me and often gave me the giggles at the wrong time. On one occasion, we attempted a creative prayer exercise which involved rubbing oil into the hands of the person sitting next to you. I was OK as I had a lady each side of me, but behind me were two very masculine male friends of mine who looked very embarrassed rubbing each other's hands with oil. I could see they were dying to laugh but with great self-control managed to restrain themselves. On another evening we spent time meditating on God with a tall candle in the middle of the floor. The aim of the candle was to represent the light of the world that would never go out. Then we passed the burning candle around. All was going well until it reached a lady who was going through a difficult time. Suddenly as the candle reached her she began to weep. It was at this point her tears instantly extinguished the candle and, try as they did, the person who was in charge couldn't get the candle to relight. I was tempted to laugh but I knew I shouldn't while one of our group was weeping. Fortunately for me, the atmosphere of serious meditation soon changed due to the endless striking of matches, and as others started to smile, I knew it was my time to laugh!

THE POINT There's a right time to weep and a right time to laugh; as Christians, we must never be afraid to let our emotions show.

 PRAYER *Lord, today help me to both laugh and weep at the right times.*

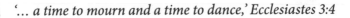

'… a time to mourn and a time to dance,' Ecclesiastes 3:4

 KEY WORDS 'dancing and mourning'

OVER THE YEARS I have built up a reputation for encouraging people to do things that they wouldn't normally do. It was never my intention to humiliate, I was just trying to encourage people to step out of their safety zone and attempt new things. I would always be there to support them, and would never ask anyone to do anything that I wasn't prepared to do myself. I was once one of 600 people attending a gospel concert watching some great bands play and some brilliant dancers perform. A band came onstage who were not only great dancers but who also performed with sticks that, when banged on to the stage, would both light up and make a musical sound. They were amazing to watch but as the band knew me, I felt revenge was in the air. After their performance it was, 'Let's embarrass Ish' time, and I was invited to join them onstage and to dance along with them while attempting to bang the musical sticks up and down. Now I may be a lot of things, but God never made me a dancer! I must have looked hilarious attempting to join in with these nimble dancers, and although it did bring great joy to all watching, it's not a ministry that I am likely to pursue!

I had just finished a round of golf and was laughing over a cup of tea with a friend when the news of the tragedy of 9/11 in New York broke on to the screen. I, like most other people, found it impossible to take in. That week I was invited to lead a family service in the West of England and my family services usually include a time of praise and some fun action songs. I checked with the organisers if this would be appropriate, as we were all experiencing a time of shock and mourning. After discussion, we decided to carry on with the service as planned, and it was a good time. Although we could never forget all those who had died or lost loved ones, we also felt that it was still important to praise God.

 THE POINT **Mourning and dance do not always fit together, but mourning and worshipping God do.**

 PRAYER *Lord, today I remember those who are in mourning. I pray even in their sadness that they will never stop praising You.*

' "Consider carefully what you hear …" ' Mark 4:24

 KEY WORDS 'listen carefully'

THE YEARS OF playing in a rock band have taken their toll on my sense of hearing. Whenever I watch television at home I get complaints from the rest of the household because the television volume rattles the floorboards! Recently, I was having a sound check on a stage and was asked how loud I would like the fold-back speakers. When I eventually settled on the volume I was told that there would be no need to use the main speakers at the front of the house as my fold-back speakers were so loud everyone in the building would be able to hear through them.

On another occasion, Irene and I were invited to speak at a conference in Switzerland and were picked up from the airport quite late at night by one of the organisers. I knew that it was going to be a long drive to our accommodation. I was tired and my ears were still suffering from the flight. Irene sat in the back of the vehicle while I sat in the front next to our new Swiss friend who was driving. In the course of our conversation he explained in his broken English that a mission had been sponsored by Horlicks. I immediately replied, 'Oh, the hot drinks company', and he just stared at me and replied, 'No, watches!' I then heard Irene giggling in the back seat. He had apparently said 'Rolex', not 'Horlicks'! It's very easy to listen to someone and to totally misinterpret the message. A lady had just become a Christian in one of the churches that I was pastoring and I announced that after the meeting everyone was invited back to the manse. She approached me afterwards and said, which man's? I wonder how many times we have said to people, 'Oh I'm sorry, I thought you meant …', but in fact that was not what they had meant at all. Jesus kept saying that if anyone has ears to hear, then let him hear. Today's verse says we must always listen carefully to what is being said to us.

 THE POINT **When we listen to family, friends or even preachers, let's listen carefully, because often we react and get hurt unnecessarily, just because we misunderstood what the person was saying.**

 PRAYER *Lord, help me today to really listen to what people say and to understand what they mean.*

'come down from the cross and save yourself!' Mark 15:30

 KEY WORDS ' **mockery and insults** '

MOCKERY, INSULTS AND cynicism are no fun. I was once invited to minister at a Christian holiday week. One evening the organiser asked someone to make the announcements and while doing so, whether he could also advertise my CDs. I couldn't believe my ears when he jokingly told the congregation that my CDs were full of dreadful music and sung by a singer who can't sing! Now even if he believed what he was saying, it was not what I wanted to hear to help promote my products. Although, strangely enough, we did have record sales that night! At another church I was invited to speak at a Bible study and as the minister introduced me he was met by a barrage of abuse from his congregation about his hair, his clothes and even his weight! It wasn't funny; it was belligerent, rude and showed a great lack of respect for the leader whom God had appointed for that church. I was with another friend at a large week-long event and an organiser asked him if he could speak at a late-night chat show. When he said yes, the organiser told him that was great because he had tried everyone else and they couldn't make it, and so, in effect, my friend was the last resort. From those who may not yet be Christians we may expect insults, but those of us that are part of the Church we need to learn to honour each other. Insults are only funny to those who say them. They can be extremely hurtful to those on the receiving end.

Jesus was hanging from a cross in total agony. He was alone because His friends had left Him, and even His Father seemed to have deserted Him. Then came the insults and mockery from the religious leaders who should have known better. Jesus could have reacted, but if He had, there would have been no way for you and me to have our sins forgiven and to be made right with God.

 THE POINT **Christians, let's refrain from mockery and insults and let's not laugh with those who use 'put down' humour.**

 PRAYER *Lord, today I want to thank You for not reacting to the mockery and for seeing Your mission through to the end.*

30 MAR ‘ *"Are you really my son Esau?" he [Isaac] asked.*
"I am," he [Jacob] replied.' Genesis 27:24

 KEY WORD ‘deceive’

BEING HUMAN, I guess we tend only to look at the outward appearance, but what I don't understand is the lack of insight from some who claim to have a prophetic gift. I have ministered alongside quite a few men of God with an international ministry who, sadly, have been involved in secret extra-marital relationships while still carrying on in ministry. Most of these men have shared a platform with some of the most well-known 'prophets' of our generation, and yet the prophets have failed to pick up from God that the man sitting next to them was deeply involved in deception and sin. I attended a conference recently where the leadership were in discussion with one of their main musicians, who was having serious marriage difficulties. They decided that he shouldn't be involved in music that year so as to give him and his wife some space to try and sort out their problems. For him to be on a platform and to encourage people to praise while going through such trauma would have been unreal to say the least. A replacement musician was brought in who knew the situation regarding the person he was replacing. A year later, it was discovered that the replacement musician was going through divorce proceedings himself at that very time but didn't mention it to the organisers. When asked why he hadn't mentioned his situation, he answered that his divorce was a very private matter and nobody else's business. Maybe not, but I believe that he was deceiving the organisers by agreeing to lead the music while knowing the person whom he was replacing had been asked to step down for a similar reason.

Isaac was very old. His eyesight had gone and he wanted to pray for both of his sons before he died. In our reading we can see that Jacob, the younger son, wanted the first blessing. He knew that by getting this he would get twice as much inheritance as his brother, so he deceived his father and pretended to be his older brother.

 THE POINT **We should never deceive or tell lies. Of course, it's quite easy to fool people, but we can never fool God.**

 PRAYER *Lord, help me today to be honest and to not try to deceive anyone.*

31 MAR *'Joseph had a dream …' Genesis 37:5*

KEY WORDS 'in God's time'

IT WAS AROUND 1980 that my old singing partner Andy Piercy invited me to London to hear a new Christian band. We arrived at the venue and, to be honest, got into such deep conversation, as we always did, that we heard little of their music. After their set the members of the band came and said hello to Andy, having heard he was the singer in After the Fire. They then moved on. Soon afterwards, I heard that this same Christian band were playing at a small pub in Brighton, so I suggested that the members of Ishmael United should have a night out together and go and hear them. It was a scruffy pub and it was empty apart from a few old boys sitting at the bar drinking and ignoring the band. The band were playing in a small room all by themselves as we sat watching them from the lounge area. The band was very good, but not quite as good as Ishmael United, I thought. I was a little put off by the singer smoking as he was singing and I thought his language seemed a bit colourful for a Christian. Afterwards, they joined us for a drink and the lead singer rambled on about some very obscure Old Testament prophecies confirming that the Lord had told them that one day the band would be very well known. I remember smiling and looking around at the empty pub; we even got more people to our gigs than they were getting. The lead singer's name was Bono, and U2 are now probably the biggest band in the world! Now that's what I call hearing God's voice! Bono must have felt like Joseph many times as he sang to sparsely filled halls, but he knew that in God's time it would all come about.

THE POINT **After thirteen years of being a slave Joseph became the governor of the strongest nation in the world. What God had told him in a dream many years previously came about in God's time. When God speaks to us about the plans He has for our lives, He rarely tells us when these things will come about. We have to wait patiently and in His time they will happen.**

PRAYER *Today, Lord, I realise that Your Word will be fulfilled in my life in Your time.*

01
APR

'The eyes of all look to you, and you give them their food at the proper time.' Psalm 145:15

KEY WORD 'food'

IT WAS EASTER and I was speaking at the Sunday service at my church in Lancashire. A friend had told me about a great Easter sermon illustration which required eating daffodils. I decided to give it a try. I began my talk by explaining that I had not had time to eat any tea. I then opened my briefcase, took out a plate, a knife, and some bread and butter, and proceeded to butter the bread in full view of an astonished congregation. Then, looking around for something to put into my sandwich, I walked over to a flower vase and pulled out a handful of daffodils. I carefully placed these on to my bread and liberally covered them with salt and pepper. By now my congregation were speechless and I knew they were thinking that their pastor was never going to eat it. How wrong they were. In no time at all I had eaten the complete daffodil sandwich. Then things started to go wrong. Within minutes my stomach started to do strange things. I had to make a quick dash off the platform and into the toilet next to the hall, and within earshot of my stunned congregation was violently sick. The worst thing was that when I finally reappeared, looking a whiter shade of pale, I couldn't remember what the daffodil-eating illustration was all about!

Moving on from daffodils, it does annoy me when I see people picking over good food and complaining about it. We have so much to be grateful for. God supplies us with so many good things to eat while so many people round the world don't have any choice.

THE POINT Not all habits are good, but a very good habit to get into is to give thanks to God before we eat each meal because once we have given thanks for our food, it will be very hard for us to complain about it. I have also learned to thank God for daffodils, but I give thanks that He made them to look nice in the garden and not in my sandwiches.

PRAYER *Lord, today I thank You for my food. Help me always to be grateful and to never forget those who are less fortunate than I am.*

‘ *"Son of man, can these bones live?"* ’ *Ezekiel 37:3*

 **KEY WORD** ‘bones’

MY EARLY YEARS were spent living in a large house in the Sussex countryside with lots and lots of Christians. For a little over a year, the Christian community also housed a small boarding school, and I was one of the pupils. At this time I also had a rather strange hobby: bone collecting.

With the help of one of my teachers, who was a keen biologist, we would scour the woods looking for regurgitated owl pellets. For the uninitiated, an owl can't chew its food and so it has to swallow a lot of its prey whole. After several hours the indigestible parts – bones, fur, etc. – are formed into a pellet that the owl eventually coughs up. These pellets would sometimes contain the whole skeleton of a small mammal that it had eaten. When we found one my teacher and I would carefully lay out the little bones in the shape of the animal and I would be taught which bone connected to which bone. This amazed me and really helped me to understand what a wonderful Creator God we have. Ezekiel was in a valley surround by dry bones and God asked him, 'Can these bones live?' Although Ezekiel answered, 'Sovereign Lord, you alone know,' we would probably have answered, 'No'. These bones were once living people but these people must have died years ago and no one could put life back into old bones, could they? Well, no one except God, that is. God put flesh on the bones, then breathed life into the bodies and they stood up and became a vast army.

After a heavy schedule of travelling and preaching I feel spiritually dry and often wonder if my family see the same exciting life of Jesus in me as others did when I was on a stage.

 THE POINT Every day I need to ask Jesus to breathe fresh life into me so that I don't become like a lifeless skeleton. Exhaustion can easily bring about the feeling of emptiness, stress and depression and if I allow these things to creep in, people won't see the life of Jesus in me.

 PRAYER *Today, Lord, help me not to be seen as a dry and lifeless Christian – whether at work or in my home.*

03 APR

'An elder must be blameless, the husband of but one wife …' Titus 1:6

'elder'

IN MY BIBLE college days, we were taught that an 'elder' must be male because of the above verse. How could a woman be the husband of one wife? I guess that makes complete sense. I tend to think it's foolish to call either a woman or a young man an elder. There are plenty of other titles to define the ministry of a female in leadership without using elder and so it is probably more accurate and sensible to use an alternative. I was once about to lead a service when an immaculately dressed young man walked in. I welcomed him and he explained that he was one of the leaders at the local Church of Jesus Christ of Latter-day Saints, and said his name was 'Elder someone.' I couldn't remember his surname. Even in those days my hearing wasn't good because I thought he said his Christian name was Elton. So for the rest of our service I kept addressing him as Elton. I'm not sure if he enjoyed the service but sadly that was the last we saw of Elton, pardon me, Elder. Following today's verse there is a list of qualifications that an elder was expected to obey and observe. When I was an elder in our local church I always tried to lead God's people by both word and example, but of course often failed miserably. I didn't want to appear aloof, superior or unapproachable but neither was I afraid of confrontation when necessary. God gave me a friendly personality and I find it easy to behave just like 'one of the boys'. In all my years of serving as an elder I wanted people to see me as I really was, including my faults. I wanted them to know that I am just another sinner saved by grace, I am not a distant saint who deems himself better than everyone else.

THE POINT Obviously we are not all called to be elders, but we are all leaders in some form or another. Let's never forget that there will always be those listening to our words and following our example.

PRAYER *Lord, today I thank You for your mercy and grace. In my position of responsibility, help me never to consider that I am in any way superior to anyone else.*

04 APR *' "I am the Lord's servant," Mary answered. "May it be to me as you have said." ' Luke 1:38*

KEY WORD > 'believe'

WAY BACK IN the early 1970s a large pop festival was going to be held near my home town. These festivals were not just about music; they were renowned for immorality, drugs and the occult. The local churches decided to hold a prayer meeting to pray against this festival. I was a very young Christian at the time and as I prayed, I felt the Lord telling me that just like Moses, I should go up on to the hills above the festival and hold my hands high in the air for a period of time. If I did this I believed that God would do something special and somehow stop the things that did not please Him. I nervously contacted the local prayer meeting and told them to forget about the prayer meeting and to join me on the hill. Needless to say, they thought that I was mad, so it was just left to a few friends and myself to climb the hill. Understandably, I got strange looks from passers-by as I stood on the hill for a long time, with my faithful friends making sure that both my hands remained high in the air. Then it happened. God opened the heavens and the rain came down in torrents. The festival was completely washed out and there was so much rain that even the bands couldn't play. Would it have rained anyway, even if we were not on the hill? I wouldn't like to say; all I know is that I believed that God wanted me to do it and the rain put a stop to a lot of evil things taking place.

Mary would have been a young teenager at the time the angel visited her and told her that as a virgin she was going to become pregnant by God, and give birth to His Son. Mary, I'm sure, would have had many questions, maybe even fears, but she believed, even though the message she had received must have sounded very strange to a young girl.

THE POINT > **When God tells us something, we must believe it and act upon it, even if at times what He says sounds crazy or humanly impossible.**

PRAYER *Lord, please help me today to learn from Mary and to believe whatever You say to me.*

05 APR *'[Jesus] gave himself for our sins to rescue us from the present evil age ...' Galatians 1:4*

KEY WORDS 'evil age'

IN THE UK today, everyone who has regular contact with children in the course of their work must be checked through the CRB (Criminal Records Bureau). These stringent safety measures are taken to ensure children growing up in today's society are kept safe and secure. When we first began working in children's ministry none of these statutes were in place. The tremendous responsibility of keeping children safe was in the hands of our team, the children's leaders. Sadly there is always the awful possibility that a paedophile might manage to gain access to a Christian event. So as well as teaching children about Jesus, our job was to keep a constant vigil for any who might wish them harm. When working at Christian camps held on an agricultural show ground, we were often warned that these people might get on site. So we had to keep checking the buildings and public toilet blocks before we could let children use them. On one occasion, we caught someone hiding in a toilet and the police came and arrested them. At another large holiday camp, as we patrolled an area behind the children's venue, I spotted a man hovering in the shadows. I politely asked him to leave. At this he lost his temper and shouted that he was going to get me. As he stormed off he certainly looked like he meant to do what he threatened. On this site was a big guy, who was an ex-CID policeman. The event organisers instructed him to guard me for the whole week. It seems strange but I am probably the only children's worker who has been given their own personal bodyguard at a Christian event! Sadly, we live in a sick world, an evil age. This is not how God intended His world to be. We could not have strayed further away from the perfect Garden of Eden that He once created.

THE POINT One day this evil age, and evil people will be a thing of the past. There will be a new heaven and a new earth, no sickness, no sin, a place of pure love where every little child will be safe.

PRAYER *Today I pray for any little children who may be in danger. Please Lord protect them.*

'snatch others from the fire and save them ...' Jude 23

KEY WORD ― 'save'

ONE OF THE many advantages of working with children and families is that when my own children were young they were able to join me on bookings. The meetings I had were fun, and they actually enjoyed being with their dad as he ministered. On one such occasion I was invited to lead a sort of teaching/adventure week in a very large house that was situated right at the foot of the mountains in north Wales. My job was to minister in the evenings while a team of young people were in charge of the daytime activities. One beautiful morning my two young sons decided to join my team as we attempted to climb Mt Snowdon. After many exhausting hours of climbing, everything was going well and the summit was in view, but then suddenly the weather changed. Almost instantaneously the sky went dark and torrential rain poured out of the heavens, turning the steep, dry mountain tracks into lethal rivers of gushing water. It was then to my horror that I saw our youngest son, Daniel, lose his footing and start to slide down the mountainside. I instinctively leapt forward, grabbed hold of his arm, and brought him up to safety. Soon after that we retreated back down the mountain, as it was far too dangerous to continue the climb. Eventually we arrived at the base soaking wet and shivering, not the best way to end a day's mountain climbing!

The Bible makes it clear that the future of those who are 'lost' and who choose not to follow Jesus is a grim one. I wonder with such a fate in store why I so rarely reach out my hand to them and offer them help like I did with my child who was in danger. It should be the most natural thing for a Christian to do, and yet so often we don't feel any urgency to do it.

THE POINT It should not be an effort to tell people about Jesus, we should do it instinctively. We should take every opportunity to reach out our hand and rescue others so that they, too, can know about the love of Jesus and enjoy the security of being saved.

PRAYER *Lord, today please give me the opportunity to reach out and share Your love with others.*

'Be imitators of God …' Ephesians 5:1

 'be like Jesus'

IN THE EARLY 1970s I was invited to play at a very large Christian event in central London. The Christian music industry was just beginning to take off and Christian record companies were looking for new 'stars' to promote. They were thrilled to find a young guy with a great voice and, for maximum exposure of his debut album, they decided to let him top the bill at this event. The company wanted their new pop idol to look a star. He was no longer a Christian nobody from some small village, he was now in central London promoting an album and surrounded by all things trendy. They decided to dress him in a smart suit, a nice flowery shirt (cool at the time) and great big high Cuban-heeled boots. I remember looking at him and smiling; I could see this humble singer was not at ease and that he was feeling very embarrassed dressed like this. It was my turn onstage, so I did my bit, dressed in my usual scruffy jeans and T-shirt (no stage image at all), and then, to rapturous applause, they announced the top-of-the-bill star. He strode on to the stage, guitar slung over his shoulder, looking very grand, and then, to everyone's horror, tripped over his new high-heeled boots and went sprawling across the stage head first. I know it's wrong to laugh at someone else's misfortune, but I couldn't help myself; it was funny, and I know the singer thought so too, a few years later!

When I was being trained for my ordination in the cathedral, I was very anxious that I wouldn't be able to be as good an Anglican as the rest of the clergy. My background and spiritual journey had been quite different from theirs. I was so relieved when the Bishop, Dean and Chapter all gave me the same reply: 'Ish, just be yourself.'

 THE POINT Always be yourself because that is the person Jesus made and loves. The only other person that all Christians should want to be like is the Lord Jesus. I wonder if those around us today can see a bit of Jesus in us?

 PRAYER *Lord, help me today to be content to be me and also help me to be more like You.*

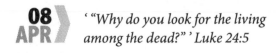

08 APR ‘ *"Why do you look for the living among the dead?"* ’ Luke 24:5

‘living among the dead’

I OFTEN WALK around the inside of our wonderful 900-year-old cathedral, and wherever I look I see reminders of the dead. There's a chapel to remember those who died at sea. Over the other side of the cathedral there's another chapel for those who died in various wars. On each wall I see plaques giving honour to past bishops, deans and other important or influential people of their day. There are large stone coffins in very prominent positions; there's one that particularly draws my attention, which has a beautiful sculpture of a knight and his lady lying peacefully side by side. And then I cannot help but notice the light pouring in from the amazing stained-glass windows, but they, too, are depicting people who are no longer alive. As I wander around these parts of the building, it can be like looking for the living among the dead. Of course it's right to remember with gratitude those who have died, and we must never forget those who sacrificed their lives in wars so that we could be free to worship in such a building. But this amazing edifice is not only all about remembering the dead. As I move to the centre of the cathedral, away from the edges and the grey stone and dark plaques, I observe the main focal point: the high altar. On it I see a cross, but with no dead Jesus upon it. Behind the altar I cannot miss the huge brightly-coloured tapestry symbolising the Holy Trinity and the extreme colour and brightness reminds me that Jesus is not among the dead, but among the living! Jesus is not lying dead in a tomb like the mortal remains in the stone coffins; He is living in believers' lives! I then notice that I am surrounded by hundreds of excited, chattering school children and guests from many countries, who are bustling around the building. The living bring new life into the ancient building.

THE POINT It is possible to find the living among the dead, but it's only those living for Jesus who will recognise life around them. The spiritually dead sadly walk around the cathedral and just enjoy looking at the dead.

PRAYER *Lord, today I pray for those who are spiritually dead; I pray that they will find life.*

'All the believers were one in heart and mind.' Acts 4:32

 KEY WORDS 'all of one mind'

WHEN I WAS in my early twenties and still a student at Bible college I was offered my first church leadership role as an assistant pastor. I was really excited by this, for two reasons. The first was that it was going to be a brand-new ministry for me. I had just spent the previous three years as a travelling evangelist, as part of the musical duo Ishmael and Andy, so being a pastor was going to be very different. The second reason was the church was in central London. Here there would be many challenges to face which I hadn't encountered before. I had not lived in a city since I was six years old. Soon after my arrival I was invited along to my first deacons' meeting with the also newly-appointed senior pastor. Here they were going to discuss my position. Within a short time I felt very uncomfortable. It was obvious they were not all of one mind and some did not really want me at all. As I sat listening they argued about whether or not I was really worth paying the suggested £5 a week as I was still 'just a boy' at Bible college. The senior pastor tried to reason with them, explaining that they were getting two pastors for the price of one. I felt like I was on special offer in a supermarket. At this point one of the deacons stared at me and exclaimed, 'No, not two for the price of one, just one and a half!' For once in my life I sat in silence and didn't react. I knew God wanted me to be there and in time I was proved right. I also became great friends with all those deacons, even the one that saw me as only half a pastor!

 THE POINT **It would be great if all Christians were so close to God that they knew His mind. Sadly, we are not, and so we often need to reason with one another to reach one mind. But let's be careful that as we discuss, we do not hurt people.**

 PRAYER *Lord, today we pray that our Church leaders will know your heart, so that in turn they can be one in heart and mind with each other and also with the rest of the Church.*

' "As surely as the LORD lives and as you live, I will not leave you." ' 2 Kings 2:2

'older people'

AT THE AGE of 21 I became an associate evangelist for British Youth for Christ. This gave me a great opportunity to meet up with older and far more experienced evangelists and I learned so much from them as I watched them minister. At this time I also met an older evangelist called Gordon Bailey. Most evangelists played safe, but not Gordon; he was without doubt the most controversial evangelist that I had ever seen and I loved him. Whenever possible I would try and be with him as he was the best (and without doubt the funniest) communicator of the Christian message I had ever met. On one occasion he was teaching religious education to a class full of riotous 16-year-olds who had no interest in religion. The class calmed down when he explained to them that they were about to see the most amazing trick. He put a glove on one side of the desk and a pencil on the other and stood a book upright between them. He then explained that he was going to perform the impossible. He was going to get the glove to leap over the book and pick up the pencil. All the class went silent as Gordon hilariously kept encouraging the glove to jump. Eventually he put his hand into the glove and picked up the pencil. He explained that a glove cannot do what it was made to do without having a hand inside it and we cannot do what we were made to do without having God living inside us. I learned so much from Gordon and I am so grateful to him.

Elisha was with an older man of God called Elijah whom he greatly respected and admired. Three times Elijah gave him the chance to leave him, and three times Elisha responded with our Scripture verse. Elisha knew there were things he could learn from Elijah and he was going to stay with him until the end.

Keep your eyes on today's Elijahs. We all need to spend time with those older men and women of God and glean from their wisdom and experience.

Lord, today I thank You for older and wiser Christians; help me to be willing to learn from them.

11 APR

'Everyone who hears these words of mine and does not put them into practice is like a foolish man who built his house on sand.' Matthew 7:26

'sand'

WHY IS IT that certain things are very 'man' things. It always seems to be the man of the house who carves the roast, even if it still tends to be the woman who cooks it. It always seems to be the man who has control over the barbecue, even though the woman has bought everything to put on it and has spent hours preparing the salads and garnishes that will accompany the cooked meat. Building sandcastles on the beach for the kids is also very much a man thing. My father always did this for his children and I always did this for my children. As a child living in Bristol we would usually travel to Devon or Cornwall for our summer holiday, but wherever we went, a sandy beach was a priority. Sometimes just plastic buckets and spades would be used but for serious sandcastle building, it meant real shovels so that the castle would be big enough for us children to sit on top of. When finished it looked great but only for a short while. It was always going to be a race against the incoming tide. First the sea would just fill the moat, then it would creep up over the high walls, and, finally, a big wave would demolish it altogether. Within minutes the powerful sea had demolished our wonderful castle which we had spent hours building and all that was left for us to see was flat sand.

The story of the wise and foolish men is by no means a children's story. It is a very frightening story. Jesus said that, for those who follow Him, it's like building our lives on a very firm foundation. For those who don't, and who choose to build their lives on other things, it's like building our lives on sand and when the rains and floods come our houses will collapse.

THE POINT Christians who really have built their lives upon Jesus can expect tough times, just like anyone else. The difference is that when they do face the problems, difficulties and pressures, they stand firm and refuse to go under!

PRAYER *Lord, today, with Your help, I will stand firm when faced with difficult times.*

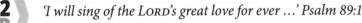

 **KEY WORD** 'singer'

WHEN I WAS a very young child someone told me that one day I would be a singer. Was this person being prophetic? Perhaps, because notice they said that one day I would be a *singer* – they never actually said that one day I would be *able* to sing! When I was ten, I attended our local village parish church and soon found myself sitting in the choir stalls. I was very grateful that I didn't have to do some sort of audition, or be asked to stand in front of Mr Baker the choirmaster to show which notes I could hit between bass and soprano. The sad truth was that I was a choirboy, but not because of my vocal ability. I was a choirboy because there was a spare cassock and someone was needed to make up the numbers! One Christmas Mr Baker courageously allowed me to sing the first verse of 'In the Bleak Midwinter' all by myself. I was thrilled at this; could this be the big singing break that my career was waiting for? Sadly not. I didn't get the words right and sang, 'In the bleak wid *minter*', which sent the rest of the choir into hysterics and was the last time Mr Baker trusted me with a solo part.

I had to face it, God had not blessed me with the voice of an angel – unless, of course, there are some angels that are better at shouting than singing! I guess it's God's little joke that over the years this gruff old voice has crooned on around 40 different albums. I encourage myself sometimes with the thought that although my voice may not be the most tuneful, at least it's sincere!

 THE POINT It's good to know that God doesn't only enjoy tuneful voices. He seems to enjoy even bad voices, if the person is singing their praise to Him. Now I am not saying that all of us croakers should rush and grab a microphone, but I am saying that when we are by ourselves, let's use our voices and have a good old sing about the Lord's love; He seems to enjoy a joyful noise as much as a tuneful one.

 PRAYER *Lord, today, as our reading says, I will sing about Your wonderful love – but maybe not in public.*

KEY WORD 'sea'

BEING AN EX-SEA Scout you would imagine that I would be good on water, but the truth is, I'm not. I'm terrible in boats and ships. While sitting on Eastbourne beach on a hot August afternoon with some friends, I suggested that Irene and I should go on what appeared to be a pleasant trip on an old-fashioned sailboat to Beachy Head. The sea looked as calm as a mill-pond and one of our friends encouraged us enthusiastically to take the trip, saying he had enjoyed the experience many times. We bought our tickets, boarded the boat, and off we went. All was fine until we neared Beachy Head when suddenly the calm sea became extremely choppy and rough. When we alighted from the boat, we were welcomed by our friend, who was laughing at our green faces. He knew the water was always rough out there but somehow had conveniently forgotten to tell us. That kind of practical joke makes you sick! On another occasion, I was invited to speak on the island of Jersey and as a special treat Irene and our three young children travelled out by air and returned by ferry. On the return crossing, everything was smooth for a time, then suddenly, out of the blue, a storm rose up. The sea instantly became rough and each time I looked out of the ferry window at the sea and sky meeting each other, my stomach began to go up and down in rhythm with the boat. It was then that everyone, except a few hardened seafarers who were dining in the restaurant, began to be sick everywhere. Not wanting to feel left out, my little family and I reluctantly, but very quickly, joined in with the vomiting party!

In Paul's day, ships were the only way to cross water and Paul not only sailed on rough seas, he also knew what it was to be shipwrecked. I hope he didn't suffer from seasickness like I do!

 THE POINT **Paul would never let rough seas stop him from taking the message of Jesus to others. Nothing should stop us doing likewise but, personally, I thank the Lord for the invention of aeroplanes!**

 PRAYER *Lord, today I pray for those who have been called to take Your good news to different parts of the world. Please keep them safe.*

14 APR *'Jesus said to them, "My Father is always at his work …" ' John 5:17*

 KEY WORDS 'always at work'

I DON'T BELIEVE there is such a thing as a Christian holiday. Whatever resort I visit I end up doing what I do at home. On one occasion, I was walking along a beach and someone called me over. I didn't know who they were, but I ended up hearing a very long life story and praying for them. On another occasion, Irene and I were in a small complex of self-catering apartments in the Mediterranean. We had just gone to the bar for a drink, when an older couple came in and the old gentleman was weeping. Just as I was enjoying sipping my drink Irene nudged me and told me that I ought to go over and see if he was all right. I walked over and started talking and discovered that they were a retired couple from the north of England, and he had just received a message that his mother had died. I gave him some consoling words and also explained what I did. I then asked him if he would like me to come to his apartment the next day and pray for him. Now I hasten to add, these two bereaved people were not in any way religious, but they jumped at the chance of me praying for him.

The following day we found their apartment and sat on the balcony with them. He had obviously been consoling himself for quite a while with his friend 'Jack Daniels'. As I started to pray, his wife jumped up and grabbed her video camera and told me that she would love to video me praying so that she could show it to her relatives back home. It was getting more and more bizarre. In the end I prayed over the gentleman while trying to smile into the camera at the same time. The amazing thing is the prayer worked and later that day the couple were very appreciative.

Father God never stops working and I think He would like the same from His children.

 THE POINT **We may have a holiday from our work, but we never have a holiday from working for God. Let's look for opportunities to serve Him at all times.**

 PRAYER *Today I thank You, Lord, for holidays. It gives me a chance to go somewhere different and yet to continue to serve You.*

15 APR *'If anyone does not know how to manage his own family, how can he take care of God's church?'* 1 Timothy 3:5

'leadership'

WHEN I WAS 15 I left both school and home to work on a farm. Having been raised in a Christian community I had lived a closeted life and knew very little about the outside world. Being a farm labourer was the best, or should I say the worst, place to receive my worldly education. Whereas the prodigal son left the farm to find excitement, I went to one to find it! Once I saw and tasted what was on offer, I was soon convinced that my parents were narrow-minded and had no idea of how to really enjoy life. I also felt that thanks to my Christian upbringing I had missed out on a lot of fun. I needed to go all out and make up for lost time. I was a very quick learner and had plenty of new friends who were happy to teach me how to live life as a 'normal person'. On the farm everyone swore, so I soon joined in and in no time I found that I couldn't control my language. I then indulged in alcohol, which led to drunkenness; girls, which led to immorality; and so the list went on. I ended up being ruder, cruder and far more excessive than my friends around me. Back at home my parents must have been heartbroken. Just as in today's verse, my godly father felt that while his son remained wayward he should stand down from Church leadership. Was he right in feeling so? Well, I cannot question what he felt he should do, but my thoughts are these: discipline in the home is very important; if we cannot lead our own family, we have no right to lead a 'flock'. My parents disciplined me well, but I chose to rebel. When a child becomes an adult, I personally don't think this scripture applies.

THE POINT **Once adult, our children are answerable directly to God, not to us. That is why it is so important to train up our children in the ways of God, while they are still young.**

PRAYER *Lord, today please help parents to be good leaders in the home and help those in authority in our churches to be good leaders in the Church.*

'The Father himself loves you because you have loved me and have believed that I came from God.' John 16:27

KEY WORDS 'father's love'

OUR DAUGHTER SUZY had been dating this wonderful guy called Adam. Adam is a DJ which means he travels the world. He was planning to travel to Australia and rang late one night to ask to see me. All sorts of thoughts went through my mind. Oh dear, something must be wrong, I told myself, perhaps he's coming to tell me that he's breaking off his relationship with Suzy. I was so relieved when I discovered the purpose of his mission was to ask my permission to marry Suzy! Of course I said yes. Then followed all the preparations for the big day. I accompanied Irene and Suzy to the bridal shop, and when I saw my little girl standing in a wedding gown, I could not stop the tears flowing. Then we had the rehearsal and there were musicians and dancers everywhere. Suzy is a dancer and choreographer so we practised our entrance and Suzy was very strict and instructed me how to walk and keep to the rhythm. Finally we had to decorate the wedding venue at midnight as it had been double-booked for the night before the wedding. And then came the big day. I proudly 'danced' in with my beautiful daughter and Adam was waiting patiently at the front. I conducted the service and the wedding vows and, of course, there was a huge laugh when I asked, 'Who gives this woman to be married?' then answered myself by saying, 'I do.' Our friend Jeff Lucas preached, and Suzy and Adam's friends played the music. I felt so proud of Suzy, and as her father I love her to bits. Although I was not so financially well off after the wedding, I have since discovered that I really am a lot better off. I have discovered that I didn't lose my beautiful daughter, but rather, I gained another wonderful son – and that's no cliché! As a father I really do love my children, but that is nothing compared to the love that Father God has for us, His children.

 THE POINT **Father God loves everyone, and those that believe that Jesus is His Son enjoy a special relationship with Him.**

 PRAYER *Lord, today I thank You for Father God's love.*

17 APR *'Where, O death is your victory? Where, O death, is your sting?' 1 Corinthians 15:55*

KEY WORD 'grave'

AMONGST MANY OTHER things, my Uncle Allan was the artist who designed the original pictures of *Glories and Miseries*. He was a wonderful, godly man, and someone with whom I felt very close. He died very suddenly and in great sadness I drove our family up to Leicester for the funeral. We arrived at the house and met with other grieving friends and relatives. The hearse arrived and the immediate family got into the funeral car and followed the hearse. I followed as the next vehicle in the procession. A long line of cars followed behind me. For a short distance everything went smoothly, then it happened. We came to some traffic lights and, while the hearse and funeral car sailed through on the amber light, I wasn't able to, and had to stop. When the lights turned green again the hearse and funeral car were nowhere to be seen. I didn't know what to do, but rather than look foolish, I drove confidently on, led by my instinct. I drove down a small road and the procession duly followed. After a few yards I entered a tyre factory and – please excuse the pun – a dead end. The others continued to follow me. I then had to reverse and drive out of the factory gates and past all the other funeral cars. All the time I was trying to keep solemn, not daring to look at any of them. They all ended up bumper-to-bumper, facing the wrong direction in the tyre factory yard. I then had to pull over and exploded with suppressed laughter. I didn't feel too guilty because I knew that if Uncle Allan could see the mourners' shocked expressions, he, too, would have been shaking with laughter. Death is always sad, and to lose a loved one is terribly painful. But let's never forget that a Christian cannot really die. A Christian just leaves this earth and continues to live with Jesus. Of course the heart stops beating and the body decays, but the real person carries on and lives forever.

THE POINT **Death is the Christian's door into heaven, where there will be no more pain or sadness.**

PRAYER *Lord, today I thank You that the grave is not the end; it's just the next part of our journey with Jesus.*

KEY WORD ❭ '**royalty**'

I HAVE NOT had the opportunity to meet personally with any royalty, and I probably never shall, although I did once get the chance to meet a knight of the realm. I was invited as a guest on to a national television programme called *Highway*. It was transmitted early on Sunday evenings and was hosted by a very famous comedian – the late Harry Secombe. Harry had recently been knighted and so was now 'Sir Harry'. The programme producers rang me and invited me over to the film set. Never having met a knight before, I asked them what I should call Harry and they said he liked to be called Sir Harry. Now I had never had to call anyone 'Sir' in my life before; even at school, we called our tutors 'Mr' or 'Mrs'. I always like to respect people's wishes, so if Harry wanted to be called Sir Harry, that was fine by me. I arrived at the studio and immediately was introduced to Sir Harry. We sat down and spent quite some time chatting together but, funnily enough, calling him 'Sir' didn't seem strange all. He was such a lovely man – full of humour, and so interesting to talk to, that I felt he deserved to be Sir Harry. He had achieved so much in life and the Queen's blessing and the honorary title bestowed on him didn't make him proud or superior; he was a humble, sincere man who knew how to make people laugh – and boyo, could he sing!

 THE POINT ❭ **When Jesus returns, unlike human royalty, He will not need a crown or robes or even a title to show us He is King. His very presence will make the whole world – including royalty, presidents and knights of the realm, fall to their knees and worship in awe and wonder.**

PRAYER *Lord, today I worship You as the King who will reign for ever.*

19 APR *'He has an unhealthy interest in controversies and quarrels about words …' 1 Timothy 6:4*

 KEY WORD 'argue'

WHEN I WAS younger I always loved a good debate. I would like to think that maturity has mellowed me into more of a peacemaker nowadays, but I will leave those who know me to comment on that. After I had proposed to Irene, we went to discuss the wedding arrangements with our minister Derek Moon. Derek was a lovely man but in my opinion was more than a little old-fashioned. During the course of our conversation I told him that I would like the Bible reading in the service to be read from the Living Bible, so that everyone attending, both churched and un-churched, could understand it. As a Bible teacher, he refused point blank to read from a paraphrase and said he would only read from a real translation like the Revised Standard Version. We had a bit of a debate about this but I decided to let it go for a while, thinking he might reconsider. The following week as he stood in the church doorway shaking hands after the service, I brought it up again. That was it, we both lost it and ended up raising voices at each other with many of the bemused congregation watching and listening! It was a war between the 'Living' and the 'RSV'; between the new and the old! I am pleased to say that in the end the Living won! The strange thing was, he and I were great pals and being an excellent keyboard player, he even played on both the 'Glories' albums, despite the fact that it certainly wasn't his style of music! He and I enjoyed the odd quarrel about all sorts of subjects and controversies, most of which were totally unimportant. It seems to me that there are two kinds of quarrelling: an unhealthy one, which results in envy, strife, malicious talk, suspicion and conflict, and a healthy one, where two people put over opposing viewpoints but stay open-minded and are willing to listen to and learn from each other.

 THE POINT If we argue, let's always listen to the opposing argument and, more importantly, let's always stay open, humble and loving.

 PRAYER *Lord, today I realise that winning an argument is not as important as loving someone I disagree with.*

20 APR *'... there is a friend who sticks closer than a brother.' Proverbs 18:24*

'friend'

I KNOW IT sounds a bit of a cliché, but I can honestly say that my very best friend in all the world, who sticks to me closer than a brother, is my wife Irene. She knows everything about me and still loves me! I find that amazing, especially when I do dreadful things. We were in America speaking at a very large conference. Like most ladies I know, Irene had spent time on her presentation, clothes, hair and making herself look great before going to deliver a seminar to a room full of people. Before she entered the room she decided she needed a drink of water from the water fountain. For the convenience of both adults and children this fountain had both a higher and a lower tap. Being only four feet ten inches tall she decided to use the lower tap. Being my usual helpful and enthusiastic self, I accidentally pressed the wrong button. To my horror water shot out from the higher spout and, yes, I somehow managed to drench Irene's clothes and her carefully coiffured hair! I thought I was dead, and decided that the wisest thing to do was to run. Amazingly Irene just smiled calmly – although behind that smile she may have been gritting her teeth. Being the great wife she is, she discreetly made her way to the ladies' cloakroom, dried out under the hand dryer, and then carried on to deliver her seminar. She even managed to turn the whole disaster into a joke which won over her audience. What a pro!

Of course the best friend we can ever have is the Lord Jesus, but it's also important to have human friends. In the story of the prodigal son we find so-called friends who only want a relationship for what they can get out of it, but not all friends are like that. Real close friends like us for ourselves, not for what we have. They even put up with us when we get moody, bad tempered, or even drench them before a seminar.

THE POINT **Good friends can be hard to come by, so when we find true friends, let's do everything we can to keep them.**

PRAYER *Lord, I thank You for all my friends. Please help me to treat them in the same way that I like to be treated.*

'We live by faith, not by sight.' 2 Corinthians 5:7

KEY WORD 'eyesight'

WHEN I WAS younger I had very good eyesight, but sadly as years have progressed my eyesight has deteriorated. Irene and I celebrated my 50th birthday in a small hotel in Dorset with my good friend Andy Piercy and his wife Judy. While the wives chatted about wife-type things Andy and I decided to go to the hotel reception and find out where the nearest Indian restaurant was located. The owner had no idea, but he gave us a telephone directory to check it out for ourselves. Then came the shocking truth. Neither Andy nor I could read the small print in the directory, even when standing ten yards away from it! Fortunately the wives were able to read it to us.

The good news is, healings do still happen. One of the most incredible healings I have ever witnessed was that of a nine-year-old boy who had very bad eyesight. His eyes were so poor he was forced to wear spectacles with really thick lenses to be able to see anything at all. He asked us to pray that God would make his eyesight better. We prayed for him and as we did so, he shocked us all by saying that prayer had made his eyes worse, and that now everything was blurred. This was not encouraging news to our prayer team! Then we realised that in fact his eyes had begun to improve, and couldn't focus through the thick lenses of his glasses. We met that boy at the same conference for the next few years and every year the lenses got thinner until in the end he didn't need to wear glasses at all. Why didn't Jesus give him instant healing? I have no idea, all I know is that I never question Jesus as I have learned that He always knows best!

THE POINT **Christians don't live just by what their eyes can see, they live by faith in the word of God. Faith is hearing God's voice and then believing that God is going to do what He says before it happens and before we can see it with our eyes.**

PRAYER *Lord, today please give me more faith to believe that You can work miracles when I pray for people to be healed.*

22 APR ‘He [Jesus] said …, "Let the little children come to me …" ’ Mark 10:14

KEY WORDS ‘little children’

OVER THE YEARS I have learned a lot from ministering to children. A long time ago I was setting up, getting ready to perform a children's concert, when I saw a young boy stand by my microphone on the stage. I spoke to the child, gently asking him to kindly get off the stage. For some reason, even though he obediently got off the stage, he kept climbing back up on to it. In the end I spoke slightly more severely and repeated that he must stay on the floor. He then replied that he was going to sing with Ishmael. As he obviously didn't recognise me, I enlightened him by telling him that I was Ishmael and I was not planning for him to join me singing onstage that night. Many years passed and I was just finishing an evening Family Celebration at the Spring Harvest Bible Week, when a message was handed to me from a steward that a very special guest was outside who wanted to meet me. As I looked to the back of the venue a young man came running up to the front and grabbed hold of the microphone. He then explained to the amazed audience that many years ago Ishmael had pushed him off the stage (this was a slight exaggeration) and he asked them if he should now push *me* off stage. Without waiting for an answer, he then proceeded, in fun, to do just that. I now realised who this person who had wanted to join me onstage all those years ago was: the successful pop singer Daniel Bedingfield. All those years ago I had forbidden him to join me onstage, but today I would say yes, Daniel, any time you want to join me onstage you would be more than welcome!

THE POINT We don't know God's future plan for all those little children in our church. That is why I am just as happy to visit churches which only have 20 children, as I am visiting those that have 200. One of that 20 may be a little future Billy Graham … or even a Daniel Bedingfield!

PRAYER *Lord, today I pray for the children in my church. May I be an encouragement to them and may they grow up to be mightily used by You.*

23 APR *'Peace I leave with you; my peace I give you.' John 14:27*

KEY WORDS 'peace of mind'

CHOOSING A HOUSE to live in can be very confusing. We spent many happy years living in a large detached house in a small village but, due to various church issues, we knew it was time to move on. We decided to join a church in the city of Chichester and we sold our large house and bought a house nearer our new church. The trouble was, in the process of selling and buying, we lost a lot of money. Property in Chichester was far more expensive than anticipated, and so we felt we could only afford a small semi-detached house. With three grown-up children, it was a squeeze. A couple of years later, a derelict old vicarage came up for sale. It was in a dreadful state of disrepair and had not been lived in for over a year. The ceilings were stained dark brown because the previous occupant had smoked a pipe; the slates were missing; and there was even ivy growing inside the house through the rotten windows. Worse still, the previous owner had kept rabbits and other pets inside the house and had allowed them the freedom of the whole ground floor. As I walked into this damp, miserable, dilapidated house where no one had wanted to live for a long time, the peace of God filled my mind and heart. I knew that this was God's house but not just for us. Since moving in we have always had an extended family living with us and, without exception, all those who have stayed have enjoyed making this house their home too. As Christians, we mustn't worry solely about outward appearance, making careful investments and using common sense. I believe that Jesus has given us an extra sense, that is a peace of heart and mind to help us to make the right decisions.

THE POINT **We all have to make decisions every day. I believe we can make certain day-to-day decisions on the spot, but any important decisions shouldn't be made until we feel that wonderful peace of mind that Jesus gives to confirm that a decision is right.**

PRAYER *Lord, when I make important decisions today, please give me that peace of heart and mind so that I know that the decisions I make are the right ones.*

'But I tell you: Love your enemies …' Matthew 5:44

 KEY WORD 'enemies'

I HAVE NO desire to go out and make enemies. When I was pastor of a church I became good friends with a local Christian businessman. He was a great help to me in building up the church and together we saw some great things happen. After a time I felt my ministry had been completed there and it was right to move on. Of course he stayed behind to carry on the work. Over the next few years that little church experienced some terrible difficulties. Sadly, my good friend was left to face a lot of the problems. I sensed that he thought I was partially responsible for some of the difficult times he encountered. Perhaps he felt I should not have involved him so much in the first place, or that I should not have moved on. Whatever the reason, he seemed to feel that our friendship had come to an end. I kept remembering the great times that we had spent together seeing God's work grow. I wrote to him and apologised, but got no response. Many years later we met up unexpectedly. I wondered if he would even want to talk to me but, thankfully, he did. It was so good to see him and we had a good time together, and I came away feeling that our friendship had been restored.

In my book *Reclaiming a Generation*, I wrote, 'I have no real enemies, but I think I may have a few friends who don't like me much.' It's true, I don't think I have any enemies or hate anyone, but I can also think of a few people who have upset me in the past and although I like to say I love them as part of God's family, the truth is I don't really like them much.

 THE POINT I think that the 'not easy to like' are the people that Jesus wants us to like; in fact, I think He wants us to go out of our way to show them that we love them. It's a hard one, but if that's what Jesus wants, that's what we must do.

 PRAYER *Lord, today please help me to show Your love to people whom I find hard to like.*

25 APR

'The LORD is my shepherd, I shall not be in want.' Psalm 23:1

'needs'

ONE OF THE reasons why Ishmael and Andy were so popular back in the early 1970s was because they were unique. Although there were many Christian singers and bands around at that time, none were playing the crazy material that Ishmael and Andy played. Later, a duo called Fish Co played similar material, but everyone else was playing quite serious music. Andy and I knew that all we really needed to fulfil the ministry that God had called us to were two acoustic guitars; we didn't even need good ones! Fame, even on a small scale, can be a dangerous thing. We were young Christians and becoming very popular with audiences up and down the country and were packing out venues. On one trip to Cornwall, we passed a workshop that had a big sign outside advertising handmade guitars for sale. We went in and talked to the guy who was making them. He showed us his craftsmanship and we were so impressed that, without any hint of prayer, we decided that we wanted one. After discussion we decided that just getting one would not be fair, we really needed one each. These guitars were very expensive, especially for two wandering penniless Christian minstrels. At this point, I must add that we didn't need new guitars, but as rising Christian stars we thought we deserved them. We waited for over a year for the guitars to be made. When they did eventually arrive, they were dreadful and unfit to play. We sent one of them back but it was no use, they wouldn't either change them or refund our money. I kept one as a souvenir of my stupidity; it would never be played, but hopefully it would serve as a reminder that what I want and what I need are two different things.

Some of the things that we want and we ask the Lord to provide for us we will never receive, because the Lord knows that we are better off without them.

THE POINT The Good Shepherd looks after His sheep and He will always provide our needs, but will not always provide our wants.

PRAYER *Lord, I know you don't provide all my wants, but I do believe that You will provide all I need today.*

26 APR *'The name of the LORD is a strong tower; the righteous run to it and are safe.' Proverbs 18:10*

'safety'

I WAS INVITED to mainland Europe where a well-known youth and children's organisation was holding a joint annual conference. The minute I arrived I felt as if I was in a war zone. There was obvious animosity between the children's and youth organisers. The children's organisers had invited me, but it seemed that the youth organisers felt that someone who worked with children had little to offer those who worked with youth. It was a packed hall with hundreds present for the first evening celebration. The band was great, and even though the atmosphere was a little strained, I felt excited as I got up and began to speak. Within a short time I knew something was wrong. I could sense that the youth organisers didn't only dislike what I was saying, but also, for some unknown reason, seemed to actually disliked me as well. I finished my talk and none of the youth organisers came up and spoke to me. I went up to my bedroom and literally hid myself away. The following day I spoke to the children's organisers and told them that I was not prepared to speak any more. I wanted to leave but they convinced me to stay and just speak with them. I'm glad they did because, for the remainder of the weekend, we had a good time together. Sadly, during my whole time there, not one of the youth organisers ever spoke to me. I returned to England totally insecure, feeling that I had little to offer overseas and, as a result of this, I refused to visit mainland Europe for many years.

Like me, do you ever have those days when you're feeling a little insecure and that people are talking behind your back? Have you ever felt like running away and hiding somewhere? Since my European experience, I have discovered the place to hide.

We can run and get protection in that strong tower, otherwise known as the Lord Jesus, whom we love and trust. It doesn't take long in the tower before our insecurity goes, and we become strong in God again.

Lord, I know that if I feel insecure today I can come to You and find protection and renew my strength.

27 APR *'The earth is the LORD's, and everything in it, the world and all who live in it;' Psalm 24:1*

 KEY WORDS 'belongs to the Lord'

NOT ALL THE concerts I perform are for nice, well-behaved middle-class Christians who live in a very select part of suburbia. Many years ago, parts of Liverpool were experiencing horrific riots and lawlessness. I was booked for a concert in a hall right in the middle of one of the roughest estates, at the height of its problems. I had been warned that police cars rarely entered this estate and even fire engines had been enticed on to the estate by false alarms just so that the residents could attack them. I drove on to the estate in fear and trepidation. The depressing tower blocks lived up to my expectations: many had boarded-up windows, and burned-out cars were littering the road just metres away from front doors. Some small children welcomed me armed with stones in their hands, and with great accuracy had no trouble hitting their target, which happened to be my vehicle. I arrived at the hall, a depressing building, which also had all its windows either boarded-up or barred, in an attempt to keep would-be thieves out. I began to set up, wondering if anyone would come to the concert but, a short while later people started to arrive. Many families came and we had a great time. The residents' attitude towards me instantly changed and they were really friendly when they realised that I had come to entertain their children. I'm pleased to say no trouble ensued. It's hard to imagine that this rough estate with its boarded-up, graffiti-covered buildings, surrounded by burned-out vehicles and some very hurt and needy people, belongs to the Lord.

 THE POINT The devil thinks he owns things and people, but how wrong he is. He can bring about chaos, destruction, and can help ruin lives, but he will never own anything or anybody. Almighty God made both the world and us, which means everything belongs to Him; He is the owner of the whole universe.

 PRAYER *Lord, everything belongs to You. At times it looks like the devil has stolen things and people from You. Lord, today I pray that people begin to realise who their rightful owner is.*

28 APR *'who [He] satisfies your desires with good things so that your youth is renewed like the eagle's.' Psalm 103:5*

'young'

WHEN I BEGAN my travelling ministry I was only 20 years old. I hadn't been a Christian for very long. I was totally sold out for Jesus. I wanted to serve him all day, every day, and nothing was going to stop me. The tours would take me all over the country; I would wear out vehicles like some people wear out shoes. It was nothing to me to drive 300 miles to the north of England on a Saturday, unload the gear from the van, set it up, do a two-hour concert, then drive 300 miles back home again. Having arrived back in the early hours and had very little sleep, I would then be at the church meeting by ten o'clock, ready to praise God! But I was a young man then; today it's not quite the same story. I am still in love with Jesus, but I have not quite got the energy I once had. The spirit is still very willing but the flesh is getting weaker. At one time I could fulfil three bookings in a day, nowadays, it takes me three days to recover from one booking! But it's not all bad news. When I first began attending the cathedral one elderly lady came up to Irene and I and commented on how nice it was to have some young people attend the service – yes, she was looking at us! Yippee, I'm back in the youth group! It's nice to know that I'm still quite young; at least I'm young when compared to some very old people! Some of us are old and are feeling very old, others of us may be young, but feeling very old. My mind never lets me believe I am getting old, it's just my body that keeps reminding me that I am no longer a spring chicken! I love today's verse; not only does God satisfy me with good things, and He does, but He also keeps me feeling young even if He doesn't keep me looking young!

Let's not feel old. Remember, we are going to live forever, so putting time into eternity we have only just begun living.

Lord, today, as an older person, I thank You for keeping me feeling young.

29 APR *'... work at it with all your heart, as working for the Lord, not for men,' Colossians 3:23*

KEY WORD 'work'

DURING THE DAYS of the band Ishmael United, our budget was very tight. Managing a band was an expensive business. As well as trying to find money to support band members, their families and a sound engineer, I also had Irene, three small children and a mortgage to finance. I had two options. I could spend the day trying to pray the money in, or go out and find a part-time job. I decided to do both. I would go and try and find a job that would also allow me time to pray. I applied to be a taxi driver and got accepted on the spot. It seemed that they didn't have many ordained ministers applying to drive taxis! I was then shown my car, it was a great big Ford Granada and was better than any car that I had ever owned or even driven before. But it was not all easy going. Taxi driving meant working very long hours and many of those hours would be spent sitting outside the railway station waiting for business. Fortunately, this did allow me the time I needed for prayer. And then there were my customers. Some were really nice and I even had a chance to talk to a few of them about Jesus, but others, especially late on a Saturday night, were not particularly pleasant, to put it mildly.

We all have to do a variety of jobs. Some that we do, we enjoy doing and so we throw ourselves into them wholeheartedly. Other jobs we find a drag and we do them half-heartedly. Today's verse is a great challenge because, whatever we are doing, we should try and imagine that we are doing it to please Jesus, not just our employer or the people around us. This would then mean that we would do the very best we can with any job we undertake.

THE POINT **As Christians we should be an example in whatever we do, however menial the task that is set before us. People can expect the very best job from us with maximum effort, because we are also doing it for the Lord.**

PRAYER *Lord, today, whatever I do, I want to do it well, because I am doing it for You.*

30 APR *'While they were there [Bethlehem], the time came for the baby to be born, and she gave birth to her firstborn, a son.' Luke 2:6–7*

'young mother'

FOR MANY YEARS Irene and I have been patrons of a charity called Education Plus. This Christian charity works with the street children in the shanty towns of Costa Rica. A while ago we had the opportunity to travel out to Costa Rica and see the work of Education Plus first-hand. A cameraman who was going to make a short film of us on location to help promote this charity also accompanied us. The shanty towns are appalling places where everyone is desperately poor. The 'houses' are just corrugated iron huts and the toilets deep holes dug in the ground. On one occasion while we were driving around, our friend Keith, who works for Education Plus, pulled up the old Land Rover outside a hut. Suddenly lots of children and babies appeared through the small doorway and ran towards the vehicle, obviously thrilled to see him. My eyes focused on a very young girl holding a small baby and I asked Keith where the baby's mother was. He then explained to me that the young girl holding the baby was the baby's mother and the whole family lived in this tin hut. There were no fathers to be seen anywhere. I was shocked; I had never seen such a young mother before.

When the Lord Jesus was born there was no palace, just an animal dwelling. No soft bed or clean sheets, just straw and a feeding trough. No medical help or nurses, just Joseph and perhaps one or two people who were nearby. But out of this poor stable a very young mother called Mary gave birth to God's Son. Once her child had been born, this world would never be the same again.

 THE POINT **We may not be rich, but very few of us are very poor. Jesus wants all Christians to remember and care for those in very needy situations. By doing this, we are following Jesus. By doing this we, too, can help change the world.**

 PRAYER *Lord, today we thank You for Your mother, Mary, who was humble and obedient and certainly was highly favoured.*

01 MAY ❯❯ *'From the rising of the sun to the place where it sets, the name of the LORD is to be praised.'* Psalm 113:3

 KEY WORD ❯ '**dawn**'

MAY DAY IS here, and in many countries people will be using this day as a day of celebration and remembrance. Some people will be celebrating the beginning of spring with fertility festivals and remembering Flora – the Roman God of spring, not the margarine. Others in England will be thinking back to medieval times and may even end up dancing round the odd Maypole. There will also be those who are far more up-to-date, and will be calling it Labour Day. These people will be remembering the Haymarket riot in Chicago in 1866 and will be considering the long and bitter struggle of working people throughout the world against their oppressors. Me, I will be thinking about Jesus and probably reminiscing back to early mornings spent in a chalk pit. Let me explain. When I was a young Christian, I was a member of the Baptist church youth group. Every year on 1 May, very early in the morning, we would drive up to a disused chalk pit and meet up with Christians of all ages from many different denominations for a time of early morning May Day praise. We would take guitars, bongos, tambourines – anything, in fact, that would make a joyful noise – and enjoy worshipping God through Scripture reading, song and prayer. To any passing professional musician, it would have sounded pretty awful and extremely amateurish. Even many of today's Christians would not want to attend as it would be seen as highly 'cheesy'. But for me it has wonderful memories. I still enjoy praising God in the open air and the May Day crack of dawn celebrations will always remain very special to me. It's a shame we only did it one day a year.

THE POINT ❯ Let me encourage you to fight off the temptation of the warm duvet, and to make your way into the open air. Praise God as you watch the dawn rise. Why not go even further and take along some food and a hot flask and treat your family to a dawn 'picnic praise' breakfast. There's nothing quite like joining in the dawn chorus.

 PRAYER *Lord, help me to praise You all day today, from early morning until last thing at night.*

02 MAY ›

'for you know very well that the day of the Lord will come like a thief in the night.' 1 Thessalonians 5:2

KEY WORD › 'thief'

IT WAS A long drive from the south of England to Lancaster. After many hours of driving I reached the city but even that was not the end of the journey for I then had to find the church building. It was early evening and the sun had gone down when I eventually discovered the front door hidden away down a quiet side street. I parked my car on the road outside the church and went in to meet the organiser. While he was making a welcoming cup of tea I started to unload my car but this of course meant leaving it unattended while I carried my gear into the building. When everything was unloaded and safely inside the church, I noticed something was missing; a large box containing all my CDs, which I was hoping to sell that night. In desperation I ran outside, but there was no sign of either the CDs or the thief who had stolen them. They were worth hundreds of pounds. I was very disappointed and, later, my audience were also disappointed because they were unable to buy any of my CDs. After the concert I reported the incident to the police and drove home, not expecting to hear any more about it. A short while later the Lancaster police phoned to inform me that they had found my CDs. They explained that the box had been thrown into a hedge just around the corner from the church and that every CD was still intact. As I put the phone down I had mixed feelings. Of course I was pleased to get the CDs back but a little disappointed that the thief didn't even keep one of them to listen to!

The Lord Jesus is going to return when we least expect it. He will come like a thief in the night when many of us may be 'spiritually' fast asleep.

THE POINT › Let's stay alert and be prepared for the return of the Lord and let's be doing things that are pleasing to Him on that great and wonderful day.

PRAYER *It will be a great day when You return, Lord; today I pray that I will be ready to welcome You whenever that time should be.*

'Is any one of you in trouble? He should pray.' James 5:13

 KEY WORD 'troubles'

IRENE AND I got married in record-breaking time. It was exactly 19 whole weeks between our first date and our wedding day. This time scale is not one we would recommend to others, but it was right for us for two specific reasons. The first was that we were both very sure that it was God's plan that we should be together, and the second reason was that this was the only free Saturday that I had in my diary that year. After the honeymoon everything was going well until we had our first major tiff. Our argument was not about our theological differences, financial problems, or even which channel we should watch on TV. The falling out was over a much more serious issue: a game of pitch and putt. Somehow Irene had managed to beat me and I was convinced that she had illegally moved her ball and her win was invalid. She was adamant that she was in the right and I was twice as adamant that she wasn't. In anger we both stormed off home in different directions. I remember thinking, 'That's it! I no longer want a relationship with someone who bends the rules of games.' I was going to pack her in, just like I had my other girlfriends in the past. Then I suddenly thought, 'I can't, I've just married her!' By the time we reached our flat, we had both calmed down. We realised how silly we'd been and after apologising, we kissed and made up, then had a time of prayer together. We learned our lesson and in all our wonderful years of marriage, we have never risked playing the serious game of pitch and putt again – we now stick to crazy golf! How are you feeling today? Is there something on your mind which is troubling you? Are you going to spend the whole day worrying or are you going to take notice of today's verse?

 THE POINT Let's stop everything for a few minutes and tell the Lord what's troubling us. Then let's leave our problems with Him. Jesus is happy to take these troubles from us and in their place leave a peace that He has reserved just for those who follow Him.

 PRAYER *Lord, please help me to sort out the things that are troubling me today.*

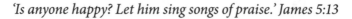
 ## 'happy'

YESTERDAY I TOLD you about our first tiff, now let me balance that with one of the happiest days of our marriage. With only a few weeks to prepare for a wedding, things can be a little rushed, but in the 1970s, weddings seemed to take far less time to prepare than they do today. The minister, musicians, best man and ushers knew what they were doing; Irene had her dress sorted; and the hotel was booked for the reception. Easy! The big day came and the sun was shining. Andy Piercy, my best man, was grinning as he stood next to me. But the reason he was grinning was because my future mother-in-law, whom I had yet to meet, had approached him by mistake, thinking he was the groom. She had told him how thrilled she was that her daughter was marrying such a good-looking young man. I refrained from going over and explaining to her that her daughter was not marrying the good-looking young man, she was marrying me! I was extremely nervous, and then my beautiful bride arrived looking fantastic. We made our vows, then sung our favourite hymns, which were probably slightly inappropriate for this occasion, for example, 'Let the fire fall' and 'Years I spent in vanity and pride'. Excuse the pun but all went off without a hitch. A couple of hours after the wedding we were on the road and off on our honeymoon. The journey was only slightly marred by us getting lost in Bournemouth, which was nowhere near our destination, but we didn't care – we were together. In our reflection yesterday, we learned that when we are feeling troubled we should pray. Today we are happy, everything is going well, and we have a smile on our face and a spring in our step.

THE POINT I wonder when we are happy and all is going well, do we actually even think of the Lord? Do we tend to only think of the Lord in our difficult times when we need something from Him? The Lord loves to be included in our happy times as well, so come on, let's sing our praises to Him, or, if we don't like singing, let's thank Him for the happiness that we feel today.

 PRAYER *Lord, today I thank You for the happiness that I often feel.*

05 MAY *'My sheep listen to my voice; I know them, and they follow me.' John 10:27*

KEY WORD 'sheep'

HAVING A SPARE couple of days, Irene and I met up with our good friends Jeff and Kay Lucas and decided to stay in a most beautiful picturesque town called Hay-on-Wye. Now for those who have never heard of this small town, it's world famous for its bookshops, so it was going to be a taste of heaven for Irene, who loves books. However, it is also known for Kington golf course, the highest and arguably one of the most challenging courses I've played on. It was a wet day but Jeff graciously volunteered to join me for a round even though he had hardly played any golf before. He filled up most of his day by scavenging in various gorse bushes playing 'hunt the golf ball' and his ball-finding proved to be far more successful than his golf. As we reached the highest point of the course, I saw a white woolly animal parked in the middle of the fairway. I jumped up and down, whistled, even yelled 'Fore!' but to no avail; the beast just stared at me and obviously didn't understand golf etiquette. I knew it was a one-in-a-million chance that I would actually hit it, so I took aim to miss it and, yep, my ball smacked the animal in the back, shot up into the air, and joined Jeff in the gorse bush. As I walked past the silly sheep, it seemed to be unhurt and it looked at me in a snooty way as if to say, 'Don't worry, I'm used to getting hit by stupid golfers!' Back at the clubhouse, I couldn't brag about getting any birdies, but I could mention I got a sheep. Jeff just got a hot chocolate.

While farming, some of the most unintelligent animals I had to look after were sheep. They would never listen to sensible instructions and they were scared of their own shadow, with the exception, of course, of the sheep above, which was not afraid of golfers.

THE POINT **Sheep are foolish and helpless and cannot survive without a shepherd. It's easy to see why Jesus likened us to sheep.**

PRAYER *Lord, today I realise that I am like a helpless sheep, and I just cannot live without Your love and guidance.*

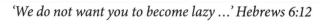

'We do not want you to become lazy ...' Hebrews 6:12

 'lazy'

I LOVE GOING on holiday with Irene, especially if we are planning to go somewhere hot. We try to book weeks in advance, because the excitement of the research and planning is almost as exciting as the holiday. I have, however, discovered one problem: if I have been working very hard beforehand, it takes a week to unwind and begin to relax and usually that's when we are getting the flight home again! For many years we loved self-catering holidays. We'd book our accommodation and we would shop and try to cook recipes based on the local produce of the country we were visiting. We rarely ate in restaurants because we enjoyed hunting around the various markets buying fresh meat and vegetables. Recently, though, we have chosen hotel holidays where we don't have to cook or even go outside to find a restaurant. We really do become very lazy for a short period of time. We spend the day just lying by the pool or on the beach reading lots of books and sleeping! However, all holidays seem to end far too quickly. On returning home, we have to wake up and face reality again!

We have always been self-employed and usually like to answer all our correspondence, but as I turn on our computer and find I am faced with hundreds of emails, I groan. Within a couple of days the holiday is just a memory – a nice memory, but within a very short time you feel like you need another one!

Sleep and rest are very important, even the perfect body of the Lord Jesus needed times for both of these, but we do have to be careful. Our time on earth is limited and God has plans for us to fulfil, and a mission for us to complete. Let's never become lazy and waste hours of our time just watching the TV or playing on the computer when there are far more important things that we should be doing.

THE POINT **Watching TV, playing computer games, and even relaxing on holiday, can be great, but spending too much precious time on any of these can easily bring about laziness.**

 Lord, today please help me to not be lazy; rather, help me to make good use of every minute in the day.

07 MAY *'My God will meet all your needs according to his glorious riches in Christ Jesus.' Philippians 4:19*

 KEY WORD 'riches'

I SEE NOW that I was very privileged to be raised as a boy in a Christian community. Although the community was far from perfect the leaders tried to base it on New Testament, Early Church principles. Even today I am grateful because it taught me so much about living by faith, trusting the Lord, and not relying on a wage packet or an employer. We had people from all walks of life join us, including commercial artists, preachers and many professional people. When someone joined the community they handed over their worldly possessions for all to share. Now although this sounds like a big deal, it wasn't, because, like the Early Church, possessions didn't mean a lot to these people who were following Jesus. The ladies were responsible for the cooking, although I must admit that nowadays this sounds sexist. But in those days the women were happy to cook and in no way were they looked upon as inferior to the men. To prove this point the men, whatever their qualifications or ministry, would be responsible for washing up! They were also expected to help farm the 11 acres of gardens and fields. It was a humble, happy environment, both in the kitchen and in the field; laughter could always be heard. All adults, including the leaders, received five shillings pocket money per week while children had one shilling; this made it easy for us all to tithe! No one had more money than anyone else. There were times when the community had very little money. Often needy people were taken in and given help and, every time, God provided all our needs, although He tended to provide carrots rather than caviar, orange squash rather than champagne. No one was rich, yet everyone felt rich.

In our Scripture verse today Paul is not saying that if we are broke, hungry, or in need of something, God must give us everything we ask for, but he is saying that God will provide our needs as He sees fit.

 THE POINT **Being rich is not just about having lots of money. Those who know and love Jesus have found riches beyond compare.**

 PRAYER *Lord, today I may not have a lot of money, but thank You for making me rich in You.*

08 MAY *'Calling the Twelve to him, he [Jesus] sent them out …' Mark 6:7*

KEY WORDS 'the disciples' calling'

ON ONE OF our many tours of Holland, Ishmael United performed in schools in the daytime and nightclubs in the evenings. Quite a strange mix! I remember in Rotterdam we were booked to sing at a senior girls' school. This must have been different for the girls. It must have been rare to have an English punk band doing the equivalent of their school assembly for them. In the evening we were booked to play in the same city at a club called The Golden Sunflower, which was as seedy as the name suggests. It was a horrible environment. It was so dark we couldn't see any of the audience and the smoke from cigarettes and drugs was so thick, it made it hard to breathe. The ideal place to try and 'shine out' the light of Jesus. During a break the lights came on. It was then I witnessed one of the saddest scenes I have ever seen. There, in this disgusting club, were some of the same girls that we had been singing to in the school earlier, being handled by old men before being taken outside to fulfil their duty as prostitutes. My stomach churned with a mixture of emotions, both tears and rage. I will never forget that night in Holland. For me it was far more than a wake-up call. Although I didn't realise it at the time, it was the start of my calling to minister to children and families which began just a couple of years after this incident took place. In today's verse we have Jesus calling His twelve disciples to Him and then sending them out to cast out demons and to heal the sick.

THE POINT I often think that we have got church meetings all wrong. Our aim should not be to see how many people we can bring in each Sunday, our aim should be to spend time with Jesus, and then see how many disciples we can send out to share the love and power of Christ with a lost world.

PRAYER *Lord, today I realise that I am in a dark world. Thank You for calling me to be a disciple and empowering me to go out and spread Your light in that darkness.*

'For the LORD comforts his people …' Isaiah 49:13

 **'comfort'**

I HAD A very special relationship with my father. He was one of my closest friends. A few years ago he became very unwell and after he had spent some time in hospital, he eventually ended up in a hospice. Now I know the hospice staff do a wonderful job and I have nothing but admiration for them, but I had this feeling that once people entered these places they rarely seemed to come out alive. While my father was lying dying of cancer I prayed every prayer I knew to try and keep him alive. Over the years I had seen many miracles and answers to prayer, but now my prayers were not being answered in the way that I wanted them to be. Just as I feared, my father died in the hospice. The following morning I sat in my study and thought, 'I am never going to laugh again.' I'd go round to visit my mother but every time I walked around the garden, it reminded me of my father and I couldn't control myself, I would just burst into tears. I feared that I had not just lost my father but I had also lost my faith. I couldn't understand why God had not answered my prayers.

Irene and my family were a great comfort to me and I tried to be the same to my mother. I think the reason why my grief lasted so long was because the main person that I should have turned to for comfort was the one I was blaming – God.

Some of us today may be suffering physical pain in our bodies. Others may be feeling very sad because a loved one has recently died. We need people to encourage, comfort and pray for us, even though the pain or hurt may still remain.

THE POINT **Earthly friends can be a great source of help, but I have since learned that I must never blame Father God for anything. He is the one who brings comfort in sorrow and nobody can comfort like our heavenly Father. He is the only one who, in time, can turn our sadness to joy.**

 PRAYER *Lord, today please comfort all who are in need of Your comfort.*

10 MAY *'Do not set your heart on what you will eat or drink; do not worry about it.' Luke 12:29*

KEY WORD 'shape'

I USED TO think that it was just women who were forever worried about their weight, but recently I have discovered this is not so. A very good friend of mine is strong, healthy and fit. He has always looked good and his faith in God is as strong as his body. I just see one slight fault in him: I believe he is totally obsessed with his weight. I don't think that he has ever looked overweight, but he went on a special diet and in doing so shed many pounds. He tells me that he feels better for doing this but some would say that he doesn't actually look better for doing it. Of course, his food intake is no concern of mine but it does get rather annoying when his main topic of conversation is usually weight and diets. If he goes out for a meal you can see him mentally counting the calories on the menu because he lives in fear of the bathroom scales. I've seen him greet rather large people and comment on how much weight they have lost, which they obviously haven't, but he lives in hope that they will say the same back to him. What annoys me most is when he taps me on the stomach and asks me if I've put on weight! Which invariably makes me think I have, even if I haven't!

I realise that obesity is a problem today and we do need to try and eat healthy, balanced meals. Exercise is also very important, but I think that we are living in a world that is obsessed with diet and weight watching. I am not sure that Jesus wants His children to be part of that world.

'Don't keep thinking about food and drink,' says Jesus. There are far more important issues that should occupy our mind.

THE POINT **If we were as obsessive about the state of our spiritual lives as we are about the shape of our physical bodies, I think that the world would be in a better shape!**

PRAYER *Lord, today help me to stop worrying about what I eat and drink and to concentrate on the important issues in life.*

11 MAY *'For whoever finds me finds life and receives favour from the* LORD.*' Proverbs 8:35*

 KEY WORD 'life'

LIKE MOST PEOPLE, my life has always been a mixture of highs and lows, great times and not such great times, but I am thankful that the good times have always far outweighed the bad times. I am also convinced that I have learned more in those difficult times, especially about trusting God, than I have learned when times have seemed to be relatively easy. At one stage in my life I found myself on the wrong end of a nasty church split. Of course it was a very painful and miserable experience for all involved, but for us as a family I knew the only way it would be resolved was for us to move away. This meant leaving the church, family and friends that I had helped to lead for many years and also moving house and town. Some days I felt really positive and excited about a new start and other days totally depressed at what I was leaving behind. Even through those days of sadness and confusion there were always little bright spots. I think the strangest thing was that while all this turmoil was going on in both my local church and in me, God was blessing my ministry more than ever. I've learned that life is never as bad as it may seem; life really is what we make it. As Christians there are choices that we must make. We can choose to live in the low times and forever reminisce on the hardships and problems we have faced, or we can get positive and think of all the blessings that God has provided over the years. Irene sometimes comments on me being ultra-positive for fear I may get disappointed. Sometimes I am, maybe unrealistically so, but I cannot be anything else. However hard the past has been, the vast majority of my memories are good ones.

 THE POINT **Life is good but if Jesus had difficult times, can we as His followers expect less? No, of course not, but we can be sure that even though we all have to walk through the odd dark valley, God has a bright future ahead for us.**

PRAYER *Lord, today we thank You for all the good things that You have given to us – most of all, that You have given us life.*

12 MAY › *'After they prayed, the place where they were meeting was shaken.' Acts 4:31*

 KEY WORDS › 'room shaking'

AS A YOUNG Christian I was not the greatest fan of the prayer meeting. Before every Sunday meeting about six of us (always the same six) would arrive early and go into the minister's vestry. Here we would take a seat, bow our heads, close our eyes, and then one or two would break the silence by offering up a prayer out loud while the others just said a very quiet 'Amen' at the end. To me, as a young person, it was hardly prayer to make the room shake. Now I am older, I see things differently; not all prayer is supposed to get the room shaking. I try and get to Morning Prayer in the cathedral at least a couple of times a week. Usually only the cathedral clergy and a couple of others attend. For half an hour all we do is read Scripture and pray. Following this, we have a short 30-minute Communion service which, again, is made up of Scripture reading and prayer, so you can see that much of that hour is spent in prayer and meditation. A lot of that time is spent in silence, and I really appreciate it. I remember when the 24/7 prayer initiative began (it was started by a friend called Pete Greig and the young people from the church he was overseeing). They decided to take over a room in the building for seven days, and at least two of the young people were praying every hour. Then, for 24 hours a day, for seven days in the week, they continued to pray. This proved to be so exciting that they didn't stop after that first week, but kept it going for many weeks. I visited that room several times myself and it was a very exciting place to be; it really was, like our reading describes, a shaking room.

 THE POINT › There is a place for quiet, meditative prayer and also praying until the room shakes. We need to experience both.

 PRAYER *Lord, please help me today to live a life of prayer and meditation. I also pray that I may experience a time when there is so much of Your power present that the room shakes.*

13 MAY *'... respect those who work hard among you, who are over you in the Lord and who admonish you.' 1 Thessalonians 5:12*

'respect'

AFTER GRADUATING FROM Bible college I was given my first church in a northern town in Lancashire. I was informed that the congregation numbered about 30 and the church had very little money. Being a keen young pastor I eagerly prepared for my first Sunday and looked forward to meeting my new congregation. My family and I arrived early at the church and then waited … and waited. Where were my congregation? Eventually two elderly ladies walked in and told me that nobody else would be coming that morning as it was Wakes Week. Wakes Week, I discovered, was a unique northern holiday where everyone seemed to disappear to Blackpool or Morecombe! Left with just these two ladies and my family, I still knew that I must give it my best shot, and it seemed to go quite well, even if the singing did seem a bit 'thin'. Afterwards, like any true-to-form-pastor, I stood at the door to shake hands with my departing little flock. It was there in the church doorway that one of the ladies stared at me and said, 'I don't like you.' I was shocked, and being an inexperienced pastor, was unsure how to respond. Then as she strode out into the midday sun, she shouted back, 'And I can't stand men with beards.' So it's fair to assume that I didn't manage to win the respect of all my congregation at my first service. A serious choice had to be made. It was either goodbye to my beard or goodbye to the old lady. Well, I still have my beard! It's easy to criticise church leaders. We seem to think that they should be perfect and always have time to meet our demands, drop everything, and come running whenever we call. Our leaders are just like us, human, sinners, and they often say things and get things wrong, but there is a difference; with all their faults they have been called by God to shepherd His flock.

THE POINT We should respect, love and encourage our church leaders: their lives are hard enough without us adding to their pressures.

PRAYER *Lord, today help me to show respect for my church leaders.*

14 MAY 'Submit yourselves for the Lord's sake to every authority instituted among men ...' 1 Peter 2:13

KEY WORD 'laws'

IN MY WILD teenage years I was leaving a folk club one night when I saw a rusty old ice cream sign. Thinking it would make a good coat hanger, I put it in the back of my car. It was a very foggy night and as traffic was going very slowly I decided to overtake the car in front of me. But in doing so, I found myself stranded in the middle of the road. It was then I saw headlights coming towards me from the opposite direction. The oncoming car swerved to miss me and went straight into a pond. Feeling guilty, I pulled over to see if the driver was all right, only to discover the car in the pond was a police car. I had to appear in court for both dangerous driving and, yes, stealing a rusty ice cream sign. My godly parents were both sad and embarrassed by their wayward prodigal son but, always wanting to help me, hired a good Christian lawyer. The lawyer instructed me on what to say and what to wear, but arrogantly I ignored his advice. I had no respect for the three magistrates and in fact ended up arguing with them. They threw the book at me, fined me, and banned me from driving. On reflection this was absolutely the right thing for them to do. No owner was found for the rusty ice cream sign, so I wasn't found guilty of theft. On leaving the courtroom I asked if I could keep the sign. They firmly told me no!

Is it OK to think we can break the law so long as we don't get caught? Do we break the speed limit, try to get away without declaring income that should be taxed, park on double yellow lines and ride our bike in a pedestrian area? God doesn't mind ... or does He?

THE POINT We are told to obey those who lay down the law and God is not happy if we don't. The only exception might be if the authorities tried to impose upon us something that would go against our Christian faith. But I don't think any of the above fits that category.

PRAYER *Lord, today help me to not to break the law, even in so-called minor ways.*

15 MAY *'… forgive whatever grievances you may have against one another.'* Colossians 3:13

'forgiveness'

MANY YEARS AGO I was booked to speak at a youth camp along with some other fairly well-known speakers. Now one of my strengths – and also weaknesses, I guess – is my sense of humour. Some love it, but I've discovered that a few hate it! I love to laugh and have a laugh and have never been offended by people laughing at me and see it as par for the course in my ministry. During this week I was to discover that one of my fellow speakers at the camp sadly did not share my sense of humour. At the end of each day the speakers and organisers would debrief over coffee. Since this was an informal meeting I would add as much humour and fun as I possibly could to stop us from getting too intense and heavy. I could see my humourless friend did not laugh once, even though everyone else was joining in the fun. I could sense that we had a personality clash – big time. But it was a good camp and at the end of the week there was no bad feeling – or so I thought. Many years later I met this leader again. The first thing he did was to take me to one side and tell me that he had never been able to forgive me for some joke I had made about him all those years ago. Of course I had no idea what he was talking about, but apologised anyway. How sad that he had lived all those years with something against me, but had never contacted me so we could have talked and prayed together to make things right.

We have all said and done some awful things in our lives to hurt others and we have all had some awful things said and done to us that have hurt us.

THE POINT Christians should be different from people who have chosen not to follow Jesus. When someone is nasty to us, we should not want revenge, we should rather try and forgive them, and win back their friendship. I know it sounds hard, maybe impossible, but if that is what Jesus wants us to do, and we cannot do it, are we really His followers?

PRAYER *Lord, I know that You forgive me, help me today to forgive others who have hurt me.*

16 MAY *'... the rain and the snow come down from heaven, and do not return to it without watering the earth ...' Isaiah 55:10*

 KEY WORD 'rain'

IT WAS EARLY winter and Irene and I had just finished speaking at a training day. It was raining when we arrived early that Saturday morning. It rained all day and was still raining as we loaded our equipment back into my Renault Espace in the dark of night. It was not much fun driving home with the windscreen wipers going flat out. Then it happened. We were about ten miles outside our home in Chichester, in the middle of a wooded country area miles from civilisation. I drove down into a valley and with no warning, splash, went bonnet-first into the middle of a deep flood covering the road. Since we were in the middle of nowhere, it was also the one place we could not get a signal for our mobile phone. The car spluttered to a halt and we jumped out to try to push the loaded Espace up a hill and out of the water. The flood water was up to my knees, so you can imagine how deep it was on Irene. It was dangerous because it was pitch black and all the electrics had gone in our car so we couldn't give a warning to anyone else. Other cars, unaware of the flood, came speeding out of the dark night towards us from both directions and joined us, marooned in the water. Eventually someone's mobile phone did work and the police came and towed us all out.

There are so many things that we complain about in life but I guess something that everyone complains about is the rain. We don't like getting wet because it stops us doing things that we enjoy doing.

 THE POINT It's God who sends the rain and snow, it's not a wicked act from the evil one. The flowers, crops and vegetables cry out for rain and, let's face it, we would not survive without it. Rain is great, but in the UK it would be nice to have a bit more sun to balance things out. Oh yes, and cars that don't get stuck in floods.

 PRAYER *Lord, today I will not moan about the rain but will thank You for sending it.*

17 MAY

'... he [God] has rescued us from the dominion of darkness ...' Colossians 1:13

 KEY WORD 'darkness'

WHEN I WAS a pastor in Lancashire I wanted to join in with every activity possible so that I could get to know our congregation better. One day the youth leader approached me and asked if I would like to join him and some of the young people on a pot-holing trip. He informed me that the caves were in the middle of the Yorkshire Dales. Thinking of my shape I did wonder if I was built for crawling underground, and dreaded the thought of getting my stomach stuck between the proverbial rock and a hard place. The youth leader assured me that I would be fine. I wasn't totally convinced when we all climbed into the minibus, since I was both the oldest and the roundest person on the expedition. It was a dark, cold, frosty January night and I thought it was a strange time to go potholing. But everyone just smiled knowing that what I called dark on the bleak Yorkshire hills was nothing compared to the dark beneath those same hills. We donned our helmets, checked our lights, and then with a rope ladder began the descent into the deep. Once we were far below ground we were all told to put our lights out, and for the first time I realised what darkness was really like. I was glad I was not alone in the darkness. I tried to imagine being by myself down there with no light. I could never have found my way out, as it seemed impossible to get any sense of direction.

Many people, either through choice or ignorance, live in spiritual darkness, and Christians can still feel the power of that darkness as it surrounds us every day.

 THE POINT Jesus is the Light and has set us free from the power of that darkness. Now is the time to share with others about the Light of the World so they too can be rescued and find their way out of their spiritual darkness.

 PRAYER *Lord, today I thank You that I need not fear the darkness and that I can live in the light, because You are the Light of the World.*

18 MAY

'Teach me to do your will, for you are my God ...' Psalm 143:10

KEY WORDS 'teach me'

I WAS SHOPPING and it was just a few days before Christmas. I couldn't help but notice that I seemed to be surrounded by lots of unhappy shoppers. One incident I saw really affected me. A mother, who was obviously with a boyfriend, had hold of two tiny little children and was shouting at her husband. The husband then stormed off and she ran after him, dragging the two little ones and screaming, 'Do you want your kids this Christmas or not? Because I don't want them.' The two children looked utterly confused as they listened to their mother and father, neither of whom seemed to want them. Because of the nature of my ministry, I often talk to children. Usually, when I see them in a meeting they tend to be on their best behaviour. I am also a father and, having watched my own children grow up together, it was a slightly different story. Of course, there were times when the two brothers and their sister argued and annoyed each other, but in family life it was expected. There were also times when they would disobey us as parents. I was never an advocate for physical punishment, using heavy smacking either with a hand or any other deterrent. After all, Solomon was the only one in the Bible who recommended 'spare the rod', and look how his children turned out! My job as a parent was to try to teach my children through both word and example, but never force.

In the Bible God clearly tells us what He wants us to do and what He doesn't want us to do. I have to admit that even as a Christian adult, I still sometimes argue with God, thinking I know best. My argument is often like that of a small child with a parent; if I want to do something, surely if Father really loves me He should let me do it. I sometimes forget that God always knows best.

THE POINT For the best life possible, we need to learn that only by doing what pleases God, will we find real happiness.

PRAYER *Lord, please teach me today to do just the things that You want me to do.*

'... he [Abraham] was about a hundred years old ...' Romans 4:19

KEY WORD 'old'

DO CHRISTIANS SUFFER from mid-life crises? I think so. At 30, I was in a Christian punk rock band and we recorded an album called *Life Begins at Thirty* because I knew God had lots more for me to do. At 40, I was at the peak days of the Glorie Company and getting invitations for all sorts of television appearances. Then came 50. Just 20 years away from my allotted three score years and ten. I realised that I had lived two-thirds of my life and I'd soon be dead, and this made me depressed! It didn't help when I watched videos I'd made many years earlier, in which I looked young. It didn't help when people told me that they hardly recognised me as I look so different to how I used to look. It didn't help to hear a child ask his mum who Ishmael was, and when she pointed me out, hear him replying, 'That's not Ishmael, that's an old man!'

I felt the ministry I loved, my days working with families and children, and jumping up and down onstage, were sorely numbered. It wouldn't look quite right for an old man to continue to do young things. But then God snapped me out of it and told me very sharply that He had not finished with me yet. I listened to Him and now think very differently. Sixty will soon come round, then 65, and so on, and while many of my peer group are already talking about retiring and slowing down, I feel even more excited about what God has got lined up for me in the future.

How old are you feeling today? You may be young, yet feeling old, or you may be old, thinking the best has gone. Let's not forget that at 100 years old Abraham was still considering the prospects of having a child; in many ways life was just beginning for him.

THE POINT Even if we have reached 100, perhaps we should stop worrying about getting old and treat every day as a new adventure with new challenges to overcome and accomplish. There is no such thing as a retired Christian.

PRAYER *Lord, today help me to realise that, whatever age I am, You still have an exciting future for me.*

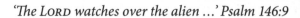

20 MAY *'The LORD watches over the alien ...' Psalm 146:9*

 KEY WORDS 'watches over'

A FEW YEARS ago Irene and I were invited to minister at a large outdoor event called the Downs Bible Week, held in Sussex. After we had finished setting up in the children's marquee we decided to walk around the fields to say hello to the campers. It was a wonderful sunny day and while adults stood around chatting, the younger ones were having great fun playing various ball games. It was then I met a friend I had not seen for years. He came rushing up and gave me the usual great big charismatic hug and soon we were deep in conversation. While we were busy conversing, Irene and our three children were slowly wandering across the field towards us. Suddenly a tennis ball came flying out of the air and smacked Irene right in the middle of the stomach. She was immediately winded and fell to the ground, gasping for air, while our three children stood watching open-mouthed in horror, wondering what on earth had happened to Mummy. Of course I was totally oblivious to Irene's injury because I was so busy chatting to this old friend. Eventually I turned round to introduce my friend to Irene who had just managed to stagger back on to her feet. Still totally oblivious of her injury I carried on chatting and laughing as though nothing had happened; well nothing had, had it? I am so glad the Lord is more observant than I am; I had hardly been watching over my wife! Today's verse says the Lord watches over the alien. Our verse is not referring to little green men from Mars, although if there are any I am sure that the Lord watches over them as well; the alien in this verse refers to a stranger.

 THE POINT If the Lord watches over everyone, He also wants us to follow His example. Let's not just watch over those around us who are our friends, let's also watch over and look after those who are more like strangers to us and who are on the fringe of things. I must also learn to watch over my wife whenever there's a chance that a low flying ball could be heading in her direction!

 PRAYER *Lord, please help me today to make a special effort to watch over those both in and out of church life.*

21 MAY *'I have loved you with an everlasting love …' Jeremiah 31:3*

 KEY WORDS 'love that lasts'

AS A YOUNG Christian I would fall in love very easily. My elders instructed me that I should only date a Christian girl, but this didn't seem too much of a hardship as there were always lots of nice Christian girls around to go out with. It was after a couple of dates that I would find myself falling in love. Yes, I was very young and very immature, and I really had no idea of what true love really was, or the responsibility that went with it. Things got worse when I started travelling with Andy. Ishmael and Andy were very popular and while travelling around the country we were in the enviable position of being single. At every concert we always seemed to be surrounded by pretty girls who also conveniently happened to be Christians. We thought nothing of dating a few at a time. In fact, I think it was an unspoken ambition of ours to have a different girlfriend in each town we visited.

During this time we had become associate evangelists for British Youth for Christ. The national director had somehow got to hear of our philandering ways and was not at all happy about it. He promptly called us to his office to see him. We tried not to giggle when he accused us of being 'Christian Casanovas'. We were unsure if that was meant as a criticism or a compliment. We never considered we were doing anything wrong, we felt we were just boys having a bit of harmless fun. We did also remind him that the girls were all Christians! We didn't realise we were playing with people's emotions.

A few years later I met Irene. I then started to learn that love is a very deep feeling, much deeper than the feelings I had experienced earlier. My love for her has not only lasted for 35 years, but I also believe that I love her far more now than when we were first married.

 THE POINT The best news for a Christian is that God's love never changes, and His love for us will last for ever.

 PRAYER *Lord, today I want to thank You for loving me with a love that will last for ever.*

22 MAY

'... I, your Lord and Teacher, have washed your feet, you also should wash one another's feet.' John 13:14

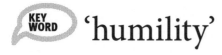

KEY WORD 'humility'

IRENE AND I were invited to do a series of teaching seminars in mainland Europe. On arrival, the organiser picked us up from the airport and seemed very pleasant. His advertising had been very successful because as we entered our first session the hall was packed with children's leaders keen to hear what we had to share. He had also arranged for a good sound system, people to help sell our books and CDs, and even a wonderful lunch. It seemed that nothing was too much trouble for him in making our trip enjoyable. He had kindly arranged that we would stay at his home, but as we arrived very late, we only met his wife. His two small children had already gone to bed. We slept well and woke up refreshed and went down to breakfast where we had the shock of our lives. I have never seen such frightened children, and they were not frightened of us. They sat silently all through breakfast. Their father would not allow them to speak at the meal table. He would issue orders to them to serve us and promptly ordered them to do the washing-up afterwards. In fact, it was like he had two tiny slaves. His wife said nothing. There was no kindness in his voice, no humility or love displayed for his children during the whole of our stay. Irene and I left that home feeling very sad; he was a great organiser but a dreadful father.

It's very easy to be full of our own self-importance. We ourselves are not special, it's only through Jesus dying for us that we have been made special. That's true of children as well. It is so easy to look down on others, and I guess the people who usually get looked down upon the most are the little ones. Often, like the organiser I just mentioned, we treat them as our slaves, ordering them to do this and that and often forgetting even to say please and thank you.

THE POINT Perhaps it's time to make children feel special, not by spoiling them, but by following Jesus' example and humbling ourselves and 'washing their feet' for a change.

PRAYER *Lord, teach me today to be humble and help me to treat all ages, including children, with respect.*

23 MAY *'All that we have accomplished you have done for us.' Isaiah 26:12*

 KEY WORD '**success**'

BACK IN THE early 1980s I believed that the Lord wanted me to get involved in television. After several conversations with a producer and director, a company that was then part of the ITV network decided to spend a budget of several thousand pounds on filming a pilot episode. This was for a children's programme called *The Glorie Train* and I was to be the presenter. It was hoped that if the pilot was successful it would go on to become a series. The film was shot on location at the Romney, Hythe and Dymchurch railway which had some superb one-third of full-size trains. We were given accommodation in a nice hotel. I had a make-up artist for my face and hair and was even bought a very smart but loud canary-yellow suit! The little station was invaded by large trucks, cranes, and even a mobile canteen, to refresh the 30 or so film crew. I was all set to become a famous TV presenter and was given star treatment. Sadly, my stardom was short-lived because soon afterwards the television company got into financial problems and was taken over by another, thus ending my very brief television career. Failure is very hard to cope with. It can be humiliating and often knocks our self-esteem. There is only one thing that can be harder to live with as a Christian than failure, and that is success. Pride is a much harder enemy to conquer because it is so easy to believe that our success is due in some way to our own capabilities and achievements. I will never know how I would have coped with television fame – maybe badly – and that's why it never happened. What I do know is that it was not part of God's plan for my life; He had something else in mind.

THE POINT I realise that anything successful that I may achieve is down to Jesus. I must give Him all the praise for everything. If I don't, I may still carry on being successful in my own eyes and in the eyes of those around me but that adds up to nothing if my relationship with Jesus has been broken.

 PRAYER *Lord, today I want to give You all the praise for every success I encounter.*

KEY WORDS 'listen to me'

I WAS MINISTERING at a large event and during that week met up with a pastor who had been a friend of mine for many years. I explained to him that I was going through a bit of a confusing time and he suggested that we meet up and have a chat. I was thrilled at this opportunity as sometimes I feel it is good to get a different perspective from someone who is neither involved in my ministry nor from my local church. We met up in a coffee lounge where all the members of the team congregated for coffee. When I arrived he was already waiting for me and I noticed that he sat on a chair facing the door where he could watch people come and go from the building. I sat facing him with my back to the door and immediately started to pour out my heart. After a few minutes of sharing I was amazed to see that he wasn't interested or even listening to anything that I was saying. He was totally preoccupied with smiling and waving at people as they entered or left the lounge. The final straw was when, just as I reached the climax of my story, he cut me off and called over one of his friends to introduce him to me. What a waste of time that was. Nice friend, yes. But good pastor, you must be joking!

I guess that many of us have had a similar encounter. At a time when we have been confiding in someone on some very important personal matter, we have discovered that they are not listening to a word we are saying, even though they are nodding their head in all the right places.

THE POINT One of the reasons why prayer is so wonderful is that we know our heavenly Father always listens to us; He never gets distracted and He always answers us. Sometimes, when answers are not instant, we relate God to the person I mentioned earlier who is not interested in listening to us. God is always interested in us, and when He says He will do something, He will, but in His time, not ours.

 PRAYER *Lord, today I can be assured that even though some people are not interested in listening to me, You always are.*

25 MAY

'... you are lukewarm – neither hot nor cold – I am about to spit you out of my mouth.' Revelation 3:16

KEY WORD 'vomit'

I HAD JUST become an associate evangelist with an organisation called British Youth for Christ and was invited to join some other young people on a retreat. It was a week of mostly training but on the Saturday night we had all been invited to join a Youth for Christ rally in the town of Crewe. I never understood why these events were called rallies when there were no cars in sight. I was pleased when I was asked to sing a couple of songs at this event. Now I had just bought some rather trendy red patent leather boots that zipped up to just below my knees – very smart, I thought. We travelled by minibus to the rally. It was one of the old Bedford models where the seats in the back faced each other and I was almost nose-to-nose with a very nice Christian girl. It happened all at once with no warning. She suddenly vomited and as I was sitting in close proximity to her, her vomit went right down my trousers. Now if that wasn't bad enough I realised that it had not only covered my lovely new boots, but it had also gone right inside them as well. Poor girl, it wasn't her fault, but I knew she felt dreadful and I smelt dreadful! When we arrived at the rally, a request was announced for perfume. I liberally sprinkled this all over my trousers but the smell didn't get better, it just got stronger. I walked onstage, with my boots squelching. The sympathetic audience were very generous with their applause although no one came up to give me a hug afterwards or wanted to sit next to me on the return trip in the minibus. The church in Laodicea made God want to vomit. They claimed to be rich and to not need a thing yet they were wretched, pitiful, poor, blind and naked. They were neither hot nor cold, just lukewarm.

THE POINT How can anyone who has known what it is to have sins forgiven ever be a lukewarm, half-hearted Christian?

PRAYER *Today, Lord, I pray I never become a lukewarm Christian. I always want to be on fire for You.*

'Two are better than one, because they have a good return for their work.' Ecclesiastes 4:9

KEY WORD 'two'

IN THE CRAZY, noisy world that I live in there are times when I love to be alone. In the evenings, whenever I can, I walk around our local golf course. There is hardly anyone about as all the golfers are enjoying the 'nineteenth hole'. Probably boring each other by passing on hole-by-hole accounts of how they have played to anyone who may care to listen. Out on the course, with the sun slowly disappearing, all is still. It's just God, His wonderful creation and me. Walking on the lush green grass I feel like St Francis as I listen to the birds singing evensong while watching the rabbits and squirrels playfully run away as I approach them with my trolley. All is beautiful; in fact, the only thing that is not beautiful is my golf, but who cares about golf, this is a great chance to be alone to think, meditate and pray. But God has not called me to be a monk and to live a life of isolation. Throughout my whole ministry I have never agreed with the idea of travelling just by myself. In the very early days I was with my close friend Andy. After that came the Ishmael United band which, although volatile at the time with personality clashes, proved to be a great learning process. Following the band I travelled with a lighting man, my brother, a dramatist and his wife, my son Daniel, and a variety of excellent musicians. Today I nearly always travel with Irene. It is not that I always needed the other people to help me minister, although everyone who has travelled with me has contributed greatly to what I did, I just believed that there was safety in having others with me. As the disciples were instructed to go out in twos, it seemed to be a principle that both Jesus and the Early Church seem to set.

THE POINT The Church is not just a group of individuals doing their own thing, it's a close body of people all working together and needing each other. A lot more can be done when two of us work together.

PRAYER *Lord, today I thank You for those who support me and work alongside me.*

KEY WORDS 'strong and courageous'

IT WAS VERY late and I was walking home through the city. The streets were deserted and the lights were very dim. I became aware of a hooded figure following me. I stopped to do my shoelace up and they stopped as well. My heart started beating faster; was I being tailed by a mugger or worse? Surely they could see that I wasn't the sort to be carrying a lot of money around at night, or could they? I quickened my pace and they quickened theirs and as I was just considering that it might be worth seeing if my legs could still run, the hooded figure ran up and clamped his hands on my shoulder. My heart leapt. Then before I could look around a voice said, 'All right, Dad? How are you doing?' It was my son Daniel. By giving me such a fright I was unsure if I should throw my arms around his shoulders or put my hands around his neck! A song that I used to enjoy playing was Morris Chapman's 'Be Bold, Be Strong, for the Lord Your God is With You'. I suppose one of the reasons I liked it was that it was so easy to play on the guitar, even though there was a sneaky F sharp minor thrown in to try and scare guitarists of my ability! This was a song that always guaranteed singing with great gusto and enthusiasm by any Christians who had happened to be with me! But there was a line in the song that would make me smile as we sang it. The line said 'I am not afraid', then everyone would shout at the top of their voice 'No, no, no'. Now I knew that most of the people standing with me, shouting out that they were not afraid of anything, had real fears of the dark, spiders, dogs, mice, wasps, church leaders, confronting fellow Christians, etc., and some were even frightened of disciplining their children.

 THE POINT If we are stating that because the Lord our God is with us we are not afraid of the evil one, surely we need not be frightened by far less destructive things. We need to be strong and courageous in the whole of life, not just spiritual warfare.

 PRAYER *Lord, today please help me to be really strong and courageous.*

28 MAY

'Why are you downcast, O my soul? …
Put your hope in God …' Psalm 43:5

KEY WORD 'upset'

THERE HAVE NOT been all that many times in my life when I have been so sad and upset that I have been moved to tears. One of those times was when we were leading the children's work at a large event and my parents had joined us for the week. Everything was going well until I was informed that my father was ill. I remember running to his chalet and being told by the paramedics that he had suffered a heart attack. This was a major shock as we did not just have a father-son relationship. We were also the best of friends and I had never imagined anything as serious as this could happen to him. But what brought tears to my eyes happened a little later when I visited him in the hospital. I was the only one at his bedside and out of the blue he started saying some harsh things to me. This was not my father speaking; what he was saying was totally out of character. Even though I realised that he did not know what he was saying due to his pain and medication, his words really upset me. Another time I cried also involved my father. It was some time later when he became seriously ill again but this time with cancer. I was praying with all my might that God would heal him, but that was not to be. I did not just cry as I saw him lying on his deathbed, I cried for a very long time afterwards. It just needed the smallest thing to trigger my memory of him and the tears would start flowing. I now know there is nothing wrong with being sad or upset. I must confess that at one time if I saw another man weeping I would feel embarrassed by this. I have learned that tears are not a sign of weakness; even Jesus wept.

THE POINT Although we will all experience times of sadness and upset, we are not called to live a life of sadness. Tears can turn to joy. We are victorious, we are conquerors, living in the joy of our Lord. The best way to cheer ourselves up is to put our hope in God … and keep praising Him.

PRAYER *Today, Lord, please turn my sadness into joy.*

29 MAY

'Can a mother forget the baby at her breast … ? … I have engraved you on the palms of my hands.' Isaiah 49:15–16

 KEY WORD 'babies'

AS SOON AS I married Irene my great desire was to begin a family straight away. At that stage I had failed to consider fertility, maturity or the enormous responsibility. I didn't even consider asking God if or when He wanted us to have children. I was quite disappointed that Irene didn't conceive on our honeymoon; after all, I seemed to be doing everything correctly that a husband should be doing in that department. It was six months later when we discovered Irene was pregnant. Why on earth did it take that long? The minute I heard the good news I rang everyone up to tell them and as they congratulated me I would reply with the old cliché 'Oh there was nothing to it.' Now I am sure my motives were not purely selfish for wanting children early in our marriage. I wanted to be reasonably young enough and fit enough to kick a ball around with them as they grew up. I also wanted to be able to enjoy the rides in a fun park in their teenage years without being so old that there would have been the chance of a heart attack. I realise that having babies is not just down to parents, it's ultimately in God's hands, but I was so thrilled that God allowed us to have children. First came baby Joseph. He was followed the next year by baby Daniel, and baby Suzannah followed after a brief interval of about four years. Irene and I love our three wonderful children. Of course they are now grown-up, but they are still as wonderful to us as they were when they were little. I, being the brave father that I am, was present at each birth. But being the coward I am, nearly fainted at each one as I am quite squeamish. I will never forget those days when they were born, and I am certain that Irene never will either!

 THE POINT God will never forget us. He was there at our spiritual birth and has our names engraved on His hand. There is no one who could know us, or love us more than He does.

 PRAYER *Today, Lord, I am so grateful to know that You will never forget me.*

30 MAY

'He [Jesus] said ... "Go into all the world and preach the good news to all creation." ' Mark 16:15

KEY WORD 'go'

MY 'WORLD' INVOLVES going everywhere and ministering in many different countries, but that's never as glamorous as it sounds. After an overseas trip people ask what I saw on my visit and often I answer, just nice people and the insides of a hall. Constant travel brings tiredness, the frustration of not understanding the language, the pressures of different cultures and, obviously, missing your loved ones at home. On one of my many trips to Germany, I arrived very late one night and went straight to my accommodation. The person who was with me explained that he didn't drink coffee but asked if I would like a cup before I went to bed. I thanked him and said I would. Unknown to me he not only didn't drink coffee, but he also didn't know how to make it. He put a few heaped spoons of percolated coffee into a mug and topped it up with a small amount of water. Out of politeness I drank the straight caffeine and spent the whole night wide awake unable to shut my eyelids! That's life on the road!

Nowadays some Christians try to justify spending money by calling a short holiday break a ministry trip. They fly off to all sorts of places believing that they are fulfilling our Bible verse. It's much easier to minister in another country than it is to minister in your local pub and show the love of Jesus to the regulars.

God does want some people to travel overseas, but for others to do so means they are actually running away from and deserting the world that Jesus wants them to reach.

THE POINT Jesus wants us to go and spread the good news to the world around us. And unless He tells us otherwise that means where we live, in our school, at the shops, or in our work place. I know it may not sound very exciting, but when one of our local friends decides to follow Jesus, that is even more exciting than a trip to anywhere else in the world.

PRAYER *Lord, today help me to go and share Your good news to all those I meet in my world, in the place where I live.*

31 MAY *'I have not come to call the righteous, but sinners to repentance.' Luke 5:32*

 KEY WORD 'sinners'

I HAVE A very close friend whom I have known and loved for years. I knew this friend when he was far from God and he was not a nice guy to know, especially after he had had a few drinks. On one occasion, he decided to travel down from the north of England where he lived to meet up with some of his drinking friends. We told him that he was very welcome to stay with us. I remember it was the night of the general election many years ago. I had already decided to sit up most of the night watching it, which was just as well. It was already into the early hours and my friend had not yet arrived. When quite a few of the votes had already come in and it looked like yet another Tory win, I heard the crash of a car door outside and saw my friend staggering towards our house. I hasten to add that this was before the strict drink driving laws of today were enforced. My drunken friend had turned his three-wheeler car over on a roundabout in his attempt to reach our house and he was very distraught about the state of his battered car. After numerous coffees he gradually sobered up and we soon ignored the election and got talking about the Christian faith. At this stage in his life, I do not think that even my friend would describe himself as a good person, but it was for people like him that Jesus came. Sinners, who were willing to change. Today that same friend is a wonderful Christian, still a sinner, but unrecognisable from the sinner of old. He is one of the most gentle, caring and kind people I know. It's amazing how meeting with Jesus can completely change a life.

On my travels, I have met people who genuinely believe that they are not sinners because, unlike my friend, they have lived a good life. They tell me they have never murdered, robbed a bank or even got drunk, so how can they be sinners?

 THE POINT If we don't admit to being sinners, there is no way that Jesus can save or change us.

 PRAYER *Lord, today I thank You that You turn sinners into saints.*

01 JUN *'Dear friend, I pray that you may enjoy good health …' 3 John 2*

KEY WORD 'health'

I PRAISE GOD that my body is reasonably healthy; sadly, I cannot say the same about the contents of my mouth. My father's teeth were never healthy so I guess he passed on his decaying teeth and gums to me as part of my inheritance. I still have bad memories of visiting the dentist when I was a very small child. The Bible says that if your eye offends you, pluck it out. The dentist back in those days seemed to follow a similar biblical principal; if your tooth aches, pull it out. A few false teeth or dentures seemed to be the answer for a healthy mouth for both young and old. The worst part of having a tooth extracted was having to breathe in the 'knock out' gas before the operation took place. The smell from that rubber mask still haunts me. On one occasion I was being driven home after the gas treatment and I remember passing out and hallucinating. Whatever sort of gas did they use? Today, of course, it's very different; it's now the dentist's desire for us to keep all our teeth, and a dental surgery is more akin to an operating theatre. I now lie almost prostrate on a bed while the dentist wears a gown and face mask. But the dreaded drill doesn't appear to have progressed over the years. It may look more modern, but it still sounds the same, and hurts the same as it did all those years ago. The main thing I object to about Christian dentists is that they always ask me some wonderful theological question and then, before I can get my teeth into answering it, they fill my mouth with all sorts of things so I am unable to speak! How unfair is that?

In our reading John wishes his readers good health. Health is not always something that is under our control but we need to keep an eye on what we eat, try and get some daily exercise, and, of course, make regular visits to the dentist.

 THE POINT **Trying to keep our teeth and body fit is important, but let's not forget to keep our spiritual life fit as well, because at the end of the day, that is far more important.**

 PRAYER *Lord, today I pray that You please keep both my body and my spirit healthy.*

02 JUN

'The end of a matter is better than its beginning …' Ecclesiastes 7:8

KEY WORDS 'finish something'

A FRIEND OF mine is a builder. Now I have met many a 'cowboy builder' who can do shoddy work, but that would not describe my friend. Without doubt he is a very good builder because he has done some excellent building work on our house. One day he invited me round to his house for tea. I was quite excited by this because, knowing how good a builder he is, I was expecting his house to be the last word; an advertisement to his craftsmanship. When I arrived, I was shocked. His house was in a terrible mess. He apologetically explained that he was still working on various jobs. This was plain to see as not one job that he had begun had been completed. They were all only half finished. I felt so sorry for his wife – she could see all the wonderful jobs he had done on other people's houses, but she had to put up with living in what resembled a builder's yard for the foreseeable future! I am useless at DIY. If I ever buy self-assembly furniture I usually end up having a fight with it and always end up in a sweat and covered in blood. However, I never let it beat me. I keep persevering until it is assembled even if, for some strange reason, I do end up with extra pieces left over and glue all over the floor. We are all like my builder friend at times, but it is not good. Perhaps it's a job we've begun in the house or garden, or perhaps it's just sorting out or tidying up. Usually it's something that needs doing, but we don't want to do it. We start something … then we give up on it.

THE POINT When we begin something we need to keep going until we finish it. In the Bible, Paul talks about the Christian life as though it is a race. Once we have started, we must not give up, even if we feel tired and have blisters on our feet. There is a great satisfaction in completing a job and an even greater satisfaction in keeping close to Jesus until we ultimately join Him in heaven.

PRAYER *Lord, today I realise that I have started following You, please help me never to give up.*

03 JUN 'Set me free from my prison ...' Psalm 142:7

 'free from prison'

I HAVE VISITED quite a few prisons in my lifetime and sometimes it was quite a scary experience. One of the most frightening prisons was the old Holloway women's prison. I was in my early 20s and had been booked to perform a concert for the inmates. I remember a warden telling me that she could not guarantee my safety if I stepped off the stage, so I didn't! During the Ishmael and Andy days we sometimes took an evangelist into prisons with us and he would often wear a clerical collar. At times we thought he was a bit lazy because whenever we had to load all the equipment into our van he always felt the call of nature and disappeared. On one occasion while visiting a maximum-security prison we thought we would teach him a lesson. Sure enough, straight after the concert and just as we began loading the heavy equipment, he disappeared. We quickly loaded our gear, jumped in the van, and drove towards the main gate, leaving him behind. Suddenly he appeared, and seeing us drive off, he sprinted across the courtyard with his clerical collar flapping. He called out to us to wait. As we passed the first of the double security gates the warden asked if the running vicar was anything to do with us. We replied, 'Vicar? What vicar?' You will be relieved to hear that we did own up that he was with us, just before he was mistakenly arrested for being an inmate attempting to escape in fancy dress!

I love the freedom of being outdoors. I feel close to God walking in the countryside or by the sea. Before I began to follow Jesus I was cautioned for dangerous driving and had to spend a few hours locked up in a very small prison cell with no window. It was horrible. The Bible tells us that before we turned to faith, we were like prisoners. Jesus died to set us free. With His Holy Spirit living inside us we can know real freedom.

 THE POINT **Although as Christians we are free, we have not been set free to do what we like; we have been set free to serve Jesus.**

 PRAYER *Lord, today I want to thank You for letting me enjoy real freedom.*

04 JUN

'Do not be quickly provoked in your spirit, for anger resides in the lap of fools.' Ecclesiastes 7:9

 KEY WORDS '**getting angry is foolish**'

AT SOME SUMMER camps I have had to oversee quite a large number of adult team members as well as children. As a team we would all sleep in a specially allocated area in tents and caravans. Being excitable young people, the team sometimes went over the top with their humour. On one occasion, after a very long day, the team was unwinding and some had become very high-spirited. Now the late summer camps were very hot in the daytime but got very cold at night. As Irene and I and our children settled down to go to sleep in our caravan I suddenly heard a scream coming from outside. I ran out to find that a couple of my key team leaders had played a trick on another leader which resulted in him being soaked, twice. He was now walking around in the cold night air, very distraught, shivering in his wet pyjamas. I rarely get angry but this was cruel, not fun. I was really angry with the two leaders and let them know it in no uncertain terms. The poor wet team member managed to dry himself off, then settled down for the night. The following morning I was still furious, I detest any sort of bullying and I was ready to send them home. However, they did apologise to the leader they drenched, and I, in turn, calmed down and apologised to them. It is one thing for me as leader to correct people, but it was wrong for me as a team leader to lose my cool while doing so.

 THE POINT

I know we must love everybody, but it is so easy to get upset by other Christians because we expect more from them. Our temper can quickly flare up and then, before we know it, we have reacted and said something in anger, not in love. For a short while we may feel quite pleased with ourselves, having given that person a piece of our mind, but then in time we feel guilty and realise that getting angry is foolish. Apologies will have to be made.

 PRAYER

Lord, today I ask that all I do and say will be done in love and never in anger.

05 JUN ›

'I tell you the truth, he who believes has everlasting life.' John 6:47

KEY WORD › 'life'

WHEN I WAS young I was never anxious about death. It never entered my mind that I could die in a serious accident on the road. First, I owned a bicycle. I would race along a busy road, weave in and out of vehicles, then see how fast I could go down a steep hill, overtaking cars. Safety helmets were yet to be invented. Next, I owned a motorbike and motor scooter. I rarely wore a crash helmet, which was complete madness because I was such a useless biker. I fell off and crashed nearly every time I tried to turn a corner. I must have given my parents nightmares. Then came tractors. They may look slow on the road but driving these powerful machines flat out, up and down steep hills and enjoying the sensation as the front wheels lift off the ground, was suicide, especially as the old tractors had no roll bars or cabin for protection. Finally, there were cars with souped-up engines and no seat belts. Lethal road races were the order of the day in the 1960s. I remember once rolling a car over and my friends all jumped out laughing and rolled it back again. We finished our journey in a very dented vehicle. I had no fear of death. Today I think and act very differently. First, I now drive a lot more carefully, not just for my own sake but for the sake of others on the road as well. Second, being way beyond the halfway mark of my three score years and ten, I often think about what is going to happen to me when I die.

THE POINT ›

The great hope that I have in being a Christian is that I believe that what Jesus said is true. He said that if I believe in Him, and live my life for Him, although I may die on earth, He has promised that I will spend forever with Him. I can't go wrong being a Christian; I not only get the best life possible while on earth, but I also get an even better life, that I cannot even begin to imagine when I die. Wow!

PRAYER

Lord, today I pray for friends who do not yet believe in You and have no fear of death. They should have.

06 JUN ❯ *'He [Jesus] committed no sin …' 1 Peter 2:22*

KEY WORD ❯ '**perfect**'

WE WERE HAVING a family holiday in southern Spain near the Sierra Nevada Mountains. It was supposed to be one of those nice reading and relaxing holidays where the only energy used would be getting in and out of the swimming pool. This all changed when I discovered that just 20 miles down the road was the location where my favourite star, Clint Eastwood, filmed Spaghetti Westerns. I soon hired a car and off we set along treacherous mountain roads in search of it. Hours later we found it, and for me it was worth the many arguments in the car. As I strutted around the set I imagined I was Clint. I was sure I'd seen some of the scenery in one of the 'dollar' movies. I looked at the barren landscape and it was easy to imagine that *The Good, The Bad and The Ugly* could have been filmed right there. It was a perfect day out, a dream come true. Watching films helps me to relax. I love epics, which must be viewed in a cinema and not on a small screen. These could be Westerns, disaster movies, or even historical films; I don't care, so long as they are epics and cost millions of dollars to make! So what do I think of biblical epic movies? Very few are accurate because they would never be allowed to be biblically accurate. They would have to contain far too much 'adult and violent' content to get passed by the censors. Mel Gibson did attempt his extremely 'bloody' best with *The Passion* but even this fell short of what the Bible really describes. I think the worst thing about biblical movies is that they always use a good-looking actor to portray Jesus. Why choose the best-looking with a perfectly toned body and hairstyle, when Isaiah prophesied that Jesus would have no beauty or majesty to attract us to him, nothing in His appearance that we should desire Him?

THE POINT ❯ **It was not Jesus' appearance that made Him special. What made Jesus different from every other person, past or present, was that He was perfect in every way. He never sinned once; He was totally pure, totally clean, totally holy!**

PRAYER ❯ *Lord, I worship You today knowing that You are the perfect Son of God.*

'Finally, be strong in the Lord and in his mighty power.' Ephesians 6:10

'strong'

I AM SO thankful to God that He has kept me physically strong. I am so grateful that I can still lift and carry amplifiers, speakers and heavy boxes up and down stairs and into the back of my vehicle. Nowadays, though, fitness is more important than strength. Years ago a few of us from our local church decided to join a gym. Before the staff would let us loose on all their fantastically expensive fitness machines they insisted that we attend an induction course to learn how to use them properly. We all turned up looking the part in our shorts, T-shirts and trainers, and followed our instructor around attentively as he explained how to use each machine and which part of the body that machine was supposed to build. This was all very informative but most of us were getting impatient, we just wanted to have a go. At last he finished his lecture by telling us very firmly that we should spend no more than ten minutes on any one machine, as our body would not be fit for longer than that. We must do things gradually. My friend Rod, who was also a leader in the church, was standing next to me. I knew that he would ignore this advice and I was right. While the rest of us spent a short time on a variety of machines Rod went straight to the running machine and stayed on it for 30 minutes, thinking that this was making his body both healthier and stronger. When he eventually got off we watched him as he went pale, staggered around for a while, and then eventually collapsed in a heap feeling really sick. I'm not sure whether he went back to the gym again. I believe he took up line dancing and golf instead.

Nowadays I still try and keep fit mostly by walking and joining my above-mentioned over-enthusiastic friend playing golf but I also realise that I need a different kind of strength; I need to be strong, but most important, I need to be strong in the Lord.

The only way to achieve 'spiritual muscles' is to read the Bible regularly and to spend time worshipping God.

Lord, help me today to become a stronger Christian.

08 JUN

'Be still before the LORD and wait patiently for him …' Psalm 37:7

KEY WORD 'waiting'

I DON'T LIKE waiting patiently. Irene and I were booked to speak at a conference in Sweden but I was not looking forward to the long trip to get there which involved planes, trains and automobiles. And for some reason or other we had to go via Denmark! Leaving home we loaded two very heavy suitcases with clothes, books, CDs, and DVDs into the back of my car. We then drove to Gatwick Airport, queued up at the ticket office and, thankfully, the cases just made it through without us having to pay extra baggage charges. Then came the long wait in the long queue to go through security, followed by the long wait in the departure lounge. The flight was fine and passed by quickly. Once in Copenhagen Airport, we had to find our way to the railway station and the platform to await our train to Sweden, dragging the two heavy cases with us. I asked if we were on the right platform and was told we were. We waited patiently. No train came. Then we were told that the train had been changed to another platform so we dragged the suitcases up and down the stairs to the other platform. Still the train did not arrive. We eventually changed platforms three times and by now I was not only exhausted, but I was also feeling faint and scared that I was going to have a heart attack! I'd had enough. I told Irene that either we got the next train, wherever it was going, or else I was going home. We got the next train, which did go to Sweden, but to the wrong part. After a few more changes and having to stand in the corridor for a lot of the journey because no seats were available, hours and hours later we finally arrived at our destination. But the conference was brilliant, definitely worth all the waiting!

THE POINT Maybe some of you are a little like me and hate waiting. I have discovered that the Lord often doesn't always answer my prayers with a yes or no, He often tells me to trust Him and wait. Waiting still does not come naturally to me, but I am learning!

PRAYER *Lord, today please teach me not to be impatient and to trust You and wait.*

169

09 JUN

'We are sure that we have a clear conscience and desire to live honourably in every way.' Hebrews 13:18

KEY WORD 'conscience'

IRENE HAS KINDLY offered to edit this manuscript for me before we send it off to the publishers, so it has fallen upon me to do the food shop, which actually I quite enjoy. On my last trip I was whizzing around with my trolley getting all the healthy foods for Irene and the not-quite-so healthy foods for me, when I spotted a very special deal on bottles of wine if you bought a box of six. As we do a lot of entertaining I thought that this would be a sensible investment so I put a box of six bottles of red wine and a box of six bottles of white wine into my trolley. When I got to the checkout I just pulled one bottle out of each box to save lifting the whole box on to the conveyer belt.

As I left the shop I suddenly realised that my bill seemed extremely low. I looked at my receipt and noticed that I had only been charged for two bottles of wine instead of twelve. For just one second, the thought crossed my mind that because it was the supermarket's fault, I would leave it. They would hardly miss the cost of ten bottles of special-deal wine, and they were, after all, the biggest food store in the UK. I thought that I should just drive off and be thankful. No way. My conscience would never let me do that. I went back into the store and walked up to the customer service desk. 'Excuse me,' I said to the young lady, 'I think my bill is wrong. I haven't paid enough.' I saw her gasp. It was obviously quite rare for a customer to complain about being undercharged. I paid my due, and she thanked me for my honesty. I really wanted to ask her what she would have done in my position but decided not to in case I was encouraging her to lie.

THE POINT There always seems to be two voices that speak into our conscience; one is telling us to do what we know to be right, and the other is telling us to do what we know to be wrong. Let's live honourably and keep a clear conscience.

PRAYER *Lord, today please help me to do that which is right and to keep a clear conscience.*

10 JUN *'I will take refuge in the shadow of your wings until the disaster has passed.' Psalm 57:1*

 KEY WORD 'protection'

ONE SPRING EVENING I decided to go for a stroll around some of God's most beautiful countryside and do a bit of praying. I also decided that God wouldn't mind if I was also accompanied by my trolley and golf clubs. It seemed a shame to walk on God's wonderful green carpet without making a few divots as I did so! The course was devoid of all human life and my only companions were God's furry little animals and birds. When I reached the third hole I was playing so badly that I decided to take a short break and wandered over to a lake to try and find a few golf balls. It was then that I was almost mugged. I hadn't noticed that Mrs Coot was taking her tiny family for a stroll just where I was searching for lost balls. Obviously I had got a little too close for comfort to her brood, because she made herself look as big as she could then she charged at me with legs flying everywhere. As she ran she also tried to hiss at me but the noise sounded more like a throttled squawk. However, her mission was accomplished as she succeeded in giving me the fright of my life; in fact, I very nearly fell into the lake. This silly but highly protective little bird must have thought she was a goose or a swan but either way, it scared me away from the lake and her chicks, so she proved to be a wonderful mother in my opinion.

When I worked on the farm, a hen with chicks always impressed me. Even when she faced all sorts of danger, the little brood of baby chicks snuggled beneath their mother's wings, oblivious of any fear their mother might be feeling. They must have felt so warm, secure, and loved.

 THE POINT This is just how God wants us to be with Him. We can't just bury our head in the sand and ignore 'disasters', but when we see the disasters approaching we must run to God who will protect us through them, and we, too, will feel warm, secure and loved.

 PRAYER *Lord, thank You that today, if I see a disaster coming, I know that the safest place to be is with You.*

11 JUN

'Dear children, do not let any lead you astray.'
1 John 3:7

KEY WORD 'led'

BEING RAISED IN a Christian community I was naïve about many things. Although frowned upon by the leaders, some of those who stayed with us smoked, but of course never in public. They would either hide behind a hedge or in a toilet because no one wanted to be caught with a cigarette in their hand. So my upbringing taught me that smoking was a definite sin and worthy of severe punishment. But with the knowledge of sin comes the temptation to do it! When I was about 11 years old, one of my school friends offered me a cigarette. Part of me said no, it was wrong and would get me into big trouble, but another part of me said, go on, give it a go. In those days smoking was the trendy thing to do and most of my friends would smoke immediately they exited the school gates. For a while I refused, then eventually, under pressure, I gave in and tried one. One leads to more and soon I was one of the smoking gang, looking pretty cool, I thought. Then one night on returning home from school my mother, who has a nose like a sniffer dog, smelt smoke on my breath and confronted me. I had to own up, I didn't want to add lying to my wickedness and remember running into my bedroom filled with guilt and condemnation, believing that I had committed the worst possible sin. Today, I do not smoke, but I think much more compassionately about those who do. Of course, it's not an unforgivable sin; there are far worse things than smoking, but we do know that it is an addiction that is very hard to break which is unhealthy, not only for the smoker, but also for those who happen to be anywhere nearby and inhale their smoke. But the main point today is not to condemn smokers, that's just my illustration.

THE POINT How easy it is to be led by others and to go off in the wrong direction. We must all learn to stand firm, to be strong and to say no. And to never allow others to change our mind on things that we feel are wrong.

PRAYER *Lord, today help me not to be led into doing things that I know I should not do.*

12 JUN

'For though we live in the world, we do not wage war as the world does.' 2 Corinthians 10:3

 KEY WORD 'violence'

AS I HAVE mentioned previously, I love watching movies. I'm not averse to a bit of violence in a movie as long as it's fiction. I rarely watch films containing 'real life' violence, as I don't consider that to be entertainment. I have always strongly disliked aggression in any form. The senior school I attended experienced its fair share of violence. This was in the days of corporal punishment where teachers were allowed to beat naughty boys with big sticks. In the playground you would often hear someone shout 'bundle'. This was the signal for all the pupils to run over and form a crowd as they watched two boys beating each other with their fists. In those days it was unheard of for weapons like guns or knives to be used. The school also had its fair share of gangs and bullies. One bully called Roger would track me down every lunch hour and would take great pleasure in fighting and hurting me for most of that hour. I used to hate those lunch times. In those days I just had to take it. There was no one to complain to and if I did complain to a teacher, Roger's gang would have turned on me and given me a proper hiding. I never physically fought back, not that I was scared to, it was just that I never saw the point in returning aggression for aggression.

Today as we watch the news we see rival football fans at war with each other, or if we walk through our city centre at night we see drunken people fighting. I can't understand how a person can get pleasure by using physical force to injure another human being.

THE POINT Christians should turn away from violence, and as difficult as it may be with some aggressive people we may meet, we are here to show them love, not to prove to them how strong we are. If you want proof just open your Bible once more at the arrest of Jesus. The bullies beat Him up terribly, but His only retaliation was to show real strength and forgive them.

 PRAYER *Lord, today help me not to react with any form of violence.*

13 JUN

'If we confess our sins, he is faithful and just and will forgive us our sins …' 1 John 1:9

KEY WORD ‘confession’

ISHMAEL AND ANDY were in Newcastle for a week of mission. Our itinerary was being planned jointly by an organisation and a local church. This all sounded fine until, when we arrived, we discovered that neither organiser got on with each other, which resulted in both of them booking separate itineraries each evening where the timing of the concerts overlapped. We did our best to fulfil two bookings each night but this proved to be impossible. Local organisers were angry with us for arriving late but when we tried to explain the reason, they refused to listen.

It was halfway through the week when the last straw broke the camel's back. It was 30 minutes before the start of a concert. Four hundred people were seated in the theatre and we were feeling exhausted and frustrated. It was then that one of the organisers began to blame the other organiser for the chaos caused. That was enough. I told Andy to pack his guitar away; we were not going to play another note until we had sat these two organisers down together and sorted things out. We left the audience to be entertained by a preacher and drove straight to the other organiser's house where the four of us talked and prayed together. We refused to leave the room until both organisers apologised to each other and made friends. This done, the rest of the week went brilliantly!

There is one thing that we all have in common. We all sin. God set a standard that He wanted people to live up to, but, starting with Adam and Eve and continuing with you and me, we have all fallen short of God's perfect standard.

THE POINT **The good news is that when we do sin, if we confess it and say sorry to God, He not only forgives us but completely wipes our wrongdoing from His memory bank. A word of advice: don't store up your confession until the end of the week or even the end of the day. It is good to say sorry to both God and people as soon as we recognise that we have done wrong.**

PRAYER *Lord, please help me today to confess my sins immediately I realise that I have done wrong.*

'Clap your hands all you nations …' Psalm 47:1

 KEY WORD '**clapping**'

ISHMAEL UNITED WERE invited to play support to a cockney duo called Chas and Dave at Brighton Polytechnic. Chas and Dave had recently had some chart hit singles so I was interested to see them perform. We arrived early for a soundcheck but the main stars were nowhere to be seen. Someone told us that they were in the bar and that we should soundcheck first. This was very unusual, but eventually they appeared and were so laid back or inebriated, that I don't think they bothered to soundcheck at all. At eight o'clock the doors opened and crowds poured in to see Chas and Dave. No one came to see us. In fact, none of this audience would have ever heard of the Christian support band. We went on and played our 45-minute warm-up set. This included new wave/punk music, which was in stark contrast to Chas and Dave's fun/boogie-woogie style. Our lyrics were also very different to theirs. Ours were all about Jesus and the Christian faith. We thought the audience were being polite by clapping at the end of each song. We simply could not believe that there might be just the chance that they were actually enjoying this overtly Christian band. After all, this was a Polytechnic audience! We finished with a song about Bartimaeus, the blind man whom Jesus healed, and then walked off stage. The audience were clapping and cheering like crazy but we thought they were just being cynical until Chas (or Dave, I never found out which was which) came rushing over and told us to go back on and play an encore. He also mentioned that the ***** Bartimaeus song was ***** brilliant!

Clapping can be a sign of gratitude. I would love to see it happen more often in some of our meetings when appropriate. Maybe applauding our church leaders and our musicians and definitely clapping those who minister faithfully to our children. God loves us to encourage each other.

 THE POINT There are times that I like to clap my hands in appreciation of the Lord. It's great to show our thanks to people, but nobody deserves more thanks than God.

 PRAYER *Lord, today help me not to be afraid to show my appreciation to both You and other people by clapping my hands.*

15 JUN ⟩ *'Make every effort to live in peace with all men ...' Hebrews 12:14*

KEY WORDS ⟩ 'live in peace'

ISHMAEL AND ANDY were due to perform at a large concert. A journalist from a local newspaper decided to come and report on the concert. The venue was full but in the back row there was a large group of young people causing a disturbance. The lights went down and everyone faced the stage. It was then I entered at the back of the theatre, dressed in black, shouting 'The end is nigh.' As the house lights came back on everyone could see that I was carrying a sandwich board with those words written on it. I continued shouting 'Prepare to meet thy doom' as I walked down the centre aisle towards the stage. Then someone jumped up from the middle of the audience waving his fist in the air and shouting, 'What a load of old rubbish, you don't know what you are talking about.' Yep, it was an angry Andy planted in the crowd. For the next five minutes we continued to heckle each other while the bewildered audience watched open-mouthed. Far from doing what today's verse instructs, we started our concert in the strangest way with a heated debate rather than peace. The journalist reported afterwards 'the concert continued in this off-beat manner throughout the evening, and by the end the disruptive element in the back row had quietened down. The obvious sincerity and joy of Ishmael and Andy had radiated out to everyone.' I still love a good debate, but I don't enjoy it if it gets 'heated' or if people begin to lose control or get hurt. That is when I tend to walk away. I think certain things are worth debating, but for Christians to get angry with each other is foolish. I will probably never stop getting involved in debates and offering my opinion, but I must learn that if I see signs of someone starting to lose control I mustn't walk away but rather speak peace into the situation and perhaps even change the subject!

THE POINT ⟩ **Christians may have differing viewpoints, but our love and friendship is far more important than winning an argument.**

PRAYER *Lord, today help me to bring peace to those who want to bring anger.*

KEY WORD 'tired'

AS A SMALL child I really believed that strength came in a tin labelled Spinach, thanks to good old Popeye the sailor man. In the cartoons he would be in the most impossible situation then suddenly out came the tin, usually tucked away inside his shirt (how many tins did he keep in there anyway?), then after a little tune and eating the contents, his muscles were bulging everywhere and he always won the day. I was invited to visit New Zealand and, as was often the case, funds were low. I took with me two musicians. When I ordered the cheapest tickets I could find, I had no idea that we would be embarking on such an epic trip. First stop was Heathrow Airport, then we flew to Amsterdam, where we changed flights for Los Angeles. In LA we had an eight-hour stopover so, being our first visit to the US, we decided to catch a bus to the beach. LA was exciting, just like in the movies! We then caught our flight to Auckland, where, on arrival, we had problems with immigration who confiscated our CDs and tapes. We had another long delay until eventually we took off for our final destination, Palmerston North. With all the time changes, delays and stopovers, I cannot to this day work out how many days our flight took or for how long we were deprived of sleep. We eventually arrived at the organiser's house only to discover that he had arranged for a few people to come round that night and meet us. It was in the middle of this meeting that I found it impossible to keep my eyes open. Still, once in bed we slept well and we were soon renewed with energy and able to play the concerts and fulfil what God had sent us there to do. It had to be His strength that made us able to do it; humanly speaking, we could never have done it!

 THE POINT **Let's always remember that if we want strength as a Christian, especially if we are feeling tired, it's not just food, pills, or even just sleep we need, we need to spend time with Jesus and He will renew our strength.**

PRAYER *Lord, help me today to set aside time to spend with You so that my strength can be renewed.*

17 JUN '... [He] increases the power of the weak.' Isaiah 40:29

KEY WORD 'power'

POWERFUL MACHINES THAT seem to be getting even more powerful surround us. Cars, motorbikes, planes, rockets, even ships and boats. But the power machines that scare me the most are power tools. Irene had decided that the carpets had to go and in their place would be the original floorboards. As for me, I thought that it was certainly a cheaper option than buying new carpets. I volunteered to do the DIY. It seemed easy enough: take up the old carpets and, hey presto, wooden floorboards. Then someone told me that to do it properly I would have to bang all the protruding nails down, then sand the boards before I could varnish them. What a horrible backbreaking job banging down those hundreds of nails was. Once done, Irene covered various parts of the room with dust covers while I went to the tool hire shop to hire the most powerful industrial sander available. My strategy being that the more powerful the machine, the faster I would get this job done.

I arrived home and proudly wheeled this expensive machine into our lounge. I thought it unwise to tell Irene that not only had I never used one before, but I had also never even seen one being used! I glanced at the instructions then carefully put the sanding sheet on the drum, plugged in the machine and switched it on. Wow, what a noise! But that was the least of my problems. The powerful machine shot off uncontrollably across the room with me in tow and ran straight into one of the curtains, instantly ripping it down from the wall and wrapping the fabric around the drum. I spent the rest of the day happily trying to cut the curtain free from the rather expensive machine!

THE POINT Powerful machines are one thing. Powerful people are another. Some church leaders love power and sometimes use this power to control and manipulate a congregation. This is a total misuse of power and does not please God. It's only when we admit that we are weak that God will give us more of His power that in turn will give glory to Him. If we misuse the power that God gives us, we can expect trouble.

PRAYER *Lord, today please let others see more of Your power in me.*

18 JUN

'Then he [Jesus] opened their minds so they could understand the Scriptures.' Luke 24:45

KEY WORD 'Bible'

EVER SINCE I was a small child I have always owned and treasured my Bible. When I was tiny I went to Sunday school in Horfield Baptist Church in Bristol. Each week I attended I was given a colourful sticker to stick in a little 'Bible book'. Receiving this little sticker was a great encouragement for me to attend. I couldn't wait to fill up one book so that I could start a new one. On each sticker was a picture of a character that I had heard about that day in the Bible story, so it was a great way for children to be reminded of what we had been taught. As I got older, someone gave me two cartoon Bible storybooks, one of the Old Testament and one of the New Testament. I spent hours and hours reading through these two books and looking at the cartoons and all the time I was doing this, I was learning more about the characters and stories that were in the Bible.

Today I have a wonderful slim-line Bible, which I bought in America many years ago. This book is very precious to me. I have underlined many passages in it which have had a special meaning for me at a certain time; I have even written little comments to remind me of certain things that I never want to forget.

The Bible is so important for Christians, but it's not just owning one, but reading and studying it regularly that's important. A few years ago, daily Bible reading became legalistic for some and they felt guilty if they didn't read it at a certain time each day. Nowadays it's the opposite. Many Christians are far more interested in listening to teaching and praise CDs rather than regularly studying God's Word for themselves.

 THE POINT Sometimes we read the Bible just like we would any other book, which is fine, but to get the best from it we need to study it and ask the Holy Spirit to help us not just to understand the passage we are reading, but to hear what God wants to teach us from that passage.

 PRAYER *Lord, today as I read my Bible, please reveal to me the wonderful truths that it contains.*

19 JUN

'He got up, rebuked the wind and said to the waves, "Quiet! Be still!"' Mark 4:39

KEY WORD 'storm'

IRENE AND I like to take our holiday at the beginning of the year. It's a time to relax and also talk about what God might have lined up for us in the coming 12 months. One January we decided to go to Egypt. Having never been there before it sounded exciting. I checked the weather forecast beforehand and it was going to be sun, sun, sun! We arrived in Egypt in the evening, so we were not able to see much, but the following morning I got up early and pulled back the curtains and the sun nearly blinded me as it shone through. I walked on to the balcony and just beyond the sand and the palm trees I could see the beautiful turquoise Red Sea. The day was spent lying on a sun bed, soaking up the sun and reading. We had a fairly early night and then the next morning I repeated the previous morning's procedure and pulled back the curtains. What a difference. Outside a howling gale was blowing, palm trees were bent almost double and the waves were crashing down on the beach. Throughout the day the storm died down. I'm pleased to say that it didn't reappear for the rest of the week, but walking around outside the hotel the storm had left its mark. Doors were damaged, trees uprooted, and it had even demolished a children's play park.

Many years ago I lived very close to the seafront. My favourite time for prayer walking was when the weather was blowing a gale and the rain was pouring down relentlessly. There wouldn't be anyone around, only fools and prayer-walkers would dare to venture out on a day like that.

THE POINT The storm in Egypt and the gales by the sea remind me how powerful God's creation is. But then I think of our verse. As I look at the power of the storm, I realise that Jesus can stop it all with just a few words from His mouth. Wind, be quiet, waves, be still. This reminds me where the ultimate power lies, with the Lord Jesus.

PRAYER *Lord, today help me never to forget that You have the power over all creation and nothing can happen without You allowing it.*

KEY WORD '**warrior**'

I HAVE BEEN to so many church family services over the years; they are called family services, but are definitely not *family* services. Most of them are just adult meetings with a short slot about a quarter of the way through where the children get a bit of attention, otherwise this meeting has little content for them. Why do people call these meetings family services? Once I was attending one such meeting, watching the many children near the front sitting quietly but looking very bored. Then the preacher got up to speak but chose not to speak from the stage. He droned on giving a very adult message for what seemed like hours on the floor in front of the stage. I again looked over at the children and felt so sorry for them. They stayed amazingly quiet and well behaved. I did notice something odd, though; they all seemed to be looking at the stage, but their heads were slowly going from side to side. After the meeting I went up to the children's leader who had been sitting with them and asked if the children had been bored. 'Oh no,' she said, 'they had a great time.' Suddenly I felt guilty. 'So they understood the speaker?' I enquired. 'Oh no,' replied the children's leader, 'they were all enjoying watching a warrior angel walking up and down on the stage behind the speaker.' Strangely enough, it was only the little ones who saw God's special messenger, and amazingly, when they all drew a picture of the angel they saw, all the pictures were almost identical.

So often the Lord is thought of just as gentle, kind, loving everyone, and someone who listens, as we tell Him our complaints and difficulties. Of course He is that, but we must also not forget that the Bible talks of Him as a warrior.

 THE POINT **Don't think that God sits doing nothing all day, He spends His time fighting for righteousness. He is with us when the evil one attacks and protects us from many dangers. But, remember, He will never take away our freewill, and if we choose to wander off or do silly things we have to face the consequences.**

 PRAYER *Lord, today I thank You for being a mighty warrior who is always fighting to protect me.*

21 JUN *'But after me will come one who is more powerful than I ...' Matthew 3:11*

'after me'

OVER THE YEARS I have had the privilege of leading many teams. Part of my calling has been to help train others in children's work and to pass on some of the experience I have gained over the years. Sadly, it has not always worked. One lady joined the team for a week-long event after being given a glowing recommendation from her church leader. On the first day we asked her to help with taking the children for outdoor games. She flatly refused to do this claiming that she was here to teach them about Jesus, not to play ball games. Later that day she packed her bags, jumped into her car, and left, never to be seen again! Then there was a guy called Doug Horley. Doug was the opposite; he had a wonderful servant heart and was always willing to learn. 'Duggie Dug Dug,' as I soon nicknamed him, later began an international children's ministry of his own. Duggie is younger than I am, and it's great to see he has followed on after me to carry on the Praise Parties I began. Someone once referred to Doug as my rival; I refer to him as one of my best friends. After a concert a small boy came up to me and said, 'Ish, you were good, but you were not as good as Duggie Dug Dug.' I just smiled and said, 'You're right.' The guy I helped to train up all those years ago has deservedly grown in popularity and now is one of the UK's top children's leaders. I, for one, think that is brilliant news!

John the Baptist was sent to prepare the way of the Lord; he also had many followers who might have thought that he must be the new Messiah sent from God. John soon put them right. 'Another is coming who is far more powerful than I am,' he told them. 'Look out for him.'

THE POINT We must never forget that popes, archbishops, apostolic leaders or church members are all just human. Christians should spend all their time diverting the attention away from themselves and towards the only one truly worthy of praise: the Lord Jesus.

PRAYER *Lord, today please help me to not want attention or recognition. Help me always to direct people's attention towards You.*

22 JUN

'He fills his hands with lightning and commands it to strike its mark.' Job 36:32

 KEY WORD 'lightning'

A FRIEND OF mine called Mark rang me up and asked if he could join me for a round of golf. Only in extreme situations could an offer like that be refused. Being a club member, I pay annually, and not for each round, but he being my guest had to pay the fee. As we walked towards the first tee I looked up and the sky looked rather dark and menacing. We were on the seventh hole, which just happened to be the hole that was furthest away from the clubhouse, when the heavens really opened up. We quickly put on our weatherproof clothing and put up our umbrellas, optimistically hoping that it would just be a shower that would soon pass. It wasn't, and it didn't. I could see that this downpour was not going to stop and decided to make my way back to the clubhouse. Mark told me that he had paid his fee, so he would finish the round. As I neared the clubhouse I heard a clap of thunder which seemed very close, and lightning streaked across the sky. It was then as I turned around that I noticed my friend racing up the fairway with his golf bag on his back. Overtaking me and in utter panic he shouted that there was no way that he was going to get struck by lightning while holding his umbrella in one hand and his iron clubs in the other!

Although some may be a little afraid of lightning, it is one of God's most fantastic displays of power. I remember many years ago a bishop from the north of England was making some rather dubious statements and soon afterwards discovered that lightning had struck part of his cathedral and set it on fire. Was this coincidence, or a bolt sent from heaven? Well, according to our Bible reading, God sometimes seems to aim the lightning at certain targets. This is both frightening and fantastic.

 THE POINT **Although I doubt whether God would have aimed a lightning bolt at my friend on the golf course, let's always remember that we serve a powerful God who has all creation within His power.**

 PRAYER *Lord, today I thank You for lightning. It is yet another reminder of Your great power.*

23 JUN *'… remembering the words the Lord Jesus himself said: "It is more blessed to give than to receive." '* Acts 20:35

'more blessed to give'

TRAVELLING FULL-TIME WITH a four-piece band plus sound engineer was always going to be expensive. Apart from paying all the personnel, there was the wear and tear and fuel for our large petrol-guzzling van and, of course, meals for hungry musicians on those long journeys. In Ishmael United we would send the organiser a contract stating a set fee. This was not a huge amount but it did help to pay the bills and look after our families. The organiser in return would sign the agreement and give us a cheque to cover that amount at the end of the concert. We had a booking in the north of England that was a very expensive, 500-mile round trip. As usual the band were not flush with cash, in fact we were quite hard up and so we were pleased that we had the work. After an excellent concert the organiser came up to me and thanked me, pushing a few notes in my hand. One glance showed me that it was a fraction of the amount that he had promised. I questioned him about our agreement, but there was no way he seemed to want to part with any more of his money, even though he could have afforded it. As the band watched me I remember pushing the money back into his hands, saying that if this was all he wanted to give us, he should have it back as his need must be even greater than ours. We then drove off.

On reflection it might not have been the best way to react. I certainly was not feeling more blessed about giving him back his money than I would have been had I been receiving the proper amount that we were due.

Maybe I should have left it for the Lord to deal with this person, or maybe the Lord used me to teach him something. The worst thing is I still don't feel too guilty about doing it.

THE POINT   **It is good to receive, but since those very difficult band days I have learned the greater joy of giving.**

PRAYER   *Lord, just as You have given to me, I pray today that I get the chance to give to others.*

24 JUN

'There is no dark place, no deep shadow, where evildoers can hide.' Job 34:22

KEY WORD 'hide'

WHEN I WAS a boy, living in the Christian community, I lived in a large house called the Old Rectory. Although at one time it would have been a real rectory, it had some very strange rooms and I often wondered who, other than a rector, had occupied it in the past. My bedroom was a very weird yet exciting room right at the top of the house. It was different from any other bedroom. As you entered it you were faced with steep steps that went up to the window and then at the top of the steps, facing the window, was a flat working surface covered with heavy slate. I always imagined that at one time it had been a laboratory used by some mysterious scientist who did all sorts of secret experiments, but then I always did have a vivid imagination! But that was not the most exciting feature. Underneath the platform was a tiny hatch that led into quite a large dark storage space. Now I was the only person in that house who was small and brave enough to squeeze through the hatch. No older children or adult would have managed it. Many a time if I wanted to be away from everyone and I didn't want to be found, I would sneak into my hideout and sit quietly until I felt I wanted to face the world again. I would hasten to add that not every time I entered that dark place was I an evildoer as described in today's verse!

In most of the movies we find that if someone is going to do some bad deed, usually they are creeping around in the dark of the night, or you see them lurking in the shadows. They do not want to be in the light, they want to be hidden by darkness so that no one can see what they are up to.

THE POINT Sometimes when we do wrong things we think that God can't possibly see us, or know what we are thinking. God knows everything about us, both good and bad, and there is no dark place where any of us can hide where He cannot find us.

PRAYER *Lord, today I know that I can never hide away from You and You will never hide away from me.*

25 JUN

'Joseph stayed in Egypt, along with all his father's family.' Genesis 50:22

'families'

MANY YEARS AGO I was involved in a church split. I was part of a leadership team and, without digging up ancient history, there were serious disagreements between members of our team. Now on most occasions like this the leaders will argue their point, each believing they are right. In the process they will often say harsh words that they will later live to regret saying. Then rival factions usually form amongst the congregation, who don't necessarily support the cause they feel to be right; more often than not they support the personality they most like. Eventually a lot of people end up confused and hurt. Then comes the crunch. Some remain thinking they have won the day while others leave the church also thinking that they have won the day. The ones who stay usually haven't a good word to say about those who leave, and those who leave haven't a good word to say about those they have left behind. A short while ago they were all close friends, but now that friendship is over! With the split that I was involved in it could never ultimately end like that because the differences were between me and some close members of my family. Inevitably even family hurts take a while to heal. Now all involved have moved on and although I realise that things can never be quite the same as they once were, I also realise that a parting of the ways could also never mean a permanent parting of our love and friendship.

Families always go through rough patches, and none, I guess, more than Joseph's. His brothers had been jealous of him and wanted to kill him, but then decided instead to sell him as a slave. You would imagine that he would not want anything else to do with his family. In fact, he wanted the opposite. Even though his family had put him through such pain, he still loved them, forgave them, and ended his days with them.

Don't let family feuds get out of hand, let's learn from Joseph and try to keep a good relationship with our families.

Lord, You created the family unit. Help us today to be examples to those around us of how families can love each other even after disagreement.

26 JUN

'The LORD will guide you always; he will satisfy your needs …' Isaiah 58:11

KEY WORD 'supply'

IRENE WOULD BE the first to admit that she has married quite a unique husband. No, I am not unique because I keep the house clean, or do all the washing up. I am sadly not even the amorous husband she would often like me to be, who presents her regularly with flowers, chocolates and romantic notes. I said I'm quite *unique*, not perfect! What makes me different from most husbands is that I enjoy going shopping with her. I find a night out shopping together getting our weekly food supply at our local superstore very enjoyable. We also go shopping in towns together but after parking the car we always split up because I rarely like shopping in the same shops as Irene. My favourite shops are charity shops. I love to rummage through those places and I buy most of my treasures and sometimes the odd bit of clothing there – except underwear, I hasten to add. In turn, I am 'Mr Recycle' because when I have finished with my clothes I drop them back at these shops for reselling. In fact, I have been known to unintentionally buy back the same shirt that I donated a few weeks earlier!

At home I realise that most of my possessions are junk. I wonder why I don't get rid of most of them. It's not that I really need any of them and very few have sentimental value. Some of my possessions I am keeping for a 'rainy day' just in case they come in handy, but they probably never will. Others I hang on to, to pass on to my children, but will they really want them? Probably not. God has not promised to supply me with all the junk I would like, but He has promised to supply all my needs. I have, however, discovered over the years that this may mean that He sometimes wants me to sell off some of my 'treasured possessions' to help provide for those needs.

THE POINT God may not supply a need if we already have the wherewithal to fulfil that need either lying around our house or sitting in a bank or savings account, or even invested in stocks and shares.

PRAYER *Lord, today I thank You for looking after my needs. The only real treasure worth having in my life is You.*

27 JUN *'The apostles performed many miraculous signs and wonders among the people.' Acts 5:12*

KEY WORD 'signs'

ONE NIGHT I was sitting by myself having a quiet drink in our local sports and social club. As usual I was surrounded by people whom I didn't know but knew that few, if any, would be churchgoers. It was then the Lord spoke to me and told me to go and speak to one of the darts team players. I waited until he had finished his game then I nervously introduced myself and started to chat to him. Following this the Lord told me to ask him if he was having trouble sleeping. I did so, and he replied yes, but how did you know? I was slightly embarrassed but had to say that God told me. The Lord then revealed to me the reason he was having trouble was because he was involved in occult activity. I passed this message on to him. By now the darts game had stopped and everyone was standing listening to what this 'strange prophet' with a pint in his hand was saying. He confessed that he was involved in this specific occult activity and again asked how I knew. Again, but now in front of a small audience, I said that God had told me. I was then able to both show and share the supernatural power of God with those very amazed darts players.

Preaching is very important – so, of course, is living a life that gives glory to Jesus. Nowadays we try and encourage those friends of ours who are not yet believers to listen to our words, but Jesus proved that for unbelievers, just to listen is never going to be enough; they need to see signs of the present supernatural power of God in action. One-third of the Gospels is taken up with Jesus performing the impossible and nobody has ever talked the talk or walked the walk like Jesus.

THE POINT If Jesus, the perfect preacher, knew that people needed to see signs and wonders before they would even consider believing, how much more do you and I need to be asking God to use us in the miraculous in this day and age.

PRAYER *Lord, please allow me today to use Your supernatural gifts so that others may come to know You.*

28 JUN

'Since no man knows the future, who can tell him what is to come?' Ecclesiastes 8:7

KEY WORD

'future'

NOW I DO believe in prophecy and I believe that today God still uses people to pass on His message to others. Sadly, a lot of what people call prophecy nowadays is just words of encouragement that sound very feeble compared to the prophecies that we read in the Bible. I also believe that there is a very fine line between a sort of Christian fortune telling and what some would call prophecy. Over the years I have had many 'minor prophets' approach me with some of the strangest 'words from the Lord'. Not so long after I really started following Jesus, a girl came up to me and told me that the Lord had shown her that we would get married. Being a very young believer I was unsure of how to react. I did know that the Lord had not given me that same message and I also knew that I was not attracted to her one little bit! I remember one couple getting married because they believed that the Lord told them to, even though they didn't like each other!

I found the hardest 'words' to discern were the ones that were warnings. Someone once approached me saying that God had told them to pass on to me that I should not go on a certain journey because disaster would happen. Again, the Lord had not revealed this to me, so I ignored it and just got on with the journey. I praise God that none of these 'disaster' words have actually come true, but they can put doubt, confusion and fear in both my mind and the minds of my loved ones. Our scripture reminds us that we don't know what is going to happen in the future and I for one am quite pleased about that. I don't want to know what is around the corner, good or bad; my life is in God's hands, and I know that whatever I have to face, He will be there alongside me.

THE POINT **Let's not worry about tomorrow too much, let's get on and enjoy serving and worshipping the Lord today!**

PRAYER

Lord, today I am not going to worry about tomorrow. Help me to live for You just one day at a time.

'What man can live and not see death … ?' Psalm 89:48

KEY WORD 'die'

PART OF A church leader's job is to encourage and help build up faith. Someone told me that a person about my age had just died and he felt that he should go and pray for him to come back to life. He asked me, as his pastor, to join him. I agreed, to support his faith, although I admitted that I was unsure if it would happen as the Lord had not revealed anything to me. On arrival at the chapel of rest, I noticed he had brought some sandwiches along, thinking the dead man, like Jairus's daughter, might be hungry when he came back to life. The first shock I had was when I saw the age of the deceased – he was years older than me! The second blow was that the coffin lid was screwed down and my friend was convinced that he should hold the occupant's hand as he prayed. I persuaded him that it was not necessary to unscrew the coffin lid. I explained that God would not stop a miracle He wanted to happen just because of a lid. I suggested that we would know if he came back to life because we would ask him to tap three times from the inside of the coffin. He prayed and kept praying, but sadly nothing happened. After a while I had to restrain myself from knocking on the side of the coffin just to release the tension and give him a bit of encouragement. I am afraid nothing happened except that we enjoyed eating the sandwiches later.

When the psalmist wrote today's verse he felt there were no alternatives. Everyone is going to die sooner or later. However, since Jesus, His followers have lived with a new hope – one day Jesus will return to earth and take all His followers to be with Him for ever … these people will never die.

THE POINT Nobody knows the day or the date when Jesus will return, but one thing we can be sure of, is that it is a lot closer now than it was in the day of the disciples, and they thought it was imminent 2,000 years ago! Stay prepared and close to Jesus, it really could happen any time and when we least expect it.

PRAYER *Lord, whether I escape death today or not, thank You that my future will be with You.*

30 JUN 'The Lord was with Samuel as he grew up ...' 1 Samuel 3:19

 KEY WORDS 'growing up'

SUNDAY WAS ALWAYS the busiest day of the week in our Christian community. It began with the worst task. As a child I would have to don my dreadful heavy woollen suit. This was the Christian uniform of the day. The suit would not have been so bad if it had not itched so much. Why was there no lining in the trousers?! Anyway, once dressed, it was off to our local Evangelical Free church. This church had a great Sunday school and I really enjoyed attending it because I loved listening to the Bible stories. After a quick lunch I then went to the Congregational church afternoon Sunday school. Again I enjoyed this meeting and what was also good about this was that after the meeting we would hunt for slow-worms on the bank outside where there were lots of them. After tea I either went back to the Evangelical church or travelled with my father and others from the community as they led services in other churches. They always allowed me to take some part in the meetings. Strangely enough I really enjoyed spending my Sundays in this way. I guess God's hand must have been upon me even way back then as a small child. But I was never going to reach the dizzy heights of Samuel.

It is true that Samuel was an exceptional child. A miracle birth, given over to God at a very early age, and then growing up to become one of the greatest prophets that has ever lived. I still meet people who think that children have no spiritual value until they are teenagers. Why don't these people read the Bible! Just as the Lord was preparing Samuel, and I believe from a very early age, so He is preparing today's children. One of my greatest thrills is to keep meeting people, now in their 20s and 30s, who became Christians at one of my meetings when they were very young and are now being mightily used by God.

 THE POINT **Let's train our children in the ways of God and start doing this when they are very young. Those early years of learning are vital.**

 PRAYER *Lord, today I pray for the children I know. Help me to encourage them to become strong believers.*

01 JUL *'and a great crowd of people followed him …' John 6:2*

 'crowd'

EVERY YEAR WE, and a few thousand others, attend Spring Harvest. For many years we ran the children's programme for eight- to eleven-year-olds. We called this The Glorie Company and sometimes we would have as many as 1,000 children attend our meetings twice a day. It was great fun but because we were resident on this site there was nowhere to hide and get a bit of peace and quiet. Our team always seemed to be surrounded by dozens of children. One day we had some free time so one of the team leaders, Anthony, and I decided to get away from the crowd and relax for an hour or two at the leisure complex. We arrived at the swimming pool, and the minute we entered the water we were surrounded by children. Obviously their parents had the same idea as us about taking some time out to enjoy the pool. The children were screaming, shouting and splashing us while the parents looked on and just laughed. This was not our idea of getting away from it all so we decided to make a run for it. We leapt out of the pool and ran straight into the changing room for safety. It wasn't until we were well into the changing room that we realised that we were surrounded by women with not a man in sight. We had run straight into the female changing room by mistake! As we walked back through the door all the children were looking at us and laughing. You can imagine the comments and, of course, they didn't let us forget our little mistake for the rest of the week!

 THE POINT **Wherever Jesus went, He too was surrounded by crowds, but not just crowds of noisy children! Many were not so much interested in what Jesus was teaching, they were more interested in seeing the miraculous deeds that He performed on people who were sick. Although Jesus never turned the crowd away, I am sure that He really appreciated the times when he was just with close friends and even more, the times when He was just with Father God.**

 PRAYER *Lord, please today let me find some time to get away from the crowd and spend time with You.*

' "Your servant has nothing there at all," she said, "except a little oil." ' 2 Kings 4:2

KEY WORDS 'nothing except'

BEING A YOUNG Christian, I knew I needed more Bible teaching. I had visited a Bible college in Wales many times on my travels and the people had always been very kind to me. I hardly looked like a typical Bible student candidate, more like a hippy with long hair and scruffy clothes, but I applied to become a student anyway. I was thrilled to get a reply offering me an interview. It was a long, tedious train journey from Sussex to South Wales. I had to change trains several times. Eventually, I arrived at the college. Nervous and excited I was shown into a small room. A man entered who appeared to be extremely unfriendly. He looked me up and down and I could see by his expression that he wasn't impressed. After interrogating me he told me that I was unsuitable for the college and showed me to the door, without even offering me so much as a cup of tea. I felt very depressed as I set off on my weary journey home. I felt like I was someone with nothing to offer. Three years later I applied to Elim Bible College and the principal himself interviewed me. He asked me what qualifications I had. I replied that I had nothing except my national diploma in agriculture and I could play a guitar. I was accepted on the spot and I got a cup of tea!

The poor widow in our verse was desperate when she bumped into Elisha. She had a major problem with debt. When Elisha asked what she had, her reply was 'nothing … except'. In other words, she didn't exactly have nothing, she had a little oil that God was going to multiply, so she could pay back all she owed.

THE POINT My rejection by the first Bible college was awful, but only then did I discover that I did have a little something. That 'something' is just the thing that God can use to help us to move into a better place. I had little qualifications 'except' I could play the guitar and that little 'except', brought me into an exciting three years of ministry as 'Ishmael and Andy'.

PRAYER *Lord, today I am so pleased that You can make a lot out of very little.*

'Then Joshua sent the people away, each to his own inheritance.' Joshua 24:28

'each to his own inheritance'

MY FATHER WAS seriously ill before he eventually died. Now Dad was the opposite of me, he was a meticulously tidy person. If you went into his shed or garage, everything not only had its own box, everything was individually labelled. Even the different-sized nails, screws, bolts and washers were in their own little jam jars. I am afraid that I just have one big box in my garage and everything metal is thrown into it. That's the reason why it takes so long for me to find anything. Having such a tidy mind my father also had everything sorted before he died. Of course most things were to be left to my mother but he did make little lists of specific items that he wanted to pass on to his three children. I was left his fishing rods and tackle although I have never felt the desire to go fishing since his death; I think it would bring back too many sad memories. He also left me his war medals, a pair of binoculars, his theological books and the family Bible. An inheritance is not something you have to work for, not even something that you have to ask for, it is something that is passed on to you, usually by someone who cares for you. When someone dies and a will is read out there can be many surprises. Some people who have not been wealthy suddenly find themselves rich. Others who were hoping to be left something find they have not and quarrels begin. Nothing in the little list of possessions that my father left me was worth a lot of money. I was certainly not going to get wealthy on my inheritance, but the memories of his fatherhood, friendship and times spent together have left me with more wealth than money. The most important thing to consider, though, is not what we leave people in material possessions but what we are passing on that will spiritually benefit those we love. Possessions will rot away but memories of our example as men and women of God won't.

 I hope my children will inherit some of my good points and not too many of my bad points.

 Lord, help me today to be a good example of a follower of Jesus.

KEY WORD 'crazy'

WE HAD A young man called Dan live in our home for a while and he became like a third son. He was always a little crazy but was always, 'sold out for God'. A while ago we were with him at a meeting at what was then acknowledged as one of the liveliest and wildest churches in the country. It was a strange meeting because the music was great, the preaching was good, the praying was powerful, but the people seemed lifeless and there was little evidence of the power of the Holy Spirit. It was at that point that Dan got up onstage and told us that God had told him to do a crazy thing; he was to just dance in front of us. We all watched as he obediently danced around the stage with no music playing. Some smiled, some were embarrassed, and others were just amazed that a young guy would get up on to the stage and do such a crazy thing. After a short while, it was like the breath of God fell on everyone present and suddenly the meeting, and the people came to life.

Now it's unlikely that Noah knew what floods were, and it's also unlikely that his garden backed on to the sea or a very large river. So to be told that he had to build a big boat would have been a crazy thing to do. It is also very unlikely that just Noah and his family would have built it. He would have to hire carpenters to come and help with the job. I dread to think what they thought of Noah or the vast project that they were working on. However, what people think is unimportant. Our young friend Dan, like King David, didn't care if people laughed while he danced before the Lord. It's being obedient to God that is all important.

 THE POINT **I guarantee that God will ask you and me to do some crazy things. We will of course be a little worried by what other people think, but we will still do them. Why? Because God told us to do them.**

 PRAYER *Lord, if You want me to do something today that some may think a little crazy, please give me the courage to do it.*

KEY WORD 'hope'

ON ONE OF my many tours of Holland, everything seemed to go wrong. It had started off well, because my younger brother Tim, who had just turned 18, had decided to keep me company and play bass for me. As we had a lot of equipment I decided to take my car, which at that time was an old Volvo Estate called Henry, which a friend had very kindly donated for my work. On disembarking from the ferry, we happily drove through multitudes of tulip fields in the warm sunshine. Then it all went wrong. The oil light came on, the engine made some strange noises, and Henry died. Even the tulips looked sad as we pulled into a ditch by the side of the road. We were in the middle of nowhere, in a country where we couldn't speak the language and with not a guilder to our name. Everything looked hopeless. It was time to call upon the Lord – we had no idea what else to do. In a very short while, the Lord answered our prayers. The car was towed to a garage, local Christians took an offering for us to cover all the garage costs and within a week old Henry was happily chugging back through those tulip fields with a brand-new engine and two happy musicians inside!

Poor Bartimaeus didn't have a lot to be happy about. He couldn't see, which meant he couldn't work, which in those days meant that he had to beg for his food and money. I guess worse than this, he was considered as a hopeless case by all who passed him by. Although he didn't know Jesus, he obviously must have heard enough about Him to believe He could help him. So a bit like us and the dead car, his only hope was to call on the name of the Lord.

 THE POINT **No one thought Jesus would have time to listen to someone like Bartimaeus, but He did. We must never be scared to call upon the name of Jesus; He always has time to listen to what we have to tell Him and to provide miraculous answers.**

 PRAYER *Lord, today when things look hopeless, I thank You that I can call upon Your name.*

KEY WORD ' age'

ALTHOUGH I CAN still think young, and sometimes can even feel young, every time I look in the mirror I see an old man looking back at me. Irene and I have always had problems finding Christian friends of our own age who enjoy a similar lifestyle to ours. Most of our age group spend their evenings either inviting friends round for dinner parties, which are evenings that I dread, or just enjoy spending the evening in front of the television with a cup of cocoa, which I equally dread! At the end of a long working day, Irene and I both enjoy relaxing in our local pub, having a drink and talking to people. This means that we make friendships with people of our age who tend not to go to church, but somehow we invariably end up talking with them about Christian things. In the pub we also meet up with a lot of younger people. I guess that is why we seem to have a lot of close friends who are the same age as our children. I was pleasantly surprised when some of these young people asked if I would arrange a regular Bible study and prayer group for them. To start with, I tried to put them off as I couldn't understand why they would want to spend a couple of hours a week with someone who was old enough to be their father, but then I realised just how wrong I was. So from that time on, regular meetings have taken place in our home and the number of young people wanting to meet up with the old man is growing steadily.

I remember my eldest son Joseph once telling me that I was not like a normal dad because I liked doing, watching and listening to the things he enjoyed. He finished up by telling me I was more like a friend than a dad. I can live with that, I'll always be his dad, but I will also always be his friend.

THE POINT **Age difference must never be an excuse for not having close friendships with young people. The age gap issue is usually initiated by us elderly ones and not younger ones.**

 PRAYER *Lord, today I thank You that You still want to use me with all ages.*

07 JUL *' "Why does your teacher eat with tax collectors and 'sinners'?" ' Matthew 9:11*

'snob'

IRENE AND I were taking a short break in the West Country. Coincidentally, our accommodation just happened to be right next to a golf course. This meant that while Irene was deep in study, I could enjoy a quiet game and my usual pursuit of hunting in bushes and hedgerows for golf balls. I spotted the clubhouse so suggested that we take a stroll and call in for a quiet drink to check it out. We were dressed reasonably smartly and entered the clubhouse lounge. It was full of men who stared at Irene as though they had never seen a woman before. We glanced at each other knowingly. This must be one of those sexist golf clubs that still have 'male only' bars. Although Irene started to leave, I refused to be intimidated and walked straight up to the bar. The barman explained that he was unable to serve us as this bar was for members only. Then a man in a blazer, obviously the club secretary, approached us and began to ask questions. I explained what my occupation was, that we were having a short break and were admiring the course while out enjoying a pleasant stroll. He immediately got out the visitors' book, said it was no problem, and promptly signed us in. He then continued, 'You people are just the sort we like in here. Of course we have to be careful what types we allow in – no riff-raff, you understand.' That clinched it, snob as well as sexist! We hastily drank up and made a quick exit – they were just not our 'sort of people'.

Jesus had just invited a notorious taxman called Matthew to join His group of close friends, and the first thing that Matthew asked Jesus to do was to come and meet his friends. The Pharisees considered Matthew and his friends as the 'scum of the earth'. Why on earth would Jesus want to spend time with 'sinners'.

THE POINT The Pharisees were the classic 'snobs' of the day. Like the secretary in the golf club they didn't want to mix with the 'riff-raff'. I am so grateful that Jesus did; He came to earth for sinners, not snobs.

PRAYER *Today I pray, Lord, that I may never be a snob. You love ordinary people; You love me.*

08 JUL

'And the child [Jesus] grew and became strong; he was filled with wisdom, and the grace of God was upon him.' Luke 2:40

KEY WORD 'childhood'

I WROTE AND recorded the concept album *Land of Hope and Glories* and decided to turn it into a proper family stage show and tour throughout the summer holidays. It had to be during the summer holidays because I wanted my little choir of singers with me onstage. August came and off we set on tour, my sister, brother-in-law and their four children, and Irene and I with our three children, plus Roy our lighting engineer. It was a two-week tour that meant we were going to travel to lots of different venues, sleep in different houses, and inevitably have lots of adventures en route. Each night we were received well and to the audience it must have appeared to run very smoothly. However, backstage was another story. No one out there would have had any idea of the chaos happening behind the scenes. Irene and my sister had to help change seven children's costumes for each scene and meanwhile the CD soundtrack just kept playing, ready or not! On one occasion, I was in such a panic that I couldn't for the life of me get my T-shirt on. It was just as I was getting all hot and bothered that Irene explained through tears of laughter that I was trying to put on her T-shirt by mistake! The tour was great and God used our children in the course of their childhood, and He continues to use them today.

Jesus was also once a little child. He enjoyed many of the things that the children enjoy. Jesus would have played games, had friends, enjoyed times of happiness and faced times of sadness. As He grew up, He became strong, probably by helping Joseph carry large trunks of wood for His work as a carpenter.

THE POINT There was one thing that made Jesus different from any other child that has ever lived; He never did one thing wrong. He was the perfect child. He was the perfect Son of God. Let's never forget that.

PRAYER *Lord, today I pray for all the little ones around me. May their childhood years be good times to remember and may they continue to be true servants of yours when they reach adulthood.*

09 JUL

'How good and pleasant it is when brothers live together in unity!' Psalm 133:1

KEY WORD 'unity'

MY BROTHER TIM is very different from me. To start with, he was a very late addition to the family, which meant that while he was growing up, I had already left home. It was a pity because although I had an older sister, Heather, to grow up with, he didn't really have an older brother. But the early years we lost out on by not being together, we caught up later on in life. When Tim reached 18 he joined me and travelled with me on the road for ten years. So in that time we soon became good friends and close brothers. But still as brothers we had our times of disunity. On one occasion Tim, another team member and I had taken time out from an event to go to a pub and watch my team, Blackburn Rovers, play Manchester United on the pub's television. Needless to say, Blackburn lost so I was not in the best of moods. We drove back and when we arrived, just as I got out of the car the seat fell on my hand. It hurt and I was hopping up and down in pain. Then I saw my brother and the other team member giggling. I was furious with them, declaring that as the seat had landed on my guitar-playing hand, it could have been the end of both my ministry and my career! Needless to say, my over-the-top reaction made them laugh even more; they both knew I was more upset about seeing Blackburn lose than the pain in my hand! We soon put things right with each other because that is what brothers have to do.

I spend most of my life travelling to different church groups and it's very sad to arrive at a church that has split because of disagreement. Now sometimes, given time these divisions work out for the best, but the sadness comes when neither party is willing to apologise and put things right.

THE POINT As followers of Jesus we are all part of God's family. This means that we are related, we are brothers and sisters. God wants us to live in unity. We each have to do everything in our power to see that we do.

PRAYER *Lord, please help me today to live in unity with all around me.*

10 JUL *'Am I now trying to win the approval of men, or of God?' Galatians 1:10*

 KEY WORD '**approval**'

PAUL CONTINUES BY saying, 'If I were still trying to please men, I would not be a servant of Christ.' There have been many times in my life when someone has wanted me to do something while God has wanted me to do something different. A youth leader invited me to speak to his youth at a camp. The subject he wanted me to speak on was 'Being free to praise God'. This would include dancing before the Lord. Unbeknown to me this was an issue with his church and the pastor was against any form of dancing. I gave my first talk and mentioned dancing. The youth leader seemed really excited about this but I was surprised to see the pastor looking annoyed. I still had no idea why. I only guessed that there must be something seriously wrong, when the pastor, who was in charge of serving the food, kept giving me a small portion! When I asked the youth leader what the problem was, he explained that he and his pastor held opposing views on dancing in church. I immediately realised here were two enemies intent on attacking one another and I was caught up in the middle. I was in a no-win situation. Whatever I said I was going to upset someone. After a couple of days I felt God tell me not to get involved. So I called both factions together. I advised them to forget about concentrating on 'being free to praise God' and to spend the rest of the week getting their relationship right with each other. I was going home! They argued with me that I couldn't possibly leave because they had booked me to stay for a week. I simply wished them well and left. This was one time when I was going to do what God wanted even though I was losing the approval of men! It's strange but after I left, the camp went down with a sickness bug for the rest of the week.

 THE POINT I don't ever plan to deliberately upset people, but I have discovered over the years that it's far more important to stay obedient to God than just to please people.

 PRAYER *Lord, today help me to do what wins Your approval.*

11 JUL ‘*In the beginning you laid the foundations of the earth, and the heavens are the work of your hands.*’ *Psalm 102:25*

KEY WORD ‘spectacular’

IRENE AND I were invited to teach in a very remote part of the Shetland Isles. The main island is not particularly beautiful, although it has its own rugged and wild charm. We gave a concert in a small village and the people were great; so enthusiastic. That weekend we were given accommodation next to a quaint old post office on the seashore. As it was still fairly early we decided to go for a drink in the village pub. We entered and all six of the locals present immediately halted their conversation and stared at us as if we were aliens. The bar décor was bland, just white walls, gaming machines and fluorescent lights. Later, the atmosphere changed slightly when a disco started up and the fluorescent lights were turned off to allow the pulsating lights to take over. Needless to say that was our cue to leave. As we walked out of the door and across the street, leaving the feeble disco lights flashing in the distance, we looked up into the sky and saw the most beautiful sight, God's disco, Aurora Borealis. We watched for ages as the skies lit up with spectacular vibrant colour and there was no way that we were going indoors while God was putting on such an amazing light show, just for us!

I smile as I listen to people trying to convince me of the theory of evolution or some other equally unlikely way that the universe was formed. I am sure they must have a lot more faith than I do to believe some of the incredible things they do. I am not stupid but have no trouble in believing what the Bible says when it tells me that a Creator God got the whole thing started, and still holds it and us in the palm of His hands.

THE POINT In a world where man has done so much damage, I can still see so much of God's creative genius. He is still doing amazing creative things, like putting on a spectacular light event just for two little people to watch it!

PRAYER *Lord, today I want to thank You for creating so much beauty around me.*

12 JUL *'And I trust that you will discover that we have not failed the test.' 2 Corinthians 13:6*

KEY WORD 'failed'

I HAD PASSED my cycling proficiency test, I had passed my tractor driving test; now the big one, my car driving test. Back in those days very few people had driving lessons. Most people learned to drive with a friend or relative sitting next to them. My father was a very good instructor. Whenever I had the chance I would tie my L-plates on to the bumpers of his Ford Anglia and persuade him to accompany me on a drive. Soon I was ready to apply for my test. The day came and I was very nervous. The examiner sat beside me in the passenger seat looking very serious. Not a smile, no friendly relaxing banter, he just put his clipboard on his lap and told me the route he wanted me to take. I was really nervous by now. After about five minutes, I started to calm down. I seemed to be driving quite well and he wasn't writing a great deal. Then it happened. A lady cyclist pulled straight out in front of me, and my car knocked her for six. I stopped the vehicle and we both ran out and helped pick up the shopping that had fallen out of her basket. Thankfully she wasn't badly injured but she did have blood running down her leg and the sight of blood always makes me feel faint. The examiner explained to her that he couldn't stop because he was conducting a test and instructed me to get back in and continue driving. By this time I was shaking, so that was the perfect time for him to tell me to do the most difficult manoeuvre, to reverse round a corner. Of course I got it all wrong and ended up on the pavement. Yep, I'd failed my test!

Paul tells the Corinthian church to test themselves to see if their faith is solid and that Jesus lives within them.

THE POINT **We all need to give ourselves a regular check-up. We may have made a commitment to follow Jesus many years ago but how close are we to Jesus today? Let's not fail the test.**

PRAYER *Lord, please show me today if I have passed the test and remain very close to You.*

13 JUL

Let everything that has breath praise the LORD.' Psalm 150:6

'praise the Lord'

IT WAS THE 1970s. After leaving Ishmael and Andy, Andy joined a fantastic band called After the Fire. Now ATF were the top Christian band of the day. They had secured a recording contract with CBS and were hitting the charts with singles. As well as being a friend of the band, I also prepared a Bible study course for them. I was keen to make a 'rock praise' album, which, back in those days, was unheard of and they kindly agreed to play for me. We decided to do a 'live' recording in a church hall in Colchester using a mobile recording studio with a young producer called John Pantry, who had already produced my highly controversial album *The Charge of the Light Brigade* one year earlier. Once set up we started recording and did we have fun! We simply praised the Lord and recorded it as we did so. There was so much laughter as we praised that by the time we were recording the final track I had completely lost my voice and had to whisper the words and sometimes not sing at all, just let the music play. Because 'rock praise' was so new, I could see John was a bit concerned, he even questioned me on whether it was 'blasphemous'. *It's Amazing What Praising Can Do* was a rough, unpolished album, but in many ways it pioneered the way for all the wonderful praise bands that we enjoy today. Following on from that, ATF backed me at Greenbelt that year and I'm told that while we were singing a song called 'Kiss the hand of Jesus' very late at night, a white dove hovered over the stage for the whole song. Powerful stuff!

THE POINT

One of the greatest things that a Christian can do is to praise the Lord. I often wonder if I had not experimented by putting rock and praise together whether today we would still be singing all our praise songs accompanied just by the piano, organ or gentle acoustic instruments. OK, feel free to blame me for introducing 'rock 'n' praise!'

PRAYER

Lord, today I am going to praise You and I know You don't mind if it is with loud rock music or gentle quiet music. The main thing is that I praise You!

14 JUL *'There is a time for everything ...' Ecclesiastes 3:1*

'a time for everything'

WHEN I WAS a pastor in the north of England I decided that I needed a hobby, preferably one that would also give me some exercise because the chips and meat and potato pies were taking their toll on my waistline. My friend Tom and I decided to visit the municipal golf course that was close by and inexpensive. Neither of us really knew how to play but we always had fun. On one occasion we arrived at the first tee and noticed a four-ball in front of us and they seemed quite slow. Now I am not the most patient of people and waiting around is not my strong point, so I was hoping that they would in time 'let us through'. We'd played a few holes and they were not getting any faster – in fact, they seemed to be getting slower, if that was possible. Then it happened. They reached a green and stopped altogether, no one was even putting the ball. We decided to go and check out what was going on and when we got near we noticed that they were all inspecting the ground. There was no way that they could be looking for a lost ball because all four balls were already on the green. Then I recognised them; it was the pastor and some of his leaders from the next town. Then I also recognised what they were doing – they were standing on the sixth green, having a prayer meeting! I hoped they weren't asking God to help them with their game, now that would be cheating! As much as I didn't want to interrupt their conversation with the Lord I did walk over to them and, remembering today's verse, I suggested that standing by a golf flag with other golfers queuing up behind them might not be the ideal time for intercession. I can't remember if they agreed with me or not!

 THE POINT God has given us specific timings to do specific things. Of course, we are told to pray without ceasing, but I think this refers more to a constant personal communication with God rather than a 'four-ball' prayer meeting in the middle of a golf course.

 PRAYER *Lord, please help me today to do the right things at the right time.*

15 JUL *'... since you are standing firm in the Lord.' 1 Thessalonians 3:8*

 KEY WORDS 'standing firm'

WHILE IN AMERICA, Irene, Suzy and I went to minister in Arkansas. We stayed with a young couple who insisted that we join them in their speedboat for some fun and a bit of water-skiing on one of their many lakes. We agreed but I had two reservations. The first was that I had heard they had all sorts of nasty creatures and deadly water snakes lurking in these lakes, and the second was that I cannot water ski! We arrived at the lake and to break us in gently we were told to sit in a large rubber inner tube that was attached to the speedboat. Once in, it was full throttle and off the boat shot with us hanging on for dear life to what looked like a large slippery grey doughnut! Then came the big challenge. Our lady host gave me a verbal lesson on 'how to water-ski in three minutes' then I donned the life jacket and skis and off went the speedboat again but this time with me in tow on the skis. I thought I was doing OK but my problem was I couldn't stand up because I have no sense of balance. I must have looked the most inelegant water-skier ever. I just stayed crouching down following the boat with my rear end merrily bouncing along on the water. Determined not to give up I kept on trying time and time again but for some reason I never managed to stand upright. It was an unforgettable experience and it was not until I was back in the privacy of my own bedroom that I happened to glance in a mirror and discovered that my behind was just one big black n' blue bruise. After that glance in the mirror I decided that water-skiing was definitely not for me. On water I would always be falling in, never standing firm.

THE POINT So often when I think I am standing firm, I start to fall. It's usually when I am feeling good that I am tempted with different sins like pride or bad thoughts ... and, sure enough, I often give in to them and instead of standing firm, I fall.

 PRAYER *Lord, please help me today to stand firm, and not to fall.*

'But he [Peter] replied, "Lord, I am ready to go with you to prison and to death."' Luke 22:33

KEY WORDS 'Lord, I will go'

IT WAS NEARLY Christmas when I staggered into my parents' house very drunk. At 19 years old I felt really depressed. Although I had enjoyed a wonderful Christian upbringing, for the previous few years I had been enjoying life as a rebel, enjoying doing all the things that the Bible said that I should not do, many times over. I use the word 'enjoying' because I did enjoy it, the problem was the enjoyment was very temporary. My life was going nowhere and if I carried on living as I was it was not going to last much longer. When my parents saw the state I was in they soon retired to bed and left their prodigal alone and in the hands of God. That night I prayed. I spoke to Jesus in my drunken stupor and promised Him that if He could change my life and give it meaning, I would try and go wherever He wanted me to go and do whatever He wanted me to do. I woke up the next morning and told my parents that I had asked God to change my life. They seemed a little sceptical. Maybe they felt that a drunk could not pray sincerely or that God didn't listen to the prayers of a drunk. Although there was rejoicing in heaven there was no fatted calf or rejoicing on earth. My mother just said, 'Well, we will see', which, on reflection, were the wisest words she could have said because now it was up to me to prove it. Two things followed that drunken prayer: Jesus answered my prayer and immediately my life began to change and, since that prayer, I have tried to be His disciple and do whatever He has asked of me.

Peter, too, was determined to do and say everything that would please Jesus and here he says he is willing to make the ultimate sacrifice. He did face all sorts of persecution and finally death for his best friend Jesus.

THE POINT **Are we willing to do what Jesus wants us to do and to go wherever Jesus wants us to go? A true disciple says yes.**

PRAYER *Lord, today and everyday, I want to be a true disciple of Yours.*

17 JUL *'… God called to him from within the bush, "Moses! Moses!"' Exodus 3:4*

 KEY WORDS 'God called'

WHEN I WAS a student at Elim Bible College, I had no money and no real home but I did have a lovely wife and baby boy. Then, just when we needed it, the Lord wonderfully provided us with a temporary home in a seaside town about 30 miles away from the college. On the Sunday we decided to visit the local Elim Pentecostal church which was just a short walk away from where we lived. There were only a handful of people in the congregation and during the service an announcement was made that a special meeting would follow. At that meeting an elderly lady announced that after months of discussion it was agreed that this was going to be the last meeting in this building. They had been praying for a pastor but none had appeared. It was then I felt God say to me to go for it. To everyone's amazement, I walked to the front of the meeting. I then frightened the life out of them all by announcing that I, a total stranger, was their pastor. I had arrived, I am he, I am the one God has called! I think some would have preferred to shut the church down than to accept that God had sent me, but in our short time in that church, we saw God do some wonderful things!

Imagine Moses standing next to a bush that was blazing away, but not burning up, and then hearing the voice of God call out his name. Now I am guessing, but I imagine that God's voice was audible. I wish that God had spoken in a loud audible voice into my situation in that church, so that the entire congregation could have heard God announce that I was His man. It would have made my entrance an awful lot easier. Nowadays God usually chooses to speak with that quiet voice into our mind, or through our eyes and into our heart as we read the Bible.

 THE POINT **Let's never forget, God always speaks clearly, it's we who are often hard of hearing!**

 PRAYER *Lord, today You have things to say to me, help me to recognise Your voice and to listen when You speak.*

18 JUL *'And Moses said, "Here I am." ' Exodus 3:4*

 'God's voice'

I WAS LEADING a special weekend of teaching to a group of eight- to eleven-year-olds about the gifts of the Holy Spirit. During the weekend I spoke on the importance of the gift of prophecy. I explained how God sometimes gives a message to one Christian to pass on to another. These messages are usually words of encouragement or words to confirm something that He has already spoken to the recipient about. This was at a time in my life when God was challenging me about some personal issues. After the teaching I called all the leaders to the front and we all knelt down. I then asked the children to come and pray over us, and that if they felt that God had given them something, they should pass it on to us in the form of encouragement or help. A young boy stood next to me and started praying for me and then, supernaturally, he started mentioning the issues that God was challenging me about at that very time. It became even more embarrassing as it seemed everyone else stopped praying to listen to what he was saying. I asked him not to speak too loudly but you know children, the more you ask them to quieten down, the louder they seem to get! This young chap was no exception! God taught me that day that there are no secrets and that He can use little ones to speak into anyone's life.

Yesterday Moses heard the voice of God, and today he says, 'Here I am.' Let's put the burning bush to one side for a moment because that was spectacular in its own right. Let's imagine if you or I were out by ourselves in a field and we heard someone shout our name. I think I would look around and expect someone to appear who obviously knew me. Moses did not look for a human being; somehow he recognised the voice of God and responded.

 THE POINT   **Let's never forget that even today God sometimes chooses to speak through people both young and old. He may use someone to speak to us in a sermon or He may use someone to speak to us in our day-to-day conversation.**

 PRAYER   *Lord, today please help me to know when it's You speaking or when it's a friend just giving advice.*

19 JUL

' "I tell you," he [Jesus] replied, "if they keep quiet, the stones will cry out." ' *Luke 19:40*

KEY WORDS

'cry out'

ON ONE OF my many trips to Holland I was put in the position where I had to cry out, I could not keep quiet! I was invited to stay with a Dutch family who had a lovely teenage daughter who sadly suffered from a serious disability. Now there was a slight problem. Not one member of the family spoke a word of English and of course I could not speak a word of Dutch. This made communication rather difficult. I arrived back late one night from a concert and had been given a key to let myself in. I crept in quietly, noticing that everyone had gone to bed. I was desperate to use the bathroom and saw that the light was on, so assumed someone was in there. For the next hour I kept returning, but each time the light was on and the door would not open. I was now in the situation where I was desperate to get in and I felt sure that the daughter had perhaps collapsed and was locked in the bathroom. I started to panic and tapped on the door. No answer. There was nothing else for it. I rushed to the parents' bedroom and knocked on their door trying to tell them that something was wrong. They both came out half asleep in their night attire. I attempted to communicate with them through word and action that their daughter was trapped in the bathroom. They followed me to the door, took hold of the handle, turned it the opposite way to which I had been turning it, and the door opened easily, revealing an empty bathroom. Did I feel stupid!

The fever-pitch excitement of Jesus entering into Jerusalem must have been an amazing thing to experience. Sadly, in just a short while, probably some of the same crowd would change the word they were crying out from 'Hosanna' to 'Crucify'. Jesus is always worthy of our praise and nothing should ever stop us telling Him how much we love Him.

THE POINT I find it odd that people can get so excited and emotional about sport and yet never show anywhere near that level of excitement and emotion when they praise Jesus. That's weird.

PRAYER *Lord, help me today to get excited about You.*

20
JUL

'... children [are] a reward from him [God].' Psalm 127:3

 **KEY WORD** 'reward'

I OFTEN FIND ministering to children is very rewarding but I do feel that there must be a place for discipline even in a Christian meeting. For most of my concerts, the songs are very interactive so the children get the chance to jump around, but there are times when I ask the children to stop running around and to sit down quietly as I tell a short Bible story. I tell them that God has things to teach them, so they do need to sit quietly and listen. I was invited to lead a family service in a large parish church. Once everything was set up and the service was about to begin, the vicar approached me and told me that in this church they like their children to be free during the Sunday service. I was not quite sure what he meant until I saw lots of children suddenly run up on to the platform where we were standing and start pushing each other off it, laughing and shouting as they did so. What he obviously meant by 'free' was letting them run riot throughout the whole service with no discipline or instruction. The climax of this 'freedom' came when he was baptising a baby. Surrounded by many un-churched relatives, he was trying to lay hands on the new little baby to pray for her while his own children were at the same time actually swinging from both of his arms! It was dreadful. The children were out of control and running the service! When it came to my turn to get up and minister I stopped all the mayhem and looked a right killjoy. Parents, especially church leaders, need to learn that children do need supervision. It's not to suppress them, but it's so that they can listen to what God is saying, and be in a position to receive from Him. Needless to say, I was never invited back to that particular church, I obviously was not 'free' enough.

 THE POINT **Children are a reward from God as our Bible reading says, and a very special prize they are too, but just as God instructs adults on how to behave, so parents and leaders have a responsibility to instruct the children in what is right and wrong.**

 PRAYER *Lord, today I thank You that children are very special to You.*

21 JUL

'Jesus spoke all these things to the crowd in parables ...' Matthew 13:34

KEY WORD 'stories'

I LOVE TELLING children the stories of Jesus. One of my favourite stories I like to tell is how the nasty little taxman called Zacchaeus became a follower of Jesus. I try to live out the story as I tell it and get the children to believe that they are actually there with me in Jericho when this was taking place. I remember once getting to the part in the story where little Zacchaeus was up in the sycamore tree waiting for Jesus to appear and when He did, Zacchaeus recognised Him and exclaimed, 'There He is!' I said this while looking at the back of the hall, pretending I was the excited Zacchaeus. The children were so caught up in the story that most of them turned around and looked towards the back of the hall, expecting to see Jesus walking in through the church door!

Jesus enjoyed speaking to people in parables. A parable is a story that has a meaning much deeper than the obvious. This meant that all the listeners had to listen very carefully because it was not written down, just spoken. They would then have to think through the meaning behind the story that Jesus told for themselves. Sadly, nowadays we are very rarely taught through stories. I think often adults miss out. Jesus told most of His little stories to the most intelligent men of His day, not to children! I also love the way that Jesus refused to disclose the meaning of His stories. You have ears, He would say, you have heard it, now go and think about its meaning for yourself. Nowadays, why do preachers, when speaking on a parable of Jesus, feel they have to give their own interpretation of it? Surely this detracts from the whole point of the parable, if we are told its meaning rather than having to think it out for ourselves.

THE POINT So much of the preaching and teaching today leaves us little to ponder on. We are just expected to accept what's said and respond accordingly. God gave each of us the intellect to think things through. Let's use it to think through those stories in His Word.

PRAYER *Lord, today I thank You that You have given me an intellect, help me to use it to learn more about You.*

22 JUL

'He [Jesus] replied, "If you have faith as small as a mustard seed, you can say to this mulberry tree, 'Be uprooted and planted in the sea,' and it will obey you." ' Luke 17:6

KEY WORDS 'little faith'

PHYSICAL HEALING FORMED a large part of Jesus' ministry while He was walking around on the earth. I believe that it's important to teach children how to pray for one another and to ask God for the impossible. One time when we had hundreds of children in our programme, they were eagerly listening to me telling them a story about healing. I felt that I should give them the chance to pray for anyone who needed prayer and then we could see some of the power of God. Two little girls got together and one explained that she had verrucas on her foot so the first thing she did was to take off her sock and shoe so that she could watch Jesus heal them. Then followed a bit of an argument as the other little girl who was going to pray refused to close her eyes to pray as she wanted to see the verrucas go as well. Eventually she did pray with her eyes open and both girls saw the verrucas disappear immediately. The little girl then put her sock and shoe back on, said 'Thank You, Jesus', and just carried on playing, believing that Jesus always did healing like this.

Take a look at a little mustard seed. You will need to be careful because it is so small you could easily drop it and never find it again. I am sure that every one of us who believes has that amount of faith. I believe we need that amount to become followers of Jesus in the first place! The problem is, we are often scared to put our faith into action like the little girls did. There are times that we need to see impossible things happen, because this will give glory to Jesus, but we are frightened to pray for others in case things don't work out.

THE POINT **We are told by Jesus to live a life of faith, and we must learn to step out and use that faith when Jesus tells us to.**

PRAYER *Lord, today I realise that I do have that little faith needed to step out and ask You to do the impossible.*

23 JUL *'But avoid foolish controversies and genealogies and arguments and quarrels …' Titus 3:9*

 # 'foolish controversies'

I WAS INVITED to lead a weekend of seminars by a church in Scandinavia. I was intrigued to hear what the Christians had to say about living in a country where there was no censorship. A great guy who spoke English well met me at the airport. I was under the impression that, because this country promoted 'total freedom', no subject I approached could cause offence or prove controversial. How wrong I was. I happened to mention alcohol in one of my seminars and immediately everyone seemed to react strongly at the very thought of a Christian touching 'the devil's brew'. This became the big debate of the weekend. Sadly, instead of just acknowledging differing opinions I, too, fought my corner and a friendly but pointless debate followed on the rights and wrongs of Christians, alcohol and abstinence. I foolishly allowed myself to be caught up in a controversy which detracted my listeners from the important teaching that I had been invited to speak on. As my friend drove me back to the airport he smiled and remarked that it was just as well I didn't bring up the subject of Christians and sex before marriage. When I asked him why, he informed me that many of those I had been arguing with believed in a 'trial marriage'. Their argument being it helped a couple discover whether they were sexually compatible before they took the marriage vows. If only he had told me that when I arrived, that really would have been something worth debating from a biblical perspective!

Genealogy simply means someone's family tree or ancestors. Here Paul is writing to his friend Titus, encouraging him to try and stop the people from this church on the island of Crete arguing about unimportant issues, past and present. Don't forget, talking and debating is not wrong, it's a way of learning, and I believe that we would learn more if we had less monologue and more dialogue in our church meetings today.

 THE POINT **When we discuss different issues, let's make sure that they are relevant and we are not just wasting time. Oh yes, and let's always keep a loving attitude towards those who think differently from us.**

 PRAYER *Lord, please help me today not to get involved in any foolish arguments.*

24 JUL

'[Timothy,] Stop drinking only water, and use a little wine because of your stomach and your frequent illnesses.' 1 Timothy 5:23

 KEY WORD 'wine'

IN THE 1980s the 'home brew kit' was a popular DIY hobby. So I thought it would be fun to have a shot at producing my own beer. I bought all the necessary equipment and when I say 'all the equipment', I didn't realise there would be so much involved. It felt like I had purchased an entire science lab! As I unpacked the kit in our kitchen I discovered I had invested in one large bucket, one glass jar, a thermometer and hydrometer, long clear pipes, a giant-size plastic spoon, rubber stoppers, corks, cleaning solutions, and lots of empty glass bottles. My first effort proved disastrous. One night I left it fermenting away nicely, the following morning, for some unknown reason, it had 'exploded' and the foul-smelling liquid had permeated and ruined our floor. So, I thought I'd forget beer making; it was far too complicated. I then thought I'd try my hand at wine making. Watch out, Cliff Richard! Easy – no sooner said than bottled. But being a beer connoisseur, rather than a wine buff, I wasn't sure if it tasted how it was supposed to taste. Soon afterwards a theologian called Roger Forster came to speak at the church Bible study. His eyes lit up when I invited him back to our home for a glass of wine, until he tasted it! As he drank it his face sort of contorted a bit as he coughed and spluttered. When I offered him a refill he politely asked if I had anything else in the house to drink! The wine-making kit was disposed of and it was back to Oddbins to refill our wine rack.

Timothy was quite young, but he may not have been particularly healthy. Suggesting alcohol for his stomach complaint seemed a little unusual advice from Paul. My expectation would be to read that Paul prayed for him, and that Timothy's stomach complaint would have been wonderfully and supernaturally healed.

THE POINT **Paul often asked God to work a supernatural miracle and at other times used his common sense. Our example above suggests he used natural healing remedies. There seems to be a place for both.**

 PRAYER *Lord, today I thank You that You use both the natural and the supernatural.*

25 JUL *'Josiah was eight years old when he became king …' 2 Chronicles 34:1*

 KEY WORD 'preparing'

AS A YOUNG boy I always loved the sound of rhythmic music. When I lived in Bristol, some Sunday mornings after Sunday school, an army band would march past our church building. The large band marched in the middle of the main road and all the cars would have to stop to let them through. I would run out and march alongside them, always getting as close as I could to the man banging the big bass drum. He was great and did all sorts of clever moves with the drumsticks when he wasn't banging his big drum. I thought it was far more exciting than church music. It's strange but at eight years old, a bit like Josiah, things happened to me that would dictate the rest of my life. No, I didn't become a king, but I was taking my first steps towards becoming a 'saint' with a small 's'! It was when I was eight and had moved down to the Christian community in Sussex that I first experienced happy Christian music played on other instruments than just the piano or organ. We had an old man visit our community and he used to play old hymns on his 'modern' squeezebox. This was fun. This happy sounding instrument brought the old songs to life for me, but it was only God who knew at that time what the future held for this eight-year-old. It was only God who knew that He was preparing this young boy for a ministry that would eventually involve him writing and playing lively Christian music.

After a line of really bad kings, along came a good one who tried to bring his kingdom back to worshipping God. Eight years old, yet already chosen for a major task in history, but we must not forget that there must have been older people around him who were giving him godly advice.

 THE POINT **Our children today are also being greatly used by God, even at eight years and younger, but they still need advice from godly older people around them. God is preparing them for their future right now.**

 PRAYER *Lord, today help me to see the spiritual potential in the young ones around me.*

26 JUL *'... he poured water into a basin and began to wash his disciples' feet ...' John 13:5*

 KEY WORD 'feet'

WHEN IRENE AND I minister together in leading all-age services, I play the music and preach and leave the creativity to her. Not only is she great at teaching creatively through visual aids, but she is also very good at making me one of her visual aids! I remember in one meeting she brought along a large tray filled with clay. As usual I had no idea what she was going to do with it. I then heard her call my name so I dutifully walked to the front to join her. Then she made a strange request, she invited me to take off my sock and shoe. It did sound a bit odd but of course I humbly obeyed. But then her next request was even more strange; she asked me to press my bare foot into the damp clay. Again, it was slightly embarrassing because I have such big feet. I did as she requested and made a huge footprint in the clay. I was also hoping that she had some water and a towel handy because my foot was going to feel horrible and I had a lot more songs to sing afterwards. As I removed my foot from the clay she called a child out. She invited the child to place their tiny footprint in the clay inside mine. When the clay set it looked amazing. It was a pictorial reminder that little ones will follow in our footsteps and do even greater things for God than we do.

Where Jesus lived the roads were dusty and people wore sandals without socks. This of course meant that feet would get very dirty. Our verse reveals the servanthood of Jesus. Like a servant He washed His friends' feet. It's interesting to note that none of the disciples had volunteered to undertake this task – perhaps they felt it was below them to get involved with such a menial act of love.

 THE POINT **Jesus is the Son of God who loves to serve others. If He serves by washing His friends' feet, how much more should we humble ourselves and serve each other.**

PRAYER *Lord, today help me never to be proud and always willing to humble myself and be willing to serve those around me.*

'Do not rebuke an older man harshly, but exhort him as if he were your father.' 1 Timothy 5:1

KEY WORD 'correction'

DURING A FAMILY service I wanted to use interactive fun with the different generations that were present. I invited two young people, two middle-aged people, and two older people to join me on the stage. First I asked them, if they could phone anyone in the Bible to have a one-to-one chat with, excluding Jesus, whom would they call? This was very illuminating. I expected Peter or Paul but was slightly surprised when a younger one said Jonah because they would like to ask him what the inside of a whale looked like! I then asked them to read me a favourite Bible verse, one that was special to them, and asked why they had chosen that specific verse. Five out of the six took this really seriously and gave wonderful little testimonies as to why they had chosen that specific scripture, but one of the older gentleman read out a most obscure Old Testament verse that really didn't fit with anything. When I asked him why he chose it, he simply told me in a very condescending tone that the whole of the Bible was special to him so he just flipped it open to a random verse. I must admit my initial reaction was a desire to flip him. He knew what I meant and was just trying to be clever. However, you will be pleased to hear that I didn't react. I knew he was an older gentleman whom I should respect so I just simply said 'Thank you, sir, how right you are.'

THE POINT **Respecting our elders is biblical, but we do need to realise that even older men do and say wrong things and need to be challenged on these things. Paul advises that correction is brought gently, but it still must be brought; everyone, whatever their age, needs to be accountable and teachable. Today the same thing must happen. Younger leaders must not be scared to challenge senior people who may have been believers for many years longer than themselves, and senior leaders must never be too proud to receive discipline from those younger than themselves.**

PRAYER *Lord, today I pray that I am always willing to receive godly correction from both young and old.*

'Israel'

IN SOME CHURCHES I visit, the leaders encourage members of the congregation who think they have a 'word from the Lord' to come to the microphone and share it. Sometimes very powerful messages have been brought but other times unfortunate things are said that leave people confused and wishing that someone had prevented the bearer of the 'word' from getting to the microphone. I was sitting near the back of one meeting when a lady spoke into the microphone claiming she had prophetic word for me. To this day I still wonder why she didn't just walk up and give me this word personally rather than blasting it through a PA system so that hundreds of other people could hear it. Anyway, in front of everyone present, she announced that she believed that from then on I should be called Israel, not Ishmael. Now, don't get me wrong, I knew where she was coming from, and that she was trying to be encouraging. She had wrongly assumed that there was some link between me and Abraham's son, the father of the Arab nation. Why him? There are millions of other Ishmaels in the world, and there are even five more in the Bible! I think that she thought that my use of the name Ishmael, somehow meant that I was God's second best. To be honest I'd feel arrogant even calling myself God's second best when Paul refers to himself as the least of the apostles. Perhaps one day people will understand that the only reason I was nicknamed Ishmael was because it was simply a play on words from my full name, Ian Stuart Smale. Although it was a nickname given me in jest when I was nine, as it means 'God hears', I have been happy to stick with it ever since.

THE POINT Isaac's Israel has always been at war with Ishmael's Arabs. Today we know that while there are millions of Christian Arabs, there are only a few hundred thousand Christian Jews. Let's keep praying for peace in the Middle East and more importantly let's pray that more Jews and Arabs find the peace that only Jesus can give to those who believe in Him.

 PRAYER *Lord, today I pray for the Jew and Arab nations, I pray for peace in their land and for peace in their hearts.*

29 JUL

'They fell down on their faces before the throne and worshipped God ...' Revelation 7:11

'prostrate'

MANY CONSIDER THE success of a church by the numbers that attend a Sunday meeting. Personally, I think that God is not too interested in head counting. I think He is more interested in those Christians being sent out from our meetings to pass on the good news of Jesus to a damaged and lost world. For many years I was a member of a church that had grown in number very rapidly and was easily the largest church numerically in the area. On reflection, I think some of us, as we looked at our packed church hall, were feeling a bit smug and thought that we were doing really well. In fact, although no one would ever dare say it, we considered ourselves to be the best and most lively church in the area. Phil Wall, who was then with the Salvation Army, was invited to come and speak to us. Phil was very brave. In his talk he warned us about our arrogance and pride. He went on to say although our numbers had grown the church itself had gone backwards. It was not what it once was. We all knew that this was God speaking and nearly everyone, including the leaders, dropped to their knees and confessed their arrogance before God. What followed was the most amazing time. The church stayed for ages just lying prostrate on the floor quietly confessing and worshipping God. In today's verse the angels standing around the throne fell down on their faces before the throne and worshipped. I wonder how much we really worship God, and I am not talking about just singing songs. If we are really in the presence of Jesus can we stay standing up, or seated on a chair?

THE POINT I somehow think that if we were really in God's presence, like the angels, we couldn't help but fall down on our faces before Him. In our meetings we know we are in the presence of our leaders, musicians and brothers and sisters, but how often do we genuinely experience the real presence of God?

PRAYER *Lord, today I realise that I will never know Your true presence if I am in any way arrogant. Please keep me humble.*

30 JUL

' "You will drink from the brook, and I have ordered the ravens to feed you there." ' 1 Kings 17:4

KEY WORD 'trust'

AS A YOUNG boy living in a Christian community, one of the most important things I learned was not to worry about the lack of money because if we walk close to God He will supply all our needs. Ishmael and Andy were ministering in Norwich and one evening our public address system died on us. Now this equipment was not a luxury, we really couldn't fulfil our ministry without it. As usual we had no money, but we decided to go down to the music shop and see what they had for sale. As we entered the doors Andy and I cast our eye on a second-hand system that we knew would be perfect for our needs. We both had a wonderful peace that God wanted us to have this equipment. A young guy owned the shop and we told him that we wanted to buy the PA system. We explained that at this present time we had no money but as we worked for God, we would be back the following day with the money to buy it. He thought we were rather odd, but agreed to hold it. We prayed and sure enough the next day someone gave us a gift of just the right amount. As we entered the shop the owner's face dropped as he explained that he had just sold it because he thought we didn't have the money. Then out of the blue he offered us a far more expensive system for the same price. We gladly accepted it and as we carried it out the door we kept on hearing him mumbling on about our celestial bank manager in the sky! Elijah had prophesied that there would be no rain for the next few years, which meant that the drought would make food scarce as well. I dare say that he may have been wondering how he was going to survive. He need not have worried. God had it all planned; ravens waited on him with food.

THE POINT Why do we spend so much time worrying about our needs? God has promised to supply them if we stay close to Him.

PRAYER *Lord, today I know that I can always trust You to supply my needs.*

'… Son, your sins are forgiven.' Mark 2:5

KEY WORDS '**saying sorry**'

SAYING SORRY DOES not always mean we are sorry. I sometimes say sorry to someone but I am not really apologising. Sometimes I am saying sorry because I am sorry that they are feeling the way they are about something. At other times I am saying sorry because I am sorry that they have found something out about me. There are even rare occasions when I say sorry just to shut them up! Many years ago my son Daniel, who was in his early teenage years and searching to find his own faith, offered to accompany me to a gig and play bass guitar for me. At this time he was not one of the most confident of people. It was raining hard when we arrived at the church building and in those days it was the trend for young people to wear baseball caps. My son was no exception. We both carried all the equipment from the car into the church in the pouring rain with the organisers just standing in the dry building watching us. As we entered the building one of the leaders approached Daniel and snarled at him to take his cap off in church! I didn't hear this but I know this is the sort of verbal assault that puts young people off ever entering a church building again. After the concert the leader again approached my son but this time to say sorry. He said he would never have said that to him if he had known that he was 'Ishmael's son'. Was he truly sorry, or would he say the same thing again to any young person who was not Ishmael's son?

THE POINT We are surrounded by some great people who share different faiths. But I personally think they miss out on the fact that Jesus, God's Son, has the authority to forgive sin. I try and live a good life, I try my best not to do, think or say things that are wrong, but I still do wrong things. It is good to know that I can go to Jesus and when I am truly sorry for what I have done, He not only forgives me, but He also allows me to start afresh.

PRAYER *Thank You, Lord, that today when I am really sorry, I know You forgive my sin.*

01 AUG

'The midwives, however, feared God and did not do what the king of Egypt had told them to do …' Exodus 1:17

 **KEY WORD** 'midwives'

WHEN IRENE WAS about to produce our firstborn we didn't own a car, only a moped. Irene felt contractions begin and so the midwife advised her to get to hospital quickly since the baby wasn't due for another three weeks. I managed to get her suitcase on to my moped and told her to walk slowly and I would meet her at the maternity hospital. Fortunately, it was only a 20-minute stroll from where we lived. The midwife looked a little shocked when I arrived with the suitcase and no pregnant wife! As Irene lay resting in the hospital a friend offered to give us a car. This was an answer to prayer but with one slight snag, he lived hundreds of miles away in Cornwall. I couldn't afford the train fare so I decided to hitchhike down, pick up the car, and be back in time for the birth. Although Irene agreed, I could see that she was a little anxious about me taking lifts from complete strangers and, more importantly, getting back in time. God really was with me because I miraculously managed to reach Cornwall in a day. Quickly and gratefully I collected the car and drove home. I arrived back at the maternity hospital just a short time before Irene started to give birth. Collecting the car was the easy bit. Now I had to stand holding Irene's hand while the midwives both delivered a baby and supported a fainting husband who was obviously very squeamish!

The evil king of Egypt commanded the midwives to destroy the infants at birth. The midwives disobeyed the king because they knew this was not what God wanted and it was morally and ethically wrong. In a similar way, attending a church, reading a Bible and believing in Jesus in certain countries is illegal but Christians continue to stand firm in their faith.

 THE POINT We must all live by the law set down by our government; in fact, that is what God wants us to do, but if the law is against the laws of God, we must be obedient to God, not to man.

 PRAYER *Lord, today I pray for those Christians in government. Please help them to stand firm and obey the teachings of Jesus.*

02 AUG *'If any one of you is without sin, let him be the first to throw a stone at her.' John 8:7*

'big sins/little sins'

WHILE LIVING IN our Christian community, I became friends with an older local boy from our village called David. As we were both in the choir, I would meet up with him on my way to the parish church on a Sunday morning and each week he would tell me about the naughty things he did. I would consider these to be big sins, as we wouldn't be allowed to commit them in our community. The more he told me about his adventures, the more exciting they seemed to me and, deep down, I would love to have joined in with him. He enjoyed smoking and as I watched him, I felt that I wanted to try smoking too. He would go on to tell me about the latest films he had seen and let me look at the glossy brochures he had picked up from the cinema. My mouth would drop open as he explained in graphic detail the things he had watched which, of course, compared with today's standards, would be very tame. And then he used bad language, but one Sunday this was his undoing. He didn't see his younger sister Susan walk up behind him. He let out an expletive and she vowed that she was going to tell their parents that he swore on a Sunday; that was a big sin! From then on David kept his profanities for weekdays only; obviously his family thought it was only a sin to swear on Sundays!

In today's verse we read about a lady caught in the act of adultery. The religious leaders clearly considered this such a big sin that she deserved the death penalty. Jesus wrote something on the ground. We don't know what He wrote, but the accusers read it and then Jesus challenged them with today's Scripture verse.

THE POINT **It's so easy to believe that there are big sins and little sins or even very wicked sinners as opposed to nice people who sometimes sin. Sin is sin and we should never judge others, because we ourselves also sin.**

 Lord, today help me to realise I should never judge or condemn others who sin, because I, too, am a sinner.

03 AUG ‘ *"Then neither do I condemn you," Jesus declared. "Go now and leave your life of sin." '* *John 8:11*

'leave that life of sin'

WHILE MINISTERING NEAR Liverpool I became friends with a church youth leader. The work he did was extremely demanding. He worked in one of the roughest housing estates I have ever experienced. Many houses had windows boarded up and we would often have stones thrown at our car as we drove through. Even the police and fire service were very reluctant to enter this estate. Then we heard some very sad news. This young Christian youth leader had been influenced by the very people he was trying to help. He, too, started to take drugs and in time became a heroin addict. On one of our trips to Liverpool we decided to help him by taking him back home with us to Sussex. We felt that the change of environment might help. A caring Christian couple took him in and looked after him. After much prayer and cold turkey he came off heroin completely. Having relocated to the south of England away from all the drug dealers in the north he started to return to normal but it didn't last. After a reasonably short period he found a local drug dealer and was soon back on heroin. He disappeared after stealing my guitar to help pay for his habit. He just couldn't leave this life of drugs, or maybe he just didn't want to. I would love to meet up with him again but it's rumoured that a few years ago he died, an addict.

Yesterday's scripture was about the lady who had sinned and when her accusers were challenged by Jesus they all went away realising that they, too, were sinners. Now Jesus faces the lady who has done wrong. He doesn't just tell her to be thankful and to go back and enjoy her life. He tells her to go and to stop doing the wrong things that she had been doing.

THE POINT **Jesus forgives us, but He is not pleased if once we have been forgiven we keep going back and doing the same old sins again and again.**

PRAYER *Lord, today I know I am a sinner but as I confess my sin please help me not to keep repeating the same old sin over and over again.*

04 AUG › *'The Lord watches over all who love him ...' Psalm 145:20*

'The Lord is watching over me'

I WAS INVITED to minister in Finland and this was my first visit. What an amazing country. It's mostly made up of water with lots and lots of islands. It was mid-summer but where was the dark of night? Even at midnight I reckoned it was light enough to play a round of golf! The organisers kindly put me up in a nice hotel. Everything was going well until one night I returned quite late to my room after a meeting. Outside the hotel was an open-air blues festival. The noise outside my bedroom window was very loud so I decided that going to bed would be a waste of time, and I might as well go and watch the festival. I personally find blues music depressing and this festival did nothing to change my opinion! Eventually it finished and I went up to bed and soon fell asleep. It was a little later that all hell broke loose in the bedroom next to mine. There was shouting, screaming, fighting, smashing of furniture, and an explosion as a television set hit the ground outside, having been thrown out of the window and off the balcony. This went on for most of the night. I have never felt so alone and surrounded by evil. I kept calling out to the Lord to watch over me with his protection. Still today, as I walk down some hotel corridors, I am reminded of that horrific night.

At times when I find I am alone and facing a difficult situation I need to remember today's reading. I may feel alone but I am not alone as the Lord is with me, and is watching over me. When stuck in that hotel room with what seemed like a taste of Hell I did remember that the Lord was watching over me, but only after I had allowed the horror of what was happening in the next room to affect me.

THE POINT Let's not allow fear to get at us. When no earthly friends are around, Jesus is always with us as our constant friend and companion. He really does watch over all who love Him.

PRAYER *Today I thank You, Lord, because I know that You are always watching over me.*

'… we have been released from the law …'
Romans 7:6

KEY WORD 'rules'

IT'S STRANGE, BUT even in the twenty-first century I still find churches with odd rules and regulations. Most would agree that a church building is no longer regarded as 'holy'. It is God's people who are holy. Yet still some treat their building as sacrosanct. Once in America I spoke to a group of children about being free in Jesus. But on the Sunday as I entered their brand-new 'sanctuary' to lead a service, I was told that the leaders had enforced two new rules. The first rule stated that the boys were not allowed to wear caps inside the building. The second was that neither men nor boys were allowed to wear short trousers, even though the temperature was 100 degrees outside. When I asked if the cap rule came from Paul's teaching in 1 Corinthians 11, they responded in the affirmative. I then asked if all the women had long hair? This was Paul's suggestion in the latter part of the same chapter, after all, and they replied, 'No.' It seems they didn't agree with that half of the chapter! Were they thinking that God could hear the prayers of a boy wearing a cap outside of the building but not inside? And with the shorts rule, King David would have been banned immediately. I refused to preach with such impractical rules that could possibly drive young people away from church, and even God. A compromise was made and we met in the old building where the new rules were not enforced. The men looked relaxed and happy arriving in their shorts and the boys with their caps on, which they politely took off every time we prayed anyway!

In the Old Testament the Law was vital to teach people about sin and instruct them about a holy God. Jesus came and taught that although we are bad we can now be made good, by believing in Him and living in obedience to Him.

THE POINT We are no longer prisoners to the Law or to sin; we do not live by written rules; we Christians are now in a love relationship with a Saviour. We must never forget that we may not be perfect yet, but Jesus still wants us to be holy.

PRAYER *Lord, today I thank You I live under New Testament grace not Old Testament law.*

'generous'

IT'S STRANGE, BUT Christmas and I have never seemed to mix well together. It's even worse nowadays with no excited small children in our family. However, the one bit I really do enjoy is giving presents. I enjoy this far more than receiving them as I really do have everything I need. I often find myself being a little unreal. Hopefully it's not a lie, when I politely say, 'Thank you, that's just what I wanted', when it's something I didn't really want at all. I used to love giving presents to our children when they were small. First there was the sack of small gifts that I delivered into their bedrooms at midnight. By five-past twelve they had all been opened. Then before breakfast I would hand round gifts from family and friends from under the tree, carefully making sure that each one received a present in sequence. When there were no presents left the children always knew there was still 'the big one' from us. That gift could not be hidden under the tree and was locked up in the garage or shed at the bottom of the garden. They'd see me leave the room and the excitement was near fever pitch! I would then return with a bicycle or large toy or game, which had been far too big to wrap up and was the gift they most desired. I know this is when they thought that Mum and Dad had been very generous. Even today, when my grown-up children call in on Christmas Day, they still ask for 'the big one' after all the presents have been opened. I'm afraid nowadays they don't get it!

The Lord is so generous, He just loves to give good things to those who love Him, serve Him and ask for things. Yes, asking is important. When children want something they do not wait until I guess what they would like, they always make their request known. Sometimes we may say they cannot have something for various reasons, but more often than not we say yes because we enjoy giving them what makes them happy.

THE POINT **Our heavenly Father loves to give His children good things and to bless them.**

PRAYER *Lord, You are so generous, please pour out Your blessings on me today.*

07 AUG *'Nobody should seek his own good, but the good of others.' 1 Corinthians 10:24*

 KEY WORD 'others'

WE WERE RUNNING a daily programme for about 300 ten- to twelve-year-olds at Kingdom Faith Bible week. We called it a New Rhythm For a New Generation and, as well as being a lot of fun, God was doing some amazing things there. As we relaxed and unwound after the evening programme the team decided to have a barbecue. Having bought all the food they discovered that one of the team claimed to be vegetarian. Of course this was no problem, many people opt to be vegetarian and have very valid reasons why they should abstain from meat. But on this occasion it did cause a slight team problem. We had a large, fairly hungry team but only a small barbecue. The vegetarian insisted that none of her food should be cooked on the grill anywhere near the sausages and burgers containing meat. This meant that she took up half the grill space. Twenty or more other team members were going to have to wait a very long time for their food to be cooked on the other half of the grill. The worst thing was, she was extremely dogmatic and got annoyed when some of the other team members tried to reason with her. I think that if I had been the lone strict vegetarian, I would have considered investing in a small disposable barbecue of my own for the good of my relationship with the other team members. What annoyed people most was that afterwards she told everyone she was only joking about wanting the meat kept separate from her food. For some strange reason none of the team laughed!

The Christian life is great. We can enjoy everything except those things that the Bible lays down as sin. Sin breaks our relationship with God. Now although we can do so many things, we do always have to be thoughtful of others.

 THE POINT **We are not living just to please ourselves, we are living to please God, and He always reminds us to think of those around and not just to think of ourselves. Sometimes this may mean us going without something we enjoy so that we can bless others.**

 PRAYER *Lord, today help me to put others before myself.*

08 AUG

'Get up and eat, for the journey is too much for you.' 1 Kings 19:7

KEY WORD 'diet'

WE LIVE IN a very image-conscious world. Until I was about 40 I never thought much about my weight or how I looked. Certainly compared with today's standards in health-conscious eating habits, I ate and drank far too much of all the wrong things. Around this time church also started to get very image-conscious. A preacher's hairstyle and hair colour became a talking point, as did the clothes and even the spectacles that he or she wore. Image became almost as important as what he or she had to say. Needless to say, for a time I, too, fell for this. I went on a strict diet – one, I hasten to add, not recommended by doctors. But people commented on how great and healthy I looked. This is one of the most dangerous compliments that people could have paid me because from then on I was under pressure to keep up this image. I knew that this would involve spending almost as much time working out how to achieve this, as I would be spending with God. Also I may have looked healthy but I was exhausted and felt weak. I lost my energy and needed to sleep most afternoons, but people said I looked good! Today I am too old to worry about how I look, it takes me all my time and energy to try and stay close to God. Yes, I do think carefully about what I eat and drink. I'm resigned to the fact that I will never be slim, but hopefully a happy and healthy 'chubby' whom God will keep using for His glory!

Elijah was hungry and tired and there was no food around, so God sent His angels to feed him. The diet God put him on was bread and water and I think Elijah was far too godly to worry about his shape or image!

THE POINT Let's not worry too much about what we eat and drink and let's worry even less about our image. It's not what we look like that's important, it's how close we are to God.

PRAYER *Lord, please help me to understand today that it's not how I look that's important to You, it's who I am.*

09 AUG *'On the first day of the week we came together to break bread.' Acts 20:7*

KEY WORD 'Sunday'

UNTIL RECENTLY I had never been a great fan of the day Sunday, probably due to my upbringing. In the Christian community it was a day of restrictive rules and regulations. While my 'normal' friends were having fun, I was told that real fun was observing God's day and keeping it holy. Each Sunday I would usually attend three church services although, in all honesty, I usually enjoyed those. But I did not enjoy the 'thou shalt nots'. Thou shalt not watch any television programmes on Sunday. A day of rest for televisions. Thou shalt not buy ice cream or a newspaper on Sunday. Encouraging shopkeepers to work is wrong. Thou shalt not go and watch a football match on Sunday. I could kick a ball but not watch a proper match. Amateur sport was fine, but professional sport where money was changing hands was sin. And last, but by no means least, thou shalt not attend church services on a Sunday wearing clothes that are comfortable. Thou shalt dress up for God and look smart, which for me meant wearing a dreadful suit that itched. I think in those days, considering the legalistic way we treated Sunday, the Pharisees would have been proud of us. It will always be a bit of a mystery to me why some Christians treat Sunday as a holy day. We read that up until Acts, the Jews had always considered the last day in the week (the Sabbath) to be the holy day, but then we discover that some of the early Christians had changed the last day to the first day, the Saturday to the Sunday, mainly because it was 'resurrection day'. Sunday was a normal working day for the first three hundred years, so for the Early Church there was certainly nothing special about the day for them. What was special was not the day, it was the meeting together to break bread and worship Jesus.

THE POINT Nowadays, although it suits most Christians to meet together on a Sunday, I believe that the day in itself is not special. It's what we do on that day that can make it special.

 PRAYER *Lord, today I thank You for Sundays, and I also thank You for six other special days when I can worship You.*

'a time to be born …' Ecclesiastes 3:2

KEY WORD: 'birthday'

TODAY IS MY birthday. When I was young, I thought about the prospect of all the exciting years ahead of me. Now that I am old, on this day, I tend to think of all the exciting years now past! One birthday, however, stands out more than all the rest. For my 40th birthday Irene was determined to do something special for me. As I had also completed 20 years of ministry, she came up with the great idea of hosting a huge party in a hotel, and inviting not just our friends and family, but also lots of people who, over the years, have had an impact on my ministry. It would be a chance to say thank you and to honour them. It was going to be a grand 'suit' affair with a specially designed cake, and a live rock band playing cover tracks from the 1960s and 1970s, my favourite era of music. All was organised; then on the day before the party disaster struck. My father was doing some work on his garden shed roof and the ladder gave way and he fell head first on to the concrete below. We all rushed around and he was in a dreadful state, covered in blood. We wrapped him in a blanket and rushed him over to Accident and Emergency. I vividly remember he was praying in tongues the whole journey. The next day we held the party and it was wonderful to welcome family, friends and our special guests but I was so disappointed that my father was not going to be there. A little later in the evening the door opened and to everyone's surprise my mother arrived with my father. His face was very bruised and he was obviously tired and weak, but I knew that he would not want to miss my birthday for anything. It was the most wonderful party and I will never have a better one, but having my dad there was the icing on the birthday cake!

THE POINT Although I still tend to reminisce about birthdays, I also believe that I still have a future. Of course, my future birthdays will not cover as many years as the past!

PRAYER *Lord, today I want to thank You that not only was I born, but also I believe that I was born to live to serve You.*

11 AUG

'Discipline your son, and he will give you peace …' Proverbs 29:17

KEY WORDS 'manage and discipline'

IT WAS A long trip up to the north of England for a concert but I was quite excited about it. This was being hosted by a church that I had not visited before. I met the vicar at the church and noticed at once that he was a really nice gentleman. Just as I expected a good vicar to be. I then set up all the equipment ready for the event that evening. The vicar informed me that his wife had made some tea for me at the vicarage. I was really hungry after my long journey and was very appreciative until I entered the house. I walked through the door and his young son rushed up to welcome me. As he did so, he deliberately hit me in an embarrassing place! While I was hopping around in agony this wonderful little chap continued to thump me continually with all his strength in every place he could possibly reach. I wholeheartedly agree with child protection, but is there such a thing as adult protection! The vicar just smiled nervously and explained that his little boy did enjoy a bit of fun and proceeded to ignore him. Eventually, much to my relief, he dragged him off me. This was the cue for him to give the same treatment to his father and then to his mother. I had never witnessed anything like it. The parents just smiled and let him carry on thumping whoever walked in the door. Neither one stopped him. Sadly, although they were a lovely couple, they had no idea how to manage their own child. Parents need to learn to discipline their children. It would make life so much easier both for teachers and Sunday school teachers if they did. We need to train up our children, while they are young, in the discipline and instruction of God.

THE POINT **All children will be rebellious at times, and if we really love them we must learn to manage and discipline them for their own good and for the good of those around them.**

PRAYER *Lord, today please help me to be able to lovingly discipline and take care of those around me.*

12 AUG *'... at just the right time, when we were still powerless, Christ died for the ungodly.'* Romans 5:6

KEY WORDS 'right time'

WE HAD A great children's leader in our Glorie Company team but he had one problem; he couldn't seem to get his timing right in the area of humour. For example, when I stood up in front of 1,000 children plus a team of 80 very excitable and energetic team leaders, I would always expect some fun and a bit of heckling. There were two especially, who are both now being greatly used as evangelists, who gave me the most grief. While I was leading something light-hearted from the stage these two would start. They were my champion hecklers and very sharp. I didn't have a clue as to what they were going to shout at me next but I would always be ready for anything! The other team members – and the children, of course – found them hilarious. They did, however, always observe my golden rule. If I was saying anything serious, especially about Jesus, I didn't want any heckling to distract the children. Well, my team member with the 'timing' problem could be hilarious also, but he usually shouted out his comments at the wrong time. Whenever he did, the rest of the team would shout out 'Timing!' – which, of course, distracted me, embarrassed him, and set all the children off laughing again.

Timing is important to me. If I am performing or speaking anywhere, much to Irene's annoyance I set off far too early, which means that we also arrive far too early and are sometimes sitting in the car for 30 minutes outside a locked venue waiting for the organiser to arrive. I feel that if I get somewhere early, this allows me time to set up, check out the sound system, have a cup of tea, and, most important of all, get to know the organisers and pray with them. God sent His Son Jesus to earth when the people in the world were very ungodly and totally powerless. God's timing was perfect!

THE POINT **God has a time for things to happen throughout each day in our lives, and His timing is perfect, but we also need to be in the right place at the right time.**

 PRAYER *I thank You today, Lord, that everything You do is perfectly timed.*

'Sing to the LORD a new song …' Psalm149:1

KEY WORDS 'new song'

I AM OFTEN asked how I go about writing a new song. Do I pray for inspiration or meditate on the Bible until God gives me the lyrics and tune? The truth is I never write a song unless I have to. It's usually for a new album and I can be involved in all sorts of other projects as I write. I have been asleep or on the golf course or walking on my way to the cathedral or even on holiday when I get the inspiration for a new song. I very rarely spend more than a few minutes writing it down because I feel that if it doesn't flow naturally then it may not be from God. One morning I was having a quick shower and some lyrics and a tune came into my head. So I quickly dried off, picked up my guitar, and recorded it. I quite liked the song but thought that it was nothing special. I decided I'd give it 'the people test', which meant singing it at a concert. If people liked it, I'd keep singing it, if they didn't, I'd drop it as I'd done with many other songs before. Before I had a chance to do this I met my friend Noel Richards and told him I'd written a new song and he said he'd like to hear it. I played it to him and he told me it was fantastic, to which I replied, 'Is it?' Not really believing that it was. That is how in 1984 the song 'Father God I Wonder' came into being! Nowadays, there are lots of new songs being produced but many just repeat the word 'Jesus' and say little else. Although I am the first to admit that I do not enjoy all ancient hymns, I do love examining the lyrical content. Sadly, many of our contemporary songs are poor in comparison to the theological substance in some ancient hymns. I agree, though, that many of our new songs do have far more catchy and popular tunes.

THE POINT There must always be times to sing a new song to the Lord, but it may also be good to balance this with some classic ancient hymns that have stood the test of time.

PRAYER *Lord, today I am going to sing to You both new and old songs!*

14 AUG *'If you are insulted because of the name of Christ, you are blessed ...' 1 Peter 4:14*

'insulted'

WE HAVE MADE several friends in our local pub and probably 99 per cent of them would never mock my faith. In fact, I'd go further than that, I would say that 99 per cent sincerely show an interest in what I do. Whenever I return from a concert, they genuinely ask how it went. My band and I performed in a nearby venue and the pub organised a minibus to drive the regulars to hear us. They said they really enjoyed it and the pub landlady, Pat, who is a close friend, even organised a reception for us all afterwards. A while later, Irene and I were amazed when Pat offered to put on a special joint birthday party for us. She provided a wonderful buffet all at her own expense. But there is one person, who is not a regular, and whom I see very occasionally. He rarely says anything complimentary to me, usually the opposite. Instead of greeting me with 'Hello', he approaches me with a cynical comment like, 'How many souls have you saved this week?' laughing as he says it. Although it gets tiresome I normally just laugh along and so far have resisted the temptation to respond with, 'Obviously not yours yet!' He's a good man and I'm sure he means nothing by it. Perhaps it's just his way of being friendly. I have a feeling that his reaction to me may indicate that he has had a bad religious experience sometime in the past.

We are often embarrassed or worried to tell our friends that we are Christians. The main reason for this is probably that we are anxious about the reaction we may encounter. Those we tell might insult us, or, worse still, gang up and mock us publicly. Our reading today tells us not to worry about what people think of us or say to us.

THE POINT If we speak about our faith when Jesus wants us to, we will be blessed by God. Those precious blessings far outweigh the impact of any hurtful words that may be said to us.

PRAYER *Lord, today I am not going to worry if people insult me because I claim to be a Christian.*

15 AUG *'Altogether, Methuselah lived 969 years, and then he died.' Genesis 5:27*

KEY WORDS 'old age'

MY GRANDFATHER WAS a remarkable man. He lived in Bristol for most of his life and from what I have gathered from my parents, he was 'a bit of a lad' in his time. He and my grandmother lived in a wonderful large house. Apart from them there was only one elderly couple that lived on the top floor. When my grandmother died my grandfather moved down to Sussex to live with my parents. He never claimed to be a religious man, so it was very brave of him at 87 years old to move into such a religious home. When I say he was not a religious man, I mean not regarding the Christian faith; he was very 'religious' when it came to certain domestic habits. He 'religiously' enjoyed his pinch of snuff, which disgusted my mother as it left brown stains on the front of all his clothing. He 'religiously' enjoyed his nightly pilgrimage to the local pub for a couple of pints. He also 'religiously' enjoyed taking valium, which began as a medication but ended up as an addiction. Amazingly, my grandfather turned to the Christian faith in his late 80s and at the age of 90 was baptised in a paddling pool in my parents' garden. Getting to know and love him made me realise that no one is ever too old to receive the love of Christ.

Now Methuselah really lived to an old age. When he was in his 500s, he would be regarded as middle-aged and he was still fathering children. He would have certainly witnessed huge changes throughout his lifetime. Today, reaching the age of 100 is a major landmark. Yet without a doubt anyone who is near that ripe old age today would have witnessed far more changes in society than Methuselah's 969 years. The sad truth is that although mankind has been extremely creative and inventive, humanity is still selfish, unforgiving, cruel and spiritually lost.

THE POINT Those around us, especially those nearing the end of their lives, desperately need to know the love of Jesus who can bring about the greatest change of all.

PRAYER *Lord, today I pray for older people I know. I realise that no one is ever too old to be born anew and to start a brand-new life.*

16 AUG

'But Moses said, "O Lord, please send someone else to do it." ' Exodus 4:13

KEY WORDS 'send someone else'

IT HAD BEEN 25 years since I had performed a live 'rock set' with a band. I had grown very comfortable playing Christian concerts for children and families. It was Dave, a young organiser, who contacted me and asked me to come and play at a music festival. He explained I would be performing to 700 young people between the ages of about 16 and 22. There would be another 30 or so young contemporary bands playing. At first I thought he was joking, but when he honoured me by saying that over the years I had been a great influence on today's contemporary Christian music, I felt I couldn't refuse. I put a band of good musicians together. We rehearsed a dozen songs which I considered were some of my most popular rock/punk songs from the past. The big day came. When we arrived at the venue we saw a large indoor stage equipped with a great PA and lighting rig. I watched brilliant young bands perform and I also saw hundreds of young people, and it terrified me! I was so nervous I felt like going home. I was thinking, 'Lord, send someone else to do it.' I was convinced that these young people didn't want to see an old man onstage playing ancient songs that were recorded before any of them were born. How wrong I was. It proved to be one of the most special and memorable gigs that I have done for years and even more amazingly, the majority of the youthful audience really seemed to enjoy it.

Some may view Moses as a bit of a coward. He had heard from God, God promised to be with him, and still he wanted to back away and for God to send someone else. As we read on we can see the mighty task ahead of him as he came face to face with Pharaoh and with the children of Israel.

THE POINT Before we condemn Moses, let's consider how we cope when God asks us to do something that is unfamiliar territory. Or when He tells us to go and witness to someone whom we don't know – or, harder still, to a relative. Have you ever thought, 'Lord, please send someone else to do it?'

PRAYER *Lord, today please don't send someone else, send me.*

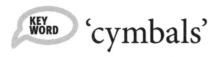

KEY WORD 'cymbals'

IN THE EARLY 1970s Ishmael and Andy often travelled and ministered with a young evangelist who had just left Bible college. This guy was a very close friend and also was an excellent preacher. I remember on one occasion we were working with him and another band in north London. The hall had a large stage with a curtain across the front, so the band set up their equipment behind the curtain ready to play later. One special talent that God gave to Andy and me was the ability to relax people, so often we would start the evening. When we had finished our set our friend the preacher appeared from behind the curtain and delivered a dynamic evangelistic sermon. The hall was full, and as our friend finished his talk he asked everyone to be quiet, to bow their heads reverently and pray a prayer of repentance. It was so quiet that you could have heard a pin drop. It was then that he turned and walked into what he thought was the opening in the curtain, only to discover that it wasn't. While the audience continued as instructed to sit silently with heads bowed in prayer, our preacher friend fell headlong into the drum kit. I guess some of those reverently praying must have almost suffered a heart attack with the noise of rolling drums and – literally – crashing cymbals. I'm sure it brought a smile to their faces when they looked up to discover our evangelist with his feet in the air lying in a heap in the middle of the drum kit.

More recently we were invited to lead a morning service in a church. While the band was setting up a lady approached my drummer to complain that it was a disgrace to bring drums and cymbals into God's house. Obviously the lady had not read Psalm 150 recently. God doesn't seem to mind drums and cymbals but I think He prefers them to be played rather than fallen over.

THE POINT **Loud percussion may not be our particular choice, but it's good to appreciate different styles of music and instruments, and not just our own preferential taste.**

PRAYER *Today I thank You, Lord, that You enjoy being praised by all kinds of musical instruments, including crashing cymbals.*

18 AUG › *'Jesus said to them, "Come and have breakfast." '*
John 21:12

'breakfast'

IN 1981 I was part of what proved to be a very controversial yet exciting tour called Let God Speak. The tour included various musicians along with two good friends – Graham Kendrick and David Pawson. Now David is without doubt a first-class Bible teacher, but he obviously was not used to the life of the itinerant musician. One morning we were all hungry and I spotted quite a scruffy transport cafe at the roadside. This was the sort of place where most of our entourage were used to eating. Everyone seemed think that it was as good a place as any for breakfast, so we parked in the large car park. As we entered the cafe it didn't occur to me that this might be an unusual stop off for a theologian like David; after all, he had proved on the tour that he was 'one of the boys'. I didn't even think twice about the fact that he would be the only one there dressed in a suit. Anyway, we queued at the counter and ordered our bacon, egg, sausage, beans and fried slice, then we each grabbed the customary mug of tea and two slices of thick buttered bread. I noticed David was missing. Then I spotted him sitting at a table. I went over and asked if he was all right, to which he replied that he was fine. He was just waiting for a waitress to come and serve him. I had to explain that in a transport cafe there was no waitress service! We have laughed about this many times since.

Jesus had risen again from the dead and was continuing to perform miracles. On this occasion He was teaching fishermen how to catch fish. Jesus had prepared the fire and told His disciples to bring some of the fish they had miraculously caught. He cooked them breakfast. Jesus was not just interested in preaching to people, He was interested in giving them what they needed, and He knew a good breakfast would cheer these men up.

Let's treat people as people. If they are hungry they may need bread on earth before they receive the bread from heaven.

Lord, today give me the chance to show practical love to somebody.

'But I call to God, and the LORD saves me.' Psalm 55:16

'call upon the Lord'

WE WERE LIVING in Lancashire and I'd had a very bad day. Everything had gone wrong and, it being a Wednesday, it was the night that I had to lead the church Bible study. I arrived at the church building and wished I could be anywhere but there, but I was the pastor so I had to be there! A small group of people turned up and I started playing the music. I deliberately played slow songs on my guitar as there was no way I felt like playing cheerful praise songs. I then suggested a time of 'open' prayer because I didn't even feel like praying. I heard some murmuring from people, along the lines of 'Pastor isn't his usual self tonight.' But it seemed that no one could get me out of this depression. It was then a young boy left his seat, and walked up and joined me in the pulpit. He then started to pray for me. Wow, someone cared! I soon apologised to the Lord, and in minutes was back to my old self, praising God in the pulpit. I heard one or two of the leaders ask whether or not it was biblical for a young boy to pray for the pastor. But I knew that God had told the boy to do this because I had failed to call upon the Lord. This was the first time that God revealed to me that He wanted to use young people. My life would never be the same again.

We all have days when nothing seems to go right and we find ourselves feeling very distressed. Certainly, David felt this way when he was writing this psalm. Let's learn from David and how he dealt with his depressing situation. He called to the Lord morning, noon and night and God heard and answered his prayer. I wonder if sometimes, after sending up just one prayer, we tend to give up praying. We then stupidly carry on living in misery, thinking that God is either too busy or not interested in our situation.

THE POINT Never give up praying. It is only God who can lift us out of our depressing day and put a smile back on our face.

PRAYER *Lord, today I will keep calling to You for help should I find myself in times of trouble.*

20 AUG

' "Who touched me?" Jesus asked.' Luke 8:45

KEY WORD 'touch'

IN THE 1990s the Holy Spirit seemed to be doing some very visual things in certain church groups. One source of this fresh outpouring of God came from a church in Toronto, Canada, and one of the manifestations of it was that when people received prayer many seemed to fall over under the power of God. As with any genuine move of the Holy Spirit there is always the counterfeit. I knew that some people who came to minister from overseas didn't just pray for people with a slight touch on the head. Some actually thought they were helping the Holy Spirit by giving the head a little push! We had one whom I suspected to be a 'pusher' coming to our church. I thought I would go and test how genuine he really was. He spoke well, then we were invited to stand in a line as he offered to pray for any who wanted to receive prayer. I stood in the front row and, sure enough, he was a pusher. Bodies were falling over all around me as he physically pushed on their head. As he approached me I braced myself; there was no way that I was going to be a pushover! He smiled as he saw me, but didn't touch me. He just blew gently into my face. I shot off the ground like a rocket and ended up in a heap on the floor. This guy was genuine, and as I lay on the floor for quite a while, I was very conscious of the presence and power of God upon me.

I can imagine why Peter thought this a strange thing for Jesus to ask, after all, they were surrounded by a crowd who would have been pushing and pressing against Him on all sides. Jesus knew someone was in need of His power and had touched Him to receive it. This act must have required great faith from the lady concerned who was ill and so it's not surprising she was healed.

THE POINT Today we cannot physically touch Jesus, but we can touch Him through our prayers and it's good to know that He still has the same power to heal and help those who believe.

PRAYER *Lord, today I need a special touch from You in many areas of my life.*

21 AUG *'Samuel said, "Speak [Lord], for your servant is listening." ' 1 Samuel 3:10*

'Speak, Lord'

NEAR WHERE WE live is a beautiful lake and I love to walk round it early in the morning when all is quiet and there's no one else around. I find this is a wonderful time and place to pray and to meditate upon the Lord. I spend the first part of my walk confessing my sin and praising God. Then when I reach halfway I start praying for my family and others and maybe throw in a few personal prayer requests. Just before I reach the halfway point, there is a very beautiful tree, and a few years ago I noticed that someone had carved my name into it. Now for some strange reason I am convinced that every time I walk past this tree an angel is waiting for me and watching over me. Please don't ask me how I know this, because I couldn't give you a rational answer; I just feel it every time I pass. I know it sounds silly, but sometimes I quickly look around, thinking that I will catch him out and get a glimpse of him, but as yet he has never appeared to me. I'd love to sit down and talk with an angel. We read in the Scriptures of people talking with angels. But then my angel probably knows that I would have so many questions, he would be listening to me for days! I often think what would be even better than that is if God regularly spoke to me in visions and dreams. I so rarely remember what I dream when I wake up. God speaks to me most often in that 'still small voice' in my mind, although sometimes I'm too busy thinking about other things to hear it.

THE POINT **I wonder how many times each day the Lord speaks to us but we ignore Him, thinking it's just our mind playing tricks. Let's not risk missing out. Even if we only think it could be God's voice, let's say, 'Speak, Lord, Your servant is listening' – we could be surprised with what follows!**

PRAYER *Lord, please speak to me today in any way You choose; Your servant is listening.*

22 AUG

'The LORD said to Moses, "Now the day of your death is near." ' Deuteronomy 31:14

KEY WORD 'death'

AS MY FATHER lay dying in a hospice bed, I felt that my prayers were not being answered. Certainly not in the way that I so wanted them to be. I was praying that he would fully recover, yet on each visit I could see he was getting worse. Then came one of the saddest moments in my life. The doctor called the close family into his office, closed the door, and said the words that none of us wanted to hear. He explained that my father was only going to live a short while longer, there was nothing else medically that could be done for him. I rarely get emotional, but this hit me like a sledgehammer. After we walked out of his office we went back and stood by my father's bed. Immediately he looked at me he knew something was wrong as I was far from my jovial self. I remember tears filling my eyes as I looked at Dad, and although we didn't explain to him all that the doctor had told us, I felt sure as he looked at me, that I gave the news away. It confirmed in his mind that his life on this earth was coming to an end. Losing a loved one is a strange thing, because even as I remember this occasion many years on, tears still fill my eyes.

Most reading this today, will have experienced the loss of a loved family member or close friend and know the sadness that this brings. God wants us to grieve and release that sadness. Even though that loved one can never be replaced and will always be missed, in time, sadness begins to be replaced by happy memories of the good times that we had with that person while they were alive. Moses' time and work on earth was completed; it was now time for him to go and be with God. Of course, it would be sad for his friends left on earth, but for Moses, he would be going home.

THE POINT For Christians, this world was never meant to be their home. Jesus is preparing an everlasting home in heaven for all those who love Him.

PRAYER *Lord, today I realise that as a Christian I have no need to fear death.*

23 AUG

'Moses threw it [his staff] on the ground and it became a snake, and he ran from it.' Exodus 4:3

 KEY WORDS 'power of God'

IN THE EARLY 1970s Ishmael and Andy were booked to play a concert in a very nice town in Surrey called Ashtead. The venue was a very nice parish church building and we were expecting some very nice well-behaved people from the area to come and enjoy our music. But a gang of skinheads arrived, and these were big skinheads, much bigger and much older than us. As they entered the church they picked up the kneelers, threw them at the stained-glass windows and caused havoc. After hiding behind a curtain for a while hoping they would go away, we realised that we would have to go onstage, and I must admit I was really afraid. We started into the first song. The audience was in darkness so we couldn't see a thing, but we could hear them shouting and then suddenly a coke tin smashed against my guitar. Obviously they had run out of kneelers! Suddenly I really felt the power of God come upon me. I stopped playing and started to preach the good news of Jesus in the direction where the noise was coming from. All went quiet. The message must be getting through, I thought. Actually, I was wrong. Unknown to me, at that very moment the police had arrived and thrown them out. That was the reason why all suddenly went quiet! Still, I had learned a valuable lesson, even in front of opposition, I had no fear once I knew the power of God was with me.

Moses at this time had a lot to learn about the power of God. Understandably he thought that if he stood in the presence of the king of Egypt he would fail. So God told him to throw his walking stick on the floor. Suddenly it was transformed into a live snake. Poor Moses, first he was afraid of Pharaoh, then he was afraid of his stick!

 THE POINT **God is all-powerful. When He asks us to do something He will enable us, by His power, to do it successfully.**

 PRAYER *Lord, I realise today that You will give me the power to do anything You ask of me.*

24 AUG

'The LORD said to him [Moses], "Reach out your hand and take it by the tail."' Exodus 4:4

KEY WORD 'snakes'

AT THE AGE of ten I was living near a large wood and most evenings I would set out on a lone adventure to explore. In today's society no parent would even consider allowing their child to do this. But things were different then. Many young lads would collect birds' eggs, although this of course is illegal nowadays and rightly so. I was never very good at collecting eggs and deep down I always felt that it was a cruel practice. I was more interested in exploring the wildlife in the woods, but the woods, especially when dusk fell, did frighten me. As I crept between the large trees that blocked out what little daylight was left, a pheasant would suddenly fly out of the bracken and make a terrible screeching noise which almost gave me a heart attack. Then I would follow the gamekeeper's tracks, and he, for some reason that I never did discover, would shoot vermin and hang the carcass up in a tree. Almost like a trophy for the rest of creation to view. But the creature that made me jump and frightened me the most was a snake, either when I spotted one slithering along the path in front of me or hanging dead from a tree having previously crossed the gamekeeper. I most certainly would not have liked to have had to face the one in the Garden of Eden!

Yesterday we realised that snakes were not Moses' favourite creatures either, in fact, he was clearly afraid of them. While his walking stick was slithering about in front of him, God told him to grab the tail. I think many of us may have found that extremely hard to do but when he did it, the snake changed back into a stiff wooden pole.

 THE POINT There are things that God may tell us to do that may look both stupid and dangerous, but if God says do something, He will also remove the danger from the situation and prove to us that He is Lord of absolutely everything, including snakes.

 PRAYER *Lord, today please take away any fear that I have of animals, but also help me to be sensible when approached by any potentially dangerous animals.*

'He calls his own sheep by name ...' John 10:3

 KEY WORDS 'individual names'

I USED TO love farming and if God had not called me to be an itinerant evangelist, I am sure that I would still be ploughing the fields and scattering! The first farm I worked on had a variety of animals, but the animals that I least liked working with were sheep. Each morning we would round the flock up into a pen so that we could check their health. We had no sheep dog so it was usually yours truly, being the newest and youngest member of the staff, who had the privilege of rounding them up. As we caught hold of them, their wool always seemed to be soaking wet from the dew, thus, in no time, our trousers were soaking wet as well. Then we had to examine them. Flies had the nasty little habit of laying eggs in the sheeps' backs so we now had the unpleasant task of removing the maggots embedded into the skin. The hoofs were usually rotten so we had to constantly clean and 'manicure' them. In fact, they had no idea how to take care of themselves. Sadly, I have found many a pregnant dead ewe which, having rolled on to her back during the night, was unable to get back on to her feet and died in that position. These sheep were not pets, they were being reared to slaughter, so none were given a name.

Jesus is the very best shepherd who has ever lived. We Christians are often alluded to as sheep. Just like the sheep mentioned above, we don't seem to have a clue as to how to look after ourselves. We seem to be constantly in need of the Good Shepherd's love and care. But there is a difference; Jesus has countless sheep but He knows our individual names. We are not just a flock or even just a church; we are individuals whom the Good Shepherd loves and personally cares for.

 THE POINT Isn't it great to know that even with such a countless number of sheep to care for, Jesus still knows us all individually by name and is our own personal friend.

 PRAYER *Today I thank You, Jesus, for being my shepherd. I am so pleased that You don't only care for us as Your flock, You care for me as an individual also.*

> *'Tobiah sent letters to intimidate me.'* Nehemiah 6:19

 KEY WORD 'intimidate'

WHEN I YOUNG I made friends with a boy about the same age as myself who was also the son of missionaries. He had spent many years alongside his parents as they shared the good news with African tribes who had never heard about Jesus. We had a lot in common as we both had devout Christian parents. We also both enjoyed hunting for fossils. A lot of time was spent fossil hunting on the beach, but one day we decided to explore the South Downs. As we were happily minding our own business, we were approached by two bullies. Neither of us knew them and they were a little older than us. For no reason they began to swear at us. Then when they saw no reaction from us they started to push us around. Of course in the middle of the countryside there was no one to come to our aid. They continued to intimidate us, demanding that we fight them. Now we had no desire to be involved in a fight. Yes, we were rather afraid of getting hurt, but we could also see no point in people beating each other. I tried to negotiate with them but they just responded with more threats. In the end I could see we had no choice. We just ran for it. Our attackers may have been good at fighting, but they were useless at the one-mile sprint! Some might say it was cowardly to run away, but I couldn't see that fighting would have achieved anything. I have never been able to bring myself to lash out and hit someone even when intimidated and provoked.

God told Nehemiah to rebuild the walls of Jerusalem. But Tobiah, who was a wealthy landowner, opposed him and took every opportunity to intimidate Nehemiah and the builders. But with all their bullying and mocking, the wall continued to be built.

 THE POINT Sadly bullying and intimidation still go on, even in church life, sometimes by leaders, other times by strong and influential people in the congregation. There is no place for this in God's family and we should do all we can to stamp this out.

 PRAYER *Lord, please help me never to intimidate or bully others, either physically or verbally.*

27 AUG > *'Keep on loving each other as brothers.' Hebrews 13:1*

 KEY WORDS > 'brothers and sisters'

AS WRITTEN ELSEWHERE in this book, I was 13 when my brother Tim was born and 15 when I moved away from home to work on a farm. This meant that I was not around for the majority of Tim's childhood years resulting in my little brother growing up a stranger to me. But thankfully that was not the end of the story. As Tim grew older he learned to play the bass guitar and for many years travelled with me as a musician and as a close friend, and that friendship is still close today. Yes, we have argued and have differing opinions, but our love has always stayed stronger than our disagreement, because we are brothers. Now Tim looks nothing like me and if you were to see us together you would never guess that we were brothers. Tim is tall and thin while I am short and – well, not so thin. While on tour we arrived to play at a concert at a YMCA in the north of England. As the venue didn't have a stage, the organiser had laid out some wooden stage blocks at the front for us to stand on so the audience could see us. Now Tim in normal life is a fairly quiet, dare I say it, even introverted character, but put a guitar in his hand and he really comes to life. I remember I was singing away at this concert and Tim was doing his usual stage antics behind me when suddenly I heard an enormous crack. I turned round to find tall, slim Tim had crashed straight through the stage block and was lying prostrate on the floor covered in bits of wood. Thankfully, only his pride was hurt, as everyone laughed. But I was also thankful that it hadn't been me jumping up and down, because with my weight I might have demolished not only the stage block but the floor as well!

 THE POINT > We are surrounded by Christian brothers and sisters and today's verse tells us that we should love all fellow believers as much as we love our closest relative.

PRAYER > *Lord, today I thank You for all my brothers and sisters. Please help me not to just say I love them, but also to show them I love them.*

28 AUG

'Do not forget to entertain strangers, for by so doing some people have entertained angels without knowing it.' Hebrews 13:2

KEY WORDS 'entertaining angels'

I WAS AN assistant pastor in Finsbury Park in central London. In those days this area was very rough. The poster outside our church declared that it was 'the friendly church with the warm welcome'. Ironically, the building was surrounded by a wall, and an eight-foot fence with barbed wire at the top of it. I think it would have also been defended with landmines had they been legal! Throughout our Sunday services a very mixed group of people would come and go. One Sunday the service was such hard work that I'd planned to just get on and preach my sermon and then get home to lunch as quickly as possible. As I stood up to launch into my sermon, a black lady walked into the church and walked straight up to the piano. I had no idea who she was and was about to say something when she started to play what I can only describe as the most heavenly music that I have ever heard. A hush came upon the congregation as she played and I could see that God was ministering to people in a very special way as they listened to the music. After a while she stood up, walked out, and I never saw her again. To this day I am convinced that an angel had walked into our meeting – and entertained us!

It's very easy to become people with a set routine. I had my service all planned, but had to be willing to change if God wanted to do something different.

We must always remain flexible, and although having a plan isn't wrong, we must always be willing to adapt if God wants us to. On a more personal note, maybe we have just planned to settle in for the evening with a nice takeaway meal and a film to watch, when the doorbell rings. We don't want to answer the door, we don't want any visitors but, who knows, it may just happen to be an angel paying us a visit.

THE POINT Let's be willing to look after and entertain strangers so that, should an angel choose to appear, they won't be sent away disappointed.

PRAYER *Lord, today help me to be a person who enjoys entertaining others as if they were angels.*

29 AUG *'In the beginning God created the heavens and the earth.' Genesis 1:1*

'God created'

MANY YEARS AFTER Ishmael and Andy had finished, Andy and I continued to be the best of friends and to stay in touch regularly. Sometimes Andy's family and our family holidayed together. We nicknamed ourselves the 'ratbags' on holiday because wherever we went we somehow managed to cause mayhem. One of our favourite holiday places is near Bridport, Dorset. If you ever drive along that hilly coastal road you can't miss the large hill with three or four trees on top. One holiday I suggested to Andy that we should climb that hill and pray together. We set off early and once over a fence the first challenge was to bypass a rather bad-tempered-looking bull who was casting a wary eye over us. Bull mission completed, we negotiated our way through countless stinging nettles, brambles and thistles, and I could see why no one else attempted the climb. Eventually, we reached the top and it was definitely worth all the effort. There was the blue sea in front of us and the rolling green hills surrounding us and, best of all, no people in sight. This is one of those times when you simply don't close your eyes to pray. Andy and I just stared in wonder at God's magnificent creation and gave thanks.

I was watching a television programme recently explaining how the world was created. With the clever application of brilliant computer-generated graphics it was fascinating to watch. It was a pity that the documentary was such absolute nonsense to listen to! Strange that today so many people invent the weirdest theories about how the universe began. Some suggest a great big bang, and amazingly it all fell into place. Great, but who caused the big bang? Others try to convince us that we all evolved from the tiniest life-form imaginable. Great, but who made the first tiniest life-form imaginable?

 THE POINT At the end of the day the Bible is the most sensible explanation. In the beginning God created. Great, but who made God? Nobody made God, that is why He is God. God always was and always will be. That is why we worship Him.

 PRAYER *Lord, today I want to thank You for being such a wonderful Creator.*

30 AUG *'So the soldiers took the money and did as they were instructed.' Matthew 28:15*

'resurrection'

MUSICAL GOSPEL OUTREACH were very influential in the 1970s. They produced a monthly magazine called *Buzz*, and they also released lots of Christian albums, in those days, of course, on vinyl! These were the years when there were lots of Christian heavy rock bands. MGO also put on an annual weekend where musicians could fellowship together and hear the latest bands. It was late on Saturday night on such a weekend and we all waited excitedly for a Scot called George Duffin to perform, since he was top of the bill. George was very dramatic and his music was extremely heavy. As the lights slowly came up all that could be seen onstage was the band playing loudly and a coffin standing upright. There was no sign of George. As the music peaked a singer was heard screaming out about the resurrection of Jesus. Suddenly the coffin opened and out came George. He ran straight to the front of the stage and leapt into the audience (I vaguely remember he was wearing some sort of grave clothes). He may have been attempting a dramatic portrayal of Christ's resurrection, but some of the audience nearly died! Some went into hysterics and others screamed or fainted. The concert ended immediately with a prolonged ministry time. While the praying over the distressed and tormented continued into the night, George just packed up his coffin, wondering what all the fuss was about. Yep, a memorable night!

The body of Jesus had disappeared from the tomb, the resurrection had taken place, Jesus had come back to life again. Of course this was last thing that the Jewish religious leaders wanted spread abroad. They bribed the soldiers on guard at the tomb. They were instructed to explain that as they dozed off, the disciples must have stolen the body of Jesus. What a crazy thing to say. How would they know who stole the body if they had dozed off?

THE POINT **Today it's still the same. People don't want to believe that Jesus is alive. Still, we know it's true, don't we? So let's make sure that the truth gets out!**

PRAYER *Jesus is alive today. Hallelujah!*

31 AUG

'He [David] won over the hearts of all the men of Judah …' 2 Samuel 19:14

KEY WORDS

'won over the hearts'

I SELECTED A team to join me one year, to work at a summer camp. I had deliberately chosen people who were young Christians and some who had never worked with me before. I felt it was a risk worth taking. As the week went on I didn't realise that one of the young men on the team was struggling with my leadership expertise. We had a team meeting and he challenged me in front of the rest of the team in a way that I had never been spoken to before. I didn't know what to say and I was shocked to the point of tears. I went back to my caravan without saying anything to him. The obvious thing a team leader would do in this situation would be to send him home. Doubts flooded my mind, maybe he was right, maybe I was a bad leader, and maybe all the team agreed with him. Soon afterwards some of my senior leaders reassured me and prayed for me. I decided not to send him home. Allowing a period of time for him to calm down and for me to get myself back together, I took him to one side and explained why I led the team like I did. I thanked him for his honesty and he allowed me to pray for him. I believe that I won him round and knew that God was changing him. Since that time we have become good friends.

King David by no means made all the right decisions all the time. But David's strength was the ability to draw people around him. Without manipulation or pressure he won over their hearts and got them on his side. Often in both home and church life decisions are made by parents and leaders, and both children and congregations are expected to agree with these without ever being won over.

THE POINT

We need to learn from David how to win the hearts of people and then we will find people agree with us because they choose to, not because they are forced to.

PRAYER

Lord, help me today to be able to win the hearts of people.

01 SEP

'When he was sound asleep, he fell to the ground from the third storey ...' Acts 20:9

'sound asleep'

I WAS ON a nationwide tour called The Banquet with friends Gerald Coates and Noel Richards. After each concert local Christians offered to accommodate us. It was a typical English winter, very cold, windy and raining. After one concert a couple told me that I was to be accommodated with them because their children loved my music. As I entered their large house I could see that the property either needed major renovation or demolition. It was very late so my hosts showed me to my bedroom, said goodnight, and went off to their room. As I entered the small bedroom my heart sank. I looked at the only window which was jammed open. It refused to close, and rolled-up newspapers lined the frame, to soak up the excess water. The wallpaper was so damp it was peeling. But, worst of all, I put my hand into the bed and all the blankets, sheets and pillows were wet with damp. I couldn't go and tell anyone, as I had no idea where they were sleeping. I certainly didn't want to risk waking up their children. I decided to keep all my clothes on and crawled underneath the top cover. In no time all my clothes were damp as well. Unlike the person in our verse, I didn't manage to get any 'sound asleep', I just lay shivering until the morning. The following day I left very early, shivering amidst coughs and sneezes before my hosts woke up. If I'd seen them, I would not have known what to say to them. The joys of touring!

A good night's sleep is important, but to fall asleep while Paul was preaching, was not to be recommended. As Paul was preaching, a young man called Eutychus, who was sitting on the window ledge, dozed off, fell out and died. When they went outside to check on him Paul threw his arms around him and to everyone's relief exclaimed that he was alive. People in those days were hungry to learn about God.

Let's try not to fall asleep during the sermon. Let's listen and learn from our Bible teachers and praise God for them.

Lord, today I thank You for those who teach me more of the truths from the Bible.

02 SEP

'And I saw a beast coming out of the sea.' Revelation 13:1

KEY WORDS 'coming out of the sea'

WE DECIDED TO go on holiday with some friends and their family to the Bay of Biscay in France. When we arrived it was beautifully sunny so we all made our way straight to the beach. My friend Rod, who is quite clever, informed us all to beware of the rip tide. We had no idea what he meant, but we assumed we would have to be careful while bathing. A couple of days later our families were happily amusing themselves on the beach. Rod and I decided to brave the sea. While I paddled about in the shallows, he swam out a short way. After a while I saw him wave at me and I politely waved back. But then I noticed he just kept on waving, and I guessed he must be in trouble. I then remembered about the rip tide he had pointed out to us earlier, which he must have forgotten about. Perhaps he wasn't so clever after all. Anyway, I waded out a short distance to try and help him and with a lot of effort he gradually got closer to the shore and to me. When he finally reached me, he was very weak and he flung his arms around me. Holding on I had to support him up the beach. I remember feeling rather embarrassed as a crowd was watching us. No doubt they wondered why two men were hugging each other in the shallow water.

I would hasten to add that Rod probably bore little resemblance to the beast emerging from the sea in our verse! Most would consider that John was referring to the Roman Empire as the beast. At this time the Caesars claimed to be gods and were demanding that the early Christians were to worship them on Caesar's day once a week. Of course this was one thing they could never do and many were martyred for standing up for their faith.

THE POINT I wonder how many of us would continue to be followers of Jesus if we were faced with persecution?

PRAYER *Today I want to thank You, Lord, for all those over the years who have been martyred because they chose to follow You. Please help me to always stand up for what I believe.*

03 SEP

'Timothy, my fellow-worker, sends his greetings to you ...' Romans 16:21

KEY WORD 'greetings'

NOWADAYS EMAILS HAVE taken the place of letters, and texting has replaced phone calls. I remember speaking at a children's leaders' conference and thinking that my seminar might be a little too controversial for some. I asked that if there was anyone who had problems with what I had said, to tell me afterwards, and then we could talk it through before I left. But no one approached me. On returning home I received what I considered to be a very unloving and critical email from one of the delegates. They demanded that I explain a few of the things that I had said. I was quite annoyed by this as there was no way I could communicate what I wanted to say cold by email. Why didn't he talk to me at the conference, we could easily have sorted things out? I sent back an equally curt email explaining this and never heard from him again. Months later I was clearing out the inbox on our computer and came across his email again. I felt that the Lord was telling me to send him greetings. I sent him another email saying that I had been thinking about him and wondered how he was getting on. In return I had a very warm reply and I felt that the relationship had been restored.

When replying to a letter or email it's good to pass on the love, best wishes or greetings of other family members or friends. As Paul concludes this letter to the Romans, he includes not only Timothy but other names to the list of those sending greetings of other family members or friends. I get many letters and emails and when replying I occasionally sign some from all the family. But sometimes my family never even read the communication I have sent because I have forgotten to show them.

THE POINT I think we must be honest in all that we say and do. I am sure most of the time our families would want us to pass on their greetings, but it's right that we ask them first and do not just make things up because they sound the polite thing to do.

PRAYER *Lord, today please help me to be honest, even in the little things like sending greetings.*

'Teach me what I cannot see …' Job 34:32

KEY WORDS 'teach me'

I ENJOY TALKING to people who have a sense of humour. I also enjoy having a sense of humour. The trouble comes when I use that sense of humour at a time when the person to whom I am talking is not in the mood to laugh. Let me explain. Many years ago I was presenting a chat show and I had the great privilege of interviewing the late Mary Whitehouse. Now when I say 'privilege' I do mean privilege; she was a remarkable campaigner who persevered against much opposition and abuse in her work to keep moral standards high. My interview was going well and the 1,500 people in the audience seemed to be really enjoying it. I then decided to bring a personal story into the conversation. I explained to Mary that I had joined a local video club but told her that I had recently resigned my membership because the last time I walked into the shop, they were previewing a blue movie. To lighten the atmosphere a bit I followed this with a little quip about how upset I had been about losing my five-pound membership fee in the deal! Poor Mary didn't understand my sense of humour. She spent the next five minutes giving me a public dressing-down on how ashamed she was that I should even consider the money involved! I still to this day cannot see what I said that was wrong. So, like our verse says, I still need people to teach me about things that I cannot see.

Today's verse continues, 'if I have done wrong, I will not do so again'. Most of the time we know when we have done wrong things because we feel guilty. Other times we can't see that we have done wrong and need friends to come and point out our wrongdoing to us, so that we can put things right.

THE POINT **If we have done something wrong and can't see it, we must be open for those whom we love and trust to come and tell us and not try to justify ourselves.**

PRAYER *Lord, today please help me to see the wrong things that I do but sometimes refuse to face up to.*

05 SEP ⟩ *'Do not give dogs what is sacred ...' Matthew 7:6*

KEY WORD ⟩ 'sacred'

WHILE I WAS a pastor in the north of England, our church held many different services during the week. One of these was given the title the Sisterhood. It sounded like some women's secret society! The meeting provided an opportunity for the senior ladies in the church to get together, share fellowship, hear from a female speaker, and have tea. In those days we were a bit uncomfortable about women preaching in the presence of men, although sometimes the ladies would invite us men to join them. I remember an Annual Sisterhood Service, where Irene was addressing the congregation. As she stood facing her attentive audience, a large rat appeared from the kitchen behind her. It was strange, because the large grey vermin seemed genuinely interested in what Irene was saying, so just sat still listening and looking towards the congregation. Fortunately, all the ladies had their eyes and concentration fixed on Irene and only a couple of us saw our uninvited whiskery intruder. If any of the older ladies had caught sight of it we could have had mass hysteria and a mass exodus to contend with. After a few minutes, it seemed to get bored with the talk and scuttled off back into the kitchen. Our verse talks about not giving to dogs what is sacred, but I don't think our rat deserved to join the Sisterhood and hear sacred things either.

Although the Gentiles were often referred to by strict Jews as dogs, the dogs in this instance may be a reference to those in opposition and outside of the Christian community. Some even think it could be a reference about not giving communion to the unbeliever. Whatever it means we must realise that what we believe about Jesus is sacred and holy. It should not be treated irreverently and should be passed on to others like passing on precious pearls. Some may act like dogs, pigs or even rats when we share this good news with them, but they will ultimately be answerable to God, not us.

THE POINT ⟩ **We must never be frivolous or flippant when talking about Jesus. His sacrifice was no laughing matter.**

PRAYER *Today, Lord, I pray for those who make fun of You and use Your name in an unholy way.*

06 SEP

'When they saw the courage of Peter and John and realised that they were unschooled, ordinary men, they were astonished …' Acts 4:13

KEY WORD 'ordinary'

I WAS ONE of the many speakers at a large conference in Florida. It was hot so while everyone else wore suits, I wore my shorts and my Blackburn Rovers football shirt to the evening meeting. A preacher called Benny Hinn was introduced. Now other speakers may have looked smart, but Benny looked immaculate. Later that evening, I was told that Mr Hinn would like to meet me in his suite. It seemed that he was soon to visit England and he had a few questions to ask me. Benny had yet to arrive and as his apartment was full of people I made my way to the food table, sat down, and started to nibble on some food. Nobody else joined me. Then the door opened and in walked Benny and his minder. Everyone stood to attention except yours truly who carried on munching. He then used the bathroom. Still no one moved. When he reappeared he walked over to the table and at last everyone else followed. He then sat down and again everyone else followed. He took some food, everyone else followed. While continuing to munch away, I said, 'Hello, Benny, nice to meet you.' You could almost hear the gasp from some around the room as I dared to call him by his Christian name. So there we sat, two opposites, best-dressed Benny and worst-dressed Ish in shorts and football shirt. Then we started talking and what fun we had. I really liked him and his wife. Outside of the big arena he was just a normal chap who liked a chat and a laugh like anyone else. He had been put on a pedestal because of his anointing but underneath that smart suit was a warm, friendly, normal guy.

THE POINT Over the past 2,000 years Peter and John have become saints, even mini deities to some. If they were on earth today, they would be put on an even higher pedestal than Benny, but would they want it? I think not. Peter and John would still want to be treated as ordinary chaps, two of the lads who'd been with Jesus.

PRAYER *Lord, today I realise that You are the only one who deserves to be put on a pedestal.*

07 SEP 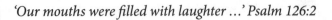 *'Our mouths were filled with laughter ...' Psalm 126:2*

KEY WORD 'laughter'

I WAS ABOUT to apply for a job which would involve selecting new songs by other writers, then recording and releasing them on CD. Irene checked that I looked smart, then off I drove to the interview. I was rather nervous because this is the only job interview that I can ever remember attending in all my life. Precisely on time, I walked into the office and shook hands with a smart lady called Sue, who happened to be the boss. I removed my coat and hung it on a hook on the door and sat down facing her. All went well. She was very friendly and we both felt that it was a job that I was capable of doing. The interview was a success and I felt Irene would have been proud of the way I had responded to all the questions without the addition of too many jokes as was my usual habit. I then got up to leave, shook hands, and confidently took hold of my coat from the back of the door. I struggled to put it on but it would not fit me. There was no way it could have shrunk in that short period of time. And then my potential new boss quietly asked me why I was attempting to put on her coat! How embarrassing that was! We both had the same colour coat and I was attempting to rip her coat apart, trying to get it to fit me! I still laugh out loud every time I think of that interview!

Good things had happened to the people of Israel and the psalmist tells us that this caused their mouths to be full of laughter. It's funny but I find that the same thing often happens to me. At the end of a praise party I am still so excited about the great time I have had that I cannot seem to stop myself laughing. It can even be a bit embarrassing sometimes! I do not need someone to tell a joke or to tickle me, I just find this comes as a natural expression of the way I am.

 THE POINT **Laughter is a wonderful, relaxing gift from God, and let us thank Him for it.**

 PRAYER *Lord, today I want to thank You for the gift of laughter.*

08 SEP *'… [Jesus] healed those who needed healing.' Luke 9:11*

KEY WORDS 'Jesus healed'

JESUS STILL HEALS people today. Yes, sometimes He uses doctors and medicines, but other times He chooses to heal supernaturally. I am also convinced that we should never make rash or false statements or exaggerate about healing, claiming someone has been healed when they haven't. I was once sharing the platform with a person who was renowned for his healing ministry. After quite a prolonged sermon he appealed for any who wanted prayer for healing to come forward. I noticed a tall gentleman respond and also a lady in a wheelchair behind him. As the tall man was being prayed for he started to sway as the Holy Spirit came upon him. Before anyone could do anything about it, he fell over backwards against the wheelchair and somehow managed to propel the poor lady up into the air and she ended up lying on top of him. Then things got worse for her. A couple of very keen members of the prayer team picked the poor lady up and, dragging her across the room, began shouting 'Look, she can walk!' It may have looked impressive from the back row but I could see that her feet were not even touching the ground! This sort of pantomime does not give glory to God. At another meeting a little girl came to the team to show us her appendix scar. She asked me to pray that God would remove the scar as she found it embarrassing when she went swimming. I did, but wasn't convinced. I felt it was just pride, she was hardly in pain. That night she approached us again and I thought oh no, she is going to want me to pray a second time. She didn't. She just pulled back her T-shirt to show us that the scar had completely disappeared. It was as if Jesus had rubbed it out with an eraser.

 THE POINT I have learned that Jesus loves healing people, even when they are not in any great pain and dying. We should never need to exaggerate the supernatural power of God. We pray, then leave Him to work the miracle so He gets all the praise.

PRAYER *Lord, today I will pray for people who need to be healed, but I will leave the healing to You.*

09 SEP

'For God so loved the world that he gave his one and only Son ...' John 3:16

KEY WORDS 'so loved'

WHEN I WAS ten years old, the Christian community where I lived took over a boarding school and my father became one of the directors. My parents decided that I should attend the school. So off I went with my father to a place that I had never been to before and to live with children whom I didn't know. We had always been a close family and I felt frightened by the prospect of being sent away. The first night I lay in a dormitory full of boys who were very wary of me. I was the odd one out because my father was the new director. Just then someone threw a stone through the window and a few of us got out of bed to see what was happening. A teacher appeared and was annoyed that we had been disobedient by getting out of bed, even if we were facing a broken window pane. He went to my father and asked permission to punish me. My father so loved me that he wanted to say no but he knew he would have to say yes as I could not be given preferential treatment over the other boys. One by one we went to the master's study and were beaten. I went back to the bedroom sobbing, not caring what the other boys thought, and found them sitting waiting for me on my bed. They were shocked that I had got punished on my first night. 'How many did you get?' they asked. 'Four,' I replied. Suddenly I became the hero as I had received more lashings of the cane than any of them. It took a painful experience to become accepted, but it was worth it, and I thanked my father afterwards.

Today's verse is the most famous verse in the Bible and, without doubt, one of the most beautiful.

THE POINT We cannot understand the pain that Father God must have felt. He knew that the only way that sinful people could be made right was if He sent His only Son, whom He loved so much, to earth and to allow Him to go through such agony. The love of Jesus is so wonderful, but remember, so is the love of Father God.

PRAYER *Lord, today I thank You that God is love.*

'... *whoever believes in him [Jesus] shall not perish but have eternal life.' John 3:16*

KEY WORD 'believe'

I HAVE NEVER enjoyed being enclosed in a building which is why I could never cope with a job in an office. I think that was one of the reasons that I did not enjoy school lessons. In class, I would always try and sit next to the window so I could spend the lesson gazing outside and wishing that I was out there. My ministry sometimes involves me in work with schools. Although I love taking assemblies in primary schools, I never really enjoyed senior school assemblies, because I recalled my own unhappy memories of senior school. However, I have had the privilege of travelling with some really good Christian schools workers and I enjoy watching them teach. Although health and safety would prevent this today, a little illustration one performed always remained in my memory bank. The object was to teach the class about belief and trust. A pupil was called to the front and asked if they trusted the schools worker and believed what he said. Most pupils would say yes. 'OK, let's prove it,' said the schools worker. He told the pupil to face away from him and to keep their feet together then, when told, to fall straight backwards and he would catch them. Did they believe that the schools worker would catch them? Then doubt was put into the pupil's mind by saying that if he did not catch them, they could break their back. 'Do you still trust me?' asked the schools worker. Some of the pupils did fall straight back and were caught, but many put a foot back just in case because they had doubts. Then the schools worker would talk about trusting in Jesus and believing in Him.

Here is the second half of the most famous verse in the Bible. To believe in Jesus means to believe that Jesus is God's Son who came to earth, who did no wrong, but ended up being crucified so that sinners could be made right with Father God. It also means believing that He rose again from the dead and is alive today.

THE POINT **If we truly believe this, Jesus promises that although our body may die, we will never perish, we will live for ever with Him.**

PRAYER *Lord, today I thank You that You promise that a true believer will live for ever.*

11 SEP *'The LORD said to Moses, "Why are you crying out to me?" ' Exodus 14:15*

'keep going'

NEARLY EVERY WEEK I get to visit a different church but I try not to get involved in the local politics. I arrived at one church at 8.30am one Saturday ready for a long 12-hour day of seminars and a concert. We received a very warm welcome from the administration team. One of the team discreetly informed me that the church was going through a very difficult time. With a full day ahead, right then was not the time for me to get involved in any of that. Throughout the day several of the children's leaders from the local church repeated the same thing to me and asked me to pray for them. I knew there was a time bomb waiting to explode somewhere. On the Sunday morning I arrived and I could really feel the tension. I could sense that harsh words had been exchanged so I got some of the leaders together and prayed for peace in the situation. If they had things to deal with they could do it later. I did not want anything to hinder what God wanted to do in that service. We had a great time with only a few walking out; that was no surprise, as I am used to that. After the meeting I prayed for the children's leaders and I could sense that some were ready to throw it all in. I advised them to keep going. They could not leave until God gave them permission. If they had been called to this work, then they must keep on doing it, despite opposition, until God said otherwise.

Moses' route out of Egypt was blocked by a vast sea. Moses told the people to stand still, while God told them to move on. So often when we face an insurmountable problem hindering our way forward, the tendency is to halt, just like Moses, to pray about it, and wait for God to remove the object. I believe that often God tells us to just keep walking and as we 'keep walking', He will remove the problem.

Don't let's stand around, but let's keep going and fulfil our calling because time is short.

Lord, today help me not to stand still when I should be moving on.

12 SEP *'A woman should learn in quietness and full submission.' 1 Timothy 2:11*

 KEY WORD 'woman'

I WAS AT a Christian Bible week overseeing 300 ten- to twelve-year-olds and supported by a good team of leaders. During one of the meetings I had been telling the young people that God had a plan for each of their lives and a ministry for them to fulfil. As the meeting continued a young girl approached me and said that she felt that God wanted her to be a preacher. As I looked at her, I was convinced that she was right. I stopped what was happening, and told everyone to sit down. I then handed the girl a microphone and said, 'OK, preach.' She looked a bit startled to begin with, but once she began speaking, everyone could hear and see that she really did have the gift of preaching. After about ten minutes she stopped and went to step down from the stage. I called her back and said her preaching required a response from her listeners and that she should make an appeal. Many children of her peer group responded. They walked to the front of the meeting where she prayed for each one in turn. A day or so later I told Colin Urquhart, who was leading the Bible week, about this and he called her into the main venue. He allowed her to preach for a short time to the few thousand adults assembled. Again, there was an amazing response as God used this young girl to communicate His message. Without getting involved in the gender 'what women should and should not be allowed to do' debate, I think, as Christians, we have to be very careful. We should never be guilty of teaching one thing to children when they are young, then changing it when they get older. For example, how many children's meetings teach that little girls should sit and learn in silence while the boys are encouraged to contribute? At all the meetings I am involved in, I encourage all the children to contribute regardless of gender.

 THE POINT **What we teach little girls in their childhood years should be consistent with what we allow women to do when they are older. We must not lead them into confusion.**

 PRAYER *Lord, please help me today not to confuse anyone with my interpretation of Scripture.*

13 SEP *'... [Elijah] bent down to the ground and put his face between his knees.' 1 Kings 18:42*

 KEY WORDS 'different positions'

I WAS INVITED to take a full band to a festival in Germany where a few thousand young people were meeting on a running track in an outdoor stadium. Several speakers and bands were included on the programme, which was presented from a very high stage. Then it was our turn. We played a few songs and everyone was really getting into the lively praise music when I felt the still small voice of God tell me to stop the music. It was as if He was saying He was bored with all the singing and He wanted us to stop playing, so that He could do something different. Much to the amazement of the organisers, and the band, I stopped playing and asked the band to come and stand with me at the front of the stage. This they obediently did. I then asked them to reach out their hands over the vast crowd. Everyone was looking bewildered, and I was praying like mad that I had got this right as we did look and feel rather silly. It was then a gentle wind started blowing from left to right and as we watched we saw the Holy Spirit touch all those below us. Some fell on their knees crying and repenting, others were leaping up and down praising, and some were lying prostrate on the grass, with their face to the ground. I have never experienced anything quite like that to this day.

Elijah had prophesied that there would be no rain for years. Then he told the king he could hear the sound of heavy rain. At this point he climbed up to the top of Mount Carmel to pray and we suddenly find him in this strange prayer position. Have you noticed how many different positions people take up when praying, some kneel, some sit or stand, some walk, some even like lying flat on the floor. At the German festival people were praying in literally every position imaginable as the Holy Spirit fell upon them.

 THE POINT The position we choose to pray in is not important, keeping our eyes fixed on Jesus is.

 PRAYER *Lord, help me to realise today that positions are not important, but the prayer is.*

14 SEP

'... the servant reported, "A cloud as small as a man's hand is rising from the sea."' 1 Kings 18:44

KEY WORDS 'waiting for God'

I WAS MINISTERING at the largest Pentecostal church in the UK at a time when I was just launching out in the gift of healing. We reached the point in the service when I said that I was going to pray for people. But first I was going to ask God, whom I should pray for. All went quiet, I waited for God to show me, but my mind was blank. As the congregation waited I felt I had to say something so I said, 'God wants to heal someone who has problems with their right foot.' No one responded. I thought by the law of averages there must be at least one person, but no. A lady said that she had something wrong with her left foot, did that count? I said no! My brother Tim who was with me whispered in my ear that he thought I'd got it wrong so, feeling very foolish, I told the lady with the left-foot problem to come forward. She explained that actually it was not her foot, it was her left ankle – I felt like crawling into a corner somewhere – and this had been broken three times and doctors had been unable to fix it. Oh yes, and she was not a Christian. I felt like going home immediately. To cut a long story short my faith had vanished but I prayed for the lady anyway and, to everyone's amazement, mostly mine, her ankle was miraculously healed and she even ran round the building to prove it! After all the mistakes I'd made than night, I was so glad I did not give up and go home, and so was the lady.

Elijah waited for God to answer His prayer. His servant looked for a physical sign. At first there was no sign of rain. Elijah told him to go back and to keep looking. It was going to take seven trips. After the seventh, he spotted the tiny cloud on the horizon emerge from the sea, God had answered Elijah's prayer and the rain came.

THE POINT Sometimes God answers our prayers straight away, sometimes we must wait, like Elijah; let's never give up praying.

PRAYER *Lord, please give me patience to pray until You give me an answer.*

‘ *"Sir," the invalid replied, "I have no one to help me …"* ’ *John 5:7*

KEY WORDS ‘help needed’

I GET SLIGHTLY annoyed when I am leading a musical event and parents don't watch their children because they are too busy enjoying themselves. It's hard enough for me to concentrate on the music and actions, let alone speak. I need help to ensure the safety of the children. Recently I was playing on a stage that had very steep, dangerous steps, and one small child kept climbing up the steps while the parent did nothing about it. In the end I was so convinced that the child would end up injured and in tears, that I stopped the concert and asked the parent to come and look after their child. On another occasion I was in a parish church building where all the adults and most of the children were joining in with the singing and dancing. But some parents had allowed their little tiny ones to wander off unsupervised to the side of the venue and to play with the kneelers. I was halfway through a song when I glanced over and saw a huge pile of kneelers tumble over on to a tiny child, completely smothering her. The other little ones then thought it was fun to start jumping on top of the fallen kneelers, suffocating the little child underneath.

Again I immediately stopped a song halfway through and told to people to get over there quick. Fortunately they arrived in the nick of time to find a traumatised, crying child. It could so easily have been a lot worse.

The poor man referred to in today's verse had been an invalid for 38 years. He was lying by the healing pool of Bethesda waiting for someone to help him get into the water when it stirred. But everyone was too busy looking after themselves to help this unfortunate person. Then Jesus appeared, making no mention of the water, and healed him on the spot. It's very easy for us to be selfish and to think only of ourselves and God and not care for those around us, be they adult or child.

THE POINT Let's keep looking around to see if there is someone who needs our help and care.

PRAYER *Lord, today I realise that it's not all about me, it's also about caring for those around me.*

'If God is for us, who can be against us?' Romans 8:31

KEY WORD 'loser'

THE DENOMINATION THAT I was first ordained into held an annual conference at a large holiday camp. They invited me to play at a concert for the youth at one of their late-night events. In those days I travelled with a guy who would do the lighting for me.

As the concert was specially targeted at the youth, I was deliberately going to make sure that it was fairly loud, and also make full use of the lighting and special effects. All was going well and the young people were really enjoying it. However, unknown to me, some of my fellow (but very traditional) pastors had crept in to watch. They were horrified by the loud noise and flashing lights. They even saw a young couple kiss and were convinced that this act of 'immorality and sin' must have been the direct result of the music and lights. To them it was Sodom and Gomorrah all over again! There was an awful uproar over the concert afterwards amongst the pastors. I sensed much opposition and aggression against me. I went back to my accommodation feeling a loser. I just wanted to hide. I didn't want to see any of these people ever again. The next day I rose very early, went to my car, and drove straight home. I felt I had done what God wanted me to do, but the aggressive pastors made me feel a loser. It took me several days of prayer and encouragement to spiritually recover from this one night.

It's so easy in this day and age to feel like an absolute loser. So often things don't seem to work out, and we feel hopeless and useless. We need to always keep in mind today's reading. The evil one always wants us to feel like a loser, to be depressed and miserable, but our reading tells us that God is for us, supporting us, encouraging us, and telling us that because of Jesus we are now winners and victorious.

 THE POINT If we are feeling a bit of a loser today, repeat this sentence a few times: Almighty God, who created the whole universe, is on our side; we are not losers.

 PRAYER *Today, Lord, I want to thank You that You are greatest encourager I could ever have.*

17 SEP 'The LORD answered, "Listen to them and give them a king." ' 1 Samuel 8:22

KEY WORD 'king'

I WAS INVITED to speak at a large church in central London and was shocked by what I found there. To start with, all the main leadership team were white, and nearly all the congregation were black. On arrival I was shown into a very nice lounge where white people sat down and black people served the food and drinks. After they had finished serving us, they all left and closed the door behind them. I felt very uneasy about this. It was then that the leading pastor explained how he ran the church. He was very much in control and because he believed that God had put him in this position, he really did believe that his congregation were put on earth to fulfil his dreams and vision. However, he even went further. He expected them to believe exactly what he believed and to like and dislike all the things that he liked and disliked. He was not open to debate, what he said was 'God's word'. I didn't like listening to this leader one little bit and was relieved when I completed what I came to do and walked out through the doors never to return. Afterwards I thought maybe I should have done more, but I was unsure what I could have done. The leader was happy playing 'king' to a large group of people and the congregation seemed happy to be his subjects and to bow down to his every whim.

God didn't want Israel to be like all the other nations. They didn't need an earthly king to rule them because He was there to lead and guide them. The people, however, kept on telling Samuel that they needed a king, and in the end God gave them one. God has given people the freedom to choose and He will never take that away from us. Often today I find many Christians who don't look to God to guide them, they rely upon the church leader or someone with an itinerant ministry who claims to be a prophet.

THE POINT **Although we respect and listen to our leaders, God is our King. He alone is the one whom we serve and who will guide us.**

PRAYER *Lord, today I realise that You are the only King whom I will worship.*

18 SEP *'John wore clothing made of camel's hair, with a leather belt around his waist ...' Mark 1:6*

 KEY WORD 'clothing'

IN THE EARLY 1970s, outrageous designer clothing was fashionable. High-heeled boots and brightly coloured garments were the order of the day. Ishmael and Andy had arrived to minister in Norwich and the pastor took one look at me dressed in my scruffy Levis and handed me some money, telling me to go out and buy a decent pair of trousers. He was obviously under the impression that the Lord had a greater love for those dressed 'smartly'. I had a feeling he expected me to invest in some smart old-fashioned cavalry twill trousers like the ones that he was modelling, but I arrived back with a pair of skin-tight cord flares with a bright red flowery design. I think the pastor now preferred me in scruffy Levis. OK, I know they sound dreadful today, but in those days you have got to believe me that they were fashionable and I was much thinner! All was going well with my new skin-tight trousers until I wore them to a ladies' coffee evening. As I bent down to pick up a coffee, the zip broke. It could not have happened at a worse meeting. I was surrounded by ladies! Fortunately, I think I just about got away with it. But I must have looked a bit odd since I spent the whole evening with my guitar strategically suspended from my neck to discreetly cover up the gaping chasm revealing my unfashionable underwear!

Keeping pace with the latest fashion and modelling trendy designer clothes never seemed like a biblical thing to pursue. In our verse, we probably have the least trendy, non-fashion victim in the Bible, John the Baptist. Even by standards in his era he was dressed rather strangely and very few people would have said, 'I want to dress like John.' John was a man who was close to God. Let's not be too fashion-conscious; the style of clothes we wear is not important, and we should never make a big deal about them.

 THE POINT **It's not what we wear on the outside of our body that's significant, it's what is happening on the inside of our lives that counts.**

 PRAYER *Lord, today please help me not to spend too much time thinking about the clothes I should wear.*

19 SEP

'The fathers have eaten sour grapes, and the children's teeth are set on edge.' Jeremiah 31:29

KEY WORDS 'taking responsibility'

MY FATHER DIED many years ago and although not perfect, I have always believed him to be a truly godly man who tried to bring up his often wayward son to walk close to Jesus. Both my father and I loved sea fishing. We would enjoy one another's company sitting on a beach or pier in all weather conditions, patiently waiting to catch a fish. Usually we just caught a tiny crab. At times, Dad was a very private man, probably because of some of the horrors he experienced as a tank commander in the Second World War. Although always humbly acknowledging his weaknesses in a general way, he would never be specific and leave himself vulnerable to his son. With my own children, I think I am the opposite. I think that they probably know me only too well. I have never tried to hide my weaknesses from them and they have all witnessed my many failings at first hand. I would never blame my father for any of my faults, and I hope that my children will never blame me for any of theirs.

Today's verse was a popular proverb of the day. This meant that a father's sin can affect his family. During Jeremiah's time, people felt that God was angry with them. Not because they had done anything wrong, but because they had inherited the sins of those who had gone before them. They were not blaming their fathers for their personal sin but were blaming their fathers for turning their backs on God. This had an effect on succeeding generations. We know that a parent's behaviour can affect their children, but we also know that God judges each person individually for the good and bad they have committed. Each adult son and daughter is answerable to God for the life they lead. No one should try to pass the blame onto others.

THE POINT A real challenge here for both young and old. Young ones cannot keep blaming their elders and older people must be very careful about what they do and say in front of their children. They must remember to set the example.

PRAYER *Lord, today help me to see that I am responsible for the things I do wrong and that I must not blame others.*

'... *Shout to God with cries of joy.*' Psalm 47:1

 KEY WORD 'shout'

ONE OF THE most important words to learn to shout if you are considering taking up golf is the word 'Fore!' Fore is another word for 'ahead' (think of a ship's fore and aft). It allows golfers a few vital seconds to be forewarned and to take cover as a wayward ball heads in their direction. But sometimes you don't get the chance to shout. I was having a round with my eldest son Joseph and his friend Dan when my ball decided to land in the middle of a clump of trees. As the boys watched the expert, I swung at the ball as hard as I could with my five iron as it was still a long way to the pin. I hit the ball well, but instead of heading towards the green, the ball hit the tree directly in front of me, then rebounded off and hit me right in the middle of the forehead. At this point in the distance I could hear uncontrollable giggles coming from my two young opponents and the giggles only stopped when they saw me fall to the ground. They came rushing over just as I was getting back on to my feet but the strange thing was, the only hurt I felt was embarrassment at hitting such a bad shot. It's just as well it hit the most solid part of my body or it might have hurt otherwise!

God gave me the voice of a shouter, and not just on the golf course. Most of you who have bought any of my albums will realise that God did not choose to bless me with an operatic or even a fine singing voice. He made me His shouter, so I guess that is why I relate so well with today's Bible verse. Maybe one or two of you are like me but consider the shouters are not quite as talented as the singers. The truth is, we may not sound as tuneful, but we are just as biblical.

THE POINT **We use our voice to shout encouragement to our favourite sports team or personality. It's even more important to use our voice to shout to the Lord because He is the only one really worth shouting about.**

 PRAYER *Lord, help me today to raise my voice to You in shouts of joy.*

21 SEP) *'Whoever loves money never has money enough ...' Ecclesiastes 5:10*

 'loving money'

THE FIRST THING that God taught me when I began my ministry was never to worry about money because He would provide. One of the first places I visited with a guitar slung over my shoulder was a town called Petworth where I had wasted most of my wild teenage years. My friend Paul and I drove into the town, not knowing any other Christians. We'd spend each day knocking on doors to try to introduce people to Jesus. Understandably we met with quite contrasting receptions. Well, would you welcome in two hippies who were standing on your doorstep preaching at you? In the evening we'd visit the local youth club with the aim of singing a few songs and sharing our faith. We had no money, no sponsors and, yes, no fuel for our vehicle. Paul had a beaten-up old Bedford Dormobile that had just managed to limp into the Petworth town car park before the last drop of fuel disappeared. It wasn't all bad news, though, because we didn't have any utility bills to pay. We were able to read the Bible with light from the car park streetlamp and we also had en-suite facilities, thanks to the twenty-four-hour public convenience located right next to our parked vehicle. It was cold in winter and sometimes we did get rather hungry. Those early years of hardship were tough, but invaluable. Hard times, good memories.

Very few people would admit to not liking money. The majority of us would like enough to live comfortably and to not have to worry about getting into debt.

But the truth still remains, the more money we have the more money we want, and this is the same for children, young people and adults. Every day we read in the media about multi-millionaires who can't possibly need any more money but they are desperately trying to earn more. I wonder why; if they live to be a thousand they could never spend it all.

 Having money is not wrong. Loving it and living for it is. Those people who live in this way will never be satisfied. So let's learn to be satisfied with what we have.

 Lord, today I thank You for money that You give to me. Help me to be satisfied with what I have.

22 SEP 'The LORD protects the simple-hearted ...' Psalm 116:6

 KEY WORDS 'simple-hearted'

JUST AS THE psalmist refers to himself as simple-hearted, I, too, would refer to myself in the same way. Whenever I write a book, preach a sermon, or compose a song, I always try and keep what I do simple so that as many people as possible benefit from my ministry. One evening at a conference in Finland I was with some young people. I agreed to sing a song for them and was amazed when a girl in her late teens requested a simple song that I had written especially for the under-fives. I could see she was serious, so I asked her why she liked that specific song. She replied that the last line said, 'Jesus made me special', and she said, with tears in her eyes, that she had never felt special. It was a sad moment and of course I sang the song. Afterwards we all prayed for her and it was wonderful to see her face light up as God answered her prayer. It amazes me how God uses such simple songs. I have mentioned elsewhere about how I wrote 'Father God, I Wonder' in the shower and yet I am again amazed how God has used such a simple song with twelve lines and six guitar chords. Numerous people of all ages have contacted me telling me what a blessing it has been to them. One young lady had been criminally and brutally raped and the words of that song really helped support her through a horrific period that many of us could not even imagine. A well-known intellectual author wrote that 'Father God' helped bring him into the Christian faith. I will never forget the time in a small jazz club in Soho where the late great Roy Castle was launching his new album which had 'Father God, I Wonder' on it. At this point Roy was suffering so badly from lung cancer that he could not even manage to play all the songs. I felt so honoured to see him blast out my simple song on the trumpet.

 THE POINT Everything doesn't need to be complex in order for the Lord to use it. God uses simple things from the simple-hearted as well.

 PRAYER *Today I thank You, Lord, that You use both the intellectual and the simple-hearted.*

23 SEP

'I will lie down and sleep in peace, for you alone, O Lord, make me dwell in safety.' Psalm 4:8

KEY WORDS 'sleep in safety'

WHEN I WAS a child living in a very secure Christian community I sometimes had very bad dreams. I could see no reason why I should keep experiencing these dreams because I was very happy and contented and surrounded by people who were very committed to Jesus. These dreams really did frighten me. They were not the usual nightmares about ghosts, monsters or nasty horrible things. I dreamed about flashing colours and lights and I always woke up shaking with fear. I had no idea what caused these dreams. I was restricted in what I was allowed to watch on the television, certainly no horror films, and the only books I read were the Bible and my junior school textbooks. I got into such a state of fear that I had to sleep with my bedroom door open. As this didn't help, I also had to sleep with my bedside light on. It got so bad that I dreaded going to bed and was scared to close my eyes. My parents became very concerned and continually prayed for me, and in time, I'm pleased to say, these nightmares left and I was able to put my head on the pillow and sleep in peace. One of my favourite songs that I have written is a song called 'What a Long Hard Day it's Been', otherwise known as 'Angels'. This song talks about God's heavenly army of angels protecting us not just when we are awake, but also while we sleep. I wrote the song in 1989 when my daughter Suzy was very young. She would join me onstage as I sang it. It was very powerful. I still hear testimonies today from those whom it has helped, and I also know that some parents still sing this song over their little children as they go to sleep as a sort of prayer lullaby.

THE POINT **I believe that at the end of each day when so much has happened during the course of 24 hours, it's a good habit to kneel down and pray before we get into bed.**

PRAYER *Lord, today I thank You for protecting me while I am asleep.*

24 SEP *'Whoever has my commands and obeys them, he is the one who loves me.' John 14:21*

 KEY WORD 'obedient'

MY FATHER LOVED practical jokes. He would often send me to the top of his garden to admire his vegetable patch only to turn on the water sprinkler and soak me. I fell for it every time. As I grew older I became wary of this old trickster and began to give him back a taste of his own medicine. Working on a farm, I was able to supply him with all sorts of bizarre Christmas presents. One year I presented him with a live cockerel which I had kindly rescued from execution. Living in a semi in the middle of a town, the cockerel got interesting reactions from our neighbours, especially when it crowed before the crack of dawn. After the cockerel, my father requested no more 'live' Christmas surprises please. But I disobeyed. Over the next few years I presented him with ducks, which turned his lawn into a mud bath and two enormous geese which attacked anyone who ventured through the back gate! Although he exclaimed 'Oh no' every Christmas when a new bird entered his life, deep down I believe he loved the excitement and actually grew attached to his fine-feathered friends.

Needless to say, I inherited my father's sense of humour and all my children have at one time or another experienced the 'water sprinkler' gag. But just like me, my children have been able to get their own back on their father. For my 50th birthday our eldest son surprised me when a farmer's trailer pulled up outside to offload a 'chicken starter kit' complete with three red hens, a coup and a bale of straw. On a more serious note, there have been times when, as a father, I have asked my children to help around the house and they have disobeyed. My children would always admit that they love me, but I would say that if they really loved me, they would show it by being obedient. Many people say that they love Jesus, but when He asks them to do something they often disobey.

 THE POINT **Jesus tells us that the only way to prove that we love Him is to do whatever He asks, without question.**

 PRAYER *Lord, today I will show You that I love You by being obedient to You.*

'The whole assembly bowed in worship, while the singers sang and the trumpeters played.' 2 Chronicles 29:28

KEY WORD ⟩ 'music'

NOWADAYS I THINK that we sometimes get confused in church meetings by what is a concert presentation and what is a praise time. A concert presentation is where Christians come to listen to and participate in music and song. After the meeting their main topic of conversation is about how good the music and musicians were. At an anointed praise time Christians make little reference to the musicians and music and prefer to talk about how powerful the presence of the power of God was. I remember attending one meeting where the large stage was literally filled with musicians playing all types of musical instruments, both ancient and modern. There were various types of flutes and whistles, Congo drums and percussion, a violin and mandolin, keyboards, drums, lead, rhythm and bass guitars, and even disco decks! For some of you this sounds like a recipe for just a noisy concert. The truth was, when all these instruments with their various sounds started playing old hymns like, 'Be Thou My Vision', the presence of God was so powerful, all we in the congregation could do was to bow down in worship to God.

King Hezekiah wanted to worship and give thanks to the Lord. He also wanted to praise God with music and singing. Out came the musicians with their cymbals, harps, lyres and trumpets. They were going to make a lot of noise as they praised. But it was not going to be a concert. As they sang, everyone bowed in the presence of God to worship Him. I finish where I began. During our services we sing a lot of great songs and hear wonderfully talented musicians, but do we really worship God?

THE POINT ⟩ **Although we praise God for talented musicians and would always want to encourage them, their job is to take our eyes off both them and their music and to encourage us just to concentrate fully on Jesus. We must never forget that the main reason that we gather together as Church is to worship God, not just to enjoy a concert, be that choral or rock.**

PRAYER *Lord, today when I am praising You, help me to think of You and not just the music that I am enjoying.*

26 SEP *'Now there was a man named Joseph, a member of the Council, a good and upright man …' Luke 23:50*

 KEY WORDS 'non-churched friends'

I MUST ADMIT, I do enjoy visiting our local pub, and not just for a pint! Let me explain. Unlike most people in a 'real' job, 99 per cent of my time is spent with church people. A few years ago I discovered that I hadn't any real 'non-churched' friends. A while back Irene and I started to visit our nearest pub regularly. A new landlady called Pat and her family had just taken over. We decided to make it our local and soon made a lot of good friends. Our new friends include an unlikely mix of people – a builder called Reg, an agnostic university lecturer called Rob, and, of course, Pat the landlady. Irene and I arranged to go on holiday to Paris with our three new friends and were a little apprehensive about how it would work out. Our friends were different from us in that none would claim to have the sort of Christian commitment that we had. So how did we get on together? Fantastically! As a group of friends with very different characters and beliefs we had a great time. Did we discuss Christian things? Of course we did. Real friends can talk about any subject, even if they don't all agree with each other.

Joseph of Arimathea was a member of the Jewish Sanhedrin, which was the top religious governing body in the country and which would later be involved in the crucifixion of Jesus. Scribes and Pharisees, many of whom hated Jesus, were the ones he worked alongside, some of whom would have been his close friends.

THE POINT **Nowadays, our advice to Joseph would be to not make friends with such people; we would advise him to mix with friends who believe what he believes. But Jesus wanted people like Joseph to stay in the Sanhedrin. He wanted His followers to befriend all of society and the best way to share the love of Jesus with people is to show people that love and friendship and not just talk about it.**

 PRAYER *Lord, please help me today to make real friends with people who may not belong to a church or believe what I believe.*

27 SEP ❭ *'Why, O Lord, do you stand far off?' Psalm 10:1*

**KEY WORDS** ❭ 'far off'

AFTER MANY YEARS of being brought up in the Christian faith, I rebelled against all I had been taught. I have never been half-hearted about anything and there was no way that I was going to be half-hearted about my rebellion. My friends who were not followers of Jesus seemed controlled and restrained by conscience. I didn't appear to have a conscience. I sinned to the extreme and rarely felt bad about it. The strange thing was that through all this rebellion, if anyone had asked me if I was a Christian, I would have responded with an emphatic yes! Another weird thing was that although my language was colourful to say the least, the one thing that I could never do was blaspheme. God was a long way off from me, but I would never dare misuse His name. My vocabulary consisted of nasty evil words, but if I ever heard someone take the name of the Lord in vain, I would cringe and reprimand them for saying such a thing.

God actually used a non-believer to bring this prodigal to his senses. One of my friends challenged me outright. In front of others he asked me how I could call myself a Christian when I was living a life that was worse than everyone else around who claimed to be pagans! I now recognise that was God giving me a wake-up call. It was at that point that I started looking for the Lord and discovered He was not far off, just a prayer away.

The psalmist believed that when things went wrong, God was far away and that was the reason why He didn't rush to help him. The great news for you and me is that since the day of Pentecost we know that God will never be far away from the Christian, because when we give our life to Jesus, God the Holy Spirit comes and lives within us. God can't ever be any closer to us than that!

THE POINT ❭ Sadly, we can drift away from the Lord. We can choose to go our own way instead of His way, but He is only a confession prayer away.

PRAYER *Lord, today I thank You that You are not far off; no one could ever be closer to me than You.*

'So we make it our goal to please him …' 2 Corinthians 5:9

KEY WORD 'goal'

AS A BOY, although I was surrounded by very enthusiastic Christians, my goal in life was to be a professional footballer, not a preacher. After school I would visit a very large council estate where most of my friends lived. It was then off with our jumpers to form the goalposts, out with the football, and the game would begin. Later, when we moved to a quiet village, my enthusiasm remained the same. Each night I would be down by some farm buildings kicking a ball around. All the time I played I imagined that I was some famous footballer and when I did a good shot, I could almost hear the roar of the imaginary crowd.

My primary school had two teams. The first team wore a very smart purple and yellow strip while the second team wore rather plain red and white. I was always in the second team. Medals were awarded for exceptional play and although I never won a gold or silver medal, I did get a few bronze ones that I treasured dearly. Then came an occasion that was to end my football career. I was not a dirty player but I was rather good at sliding tackles and on one occasion I did a sliding tackle on the first team's star striker, which saw him go limping off the pitch. The games teacher shouted in front of everyone that I would never make a footballer. He promptly announced to everyone that I was rubbish. I was about 11 years old at the time and I remember as I left the pitch and headed back to the changing room I started to cry. My dream had been blown apart and I would never forget those words for the rest of my life. Of course my dream as a boy of being a professional footballer was not to be my goal in life, God had other plans for me, but we must be so careful what we say to people, we really can scar them for life.

THE POINT **Whatever our career maybe, the Christian's goal should always be to please God, but let's never rob people of their dream.**

PRAYER *Lord, I thank You for my dreams even though many of them may not have materialised.*

29 SEP *'Now Jericho was tightly shut up because of the Israelites.' Joshua 6:1*

'feeling safe'

TWO BAND MEMBERS joined me on one of my many ministry trips to Gibraltar. While there we had a free day so we decided to take the short trip across the straits and visit Morocco in North Africa. We were in for some surprises. To begin with, the flight was shaky to say the least. We were transported in a tiny little plane that resembled a flying bus. It hovered just above the sea and the pilot insisted on turning around to talk to us. When we arrived in Morocco we decided to break away from the guide and do some exploring off the beaten track. We discovered a butcher's shop with cows' heads hanging outside, children playing with live canaries tied to a piece of string, and a whole street of people shouting. It was not a very pleasant experience. I suppose being the only white people speaking English in this part of the city we must have stood out like three sore thumbs. Some youths approached us and tried to sell us some drugs. We politely refused but then they started to get aggressive. After a quick glance at each other we all knew it was time to make a quick exit, and run we did. They chased after us for a while but gave up as we returned to join our tourist party. We were pleased to rejoin our guide but we only felt safe when we arrived back in Gibraltar.

Jericho was a vast fortress. The newly-formed Israelite army had no hope of conquering it without the help of God. Jericho's gates were tightly shut, the people inside felt very safe. Sometimes we can sit secure inside our house with all the doors and windows locked, the burglar alarm on, and feel that no one can get at us.

THE POINT Safety does not come just by being protected by strong walls, guards and security alarms; we can find real safety in the most dangerous places when we do what Jesus wants us to do and stay obedient and close to Him.

PRAYER *Lord, today I realise that it is only when I am close to You that I am really safe.*

'I am not ashamed of the gospel ...' Romans 1:16

KEY WORD 'ashamed'

OVER THE YEARS my wife Irene has had to put up with a lot being married to me. In her seminars she explains that because of my itinerant ministry, she was often left alone to bring up our three children. She continues to confess that bringing up our three children has been a piece of cake; being married to me for over 35 years has been her biggest challenge. I know there must have been times when she has been embarrassed at my crazy behaviour. The frightening thing is that the older I get, the less chance there is of me ever being a sensible, mature, adult. One of the great things about our marriage is that Irene and I enjoy so many of the same things. We both like sitting on the beach in the sun reading books. We both like the same food and going out to enjoy a quiet drink. We even enjoy the same movies, except that Irene's not a great fan of Westerns. We even both enjoy our regular early evening food shop at our local supermarket. But we have rules. As we enter the supermarket we each take a separate trolley and then disappear until we meet up again at the checkout. On one trip I felt slightly mischievous and decided to have a bit of fun. As Irene disappeared up the aisle I went to the information desk and asked them to help me find Irene Smale. Of course they assumed that I had lost a little girl, so in no time a loud booming voice echoed all around the supermarket public address system, 'Could Irene Smale please come to the information desk.' It took a little while, but eventually poor Irene arrived red-faced and, of course, I was in hysterics. I guess you could say I was literally off my trolley! I did apologise afterwards as I knew it was a naughty thing to do and Irene had every right to be embarrassed and ashamed of me. I'm sure she's absolutely right when she says that living with me is not easy!

THE POINT **Jesus never did anything wrong; we should never be ashamed to tell anyone about the good news of Jesus.**

PRAYER *Lord, I am not ashamed of the gospel; please give me the opportunity to share Your good news with someone today.*

01
OCT

'Do not say, "Why were the old days better than these?" ' Ecclesiastes 7:10

'the old days'

I TRY TO visit my mother once a week and take her out to coffee. Our conversation always begins with her telling me in great detail what happened the previous Sunday at her church meeting. My mother is always brutally honest in her review, although she usually tries to be extremely positive about everything – sometimes, in my opinion, unrealistically so. She would never want to sound disloyal to her leader. However, although my mother appreciates that God is doing some great things today, nothing will ever match up to what she experienced God doing back in the old days, when my father was alive and our family lived in the Christian commune. After she has finished talking about Sunday, the conversation usually reverts to those good old days, sometimes in a sentimental way but more often than not in a way that shows she is longing to see what happened then happen again today. I know she often tells her friends about the things she experienced God doing all those many years ago, but most wouldn't have a clue what she was talking about. You really did have to be there to experience it.

Like my mother, I enjoy reminiscing about the 'good old days'. I often look back over the years, during most of which I have been involved in Christian ministry, and I praise God that my life is so full of happy memories. I have seen God do so many exciting things in the past. Why does the past always seem so rosy? I think most of the time our mind chooses only to remember the things we enjoyed, the exciting times, and the times when things were going well. If we thought about the past for a bit longer we might also recollect the sad times, the bad times, and the times when things were even worse than they are today.

THE POINT

As our verse reminds us, let's not be fooled. The old days were no better than today; today is far more exciting. Jesus is the same yesterday, today and forever; let's get on and live for today.

PRAYER

Lord, it's good to remember the past but help me to live for today.

02 OCT

'Give proper recognition to those widows who are really in need.' 1 Timothy 5:3

 **KEY WORD** 'widow'

THROUGHOUT THE WORLD there are millions of people in desperate need and on the point of starvation. Some of the most deprived places that we have ever visited were the shanty towns in San José, Costa Rica. Here most mothers live in tin huts, having been abandoned by their 'men' who have moved on and left them to fend for their children. The mothers have no idea when, or even if, they will ever see the fathers of their children again. Irene and I are patrons of a Christian charity called Education Plus. They not only provide the means for children's schooling, but they also give pastoral care to deserted 'widows'. We were privileged to visit many of the children there and they were some of the most lovely and appreciative children we have ever met. During our stay we took a group of them to a burger bar. This was a very special treat for them. We watched one 12-year-old boy eat only half of his beefburger and wrap the remains up in a napkin. We asked him what he was going to do with the other half and he told us that he was going to take it home as a treat for his mother. I wonder if any hungry child in the UK would ever think of doing that.

Paul was very concerned that the poor (in this case the widows) were looked after and didn't go without. Nowadays a lot of Christians, certainly in the UK, are fairly well off financially. We have a roof over our head, a car, nice clothes, and a bit of money in the bank. Most of us do believe that Jesus wants us to be generous to the genuinely needy, and to support missions and charities in the poorer parts of the world.

 THE POINT Of course it is very important that we carry on doing this but it may also be worth glancing around at your next church service because there may just be a 'widow' or genuinely needy Christian sitting just a few seats away from you. We must give worldwide, but we must never neglect our neighbour either.

 PRAYER *Lord, help me today to care for the needy, whether they be here at home or in some far-off part of the world.*

03 OCT

'Now if we are [God's] children, then we are [his] heirs.' Romans 8:17

KEY WORD 'heir'

DURING MY MINISTRY I have often wished that I had some very wealthy relative, who, when they died, would leave a vast inheritance for me to invest in the work of God. If ever there was a time when finance was desperately needed, it was in the Ishmael and Andy days. For quite a time we drove around in an old Ford Anglia van which was so rusty that water came through from underneath the floor and, if it was raining, we would arrive to do a concert with soaking wet feet. When our van finally died we took it to a scrap yard and we got the bus home holding the only thing that was worth salvaging, the steering wheel. Later that week we had a concert but no vehicle and little money. We were convinced that God would supply a vehicle by the Saturday but He didn't and no wealthy benefactor did either! So we travelled by train, with our guitars slung over our shoulders. On reaching our destination we had the shock of our lives. There were hundreds of people queuing to fill the venue and of course we had no PA system. There was no way that we could carry that on the train as well, and so we had left it at home. How did that booking go? Quietly!

Although I have never experienced what it's like to be so wealthy, the truth is I am rich because, as our verse reminds us, as a child of God I am also one of His heirs. He has more riches than we could ever imagine and at the right time He wants to pass these on to us. There is one snag; as heirs we will also share in His suffering in order that we might share in His glory. In other words we have a great future ahead but can expect some hard and difficult times while on earth.

THE POINT **It's worth hanging on in there, even though at times we may feel like giving up. As His children we must realise that our Father is there to help us every step of the way, especially in those difficult times.**

PRAYER *Lord, today I thank You for making me Your son/daughter and heir.*

04
OCT

'Then Peter stood up with the Eleven, raised his voice and addressed the crowd.' Acts 2:14

'preaching'

IN OTHER PARTS of this book I have explained how bad I was throughout my farming years. After I decided that I really did want to be a follower of Jesus, my life began to change. No, of course I didn't become an angel, but some parts of my life were very different. Not all parts, however. I stopped using expletives and telling foul jokes. But other memories from the past will continue to haunt me. As a very young Christian I felt that the first thing that I must do was to go back to my farming friends, who had known me at my worst, and to let them now see what a real Christian was like. My return was not a happy one as I did it all wrong. I remember preaching at them, waving my Bible with one hand and pointing my finger at them with the other. They needed to know that they were sinners and they needed to change their lives just like I had done. I showed them no love or compassion. I had turned into a hellfire preacher wanting to save their souls but not showing any interest in them as lost friends. Needless to say, in a very short time I had no unbelieving friends left. Many of them even said that they much preferred the old me to the new me, as I was a much nicer person and a real friend before I started following Jesus. Thankfully, since then I have learned from that experience.

Peter was on his feet preaching at the top of his voice. Have you ever thought how long it took him to prepare his talk? It was not so much a talk, more a diary of events with a bit of accusation thrown in. Now although the words he said were important, what really challenged his listeners was that this fisherman Peter was powerful; in fact, he was full of the Holy Spirit as he spoke.

When we have the chance to share the good news of Jesus with people today, let's pray that we are both full of the Holy Spirit and full of love for those we are talking to.

Lord, today let me speak out for You, in power and in love.

05
OCT

'When the people heard this, they ... said,
"What shall we do?"' Acts 2:37

 KEY WORDS 'what should we do?'

I HAVE MANY people who ask for advice, especially couples asking me the question 'What should we do?' and, sometimes, although I try and be prayerful in my answer, I often wish on reflection that I had given them a different one. Many years ago a young couple decided to follow Jesus. Of course there was great rejoicing in the whole church. They also had a little child. After a while they asked to become members and it was only at that point that we discovered they were not married. Now it's not a leader's job to tell two people to get married, even if they have a child. We had no idea how much they loved each other and so marriage could pose even more problems. On the other hand, we couldn't agree with an unmarried Christian couple sleeping together. They asked us, 'What should we do?' After much thought we advised that the man should live elsewhere until they married. Understandably, they felt they could not do this as they had been a family for years, and so they left the church. Soon after, they did marry and joined a more sympathetic church. I think they would always regret asking us what they should do, and I think that whatever answer we would have given would have been considered wrong.

Yesterday we read that Peter was full of the Holy Spirit and preached to a very large crowd; today we see how the crowd reacted. The Bible says that they were feeling very guilty and heartbroken that they had done wrong things and most of all that they had been involved in crucifying Jesus. 'What shall we do?' they asked, and Peter told them that they had to be sorry, to turn around, to start a new life following Jesus, and to be baptised. And 3,000 did just that.

 THE POINT Often today we ask people who are not yet Christians to respond if they want to know more about Jesus. I am looking forward to the day when, like Peter's listeners, people are so challenged by what they hear that they ask us 'What shall we do?' without any pressure or appeal.

 PRAYER *Lord, help me today to have the right answer*
if someone asks me 'What shall I do?'

06 OCT

'In the desert the whole community grumbled against Moses and Aaron.' Exodus 16:2

KEY WORD

'grumblers'

I TRIED TO be a good pastor but I knew that as a southerner living in a northern town it would always be a challenge to get some people to like me. Over time I felt I had managed to win the trust and friendship of the majority of the church, but there was one older couple that, from the word go, didn't like me at all. Because the church was paying me a very small wage, they felt that they were personally employing me. At one time they even threatened to stop putting their weekly £1 into the offering if I went against their wishes. After less than two years the congregation of less than 30 had grown to well over 100 and a lot of the new Christians were young people. 'You've turned our lovely church into a youth club,' they grumbled. I often visited their home to try and make peace but the obnoxious husband would just insult me with detrimental personal comments. The last straw came when, one Sunday morning, I moved the artificial flowers that his wife had donated many years earlier, to make way for a speaker cabinet. As she entered the church for the Sunday service, she stormed up the aisle, grabbed her plastic flowers, and then her husband on the way out, and grumbled in a loud voice, 'That's the last time we're coming here.' I don't think anyone except God heard the little hallelujah I muttered under my breath.

The children of Israel had been slaves in Egypt and had been treated very badly. After Moses led them to freedom they saw the power of the Lord against Pharaoh, then they saw the sea open up for them, then they saw bad water become pure, and now they grumbled. How could they do such a thing when they had seen God do so much for them? Sadly, quite easily, and they are not a lot different from us.

THE POINT

We have all seen God do wonderful things in our lives. He's changed us into brand-new people and given us a reason for living, yet still we often moan and groan about all sorts of things. Let's stop being grumblers and keep being a thankful and praising people.

PRAYER

Lord, please help me today not to grumble.

07 OCT

'But God demonstrates his own love for us in this: While we were still sinners, Christ died for us.' Romans 5:8

KEY WORDS

'God's love never changes'

PEOPLE THINK I never get depressed but that's not true. I do get depressed but am so grateful to God that so far my depression never lasts for long. It seems the closer I try and get to God, the more my sin and shortcomings are brought to mind. When this happens, I can easily feel down. I was about to lead a children's concert after a particularly depressing day. I felt like a lousy sinner who was once used by God but who was now just going through the motions. I had tried to reassure myself about grace and mercy but nothing was getting through. The concert went fine, I could have managed it blindfolded, but then at the end a parent came to talk to me. This person, whom I had never met before, seemed very excited. She told me how wonderfully anointed I was, how she felt the Holy Spirit's power in what I was doing and how she saw the love of Jesus in me as I ministered. I felt like saying are you sure? Then I realised that this was Jesus speaking to me through this lady. Jesus was saying, 'Cheer up, I love sinners just as much as I love saints!'

Although I have always loved my children and always will, when they have done something wrong and I am feeling disappointed with them, they may think otherwise. They may feel that I love naughty children less than I love good children. That is never the case. It is the same with God. His love for us never changes. The fact remains that even when we were at our worst and had no good in us, God showed us just how much He loved us by allowing His only Son Jesus to come down to earth and to die so that we could be made clean inside and made right with Him.

THE POINT

It's important that our love remains consistent to those around us. We do not love them less because they are not churchgoers or of the Christian faith.

PRAYER

Lord, help me to love people today, not for what they do, but for who they are. They are all loved by You, even if they don't realise it yet.

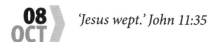

08 OCT *'Jesus wept.' John 11:35*

KEY WORD 'wept'

THERE HAVE BEEN many so-called biblically-based musicals and movies. I enjoyed *Jesus of Nazareth*, starring Robert Powell, but after laughing at his antics with Jasper Carrott in *The Detectives* I can no longer visualise Robert Powell's portrayal of Jesus in all seriousness. As a musician my criticism of *Godspell* and *Joseph and His Amazing Technicolor Dreamcoat* is that they were musically weak. However, I did enjoy the music in *Jesus Christ Superstar*, although it's the least biblically accurate of all those mentioned.

In the 1970s Irene and I were invited to visit some friends who lived in London. We had seen very few live stage shows so that evening they suggested that we go along and see the musical *Jesus Christ Superstar*. I was very impressed with the show – great performance and music – but I was even more impressed with the curry that our friends cooked for us when we returned to their home afterwards.

Very recently when I was driving up to Lincolnshire I found a copy of the *Jesus Christ Superstar* CD and decided to play it to help break up the long journey. As I listened, all these years on, I still loved the music and still winced at some of the lyrics, but then came the 39 lashes. As I sat listening to a secular recording, I began to feel very emotional and even had to stop the car. As I sat in the driving seat my eyes welled up as I imagined Jesus going through all that pain.

Jesus' friend Lazarus had died. His sister Mary told Jesus through her tears that if only He had been there earlier, Lazarus would not have died. Jesus looked at her and all her Jewish friends weeping and was deeply moved, He then began weeping Himself. I do not cry a lot, but I am sure there are times if I could see things as God sees them that I would be weeping a lot more.

THE POINT **Maybe we should weep more. As we see those around us rejecting Jesus or those who have 'given up' following Christ, perhaps tears should fill our eyes.**

PRAYER *Lord, today please help me to see some of what You see and help me not be afraid to weep just as You did.*

09 OCT

'So you too should be glad and rejoice with me.' Philippians 2:18

KEY WORDS 'be glad and rejoice'

IN ABOUT 1979, I formed a rock-punk band with a group of friends that we called Ishmael United. We were very loud, and often the music was enhanced by strobe and multicoloured lighting. I remember one concert when, just before we were due to appear onstage and face a large noisy audience, I suddenly felt a migraine attack coming on. I rarely suffered from nasty headaches and this was the very first one that I can remember having just before a concert. The organisers looked concerned and wondered, since my face had turned ashen grey, if they should cancel the event. I didn't agree to this, even if the audience was going to appear to me as one big blur. I was going out there to praise God and encourage them to join in with me. Once onstage a mixture of the noise of the band and the bright flashing lights instantly made my head start to pound. Then the blurred vision deteriorated so I couldn't see clearly at all. I was singing while trying to stop myself from being sick and all the time praying. I kept on believing that God had called me to be in this band to pass on His good news to others and so He would help me through it. The very last thing I felt like doing was praising God or rejoicing, but I felt that once I could put God right in the foreground, maybe the migraine would start disappearing into the background.

And I am so pleased to tell you that that is exactly what happened. Just a few songs into the lengthy set my eyes began to focus again, my head stopped throbbing, and the nauseous feeling disappeared. I was then able to continue praising God even more energetically!

Paul was saying some serious stuff to the Philippians but he also said that he felt glad and rejoiced with all of them and encouraged them to rejoice with him.

THE POINT However we feel, let's cheer up and be happy together. I must admit, rejoicing doesn't always mean that our suffering will instantly disappear, but it certainly will seem to go a lot more quickly than if we just sit around feeling sorry for ourselves.

PRAYER *Today I am going to be glad and rejoice, however bad I feel.*

'The Lord said [to Abraham], "I will surely return to you about this time next year, and Sarah your wife will have a son." ' Genesis 18:10

KEY
WORDS
‘conceiving a child’

WE KNEW A nice young couple who were experiencing difficulties having children. The wife invited one of the church leader's wives and myself to pray for her. Now let me explain. We were not going to pray that she could conceive, because at the end of the day that is in God's hands not ours. We were thrilled that she had asked for prayer and hopefully our prayers would be an encouragement to her. We spent quite a time praying and we felt that the Holy Spirit revealed to us a few things that we should pray specifically about, so this we did. Eventually we left the house and both she and we were feeling at peace that God had been doing some healing in her life. Some time later we heard that her husband was not at all happy about us being in his house praying for his wife and obviously was not happy with the prayers that we had prayed. We had turned up in all innocence at the wife's request, imagining that she had talked this through with her husband and that this was what they both wanted. Obviously it was not what he wanted.

From that time on we heard very little from them. The great news is that soon after our prayer together the wife conceived and now I believe there are quite a few tiny footsteps pattering around the house. Sadly, I doubt if the husband still thinks it was anything to do with answered prayer.

Abraham had a visit from three messengers from heaven. They told him that in one year's time, he and Sarah would have a baby boy. Abraham would have been surprised by their words as both he and Sarah were far too old to have children, but He knew that when God says something, even though it sounds impossible, He will do it.

THE POINT **God still speaks to us today, and sometimes through people and prayer. Always listen out for that word from Him and try not be too surprised if what He says sounds unlikely or even impossible.**

PRAYER *Lord, today when I speak to You, I believe that You also want to speak to me.*

11
OCT

'The LORD said to Abraham, "Why did Sarah laugh and say, 'Will I really have a child, now that I am old?' " ' Genesis 18:13

KEY WORDS 'you are joking'

ONE EVENING IRENE and I were enjoying our weekly supermarket shop. Realising I'd hardly eaten all day I was suddenly overcome with hunger. I decided to buy a carton of chicken nuggets to nibble on the way home. It was dark when we got back to the car and in no time I was happily munching away. They tasted brilliant and although I offered one to Irene she refused as she didn't like them. Once home I realised that I had eaten nearly all of the carton. Not wanting to appear greedy I offered to share the rest with my eldest son. He got one piece of chicken halfway into his mouth and then instantly spat it out. 'It's raw!' Sure enough, it was raw. The chicken was translucent inside. It was then that I read on the carton that it should be cooked in the oven for fifteen minutes. We all knew it was dangerous to eat raw chicken and suddenly I was thinking I should be feeling really ill. Strangely enough I went out that evening and felt fine. All those curries must have given me a cast iron gut. Later we were recounting the tale to friends and all they could say was, 'You are joking.' Realising that I wasn't they went into convulsions of laughter. I thought it was quite a funny story, but not that funny. I could easily have ended up in hospital with food poisoning!

Sarah heard the angels tell Abraham that she would give birth to a baby boy within a year. She also knew she was an old lady and so laughed, thinking they were joking. We can tell from our reading that the heavenly visitors had not come to tell jokes, but to bring the word of the Lord. They seemed disappointed that Sarah wasn't taking them seriously. The next verse says 'Is anything too hard for the LORD?'

THE POINT Let's think about that for a minute. Do we think when God says He's going to do the impossible, that He's having a laugh? I hope not or we are as guilty of scepticism as the unbelieving Sarah.

PRAYER *Lord, help me today to take the things You say seriously.*

12 OCT

' "Come, follow me," Jesus said, "and I will make you fishers of men." ' Matthew 4:19

 KEY WORD 'fisherman'

YOU WILL GATHER from elsewhere in this book that my father was a keen fisherman. I used to love going fishing with him but we always had to complete a set routine before we got anywhere near the sea. First, he would make up his sandwiches and coffee flask, always sneaking a couple of bars of chocolate into his bag. Then he would load all the tackle into the car along with a library of sea-fishing magazines to read in between catches. The last stop was the fishing tackle shop. Here he would stock up with hooks and weights, even though he already had enough of these to last a lifetime. Then while I was talking to the shopkeeper my father would appear at the counter with some special oil that proudly boasted on the side of the jar that this product was guaranteed to attract fish. Anything that claimed fish would find it irresistible, my father would also find irresistible. Once at the pier we would cast off, then he would open up his large fishing bag, and we would start on the coffee followed by the sandwiches. I have watched my father catch seaweed, seabirds, sea rubbish, trees – he even once hooked his own jacket that was behind him as he attempted to cast – but never fish! But he never seemed to mind. He was happy to let his line sit in the water while he sat on his bag and read his fishing magazines and chatted away merrily. As the day drew to a close with no fish to take home for supper, the chocolate proved adequate compensation for the well-equipped fisherman with no catch. It was a bit different with Peter and Andrew; they were real fishermen. If they didn't catch any fish, they would have no income. Fishing was their life, until Jesus came along. 'People are more important than fish,' said Jesus, 'so from now on put your nets down and follow Me', and they did.

 THE POINT
My dad didn't catch fish, but he was good at catching people. Through the testimony of his life, his words, his love and his faithfulness, he encouraged many to become followers of Jesus.

 PRAYER
Lord, today I want to be in the right place to 'catch' people for You.

13 OCT *'An honest answer is like a kiss on the lips.' Proverbs 24:26*

KEY WORD 'kiss'

I REMEMBER ONE of my very first kisses. I was nine years old and had recently moved to the Christian community. Miriam was a girl who also lived in the community and I thought she was really pretty. One night, while the adults were enjoying a prayer meeting, I was with my sister Heather, my cousin Lyn, and Miriam. I suggested we should play a game of dare. I then dictated the rules. We would switch the lights off and then everyone except me would hide in the room. My dare was, I would close my eyes while they hid, and the first hidden person whom I found I would have to kiss. All agreed, although it wasn't going to be much of a treat if I found my sister or cousin first. But with my cunning plan in mind there was no way that that was going to happen. I confess I didn't close my eyes tight as they all ran off. I saw Miriam disappear behind the curtains. When I had counted to 50 I shouted 'Coming!', made a beeline for the curtains and found her standing behind them. Mustering up all the bravery a very embarrassed nine-year-old boy could, I kissed her quickly on the lips and ran out of the room. I felt so proud of myself, what an achievement – although I never did discover how Miriam felt, as it never happened again.

A kiss on the lips with the person we love is a beautiful experience. But for children a kiss on the lips may seem quite revolting. If I give a brotherly kiss on the cheek to a Christian sister nowadays, I notice that they always react. Their reaction is not one of joy, it's pain, due to the short hairy spikes sticking out of my chin. Today's verse tells us that being honest is as pleasant as a kiss on the lips. The Bible doesn't seem to agree with telling half-truths or little white lies; it seems God wants us to give honest answers at all times and that is not always easy.

THE POINT Let's remember that when we give honest answers we must give them in loving and caring ways; we never want to deliberately hurt anyone.

PRAYER *Lord, today help me to give honest answers in a loving and gentle way.*

'This is good, and pleases God our Saviour, who wants all men to be saved …' 1 Timothy 2:3–4

'saving lives'

I BELIEVE THAT Christians who just meet together for church services really miss out on friendship. Having fun and socialising together is vital. It was a lovely sunny day so most of our church and their friends met up for a barbecue at the local beach. The beach was pebbly but surrounded by beautiful sand dunes. While some of us stayed on the beach talking and preparing the food a group went down to the sea to have fun. Our daughter Suzy, who was tiny at this time, tagged along with the sea group. As we continued talking we could hear all the shouting and laughter in the distance. They were all waist-deep in the water having fun messing about. But as we gazed down towards the swimmers we could not see Suzy. We kept looking, and suddenly I spotted her. I could see her falling over into the water head first. She was unable to swim and no one had noticed her. We could see that she was in serious trouble.

In panic, I ran as fast as I could, shouting towards the sea knowing that I would never make it to her in time. It was then that one of the older church members nearby turned around and saw Suzy struggling. He scooped her up out of the sea and rescued her. She was shaken, coughing and crying when he carried her to the shore, but she was alive. I was so grateful to this person for rescuing her from what could have been a tragic situation.

Although we might be able to rescue one other from human danger, the real life-saving is down to Jesus. He is the only one who can save us from being lost for ever. Although He is our best friend, he is also the King of kings who sits on a throne in heaven and also the perfect Lamb of God who died on a cross, the only perfect, holy Person qualified to save us.

THE POINT   **Let's never forget what today's verse says. God really does want all men to be saved, not just a select few.**

PRAYER   *Lord, today I want to thank You for saving me and I pray for others who need saving.*

 **'talking'**

I RARELY GO out to dinner parties any more because I have one big problem; I never know when to be quiet. The last one Irene and I went to was with four friends of ours who kindly invited us to join them for the evening. As we sat around a meal table and everyone was being polite and saying very little, I thought that that was my cue to start talking. Now all my friends will tell you I can talk and once I start, there is no stopping me. It's not down to nervousness. I just consider any silent gap needs to be filled and I am never short of stories to tell, as you may have discovered from reading this book! That evening I talked and talked and talked. In fact, I cannot remember Irene or our four friends saying a word. I was totally unaware that I had completely taken over the evening. As we drove back home in the car Irene gently reminded me that I hadn't stopped talking from the minute we went through the door until the minute we left. She even explained that I was sitting too far away from her for her to give me a gentle kick under the table to make me shut up. Did I learn my lesson? Of course I did. As I said earlier, I have given up going to dinner parties and now just meet friends in places where I can talk, and they can walk away!

God also loves talking and I believe that He never stops talking either. He always has so much to say to us His children. We must be a little careful though. Let's never be so busy talking and listening to other people that we ignore Him and do not hear what He has to say to us. As an ordained clergyman, I have been informed that I will be expected to go on prayer retreats where silence is kept. Now that will be a real challenge for me!

 THE POINT **I talk a lot, and sometimes what I say is a lot of rubbish. God also talks a lot, but everything He says needs to be listened to.**

 PRAYER *Lord, I can talk, please help me also to listen.*

16 OCT

'Who shall separate us from the love of Christ?' Romans 8:35

KEY WORD 'separation'

WHEN WE MOVED to Chichester we joined a very large church where God was really moving. Irene and I were so excited about joining and, for the first time for over 20 years, I was not part of a leadership team. This left me free to develop my itinerant ministry. Although this church had one core leadership team, it was divided into three congregations, each one planted in a different town. Meeting as three separate congregations was good, but I loved it when over 600 of us would have the monthly get-together in a large hall for a united church meeting. Of course friendships crossed all three congregations, so when we got together not only did we have wonderful times of worship but also great fellowship with those from the other congregations whom we rarely saw. Sadly, as time went on, the leaders discovered that they were not of one heart and mind. Although friendships had been rooted for years, the disagreements were becoming stronger than the friendships. Leadership meetings and people were called together but by then it became clear that there would be no reconciliation. Division really had set in and separation was inevitable.

The three congregations split, each going their own way and, as usually happens in these situations, many individuals wandered off disillusioned. Personally, I felt it was very sad, but I still hold on to the wonderful memories of when the three congregations were united. I have seldom enjoyed church business meetings at any church where I have been in membership. I cannot remember one where everyone has been in agreement. There always seems to be a group or a person who wants to separate themselves from the rest. Why do people always want to act in opposition? The great news is that nothing and no one can separate us from the love of Christ, if only we could love each other like He loves us.

THE POINT I think the only way to stop church separation is to get closer to Jesus. The more we know Jesus and become like Him, the more humble we will be in the presence of others. We will then start washing each other's feet rather than washing our hands of each other.

PRAYER *Lord, today I thank You that nothing can stop You loving me.*

17 OCT

'No-one claimed that any of his possessions was his own, but they shared everything they had.' Acts 4:32

 KEY WORD 'shared'

IT WAS AN amazing experience growing up in a community where this scripture was put into practice, but it didn't always work. The adults in the community were given a weekly allowance of five shillings and the children were given one shilling. Bearing in mind that everyone's food and lodging was provided, this was like pocket money. It allowed everyone to buy their own little luxuries such as chocolate, sweets, etc. All the adults received the same, regardless of whether they were directors or housewives. Today five shillings sounds like peanuts but way back in the 1950s, five shillings went a long way. When people entered the community they donated all their worldly possessions to be shared by all. We had all sorts of people from a wealthy naval commander, who donated everything, including a vast collection of silverware, to wandering travellers who drifted in with nothing to donate.

But the community was not just made up of godly, Bible-reading intercessors; we also had the odd person join, who proved to be far from godly. Five shillings a week would never be enough to cover their kind of lifestyle. On one occasion a canny Scot joined the community. He arrived with nothing to donate but he did seem to have a rare talent. The rest of the community began to notice that he seemed to be able to make his five shillings go further than anyone else. As well as being able to afford his smoking habit he had money to travel to wherever he wanted, whenever he wished. No one said anything until by accident someone discovered a stack of pawn tickets belonging to him in the laundry basket. While all the rest of the community had been scraping through on their meagre allowance, our canny Scot had been pawning the community silverware to allow himself a little bonus! In heaven this will never happen. I guess that, even with all its little idiosyncrasies, and except for the thieves, the community was a tiny taste of what heaven might be like.

 THE POINT The day will come when we will all be one big happy family worshipping God and sharing everything. I look forward to that day.

 PRAYER *Lord, today help me to share what I have with others.*

18 OCT

'… As surely as the LORD lives and as you live, I will not leave you.' 2 Kings 2:2

'learning from others'

ALEX AND FLORA (Peggy) Buchanan are a couple who are a little older than I am and a lot wiser! They are mostly known for their prophetic ministry but they have taught me so much just by their daily walk with God. Over the years this couple have known what it's like to experience extreme physical hardship and pain. Alex is a bit like the bionic man after all the operations and surgery he has patiently endured. I have never heard either of them complain to God about their suffering – in fact, they both always seem to be praising Him! A bit of a personal challenge there! However, the reason I most like meeting up with them is that as the three of us sit and talk, it is always like there are four of us sitting and sharing. Jesus makes up the fourth Person. As we talk, Alex rarely makes the formal announcement 'Let us pray'; halfway through a sentence to me he suddenly starts talking to Jesus and brings Him into our conversation. This godly couple really do have an amazing relationship with Jesus, talking and listening to Him and really believing that He is with them every day and night.

As I am getting older I, too, have younger people ask me if I could regularly offer some spiritual direction into their lives. This is one of the blessings of getting older. We have the opportunity to pass on our experience of life to encourage younger ones. What a privilege yet great responsibility this is. Elisha was walking with an older man of God called Elijah whom he greatly respected and admired. Three times Elijah gave him the chance to leave him and three times Elisha gave the reply in our Scripture verse. Elisha knew there were things he could learn from Elijah and he was going to stay with him, and keep learning until the very end.

THE POINT Those who are younger need to spend time with older, more experienced 'Elijahs'. They would find it a great benefit to listen to older Christians and to glean from their knowledge and walk with God.

PRAYER *Lord, I thank You today for those who have walked faithfully with You for longer than I have.*

19 OCT *'I also want women to dress modestly, with decency and propriety …' 1 Timothy 2:9*

'appropriate clothes'

CHRISTIANS IN DIFFERENT countries each have a different set of rules regarding dress code. I was the main teacher at a weekend residential camp in America where hundreds of people had come to be taught. The accommodation and grounds were beautiful and it also had a large outdoor swimming pool. One hot afternoon I decided to put on my swimming trunks and join the delegates for a nice cool dip. I got as far as the gate when the lifeguard, who worked for the centre, stopped me. 'I am sorry pastor,' he said, 'but we cannot allow you to enter the pool dressed like that.' I had no idea what he was talking about until he explained that I was wearing 'speedoze' (swimming trunks), and Christian men were only allowed in if they wore swimming shorts. When I asked him why he explained that they were too provocative and might cause the women to stumble. As I walked away to find some shorts I had to laugh at the thought that there might be some women in the pool who would find a middle-aged, overweight preacher in swimming trunks a turn on! I was hardly Mr Universe! Later that year I went to Scandinavia and was again asked to leave the pool but this time for the opposite reason, swimming shorts were not allowed, only trunks! To top it all, while in Finland, the Christian brothers invited me to join them in the sauna. They wore neither trunks nor shorts and, I hasten to add, I did turn down this invite!

Don't forget, Paul was not God. When he was writing to the churches he was not setting out more laws and commandments, he was just giving practical advice that he felt would help individuals to be more like Jesus. In our verse Paul is not entering into the world of the female fashion critic and he is not saying that women should not dress nicely, but he is saying that ladies should think about what they are wearing.

THE POINT **As Christians, none of us should be wanting people to look at us, we should be always pointing people to Jesus.**

PRAYER *Lord, today I thank You for clothes; help me to wear the appropriate ones for each occasion.*

20 OCT

'… to another the message of knowledge by means of the same Spirit,' 1 Corinthians 12:8

KEY WORDS 'supernatural gifts'

WE WERE INVITED to a summer Bible week to lead the children's meetings. At one of the sessions I was teaching about the gift called 'a word of knowledge', which Paul mentions as one of the gifts of the Holy Spirit. As I finished the morning session a small girl came up to me saying that she believed that she had a word from God. She believed she should pray for someone who had a bad back. I asked her to speak this into the microphone, then asked if the person with the bad back could come forward so she could pray for them. No one responded. She then said that the person had hurt their back in the gym at school. Still no one responded. I told her that maybe the person was shy or maybe she had got it wrong and we left it at that. During the evening meeting she came to me and said the same thing. By now I was getting a bit embarrassed but she announced it again and still no one owned up to having a bad back. I could see this was a very spiritual little girl so I told her to ask God who the person was and then to go into the crowd and find them. She said a short prayer then left the stage and immediately a few children came up to her saying that it might be them. She told them it wasn't and walked to the back of the hall and went up to a boy whom she had never met before and told him that he was the one with the bad back. He admitted he was and when she prayed for him, the pain instantly went from his back. I don't know what was the greater miracle, the little girl using her 'word of knowledge' from God, or the little boy getting instantly healed! God's supernatural gifts are not just for adults or church leaders. God gives His gifts to any that ask for them and that includes children.

THE POINT **People need to see God's supernatural gifts today. Let's be ready to step out and use them as God gives them to us.**

PRAYER *Lord, today please use me in both natural and supernatural ways.*

'And after the fire came a gentle whisper.' 1 Kings 19:12

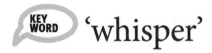

KEY WORD 'whisper'

I LOVE HEARING the sound of a wild storm raging outside my house, especially if I am sitting feeling cosy in a comfy chair. I feel very safe knowing that the outside elements cannot hurt me thanks to solid brick walls. But I remember feeling very different in the middle of the night way back in October 1987. As we sat in our house in Sussex we first experienced a gentle breeze outside but within a very short time the gentle breeze had whipped up into the strongest storm for about 300 years. Now this was frightening, and we were unsure if even the brick walls and double-glazing would be able to cope with such a hurricane. The noise was so loud that shouting to each other sounded like a whisper. Living in the south of England we were not prepared for something of this scale. That storm caused 15 million trees to be felled, ships were driven up high on to the shore and beaches and homes were severely damaged. Sadly some people even lost their lives as the storm raged. The following day many roads were impassable due to fallen trees and chainsaw sales went sky high. The storm left devastation everywhere. I know that even this was quite a minor catastrophe compared to other countries where hurricanes have struck. From that day onwards I realised the power in a mighty wind.

Elijah was in a cave when he felt the power of a mighty wind. He saw the devastation caused by an earthquake below him and experienced the heat from the blaze of fire around him. God is powerful and often, when we see the awesome power of the weather and the elements, it reminds us of this. But God was not in the wind, earthquake and fire. His power was found in a gentle whisper.

THE POINT **It's worth remembering that almighty God, the Creator of the universe, has not come to shout at us or frighten us with His power. He has all that power within His grasp, yet He loves to gently whisper His plans to us, like a father speaking to his small child.**

PRAYER *Lord, today help me to be ready to listen to that still small voice.*

22 OCT

'So if you have not been trustworthy in handling worldly wealth, who will trust you with true riches?' Luke 16:11

'untrustworthy'

THINGS WERE GOING really well. I had a very full diary, my books and my albums were selling like hot cakes, and I was working on the pilot for a children's TV series for national television. It was then a friend approached me and believed that they had a message from God for me. He said that my image needed to live up to my calling and that meant that the old car I was driving around in was not suitable for my status. He said that I needed a 'car for a star'. It's strange how gullible we become when we hear some words that we want to hear. I felt this must be from God, so I emptied our bank account to buy a top-of-the-range second-hand vehicle that was, yes, even gold in colour. This really was a car for a star. Sadly, almost immediately after purchasing it, it broke down and a few miles later the engine completely gave up the ghost. I took it back to the garage where I had bought it and they spent the next six months trying to find the spare part that it needed. In the end I told the garage that they could keep the car. I didn't want to ever see it again as it was a golden reminder of how untrustworthy I had been with God's money. Since then I have never been fooled again into thinking myself as anything other than just a normal Christian.

The amount of money we have is unimportant; it's what we do with that money that will prove if we are trustworthy or not. Whether we earn a large wage, or pocket money, if we waste what we are given, we cannot expect God to believe that we are ready to receive riches of greater value. Now this does not mean that we cannot spend some of it on little luxuries; what it does mean is that, as Christians, we should ask God how we are to spend it, or to whom we should give it.

THE POINT When we can prove that we are trustworthy with our money, then will come the true riches from heaven.

PRAYER *Lord, today please help me to be trustworthy with my money.*

'He spreads the snow like wool ...' Psalm 147:16

KEY WORD 'snow'

MAYBE IT'S DOWN to global warming, but every year there seems to be less and less snowfall in the winter in the part of Sussex where we live. The weather seemed to be very different back in the early 1970s. Ishmael and Andy would never let the weather stop them getting to a gig or returning home again. Norwich is a city in the east of England and, because Norfolk is so flat, bad weather can be very bad. We had a booking at a large church in Norwich but the weather forecast was heavy snow. As we travelled the 200-mile trip, sure enough the snow did start to fall. We made it to the church, convinced that God wanted us to be there, and had a wonderful evening before setting off back down south. The organisers warned us that the weather had got worse and due to the wind snowdrifts were forming which would be likely to make roads impassable. We thanked them for their concern, but as always in those days thought that we knew best, and ignored their advice as we wanted to get home. After a few miles we started skidding and sliding all over the road; our little van could not cope with the deep snow on the roads. It was getting very dangerous and eventually we skidded to a halt. In front of us was a long line of lifeless cars and lorries wedged in drifts waiting to be rescued. Neither Andy nor I felt like spending the night in the freezing van and somehow we managed to turn the vehicle around and skid back to Norwich. Unfortunately, we couldn't remember the church leader's address so we gratefully spent the night in the shelter of the local YMCA. Sun shining on freshly fallen snow can look very beautiful. Even the most depressing scenery can be transformed by a covering of snow. Snow makes everything that it covers look pure and clean.

THE POINT It is easy to see why the psalmist says that God spreads the snow like wool, and it's yet another part of God's creative beauty that we can enjoy.

PRAYER *Lord, thank You for the beauty that can be seen in fresh fallen snow but today we do pray that a way may be found to stop global warming.*

24 OCT *'God opposes the proud but gives grace to the humble.' 1 Peter 5:5*

 KEY WORD 'proud'

AFTER A YEAR or so we decided to change the name from Ishmael United to Rev Counta and the Speedoze. We thought the name change might help us get into more secular venues. Rev Counta and the Speedoze were touring Holland. It was a hard tour because we had to play in venues where the audience were often anti-Christian. We were then invited to play live on Hilversum Radio, which was a very popular Dutch radio station with millions of listeners. This was going to be exciting for the band, or so we hoped. On arrival I was shocked when I saw the ageing studio audience. I just knew that energetic Christian punk rock was not really going to be their cup of tea! The producer told us that there would be no time to sound check or try out the studio equipment, we were to go straight on and perform. When in position I counted in '123', expecting the usual wall of sound from the band, but no sound transpired. All that could be heard was drums, my acoustic guitar and me singing. The keyboard player could not work out how to switch on the keyboard, while the bass player could not get any sound at all from his amplifier. So the punk set turned into a drum and acoustic guitar duet. The audience did not applaud, but who could blame them; it must have sounded dreadful. We left the studio totally embarrassed and totally humiliated. Christian fans who had listened to it on the radio just politely commented that it was 'different'. Thankfully, it was not always like that. It was a great feeling being in a band and standing on a stage in front of hundreds, sometimes thousands, of people and watching appreciative faces as they applauded our performance. That was when I had to be on my guard, so as not to become proud. Sometimes organisers introduce me as 'one of Britain's leading children's workers'. Although I know they are trying to be nice, I just have to ignore what they are saying, because the minute I start believing my own publicity I will be of little use to God.

 THE POINT **We must all beware of the dangers of this thing called pride and it doesn't just affect people who spend a lot of their lives in front of an audience, you know.**

 PRAYER *Today, Lord, help me not to be proud.*

25 OCT *'Whoever believes and is baptised will be saved ...' Mark 16:16*

KEY WORD 'baptism'

MY CHURCH BUILDING in Lancashire was in a terrible state when I arrived, but that was not important. The important thing was that God was using me. In a very short time the little church began to grow numerically as many people, mostly teenagers, became followers of Jesus. Being a keen believer in baptism, I instructed new believers that they needed to be baptised and, after explaining to them what baptism was all about, I decided to hold my first baptismal service in this church building. Our denomination believed in baptism by immersion and under the carpet below the platform at the front of the building I was told there was a baptismal tank.

After taking the carpet and lid away I discovered they were right. I found this deep hole but it hadn't been used for a long time. It was dirty, and covered in rat excrement and mildew. We cleaned it out as best as we could and on the Saturday night filled it with water and lowered in the immersion water heater that nowadays would never pass health and safety regulations. We then put the lid back on because if anyone had fallen into the water with the heater in action they would have been instantly electrocuted!

The following evening during the service the baptismal candidates stood in a line while we took the lid off the tank. I noticed that one of the teenagers was wearing a 'Jaws' T-shirt, and although I considered the shark did seem appropriate, the naked lady swimming away from 'Jaws' did not! As the lid came off steam poured out. The tank had leaked and now there was only a small amount of water left in the bottom. The baptism went ahead but it was more of a rolling in water than immersing and everyone came out bright red as the shallow water was now boiling hot!

Nowadays the debate still continues between denominations, about how much water should be used and should it be infant or adult baptism. As I said, at my first service I did neither sprinkling nor immersion, I did 'rolling' and I don't really think that upset Jesus.

THE POINT **One thing we all can agree on is that baptism is important!**

PRAYER *Today, Lord, I want to thank You for the importance of baptism.*

'When Elizabeth heard Mary's greeting, the baby leaped in her womb, and Elizabeth was filled with the Holy Spirit.' Luke 1:41

KEY WORDS 'unborn babies'

IMMEDIATELY WE GOT married I wanted Irene to conceive. As I have mentioned earlier, I was very disappointed to discover that she wasn't pregnant when we returned from our honeymoon. It took six long months until the miracle took place. I still to this day cannot understand why it took so long! Of course in those days I knew nothing about children or babies; I was only 24 and my ministry was to youth. I had never actually had anything to do with children and at this early stage of my life had never considered that I would. However, I did have high hopes for my own children. I was already imagining Irene giving birth to a mighty man or woman of God who in no time would join Dad ministering for Jesus on the road. Then came the visual transformation. Irene, being only four foot ten inches high, was getting as wide as she was tall. She still looked so young that the bus driver would ask if she wanted half fare, until they saw her protruding middle. I loved listening to the little one's heartbeat and got more and more excited as the big day drew near.

After eight months and one week, my beautiful little 21-year-old wife gave birth to our first little baby, Joseph. Our lives would never be the same! Although none of my children travelled with me at birth I am thrilled to say that all three have ministered with Dad many times over the years. I enjoy seeing pregnant ladies at meetings because although I only see one chair filled, I know there are at least two people sitting on it. And even more important, two people who are going to feel the presence of God. I believe that little life in the womb enjoys being in the presence of praising Christians – just as John the Baptist in Elizabeth's womb couldn't resist having a good old jump for joy when Jesus appeared in His mother Mary's womb.

THE POINT **Let's never forget that these little ones need spiritual attention even before they come into this world and let's pray regularly for both mother and baby.**

PRAYER *Lord, today I pray for unborn babies, that they sense Your presence around them wherever they are.*

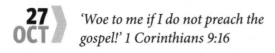

'Woe to me if I do not preach the gospel!' 1 Corinthians 9:16

KEY WORDS 'preach the gospel'

I HAVE ALWAYS been a keen evangelist and love sharing the good news of Jesus with people. I think today I may be a little more subtle in my approach and I am not sure if that's a good thing or a bad thing. Many years ago I decided to revisit a town where I had spent most of my wild youth. I wanted to share my new-found faith with my old drinking friends. Being a Saturday afternoon, I knew they would be lazing around the market square, just smoking and chatting. So this would be a great chance to talk with them. When I arrived I knew they were wary of me, as they had heard that I had 'found religion', and they were surprised that I no longer swore.

After a while I could see that I was really getting somewhere. Instead of making fun of me they were actually listening to what I had to say and were asking all sorts of deep questions. I had literally got to the point of asking them whether they would like to become followers of Jesus and then it happened! I really was in full-flow preaching mode when a miserable, unthinking, and, dare I say, demonic, enormous seagull flew over and did its business right on to my head! Splat, and I don't know what it had been eating, but there sure was a lot of it. Of course that was the end of my evangelism! My listeners were in hysterics, practically rolling around on the pavement with laughter. I just got out my handkerchief and tried to remove the sticky mess from my long hair. My friends were hungry to know the truth so a little mishap like that was never going to quell my enthusiasm. In fact, I think it fired me up all the more.

THE POINT **A bit of opposition from people or even seagulls means that we must be doing something right. Let's try and feel how Paul felt in today's reading and understand that we are not fulfilling what God has put us on this earth to do if we are not sharing the good news of Jesus with others.**

PRAYER *Lord, today help me to see the importance of preaching Your gospel to others.*

28 OCT *'Do not store up for yourselves treasures on earth …' Matthew 6:19*

KEY WORDS 'treasures on earth'

I HAVE ALWAYS loved new technology, even though my son Joseph often affectionately refers to me as the 'computer bozo'. Way back in the early 1970s colour televisions were just in vogue. I remember that many people in the church thought that these were very worldly and would never catch on. Of course they were quite expensive in those days, but it just so happened that a good friend of mine was the owner of a local TV shop. When our old black and white box died on us, he gave us a second-hand colour set for a very reasonable price. To be honest, one of the main reasons that I wanted colour was for the football, as it was impossible to decipher which team was which when they all appeared to be playing in black and white! I remember carrying the huge, very heavy set into our lounge and setting it up. It was slightly disappointing as it was an extremely fuzzy picture and nowhere near as sharp as the old black and white set. But that didn't matter, at least the fuzzy picture was in colour! It was exactly the same when satellite television first hit the scene. I was one of the first people in the church to invest in one of those enormously ugly dishes and again was criticised for worldliness. I actually found it very helpful being the owner of such technology. Our children were of the age when they were beginning to enjoy films, so instead of going to a friend's house to watch all sorts of rubbish, their friends would come to our house where I could monitor what was being viewed. These days I seem a lot busier. I rarely have the time or the desire to watch much TV, and if I watch it for too long I soon begin to think that there are far more important things that I could be doing with my time. Possessions and 'things' are fun, but hardly treasures.

THE POINT 'Things' may be exciting for a short while but real treasure can only be found when we are living our lives for Jesus, and that treasure will last forever.

PRAYER *Lord, today help me not to live for treasures on earth, but to live for You.*

'Your beauty should not come from outward adornment …' 1 Peter 3:3

KEY WORD 'beauty'

WHEN WE FIRST visited America I had no idea that US and UK Christian culture could be so different. We were booked to speak and sing at a large conference held in a very grand hotel. The organisers and delegates were fantastic, really friendly and very encouraging. The seminars were well received, except that I spoke too quickly and because of my accent some couldn't understand what I was saying. Then came the musical performance on the first evening. We were booked to play near the start and other American children would be singing after us. Now my daughter Suzy had travelled over with us. She was very young but I thought it would be helpful to have her onstage with me, to help teach the actions and dance movements. We then had to find something suitable for her to wear. We thought that it would be nice if she fitted in with the American culture so we bought her some trendy cycling shorts and a special T-shirt from the shopping mall which had the American flag on the front. I thought she looked stunning! The time came to perform and as we got on to the stage the hall was packed. I noticed, though, that the audience seemed a little shocked but didn't know why. Perhaps it was the 'rock music', perhaps they just weren't used to that style. As we sat down afterwards we discovered that it wasn't the music. All the other girls onstage that night were dressed in what could best be described as 'bridesmaids' dresses. So I guess that the shorts and T-shirt that Suzy was wearing may have been trendy, but were certainly not what this audience was expecting.

THE POINT Paul states in our Bible verse that real beauty is not found in what we look like or in what we wear, it's found in our inner self. Many adults sadly base a relationship on looks. My advice to those who perhaps are considering marriage is to look at the inner person; this is the person with whom you need to fall in love, not just the person you see with your eyes.

PRAYER *Lord, today I thank You that You have given me an inward beauty.*

'Let them praise his name with dancing …' Psalm 149:3

KEY WORDS 'praise and dancing'

I WAS VERY pleased with the way things were going at our Pentecostal church in Lancashire. Many people were becoming Christians and getting baptised and our services were the liveliest around, I thought. One Sunday night I noticed two men sitting in the congregation whom I did not recognise. As we sang our first hymn I was shocked to see them both leave their seats and begin to dance in the aisles, bashing tambourines as they did so. Now we were free, but none of my people would think of jumping around while singing and looking strange. I found them rather frightening and intimidating so as soon as the service finished I hid in the vestry. Within minutes they knocked on the door and entered. First they gave me a hug. We were free but we shook hands in our church. They then said how much they enjoyed my teaching and asked me to preach at their 'fellowship'. Unsure of what I was letting myself in for I fixed a date. Their hall was in the middle of nowhere. As I walked in, one of their leaders rushed up and not only hugged me, but also kissed me! What on earth had I come to? I quickly went to one side and stood firmly against a wall. I then looked around the room. It was full of young people praying and reading the Bible; I had never seen so many 'spiritual' young people in one room before. When the music started up everyone began dancing and praising – except me. I remained seated, pretending to read my Bible. Suddenly I realised I was not as free as I thought I was. Over the next year I became very close with this fellowship and I will be for ever grateful for the many things they taught me.

THE POINT I thought I was really free to praise God, until I met others who, like King David, seemed to have no inhibitions at all. We don't all need to be dancers, but I do think that we need to be released from any inhibitions we may have that might be hindering us in expressing our praise to God.

PRAYER *Lord, please today take away any inhibitions that might be restricting my praise to You.*

31 OCT

'But David continued up the Mount of Olives weeping as he went …' 2 Samuel 15:30

KEY WORDS 'parents and children'

WHEN I LEFT home at 15, I knew my parents would have preferred me to stay with them for a little while longer as I was very young and inexperienced to cope with the big wide world. The career I had chosen was farming, and they lived in Littlehampton, a seaside town, not a farming community. I needed to move into the country to fulfil my ambition. The main fear that my parents had was whether my spiritual life would survive. For all of my life I had been surrounded by Christians. Now I was going to a place where I didn't know any Christians. The family that I was going to live with were really nice people, but would not claim in anyway to be followers of Jesus. For a while I travelled home at weekends to see my friends at the Baptist church. But then as summer and harvest came, I had to work Sundays. I gradually got into the habit of not going home and lost the desire to attend church services at all. I discovered there was a lot more fun to be had on a Sunday with my newfound friends. For the next few years I must have caused my parents a lot of heartache and tears, but they never stopped praying for me. If anyone was to ask me what turned my life back to Jesus a few years later, I would have to say the continuing love my parents showed me, and the prayers that they never ceased to pray.

David loved his children. Absalom his son decided that he wanted to take his father's place and become king. So he conspired against him and took over the palace in Jerusalem. David was heartbroken as we can see from our reading, but rather than cause trouble he and his followers moved out of the city. Absalom came to a very sad end, but David never stopped loving him.

THE POINT **Parents are often hurt by what their children say or what their children do. But because our children are a gift from God, like King David, we can never stop loving them.**

PRAYER *Lord, help me today to love my family and to never stop praying for them.*

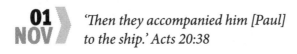

01
NOV

'Then they accompanied him [Paul] to the ship.' Acts 20:38

KEY WORDS 'life on the ocean waves'

ISHMAEL UNITED TOURED quite a bit in Holland. We always had to take our own musical equipment which meant a tedious ferry crossing to the Hook of Holland. The Dutch gigs were nearly always tough. We often found we were playing alcohol-fuelled rock clubs, 'druggy' nightclubs, and even totally gay clubs. We played anywhere we had the opportunity to spread the good news of Jesus. But it was exhausting and most of the time very stressful. Then came the return crossing, which was even more boring than the outward one because we were now feeling tired and irritable. This is when we sometimes went a bit silly and decided to dare each other to do crazy things just to help pass the time. I still to this day cannot believe how mature evangelists could get up to such mischief! People on the ferry looked miserable so we decided to liven things up a bit. We dared Laurie our bass player to run through the bar in just his underpants, pretending that someone had run off with the rest of his clothes. After a bit of persuasion he agreed. The rest of us went into the bar and, sure enough, right on time in ran Laurie wearing nothing but his underpants. He ran through the bar shouting 'Has anyone seen my clothes?' Of course we were all in hysterics, but the amazing thing was, all the drinkers hardly even looked up from their drinks. There wasn't even a smile. It was just as if this was an everyday occurrence on the ferry!

Of course, in Paul's day, you would never do such a crazy thing on board ship! The ship was the only way to cross water and Paul would not have had the chance to get bored. When he wasn't trying to cope with the rough sea he would have been contemplating a potential shipwreck.

THE POINT **Paul would never let rough seas stop him from taking the message of Jesus to others, and although the trips may not have been pleasant, the opportunity to pass on the good news, always made it worthwhile.**

PRAYER *Lord, today I thank You for transport and for the opportunity of being able to take Your good news to all parts of the globe.*

02 NOV

'When his master [Potiphar] heard the story his wife told him … he burned with anger.' Genesis 39:19

KEY WORDS 'wrongful accusation'

I WAS INVITED to speak at a church which had a reputation for being very wary of the gifts of the Holy Spirit. I realised that I would have to be careful what I said. After I had finished my talk I invited anyone who would like to commit themselves to Jesus to join me at the front of the hall and I would pray for them. A young girl and her mother approached me and before I prayed I asked the mother if she would like to stay with us as I did so. She refused, thinking that her presence might make her child feel inhibited, and so retreated to the back of the hall. I prayed over the little girl and asked her to just say thank you to Jesus because I believed that He had heard her sincere prayer. Then two supernatural things happened. The first was the little girl started praising God in tongues. Now this was nothing to do with me, I hadn't even mentioned this gift let alone used it. The second thing that happened was the mother seemed to have supernatural hearing and ran to the front shouting, 'What have you done to my little girl?' I tried to explain that I hadn't done anything but she wouldn't believe me. While the mother was fuming and wrongfully accusing me, the little girl continued smiling and praising the Lord in her newly-discovered language. As I have often found, adults often need more help than the children.

Poor Joseph. Potiphar's wife was a nasty lady who told her husband that Joseph had tried to seduce her, when it was the other way around. Sadly, the husband believed his lying wife and Joseph was in trouble. We may get falsely accused of things and sadly there are always people who want to believe the worst about us.

THE POINT **Let's not turn wrongful accusations into a debate. We just simply need to tell the truth because at the end our accusers will believe what they want to believe anyway. The good news is that God knows the truth and He will always stand by the innocent.**

PRAYER *Lord, help me today to love those who wrongfully accuse me of things that I haven't done.*

03 NOV

'Do not be carried away by all kinds of strange teachings.' Hebrews 13:9

KEY WORDS ‘strange teaching’

I GET SOME strange reactions from people in meetings. I still often experience the 'walk-outs' as I travel. At a Sunday morning family service I go to great lengths asking everyone to be tolerant of one another, especially the children, because during the service I will be doing songs that will be especially aimed at the little ones. Then as I begin to play a Scripture-based, child-friendly song with actions, up they get and out they stomp, slamming the door as they do so. Did they not hear the few words I said about tolerance just a few minutes earlier? On one occasion, I was preaching when a man jumped up and started to shout back at me, vehemently disagreeing with what I said. The leaders and congregation just stared in astonishment and didn't know what to do. I had no problem with this. I had experienced it a few times before and actually it can have a positive effect, because it always wakes people up. I politely said, 'Sir, please sit down and stop causing a disturbance.' I continued to say that the leaders had invited me to speak, not him, so please could he listen to what I had to say, and then, at the end, if he still disagreed with me, we could discuss it rationally together. Of course he didn't stay, he was more interested in making a statement by stomping out and slamming the door.

Whenever I speak, I always tell people that I don't expect them to agree with everything I say. I encourage them to read the Bible for themselves and to check that what I am saying is true. Nowadays some Christians still listen to preachers who teach strange things without thinking through what they are being taught. The worst thing is, just as today's verse highlights, they get 'carried away' by what they have heard. Before long they are encouraging everyone else to also believe this strange teaching. This can be dangerous.

THE POINT We must check out everything that we are taught with the Bible and even then we have to be careful that Scripture is not being misinterpreted. We need sound teaching, not strange teaching.

PRAYER *Lord, today help me to think about what I am being taught, and to check it out with the Bible.*

'… Peter was sleeping between two soldiers …' Acts 12:6

KEY WORDS 'sleep without fear'

I WAS SPEAKING at a conference in France and was really enjoying it. The room was full of children's leaders and all seemed to appreciate my teaching. In the evening a German senior pastor joined us and after a time of praise everyone in the room felt the presence of the power of God. I had met the pastor before and he was a leader in a large church in Berlin. People started asking for the senior pastor and myself to pray for them. There were many people gathered, with many different needs and without rushing, we spent time praying for each one individually, that God would answer their prayer. It was getting very late and there was just one lady left who looked extremely distraught. The pastor and I began to pray for her and as we did she explained to us some of the terrible things that had happened to her in her life. She was totally gripped by certain fears. We prayed for quite a while and as we did so we saw the wonderful miracle that only Jesus can do as He sets the captive free. It was now about midnight and we were facing a smiling lady who looked like a ton weight had been lifted from shoulders. I was exhausted and made my way up to my bedroom. But as I did so I had a strange feeling that I was being followed. As I lay in bed I began to shake. I felt that there was something in my room. Suddenly I realised that the fears that had been so affecting the lady we had just been praying for, were now affecting me! There was no way that I was going to sleep. I then had to pray the same prayers that I had prayed over this lady over myself, and in a short time the shaking and fear had completely gone.

 THE POINT **Peter was so close to Jesus that he could sleep like a baby in prison chained to two soldiers, even though tomorrow King Herod might have him killed. If we keep close to Jesus we, too, should be able to sleep like Peter – with no fear.**

 PRAYER *Lord, please help me to sleep soundly tonight.*

'Neither do people light a lamp and put it under a bowl.' Matthew 5:15

KEY WORDS 'shining lights'

I AM STILL unsure if Christians should celebrate bonfire night when its roots are a celebration of the burning of Guy Fawkes or, worse still, the Pope. Nowadays I can't say that I am the greatest fan of firework displays either, but this is down to the flashing lights which can bring on a migraine attack. Strange as it may seem, I never suffered from migraines when I was younger; it seems to only have appeared as I have grown older and have allowed the occasional stress attack to get to me. Anyway, let me take you back to a bonfire night in the late 1950s when I was a boy and really enjoyed them. Our Christian community was based in a small village and every year our village hosted one of the biggest and best firework displays in the whole of Sussex. Hundreds would come to join in the procession that began right outside the gates of our big house. The main street was packed with music bands, organisations, people in weird and wonderful fancy-dress costumes and, of course, lots of people rattling tins for charity. As we stood in the dark in long lines we would be given a flaming torch and we would all set off on a long procession. I loved marching around, following the bands with a flaming torch in my hand. At the end of the procession everyone threw the torch on to the unlit bonfire and in no time the massive fire lit up the whole sky. This brings us back to our Bible verse. What could be more crazy than to get a torch, go into a dark place where you want to be able to see, then to cover your torch with a bucket. Everyone would still be in the dark!

Jesus says that those who love Him are like His lights in a dark world, so we should never hide the fact that we are Christians.

THE POINT I don't think that we should just preach at everyone; we shine God's light by the things that we do and the people we are. It's when people see our changed lives that they will want to know more about Jesus.

PRAYER *Lord, help me today to shine out Your love to others.*

06 NOV ❯ *'There is the sea, vast and spacious, teeming with creatures beyond number ...' Psalm 104:25*

 KEY WORDS ❯ '**sea creatures**'

IRENE AND I had just arrived with my cousins on the beautiful island of Tenerife. On the first day we hired a car and set off to the nearest beach to cool off in the bright blue sea. When we arrived I was the first one to dive in and then I spotted a pontoon quite a distance out complete with diving board. I needed to swim out to that! Sitting on the edge of the pontoon I could just make out a few young people shouting and waving. It was nice to see friendly people so I waved back and headed out towards the floating raft. As I got nearer I could hear that they were not shouting greetings but something about fish. Then I saw them. I was surrounded by what looked like floating underdone fried eggs. Jellyfish! I carried on swimming and felt the horrible creatures sting me all over. As I jumped up on to the pontoon the young people asked me why I had swum out when they were warning me about the jellyfish. I couldn't reply as I was in so much discomfort. I saw my family sitting happily on the beach, waving at me and totally oblivious of what my slimy persecutors had done to me. I had to get back to shore but this meant diving back into the shoal of jellyfish. In I went, and my body seemed to act like a magnet to these wonderful specimens of creation. Eventually, I reached the beach and dragged myself out of the water. My skin was covered in swollen red blotches and I imagined the pain to be on a par with jumping headfirst into a beehive! Of course, I was given a strong but sympathetic rebuke from Irene and a lot of teasing from my cousins, but I failed to see the funny side of it for at least five days!

 THE POINT ❯ **We can never imagine how vast the oceans are, let alone the millions of amazing creatures, apart from those nasty jellyfish, that live in them. God created every living creature even in the darkest depths of the ocean, some that after thousands of years have still never been discovered by man.**

 PRAYER *Lord, today I thank You for vast seas and for the amazing creatures that inhabit them.*

'[Peter asked,] "Lord, how many times shall I forgive my brother … ?" ' Matthew 18:21

KEY WORDS

'forgive my brother'

MY YOUNGER BROTHER Tim takes after our father in many ways. One of the ways that he is like him is that he is very fussy about keeping everything tidy and in its place. He and I spent many happy years touring together, and to help fund his ministry, I gave Tim the responsibility of running my bookstall. While he sold my products he also used his own initiative and made a few extra pounds by selling badges, notebooks and even rainbow braces! Now the teams we worked with were great fun. We were setting up for a week's camp with the eight- to eleven-year-olds at Kingdom Faith Bible Week. This was held on a county showground and our venue was a very large animal auction hall. While the venue was being decorated Tim was meticulously setting up and arranging the bookstall. When he went off somewhere I saw a few of the team rush over, dismantle the bookstall, and reconstruct it on a platform about 20 feet off the ground where the animal auctioneer stood. I suppose as leader I should have stopped it as I guessed it would upset Tim, but I didn't. When he arrived back he couldn't find his stall. He looked everywhere except up towards the roof. He was getting annoyed while everyone was laughing. Eventually, we told him where it was and it was brought back down to earth. As I said, I could have stopped it. I was both his older brother and team leader, and I think that he would have expected me to. Fortunately, however, it didn't spoil a great week of ministry and also a great week of sales for Tim's stall. Throughout our years working together Tim has probably asked the same question as Peter asked many times!

The bad news is that try as I do I cannot seem to stop sinning. The good news is that Jesus will never stop forgiving me.

THE POINT

This does not mean that we should not worry about doing wrong, of course we should, but it does mean that Jesus never stops loving us when we do sin.

PRAYER

Lord, I know today that You will forgive me.
I also know that I must forgive others.

'The wings of the ostrich flap joyfully ...' Job 39:13

KEY WORDS 'little bird – big bird'

WE ALWAYS SEEM to live next door to nice neighbours. One particular neighbour kept an aviary and bred birds. She very kindly offered to donate one of her newly-hatched chicks to our little family as a pet. We went out and excitedly bought a cage and all the accessories. But the problem was that this bird had a slight flaw: it only had one leg intact! When we got our feathered family pet home our three children, Joseph, Daniel and Suzy, were fascinated by it. We had never seen a budgie with one leg before! We felt really sorry for him because it was a major struggle for him to even balance on his perch. But he was warmly welcomed as one of the family and named Joey because that was the only budgie name we knew. The following day I went off on my travels and dutifully said goodbye to our family, which of course now included Joey. It was a very tiring tour and I arrived back home exhausted and drained. As I entered our lounge there sat a tearful-looking Irene who greeted me with the words, 'Joey is dead.' I failed to hear her correctly and my immediate thought was that my eldest son Joseph had died while I had been away. I suddenly felt traumatised. Then Irene pointed to the birdcage and, lying stiff on the floor, was Joey our little budgie, with his one leg stuck in the air. I breathed a sigh of relief as I sat down, a little sad but extremely relieved!

When we think of an ostrich, joyful flapping wings hardly springs to mind, as described in today's verse: most of us would tend to think of a rather silly bird that buries its head in the sand when it meets any problems hoping that by the time it takes its head out, the problem will have disappeared.

THE POINT **Let's not be like an ostrich. When we face difficulties and problems, let's take them to Jesus and tell him all about them. He will lead us through them and even help us to rejoice while we face them.**

PRAYER *Lord, thank You for pets and even joyful, flapping ostriches, but today help me to take all my problems to You.*

09 NOV

'Until I come, devote yourself to the public reading of Scripture ...' 1 Timothy 4:13

KEY WORDS 'reading out loud'

WHEN WE FIRST started to attend services at the cathedral I found it amazing. I had never experienced anything like it before. It was full of ritual, ceremony and mystery. I even exclaimed to the bishop how dramatic it was. It was very formal and I had been used to total informality bordering on chaos. This was a different world. Yet everything that was said and done had a significance and meaning. I loved it because each service was full of Scripture, either sung or spoken, and I felt the presence of Jesus there in a very different way. Irene and I soon became friends with the Dean and Chapter and were asked to offer the prayers of intercession at a very special anniversary service. Now I haven't experienced a case of nerves for years. I have performed in front of thousands with no fear, but here, suddenly I felt nervous. It seemed as if we were the only ones dressed in ordinary clothes. We were surrounded by bishops in mitres, the Dean and canons in flowing robes, and almost everyone else in sight wore a black clerical shirt with white collar. The time came for us to offer our prayers. As I stood up to pray my throat went dry and I tried to speak but no noise came out. I felt like giggling with embarrassment. I managed to control myself and to pray sensibly – well, almost, probably due to the fact that Irene was glaring at me!

Paul gives young Timothy advice and we can see by our verse that he encourages him to commit himself to reading the Scriptures out loud to others so that they can learn more of God and His wonderful love. Nowadays when I have my personal devotions, I have found it very beneficial to read the Bible out loud to myself. Do give it a try.

THE POINT It is good to read the Bible out loud to each other, so while one reads the others can listen and take in what is being read to them. We see it happening in most church services, let's try it in our homes.

PRAYER *Lord, today I thank You for my Bible. Please teach me more about Yourself as I read it, either quietly or out loud.*

10 NOV

'When times are good, be happy; but when times are bad, consider: God has made the one as well as the other.' Ecclesiastes 7:14

KEY WORDS ▸ 'good and bad times'

VE DAY WAS approaching rapidly. This was going to be a great day for our local church as ITV wanted to film our live family service, which would be viewed by millions. Sometimes 'live' does not mean 'live', because certain parts have to be pre-recorded. But on this occasion everything during that hour would appear directly on to the viewer's screen at home, just as it happened. I was so excited because I have always believed in the importance of the family service. Now the nation could see how one of these meetings could work, being fun, yet remaining reverent. It was decided that my brother-in-law, the full-time elder, would give the introduction, my father would pray, another couple would give the children's talk, Irene would give the Bible reading, and I would do most of what was left. We had good musicians so I knew the music would be excellent. I am pleased to say that the service went off brilliantly except for a couple of small hitches. We spent the day before rehearsing everything very carefully. A very nervous Irene had practised several times, walking up to the stand where the Bible lay open at the correct page to give her reading. Being a live broadcast she was extremely anxious that one wrong word could prove a potential disaster. The big day arrived. All was going smoothly until my father started praying an 'epic' prayer and, in the end, I had to grab the microphone from him to bring it to an abrupt end. Then came Irene's turn to read. As she approached the stand she looked down at the Bible and, to her horror, someone had turned over the pages. Poor Irene's mind went blank. Where was the reading taken from? Fortunately she suddenly remembered and thankfully no one noticed the elongated pause as she kept her cool and calmly found the correct page. It all turned out well in the end and I was so happy and extremely relieved.

THE POINT ▸ **As our verse tells us, although it's sometimes hard to take, we do need both good and bad times because the bad times make the good times seem even better.**

PRAYER *Lord, today I thank You for both the good and the bad times.*

11 NOV *'They [the Pharisees] said, it is only by Beelzebub, the prince of demons, that this fellow drives out demons.' Matthew 12:24*

KEY WORD 'demons'

I HAD JUST finished leading the Sunday morning service when a lady who was also a children's leader, came running up to me looking very hot and bothered. She was dragging another lady with her. She informed me that there was a boy sitting at the back of the building who was demon-possessed. She then pulled the other lady alongside her. 'This is his mother who is a "witch",' she continued, 'and his father is a "warlock".' The 'warlock' was obviously not present this Sunday. 'That demon-possessed boy', she said, getting more and more flustered, 'just swears at me.' I said that I would talk to the boy and when she offered to accompany me, I told her she should stay and keep the 'witch' company. As I walked over to where the boy was seated I could see he was very agitated and his eyes were fiery as they looked at me. Before I could say hello, he said, 'You won't cast anything out of me.' I smiled and said I didn't want to, I had just come over to ask if he had enjoyed the meeting. Gradually, as we talked, he calmed down and he allowed me to pray peace into his life. Here was a young lad who was far from demon-possessed. He was just a hurt young person who was full of fear. The children's leader who had been trying to cast demons out of him had only been adding to his hurts and fears. We must be so careful what we say to people and also how we pray for them. Making public accusations about people and claiming that they are involved in witchcraft or that they are demon-possessed is not exactly helpful. In fact, it can be extremely damaging. In today's verse Jesus had just wonderfully healed a man who was blind and could not speak. But the Pharisees accused Him of doing this by the power of Satan. They were treading on very dangerous ground!

 THE POINT **We must be very careful when we talk about people being demon-possessed. Through wrong discernment we can end up being the ones doing the enemy's work for him.**

 PRAYER *Today, Lord, please give me the true gift of discernment.*

12 NOV

'Elisha said, "Hear the word of the LORD." ' 2 Kings 7:1

KEY WORDS # 'word of the Lord'

I WAS ATTENDING a children's leaders' conference in America where a very well-known, highly respected, extremely expensively dressed preacher had been invited to preach at the evening session. This speaker was not known to be involved in children's ministry and so I was surprised that he had been invited. It was not usual for children to be present in his meetings but, as there were a few leaders' children there, he allowed them to sit near the front. His talk was excellent and even the children listened intently. At the end of his talk he came to the part that many of the adults had been waiting for, the ministry time, where he would pray for people. But then I saw, even with all his powerful words, like the rest of us, he, too, did not always do and say the right things. At this point he announced, 'Get those kids out of the way because it's time to pray for people.' I and many others were shocked. Were children not people? Were children not worth praying for? Maybe I am being a bit harsh on the man. He certainly knew how to preach the Word of God, perhaps he just needed to learn how much God values children. Of course I would have challenged him, except he had an armed bodyguard standing near him onstage. I thought I would leave it to one of his friends to tell him!

Most of us have witnessed people grab a microphone and tell us that they have come to bring us a word from the Lord. Sometimes they have, but many times they haven't. Elisha was different; when he had a word from the Lord he often went and proclaimed it to the most important person of the day, the king.

THE POINT > **God has things to say to us as Church, but He also has things to say to the leaders responsible for running our country. My prayer is that God raises up some 'Elishas' who really do have a word from the Lord and who have the courage to pass it on to those in positions who can change things for the better.**

PRAYER *Lord, today I pray that the leaders of my country hear a word from You.*

13 NOV ›

'The fruit of the Spirit is … self-control.' Galatians 5:22–23

'restraint'

ONE SUNDAY JUST after we had started attending the cathedral we heard that one of the clergy needed a manuscript to be typed. Irene was pleased to be able to offer to do this work for him. When completed, he was very grateful and asked her if there was any way that he could thank her. Now Irene knew there was an amazing library containing some very ancient and special books kept under lock and key in the cathedral. Irene also knew that this member of the clergy was in charge of the library. As she loves books she asked if she could see the library. When she told me about this, I, too, wanted to go and see it with her. Not just because of the books, but because I was also curious to see this special part of the cathedral where access is not normally given to the general public. I could sense that she was slightly wary about letting me near such valuable treasures. In the end she agreed to take me as long as I behaved myself, didn't touch anything, and didn't ask embarrassing questions. I promised to keep my hands behind my back and to not touch or say anything. The big day came. We followed the member of the clergy through a small door, up a narrow spiral staircase, and into a very old room that was filled with shelves of ancient books. It was amazing; so much so that I immediately forgot about restraint and started firing questions. Finally, I asked if I could see the oldest book. We watched as he took out a key, unlocked what appeared to be a safe, and very carefully placed this invaluable ancient manuscript in front of us. Self-control vanished, curiosity got the better of me, and, before Irene could stop me, my hand instinctively shot out and excitedly tapped the cover, exclaiming how tough it was! The member of clergy was an extremely gracious man and didn't rebuke me or even tell me off for touching such a precious book. Probably because he guessed that Irene was going to do that the minute we got outside the cathedral!

THE POINT › We must all learn self-control or we could end up in big trouble with both God and man!

PRAYER › *Lord, help me today to exercise self-control.*

**14
NOV**

*'All the days ordained for me were written
in your book …' Psalm 139:16*

 'freewill'

I HAD MINISTERED to teenagers, graduated from Bible college, pastored churches. I'd even spent a few years in a punk rock band. Did God now want me to minister to children? Spring Harvest was a large family event that met in various holiday camps. I had been involved in running the adult programme, but now, having young children of my own, I was wondering if I should be involved with the children's work. This was something that I had never attempted before. The executive committee met up with me and interrogated me as to why I wanted to work with children. To be honest I didn't look like a typical children's worker and certainly didn't talk like one. I suggested that for the eight- to eleven-year-old programme I bring along a rock band and offer the children similar music to the adult programme. Actually, what I was intending was far more radical than that because I had recently left the punk band! They agreed to give me one year's trial. That was when the Glorie Company was launched. God used the Glorie Company as a catalyst for many others to develop. I believe that our programme helped to radically change the whole concept of children's work and thousands and thousands of children were reached over a number of years. The big question was, did I choose children's work or had God ordained it, and I had no choice but to work with children? Freewill is a subject that theologians have debated for centuries. Has God preordained my life for me? If He has, that must mean that I have no choice over what I do and don't do. I don't believe it's that complicated. God has given us the opportunity to choose what we do. Sometimes we do what is right, sometimes we don't. He never takes that freedom of choice away. But God also knows everything. This means that He knows all about the choices that we are going to make before we are even born. But He doesn't make them for us.

**Let's try and choose to do the right things
that we know will please almighty God.**

Lord, today help me to choose to do what is right.

15 NOV *'Miriam … took a tambourine in her hand, and all the women followed her, with tambourines and dancing.' Exodus 15:20*

KEY WORD 'noise'

I WAS INVITED to speak at a family service where local musicians were to play the music. This sounded good, and I was also keen to see how they managed to involve all ages. I was told that all the children stayed in for the whole meeting and that they would be kept involved. After a few notices, the band began to play, and they started with a song that I would not consider to be especially child-friendly. Then the children were each given a flag and the children's leader lined them up behind him. At his command the children followed him around the hall, marching in a line, waving their flags as they did so. I thought that this was great and everyone was smiling as they marched. Then eventually I noticed a slight problem. The 'worship' went on and on and on, and for the whole time the children continued to march around the room non-stop. They appeared to get more and more exhausted. By the time the band decided they had played enough, the children looked like they could do with a good sleep! When I encourage adults to involve children in a family service, this is not quite what I have in mind!

Miriam, Aaron's sister, was having a great time giving thanks to the Lord along with all the other women. To express their thanks they danced and played that jingly percussion instrument called a tambourine. Now today some churches have banned the tambourine for two reasons. The first is that when it is played out of time, it's really hard for the musicians to play in time, and the second is that if the meeting is being recorded, again, even a slightly out-of-time tambourine can spoil it for the listener. I can understand both of those issues. But I think that sometimes we ought to consider the tambourine player that is getting blessed and not just the listener who isn't.

THE POINT **The Bible talks about making a joyful noise and doesn't mention that it has to be either in tune or in time.**

PRAYER *Lord, today please make me as free as Miriam as I praise You, with or without a tambourine.*

KEY WORDS 'we are all children'

AS I ARRIVED at a weekend Christian conference, I noticed that most people were wearing suits and clerical dress, while my friend and I were wearing our usual jeans and trainers. We looked out of place, but then that was not unusual for me. I always wonder why miserable faces so often accompany clerical dress? This weekend didn't promise to be a barrel of laughs. As we had a few minutes to spare my friend and I decided to explore the large building. Then we found it. In a basement room was an inflated bouncy castle. We looked at each other, each knowing what the other was thinking. Come on, we're over 50 years old, surely we are not considering we should try out the bouncy castle? In no time at all we were bouncing around like a couple of ten-year-olds, and did we laugh as we rolled around all over the place! All was going well until a caretaker must have overheard our laughter. He was furious! He shouted to us that the bouncy castle was there for children, not old men! We walked back towards the conference hall grinning. Of course we should have felt ashamed of ourselves but we didn't. Deep down we both just wanted to go back and have another go. But then we thought it may not look good if two well-known ministers were expelled from an adult conference for jumping on a bouncy castle!

I have a close friend who is a Baptist pastor and I usually do a booking for him each Christmas. Before the booking we enjoy tea and cakes at his house and then he gets out a special Christmas train set explaining that the grandchildren are coming round. Sure enough they do come round, but it is he and I who end up playing with the train set, the grandchildren prefer to watch the television!

 THE POINT **Today's verse reminds us that Christians never become adult, we just grow to become more mature children of God. Being children means whatever age we are, we will always be full of fun, very excitable, and totally dependent on our heavenly Father.**

 PRAYER *Lord, today I thank You that You are my patient Father and I am Your excitable child.*

'It took Solomon thirteen years, however, to complete the construction of his palace.' 1 Kings 7:1

 'building'

AS I HAVE already mentioned, a few years ago, we decided to buy an old vicarage. It really was in a dreadful state when we first moved in. The house was damp and very run down but had great potential. Someone had prophesied over us a short while earlier that we were going to 'father and mother' young people. This property had enough rooms not only for our family but to take in others as well. We needed to replace the roof so we decided to incorporate a couple of rooms into the loft at the same time. We chose a builder who was a friend of a friend and that's when the nightmare began. A job that was supposed to take about nine weeks took nine months and cost double the estimate. We had no roof for many weeks. Irene and I had to sleep in a dust-filled room with half a wall missing. The builder ordered two separate staircases that were both the wrong size and insisted we pay for his miscalculations. The final straw came in the middle of the freezing winter, two weeks before Christmas. Just after the builder had 'finished', the gas company arrived and immediately disconnected our supply, saying that the builder had put the wrong pipes in the wrong place and we could all have been killed by lethal carbon monoxide fumes. Needless to say, we have not ventured into any building work since!

In the previous verse to our reading for today, we see that Solomon had spent seven years building what was God's house in those days, the Temple. It's interesting to note the word 'however' in today's verse. What that meant was that Solomon spent nearly twice as long building his own house as he did building God's. I think today, sadly, we are no different. Although we say we love the Lord, we spend far more time thinking about our family, our possessions and our leisure activities than we do thinking about God.

 THE POINT **God knows our faults, and the wonderful thing is that He loves us knowing our faults, but let's make the effort to try and give God first place in our lives.**

 PRAYER *Lord, please help me today to give You a greater place in my life.*

'To act justly and to love mercy …' Micah 6:8

KEY WORD 'mercy'

IT WAS SUPPOSED to be a 'friendly' game of golf involving a few church friends. It's strange how competitive even very shy Christians can be when they become absorbed in games and sport! I was playing with one of my sons and a couple of his friends. We had just completed the first hole and I had been pleased with my second tee shot, as it had gone a good distance and was fairly straight for a change. The four of us walked up the second fairway laughing and chatting. My second shot was about 150 yards to the green and I did a sweet shot with my eight iron that landed right on the green and quite close to the flag. As I was congratulating myself my son shouted out, 'Disqualified!' I thought he was joking but he wasn't. He walked over and informed me that I was disqualified because I had hit his ball by mistake. 'Why didn't you tell me before I hit it?' I pleaded, but it was too late to appeal. The other lads thought it was hilarious that I had hit such a great shot and was about to lose the hole because of my son! Of course he was playing to the rules, but I had hoped, as it wasn't a competition, that he might have shown Dad a bit of mercy. No chance, this was golf!

It's so important that we are fair with people and treat them justly. I sometimes meet parents who spend more time with one child, not realising that they are ignoring the other. Sometimes they give one a better present than the other because deep down they consider they deserve special treatment. This is not good; we must be fair and show equal love at all times.

THE POINT We must also show mercy to people who hurt us and not retaliate and seek revenge. We have all done bad things to hurt God, and there is no reason why He should show His mercy to us, yet He does. Why? Because He loves us. We must try and be more like Him.

PRAYER *Lord, today help me to be fair and show mercy to all I meet.*

KEY WORDS 'frightened to speak'

WE HAD ARRIVED at a lovely hotel for a week's holiday but while travelling from the airport we noticed a married couple about our age, sitting behind us. The husband was obviously inebriated and although he was not abusive, his behaviour was very loud and embarrassingly demonstrative. Later that day we saw the same couple sitting in the hotel bar. He had now sobered up somewhat so we decided to go and talk to them. It didn't take long before he was telling us about his profession and was asking me what I did. Now I often find it difficult to explain exactly what I do, because I have learned invariably through bitter experience that the minute I say, 'I work for God', everyone ignores me for the rest of the week, obviously thinking that I am out to make them feel guilty and to ruin their fun. I said to this couple that I would tell them later, maybe on the last day of the holiday, but that made them even more inquisitive. The longer I stalled the more curious they were to know. In the end, when they were convinced that I was working for MI5, I had to tell them. Guess what, they looked totally shocked and avoided us for the rest of the holiday!

The Pharisees certainly knew how to spoil a party. Our verse relates to a story where Jesus healed a man who was born blind. Just think how excited and thrilled his parents must have felt. Then along came the Pharisees like a wet blanket. They interrogated the parents because they didn't want to believe that Jesus was God's Son or that He was capable of performing such a miracle. The parents lived in fear of the Pharisees and were scared to speak out the truth. All their excitement was overcome by fear.

THE POINT We must not be frightened to tell people about our friendship with Jesus. Let's never be scared to tell people that it's Jesus who is the One who cares for us and looks after us, even if it loses us friends on holiday.

 PRAYER *Lord, today help me not to be frightened to speak out and tell people about the wonderful things that You have done in my life.*

20
NOV

'A champion named Goliath, who was from Gath, came out of the Philistine camp.' 1 Samuel 17:4

 KEY WORD '**giants**'

OUR LOCAL CHURCH asked me to organise an all-age meeting and I decided the theme should be David and Goliath. We arranged the chairs into three separate areas so that when people arrived they were automatically divided into three teams. I then invited the children on to the stage, to build a life-size Goliath out of cardboard boxes. One of the young people had drawn Goliath on to the separate boxes and not until they put the head in place did I realise that they had put a photo of me where Goliath's face should have been! After Goliath was built, three of the church's top golfers walked through the door. They were dressed complete with golfing gear and each pulled their trolley of clubs behind them. Individually, they took up their place in front of each of the three groups. The groups cheered as they did this. In front of each team stood their 'champion'. Then we turned Goliath's head around to reveal a large hole in the box. This was about 12 feet off the ground. Each golfer was given six tries at pitching a golf ball, a plastic ball of course, into Goliath's head. Finally one did it. Everyone cheered as he was paraded around the hall while seated on the other two golfers' shoulders. I went on to speak about 'hitting the target for Jesus'. Jesus often used visual aids to illustrate His point. No one would ever forget that meeting!

Goliath was seriously big, big enough to frighten the whole Israelite army. But he was still only a man. It's hard to understand why God's army was afraid of one man, even if he was a giant. It's very easy for us today to allow something to become a giant in our lives and we sometimes feel that this giant is impossible to conquer. This giant is just another challenge that is facing us; it may look bigger than all the others we've faced in the past but it's not.

 THE POINT   **All giants soon look very small if we ask Almighty God who holds the universe in His hands to come and deal with them. Let's never forget that.**

 PRAYER   *Lord, today I realise that You're the only one who can help me sort out all my problems, both big and small.*

21 NOV

'The king said to the girl, "Ask me for anything you want and I'll give it to you." ' Mark 6:22

KEY WORDS

'keeping a promise'

A MIDDLE-AGED MAN and woman belonged to my congregation. Both had been married previously and were now living quite lonely lives. They were attracted to each other and soon fell in love. She was a very warm lady while he appeared to be a godly man who knew the Scriptures well. So much so that he was forever quoting Bible verses. After a while they informed me that they wanted to get married and asked if I would be willing to bless the ceremony. As they were both Christians I sat them down and had a long talk with them. We all agreed that pre-marital sex was not right for Christians and they promised me faithfully that they had not, and would not do this before their wedding day. The big day came, everyone was happy, and the service was a wonderful occasion. A while afterwards I discovered that not only had this couple had sex before the wedding day, but they were also already having sex before our pre-marital discussion together. They had lied to me and the promise that they made to me was worthless. If their promise to me meant nothing, I question how sincere their promises to each other were during those actual wedding vows.

King Herod was not a good man and John the Baptist had never been frightened to point this out to both him and his queen. King Herod was at a party, where he probably had too much to drink and was watching the queen's daughter dance in front of him. The king enjoyed it so much he promised to reward her with whatever she wanted. She told this to her mother who said she should ask for John the Baptist to be killed. The king was upset by this but had to do what she asked because he had made a promise.

THE POINT

Let's be very careful what we promise people, especially if we are having fun with friends who may not be followers of Jesus. They may ask us to promise things that we may regret later.

PRAYER

Lord, today please help me not make any promises that could lead me into doing wrong things.

'Such knowledge is too wonderful for me ...' Psalm 139:6

'awesome'

THE MINISTRY OF Ishmael and Andy during the early 1970s was a fun ministry; we even once did a whole concert playing guitars while wearing gloves! Apart from two friends of ours, the two Steves, better known as Fish Co, most of the other early 'modern' Christian music was fairly serious and intense. Remember that at this time 'worship songs', as we know them today, were unheard of; most of the songs being written were songs that had a message usually for the non-believer. The range of music was vast, from folk music to very heavy rock and everything else in between. This really was an exciting time to live and the era was labelled as the Jesus Movement. But as I said, Ishmael and Andy never followed the mainstream Christian music of the day. At one concert some of the other groups that were going to perform were having a debate about who was going to sing 'Streets of London'. They had all included it in their repertoire. While they argued, Andy and I were writing out our list, including such titles as 'The Grunting Song'! It was while Ishmael and Andy were famous for performing such 'wacky' songs as 'The Grunting Song', that we put a tune to some of the verses from Psalm 139. I still rate this song as one of Ishmael and Andy's best. I suppose that being the very first Scripture song which I co-wrote, it could well have been the inspiration behind the many Scripture songs that I would be writing later.

Psalm 139 is still one of my favourite psalms and in it King David explains how God is way beyond his human comprehension. He is amazed that God knows everything about him and he is also well aware that there is nowhere he could go in the whole of the universe where God could not see him or find him. Sometimes I think we forget how big and powerful God really is and this can easily happen if we try to get over-familiar with Him.

THE POINT
'Awesome' is a great old-fashioned word to help define God. It means overwhelming wonder and admiration, and we should always be in awe of God.

PRAYER
Lord, today when I think of You I am filled with overwhelming wonder and admiration.

23 NOV 'You have heard that it was said, "Eye for eye, and tooth for tooth".' Matthew 5:38

'retaliation'

IN THE 1970s there was a popular northern Christian rock band whose lead singer Mike became a very close friend of mine. He was at the time a non-conformist Baptist minister with shoulder-length hair at the back and a bald forehead. Now this band really was outrageous! They were never afraid to speak their mind and always gave back as good as they got. I remember at one festival they believed that the Christian organisers were doing some ungodly things. So Mike preached the gospel directly to them from the main stage! They were fearless in front of any audience. I travelled with them to a school to watch them perform. They were loud, dramatic, and very powerful. Halfway through the concert and during a song introduction Mike started to share the good news of Jesus with the very rowdy non-churched audience. All went quiet except for one very loud girl right near the front who kept shouting at the band, determined to distract people from hearing about Jesus. After a while Mike could take no more of it. He jumped off the stage, stared the girl straight in the face, and through the microphone gently whispered, 'Gob it, luv, or I'll lay one on ya.' The Lancastrian pearls of wisdom delivered in a heavy Lancastrian accent seemed to do the trick, although he would probably be locked up for saying that today. The girl went silent immediately and many decided to follow Jesus that night. Effective, yes, but I'm not convinced that those would be the exact words that Jesus would have used even if He was in Lancashire!

Jesus taught a whole new way of thinking. In the Old Testament as we can see in today's verse, they would have retaliated with as good as they got. Jesus does not want His followers to retaliate or fight back. He wants us to return love for aggression and hatred. This is very hard to do as it goes against our instinct.

THE POINT **We will need to ask Jesus to help us to be able to love our enemies as it not the easiest thing to do.**

PRAYER *Lord, today help me to be able to turn the other cheek and not to fight back.*

'Let the blame rest on me' 2 Samuel 14:9

 KEY WORD **'blame'**

I AM NO mechanic but Irene's car windscreen washer was not working so I thought I had better try and fix it. I tried cleaning the nozzle but it simply gave a pathetic squirt and a few drops of water appeared. So I opened the car bonnet to see if there was another way to fix it. There wasn't. So for about half an hour I prodded and squirted the nozzle by turn, and gradually I got it sort of working; at least a dribble of water was reaching the windscreen. Later that day as Irene was about to drive off to work I proudly told her that I had fixed her windscreen washer and she seemed very appreciative. About 20 minutes later I received a phone call from a very distraught wife. She explained that she had been travelling quite fast along the dual carriageway when suddenly the car bonnet flew open and her vision had become totally obscured. She had just managed to pull over to the side of the road but the hinges had buckled on the car bonnet and it was jammed in an upright position blocking all visibility. I suddenly thought, 'Oh no, I didn't fasten the bonnet down properly.' I felt awful. I could have caused a terrible accident and injured my wife or worse. I raced over and was relieved to see that she was not hurt, only shaken. I then managed to jam the car bonnet down buckling the hinges even more in the process. It was a costly mistake but it could have been a lot more costly. A couple of weeks later a television programme ran a documentary on a car that was the same model, make and year as Irene's. And would you believe it, the programme accused the car manufacturer of using faulty bonnet locks. Dozens of accidents had been reported because of this particular car bonnet flying open. So who was really to blame, me or the manufacturer? Needless to say the manufacturers are refusing to take any blame!

 THE POINT **Nowadays people tend not to want to take the blame. They try to pass responsibility on to others. If we have done something wrong, we need to acknowledge it.**

 PRAYER *Lord, today help me not to blame someone else for something that I have done.*

'Blessed is the king who comes in the name of the Lord!' Luke 19:38

'the king and his kingdom'

ALTHOUGH I HAVE never been in close proximity to a king, I have been in the same room as a queen. When I was part of the Pioneer team we would meet regularly together to give updates on our various ministries, then share Bible teaching and prayer. When we met together with Gerald Coates and the team it was always great fun. On one such occasion, in the afternoon I remember feeling a bit sleepy having recently enjoyed a nice lunch. Gerald explained that a very special guest was going to join us that afternoon. Now this was no surprise to us; Gerald has many famous friends. Was it going to be Sir Cliff Richard or maybe an MP? He was determined to keep it a surprise, which also kept me awake. Later we saw a car draw up and a lady get out. I had no idea who she was; she certainly didn't look as if she was in the entertainment business. Gerald went to greet her and as he led her into the room he announced, as only Gerald could, 'Please welcome Her Majesty, the Queen of Romania.' It really was a queen, although I must confess I had never heard of her. We discovered later on that her kingdom was experiencing great hardship. I felt it was a great honour to be in the same room as her, and prayed both for her and her country.

History is full of kings of varying character, culture and type. Some ruled very successfully while others misused their power. Some treated the poor very badly and were only interested in making themselves rich, while doing things that would make God sad. King Jesus was very different. He loved everyone but seemed to have a special place in His heart for the poor, the vulnerable and the lonely. When Jesus entered Jerusalem on a donkey people shouted out, 'Blessed is the king'. A very short while later some of these same people would shout 'Crucify him!'

 Two thousand years on Jesus is alive. He is still the King and His kingdom is expanding day by day.

 Lord, may Your kingdom come on earth as it is in heaven.

26 NOV

'... [Moses] said, "Whoever is for the Lord, come to me."' Exodus 32:26

KEY WORD 'decisions'

IN APRIL 1978 I had to make a huge decision which, unknown to me at that time, was going to affect me for the next 16 years. Having been ordained and been the minister of a church for several years, I had moved back to the south of England. We were worshipping at a very small church which met in the local village hall. This was a church that had been started by two elders who had been sent out by the local Baptist church situated a few miles away. The aim of this church plant was to reach into the local village community. As a family we were very happy in the church because most of my relatives were there. Soon after our arrival the two elders felt it right that God wanted them to ask me to become part of the eldership. This was when I had to make a big decision. On the one hand, I believed that this is what God wanted me to do, even though I had an itinerant ministry. However, on the other hand, the other two elders were my father and my brother-in-law. I knew that if I agreed some of the congregation would consider it was unwise for three members of the same family to lead a church. I prayed and felt it was right. And, sure enough, although we saw great blessing over the next 16 years, we also received much criticism because the three of us belonged to the same family. We are all faced with decisions, although we often hate making them. Some would prefer, or find it easier, if a member of the family, a friend or even a church leader made all the decisions for us.

The Israelites had sinned against God by worshipping the golden calf and Moses said they had to make a decision. If they wanted to really follow God they had to stand with him. Some did, and some chose not to.

THE POINT Supposing Moses said the same words to us today, would we stand with him? There is a high cost to being a follower of the Lord and each day as Christians we have to make important decisions about following Him.

PRAYER *Lord, please help me to make the right decisions about following You today.*

27 NOV

'Then their eyes were opened and they recognised him ...' Luke 24:31

KEY WORDS 'not recognised'

IN THE EARLY days of Spring Harvest I led the late-night praise events for adults along with my friend Dave Bilbrough. These were lively praise times. And as people had been sitting listening to seminars throughout the day, this was a great opportunity for everyone to let their hair down. It was always packed to capacity and each night people had to be turned away. Every night before anyone was allowed in, Dave and I had to have a sound check, to make sure that all the volume levels were correct. One night I was onstage testing the microphones and I asked Dave to stand at the back of the hall to see if the sound was clear enough. I heard him shout out yes, then immediately the lights went down, the doors opened, and hundreds of people rushed in. We liked to pray before the event and I started to get anxious because Dave had not returned and we were due to begin the programme in a very short time. What on earth had happened to him? Then, just seconds before we were due to start, he came rushing up to me all hot and bothered. He explained that when the crowd rushed in, somehow he got pushed outside the door and the stewards, not recognising him, said they could not allow him back into the hall as the venue was full. He kept telling them that he was Dave Bilbrough who was hosting the show, but obviously the stewards didn't think that Dave Bilbrough looked like Dave Bilbrough!

Jesus had been crucified and some of His friends did not believe that He had come back to life. In today's verse two of Jesus' best friends are walking along the road talking to the resurrected Jesus, but not recognising it was Him until He gave thanks for some bread and handed it to them.

THE POINT **Jesus may not appear to us so we can see Him with our eyes, but every day He is with us; that is a fact we need to recognise, and believe.**

PRAYER *Lord, please help me today to recognise that You are with me all through the day. You are with me in the good times, and You are with me in the difficult times.*

'I am the LORD, who heals you.' Exodus 15:26

 KEY WORDS 'the Lord heals'

MANY YEARS AGO I was invited to teach at the Elim youth camp on the Isle of Wight. Roy, my lighting engineer, accompanied me. We took the ferry crossing then decided to have an early night in the luxury accommodation provided for us in the form of an old tent! Early Saturday morning I woke up feeling dreadful. I had a terrible pain in my lower back and felt very nauseous. I knew I must be ill because I couldn't even face the cooked breakfast! I was driven to the Accident and Emergency department of the nearest hospital and immediately rushed into a little cubicle. They tried to lay me down on a bed but I couldn't physically lie down. I just walked around the bed in agony, praying in tongues. They diagnosed kidney stones in both kidneys and a kidney infection. After inserting a catheter into me (ouch) they raced me over to another hospital. I was put in a ward and at last given some painkillers. After one night I decided to discharge myself because I just wanted to get home. If all I had to do was to wait patiently until the stones rolled away, I may as well do that in the comfort of my own home. The doctor explained that my problem had been caused by dehydration and advised that I should drink at least two pints of fluid each night. I remember smiling and saying I'd try! Once home in my own bed I had visitors galore coming to pray for me. Our own children and their cousins decided to hold a little prayer meeting for me in the garden shed. Their prayers were answered and within hours those stones were rolled away and I was back on the road again.

THE POINT Throughout all my years of travel God has kept me wonderfully fit, so this kidney problem came as a major shock. I praised God for the doctors and the medical staff and I also praised God for those adults and children who prayed for me. The drugs calmed down the pain and the prayers got rid of the kidney stones in double-quick time!

 PRAYER *Lord, today I think of those in hospital. Please use the medical staff and also our prayers to bring about healing.*

29 NOV ‘ *"Follow me," Jesus told him, and Levi got up and followed him.' Mark 2:14*

KEY WORDS ‘follow me’

ANDY PIERCY, THE better-looking half of Ishmael and Andy, had been a friend of mine before either of us started following Jesus. I became a committed Christian before Andy, but when he eventually turned to the Christian faith, he wanted to be a true disciple. He read in the Bible about Jesus telling His followers that they would only need one set of clothes. Much to his parents' horror, one of the first things that he did as a Christian was to take all his clothes, except one article of each, and drop them off at the local charity shop. Andy was just a few months from completing an apprenticeship with the Post Office that would qualify him for a very good job. But he believed that God had called him to work with me, so told his parents that he must leave his job straightaway. Everyone, including church leaders, told Andy the sensible thing to do would be to complete his qualification and then, if things went wrong, he would always have a job to fall back on. Andy just told them that God wanted him to start working for Him now, not in a few months' time, and if God had called him, there was no way he would ever need to fall back on the Post Office. To this day, Andy has never needed those Post Office qualifications because God has called him and qualified him in a wonderful ministry of music.

Matthew had a very good job, collecting people's taxes. Although it was not a career that would make him popular, in all probability he was set for life with a regular income. Then along came Jesus. We do not hear that Jesus had a long conversation with Matthew, or even promised him a better job, He just simply said, 'Follow me,' and immediately Matthew did so.

THE POINT   Jesus stills calls you and me to follow Him today. For some it will be to follow Him as we study or as we work, for others it will be to follow Him with no promise of any income except to trust that He will provide all our needs. Either way Jesus has said the words 'follow me' to all of us at one time or another.

PRAYER   *Lord, today I am going to follow You.*

30 NOV *'Then Abram gave him a tenth of everything.' Genesis 14:20*

KEY WORDS 'giving money'

RECENTLY I WAS invited to lead a school assembly and a family event. I did the assembly and had a great time. After the assembly the organiser asked me if I would visit his parents as they'd been at Bible college with me many years earlier. They had spent a lot of their lives overseas doing missionary work. He also explained that they were now quite old and almost blind. I went with him and when we arrived at their house and I saw their faces, memories came flooding back. They were frail and could hardly see me, but were obviously thrilled that I had the time to call in and visit. After a bit of talk and prayer I got up to leave, but as I did so the husband pushed a lot of money in my hand. At first I didn't want to receive it as this couple were far from wealthy, but then I saw that they would be offended if I didn't take it. I thanked them so much and also thanked the Lord, because in my work every gift is gratefully received. As I left, their son was so grateful to me for visiting them and told me just this small act had added a lot of joy to their lives. I told him that even without the gift, seeing his faithful, godly parents had also added a lot of joy to my life.

Today's verse mentions giving a tenth, which nowadays in church life is called a tithe. Abraham gave it to Melchizedek about whom we really know very little. Certainly Abraham must have thought he was very special, to give him a tenth of all he owned. Nowadays, we are encouraged to give a tenth of our income to our local church as a minimum of our giving. Some agree with this, others may not, but let's never forget that Jesus today does not want just a tithe, He wants our whole life, which includes all of our possessions and money.

THE POINT All we have belongs to Jesus so it should not be too hard to pass His money on to bless others.

PRAYER *Lord, today I realise You do not want 10 per cent, you want 100 per cent of all I have.*

01 DEC

'You were running a good race. Who cut in on you and kept you from obeying the truth?' Galatians 5:7

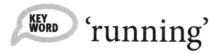

KEY WORD 'running'

I DECIDED IT was time to shape up. All my middle-age flab appeared to be getting flabbier and this 'temple', although not quite turning into a ruin, was certainly in a state of disrepair. One of the younger men in our church was keen on jogging and heard about my desire to get fit. He was soon on the phone telling me that he was sure that he could be of some assistance in this matter. A few days later he appeared on my doorstep in tracksuit and trainers and I had obediently, at his request, purchased similar attire. I felt fitter just by putting these fitness clothes on! Then off we set. Now, I struggle to identify my limitations. If someone else can do something, my mind assures me that I can do it too. I asked him how far he usually jogged and he told me a few miles. 'Let's do it, then,' I said. He was a bit wary about my enthusiasm since this was my first jog and also after surveying how unfit I was. But he also knew that I was not one to be argued with. Well, needless to say, I only just completed the run. As I staggered across the threshold of our house, Irene saw by the colour of my face, that I was about to faint. I had to lie down to recover. Then, worse, for the next few days the aching muscles were dreadful. From that time on, I decided that maybe jogging was not for me. Perhaps football was the answer – watching it on the television that is!

Running in lanes looks quite straightforward, until another runner cuts in front and causes an obstruction. The Galatians were obviously running well for Jesus and then someone cut across them and slowed them down by telling them lies. We must beware of this today.

THE POINT **Real truth can only be found in God's Word, and if someone tries to pass on 'good ideas' which are not biblical, we had better watch out. Lies will slow us down and mess up the 'race we are running' to live our lives for Jesus.**

PRAYER *Lord, don't let anyone obstruct me today as I run the Christian 'race'.*

'Sing to God, sing praise to his name ...' Psalm 68:4

 KEY WORDS **'happy faces'**

PUPPETS ARE GREAT. Puppets can be used to great effect to communicate the Bible to children, but I have never quite understood how people imagine that lifeless things could ever teach anyone to praise God or to reflect the joy of the Lord. At one church in America I was amazed by what I saw. It was a children's meeting and the children's leaders did all the fun stuff with the children. So far so good. But then came the serious bit. It was then that the puppets took over. A puppet preached and then even gave an appeal and invited children to come forward for prayer. I'm sorry, but I just can't get my head around that! At another meeting the puppets performed and were miming Christian lyrics to well-known sixties pop songs. Why were they ruining some of my favourite sixties songs by adding cheesy 'Christian' lyrics? However, the worst thing of all was that not one of those puppets had a happy face. They either looked downright grumpy or downright scary! Perhaps they were meant to represent adult Christians singing their praise in church. I certainly hope not, hardly good role models for little children! Singing and praising God brings joy to my heart and a smile to my face and I know even just looking happy can cheer up people around me. Moving on from puppets, as I travel I have experienced various types of praise. I have enjoyed listening to excellent choirs who sound majestic but who look so glum. I have enjoyed listening to brilliant soloists with the most wonderfully trained voices, but downcast expressions. I have heard the very best Christian 'worship' bands, but who always look miserable because it's the cool way to look. I have also seen children who will never sing in a choir or be soloists or rock singers, but they sing with a huge happy smile on their faces. Their facial expression reveals that they really enjoying praising God. You can guess who I enjoy watching and listening to the most, can't you!

 THE POINT **When we sing to the Lord let's show our joy towards Him not just in words, but also in our face.**

 PRAYER *Lord, today please let my happy face reflect my thankful heart.*

03 DEC

'Everyone who hears these word of mine and puts them into practice is like a wise man who built his house on the rock.' Matthew 7:24

KEY WORD 'underwater'

I LIVE NEAR the picturesque village of Old Bosham. This village has a very quiet, pretty harbour and thousands of tourists come and visit each year. It is my mother's favourite place. But I think the reason for that is the quaint little tea shop which attracts her like a magnet. The village boasts relatively few houses which makes it one of the most expensive areas in which to live. As well as the teashop, there is one of the oldest church buildings in Sussex, Holy Trinity. Buried in the graveyard is the young daughter of King Canute, who sadly drowned in a nearby pond in the eleventh century. It's also believed that this may have been King Harold's final resting place after his battle at Hastings. The Venerable Bede even informs us that St Wilfred, who came to convert the southern Saxons to Christianity, spent quite a bit of time here. But that's history. What fascinates me today is the harbour. At low tide there is no sign of water so people assume it's safe to park on the shore as they explore the village. But that's where many have become unstuck, or should I say stuck! The tide comes in very quickly and if a car has been left on the shore, in a short time it will be underwater! In the little village pub there are lots of photographs of the cars that have ended up submerged.

The story of the wise and foolish men is a favourite story that is told to children but, as I've said before, it's a frightening story. Jesus said for those who follow Him, it is like building their life on a solid rock and a very firm foundation. However, for those who choose to build their life on anything else, it's like building on sand and when the rain and flood come, their house – in other words, life – will be sunk, literally, underwater!

THE POINT This story should make us all the more thankful that we are followers of Jesus, and all the more urgent in telling our friends, who may have built on the sand, the good news of Jesus.

PRAYER *Lord, today please give me the opportunity to pass on Your good news to those who at this time may be living on sand.*

04 DEC *'As Solomon grew old, his wives turned his heart after other gods ...' 1 Kings 11: 4*

KEY WORDS 'turning hearts'

SOME OF MY closest friends are young musicians. A while ago a group of these young musicians formed a band and were determined not to fall into the oversubscribed 'praise and worship' category. They were really determined to take God into the secular rock world. Each one of them was an excellent musician. When they started touring with some name bands, Irene and I had the privilege of going to see them in concert, and they were very good. As time went on they became even more totally dedicated to the band, but this was when things started to go wrong. It was a dedication to their band and their music, which is not the same as a dedication to the Lord and His plans for them. The band rehearsals and recording became a priority over everything else, and it was easy to notice that some of the members were not as strong spiritually as they once had been. Then God did a wonderful renewal work in their lives. After a lot of honest soul searching some of them realised that their commitment to the band was actually turning their heart away from God. Although it was going to be a struggle because of their love for music, they were willing to put things right with God even if it meant finishing a very successful band.

Solomon may have been one of the wisest guys ever, but I wonder how wise he was when he chose to marry 700 wives of royal birth. In addition, he had 300 'sleeping partners'. I guess he thought that to marry all these royal ladies from other nations would bring peace and prosperity to his kingdom. Sadly, his wisdom seemed to ignore the fact that they worshipped other gods, and they brought them into his palace. We should all be peacemakers but not at the cost of breaking God's word or of compromise. How sad that God's friend Solomon in the end allowed these ladies to lead him in the wrong way.

THE POINT **Remember that things that begin with Godly intentions can be the very same things that turn our hearts from Him.**

PRAYER *Lord, today make me wiser than Solomon; I won't let anything turn my heart from You.*

05 DEC 'Those controlled by the sinful nature cannot please God.' *Romans 8:8*

 KEY WORD 'controlled'

SPRING HARVEST IS the largest Christian holiday event in Europe. At its peak there must have been nearly 100,000 people attending the holiday camps where it was being held. One year I volunteered to do all three weeks, and even said that I would stay on for a fourth week to minister at the Assemblies of God Bible Week which was held on the same site. That would mean four weeks living in a not very nice chalet and eating not very nice food. But I loved the challenge. The three Spring Harvest weeks went very well but were totally exhausting. Irene and I were responsible for overseeing 1,000 eight- to eleven-year-olds plus a team of 80 adult helpers for many hours each day. We did see God do some great things in the children's lives, but that did not take away the extreme exhaustion I suffered. The fourth week was a much harder week. I didn't know the site leaders or their expectations and being overtired did not help. On the Sunday they put all the children in one venue and asked me to look after them, practically single-handed, while all the adults held a Communion service. By this time I knew I was running on both spiritual and physical autopilot. When I eventually arrived home exhausted I knew I was going to be battling away with my sinful nature. I was far more likely to snap at Irene and the children. I was far more likely to have selfish thoughts. I was far more likely to do and say things that I would not normally do or say. With God's help I knew that I must try to overcome that old nature, but I knew that it was not going to be an easy thing to do.

But it's not just when I am tired that my old sinful nature tries to drag me down; strangely enough, it can happen when I have been involved in doing something that God has really blessed, which is another time when I become vulnerable.

 THE POINT We must try not to let our old nature take control again, but we'll need God's help to stop this happening.

 PRAYER *Lord, please help me today not to allow my old nature to take control.*

06 DEC *'We remember the fish we ate in Egypt at no cost – also the cucumbers, melons, leeks, onions and garlic.' Numbers 11:5*

'interesting food'

I WAS INVITED to Amsterdam to lead a weekend at the Youth With A Mission base and I took a friend with me for company. Now having worked with YWAM many times before, I know at times they can live quite frugally, so I thought I was prepared for anything. On arrival everyone was very welcoming and I was shown to the lecture room where I gave my first teaching seminar. Following this it was lunchtime and we were pretty hungry. We were then served up a little rice and very little else. I began to think that times must be really hard for these students over here. After the lunch I did some more teaching and, I must admit, I was getting really hungry and counting the hours until the evening meal. At last six o'clock came and again we sat down with the students, and again out came a small portion of rice and very little else. I'm afraid that was it. My friend and I sneaked out and found a café selling frikkadels and fries and we heartily tucked into a large portion each. When we arrived back the director was standing on the doorstep. We hadn't met him yet and we wondered if he could detect the smell of frikkadels and fries. He then apologised about the food and explained that the students were experimenting by living on the diet and rations of a country in Asia that they were soon to visit and he had not expected us to live on the same diet. We laughed and said it was no problem, but still did not confess to him about our hearty supper.

The Israelites were bored with the Lord's provision of manna. Reminiscing about their past they longed for what they used to eat back in Egypt. What an ungrateful people they were. They had forgotten how God had rescued them from slavery and could only remember the good food they once had.

THE POINT **Remembering the past is important as it is our history, but we must not live in it.**

PRAYER *Lord, thank You for today. Help me not to live in unreal memories of the past.*

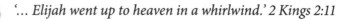
 # **KEY WORD** 'whirlwind'

IRENE AND I were enjoying a winter sunshine break and our hotel was quite a distance from the beach. Now although there were only the two of us on this trip we carried our towels, sun cream, books, goggles, bottles of water, MP3 player, mats, beach umbrella and my folding chair all the way to the beach. Much to Irene's embarrassment, for some reason or another my folding chair always accompanies me on holiday. We trudged about a mile over rough terrain until we reached the sand. The beach was beautiful, surrounded by stunning cliffs and a bright blue sea. We found a good space between two families. Then I put up our umbrella, set out our mats and towels, set up my chair and sank into it, ready to tuck into my holiday reading. Ah bliss, at last. After a while I looked up from my book and in the distant hills I noticed a cloud of dust blowing up. As I looked more closely I could see it appeared to be a small whirlwind. Soon most other people on the beach were also staring at it. Then we noticed it was heading downhill and rapidly approaching our beach. It was a tiny cloud not much taller than me, so no great alarm. It got closer and closer then, would you believe it, out of miles of beach, it was heading straight for Irene and me. As it hit us I grabbed the umbrella and everything else that was being whipped up in the air, while Irene just grabbed hold of me! She knew she was safe hanging on to a 13-stone anchor. Then the miniature tornado just disappeared into the sea whipping up waves en route.

 THE POINT On reflection, it would have been a nice way to go had it been God's time that we should join Him in heaven. Just like Elijah in today's verse, going up on a dusty lift that goes right up to heaven itself, with no pain involved. God has a set time for when we will leave this earth and go and live with Him for ever, and we do not know when that time is. Are we ready to meet Him if it's today?

 PRAYER *Lord, I want to be ready to meet You, be that today or in many years' time.*

08 DEC *'It is unthinkable that God would do wrong ...' Job 34:12*

 KEY WORD 'unthinkable'

I REALISE THAT everyone, including Christians, must die, but what I cannot understand is why some Christians have to go through so much suffering and pain before they die. It cannot be counted as persecution and it doesn't even seem to give glory to God. In the last few days of my father's life I tried everything to keep him alive. I had seen God do so many healings that I was really convinced that He was going to do another. At times my gentle father, who had served God faithfully for many years, looked as if he was in turmoil and great pain. Why didn't God step in at this point? Why did he have to rely upon an ever-increasing dose of painkillers to reduce the agony he was suffering? I didn't blame God for the pain and suffering that he went through, although for a while I did wrongly blame God when my prayers were not answered and he died. I just couldn't understand why God could let his life end in such a way. Years later, I realise that God's timing was perfect; it was my father's time to go. A lot of things happened after his death that I think he would have found very hard to cope with. I still have questions, but one thing I firmly believe is that God can do no wrong. Today's verse reminds us of this. It is not only unthinkable, it's also the greatest impossibility in the world; God is perfect in every way.

But do we all believe this? Our newspapers are full of people blaming God for every war, every famine, in fact, every terrible thing that happens. Notice the same writers never thank Him when there is good news and things are going well. But even you and I need to be careful. Sometimes God does not answer our prayers in the way we would like Him to, so we may accuse Him of not listening or even not caring. It is unthinkable that God could do wrong!

 THE POINT **As I said earlier we may not understand some of God's decisions but we must believe that He always makes the right ones. He can do no wrong.**

 PRAYER *Lord, today I know that You are God, You can never do any wrong thing.*

09 DEC *'Much dreaming and many words are meaningless. Therefore stand in awe of God.' Ecclesiastes 5:7*

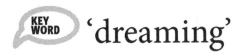 **KEY WORD** '**dreaming**'

MANY PEOPLE, ESPECIALLY during the 1990s, experienced the power of God come so strongly on them that for some reason or another they have ended up crumbling flat on to the floor. This experience has been called many things, including 'slain in the Spirit', a description I am unsure about. It sounds more like God's punishment rather than just peacefully resting in God. It happened to me many times, usually when someone prayed for me, but there have been times when I have ended up lying on the floor just because of the sheer power of God that has been present in a meeting. My legs just seemed to give way and down I'd go, feeling a wonderful sense of God's peace. One of the most amazing experiences I had was when I decided to have one of my many short afternoon 'power' naps. As I lay on my bed I felt really relaxed and soon dozed off. Then I started to dream, and I dreamt that someone was praying for me and as they prayed, I ended up lying on the floor. It was a strange dream because I was lying on my bed, yet dreaming that I was lying on the floor and feeling totally, totally relaxed in the presence of God. This was a unique experience. When I woke up from that sleep I felt indescribably relaxed and full of God's power. Most of my dreams are meaningless and rubbish and I forget them very quickly, but occasionally God speaks to me in a dream and in the morning that dream is still very vivid. I remember one night I dreamt I was writing a song and the words and music were so clear I woke up in the middle of the night and went downstairs and recorded the song straight away as I was frightened that I would forget it by the morning.

 THE POINT One little warning, though: we must be careful what we watch on the TV or what we read before we go to bed, because sometimes this can cause our dreams not only to be meaningless – they can be really nasty.

 PRAYER *Lord, if I dream tonight please help my dreams to be pleasant ones.*

'Let them praise his name with dancing ...' Psalm 149:3

KEY WORD 'dancing'

WHILE MINISTERING IN Durban, South Africa, we were invited to go and visit a Zulu reservation. Now as well as Irene and I on this ministry team there was an intercessory prayer group from Australia, made up of children and their parents and also a rather well-built American preacher. On the free day our hosts treated us all to the Zulu experience. I could sense that the prayer team were a little unsure about even being there because they felt the Zulu dances might be linked to the worship of pagan gods. I, however, not being quite so spiritual, just wanted to enjoy the show. I love rhythmic music and I knew that the Zulu drumming could teach some of our Christian drummers a thing or two. All was going very well and then came a scary bit. When I say scary, it was only scary for our American preacher. As we sat observing the crowd it was obvious that the Zulu women, who themselves were hardly size 10, had a theory about large men. We were informed that they believed that the more a man weighed the more prosperous he must be. Near the end of the performance one of these large dancing ladies took hold of our American preacher and forced him to dance with her. He looked terrified – not of pagan gods, but of her! I found this hilarious and immediately left my seat and joined him on the dance floor. I hasten to add that I was not dancing, I was filming him with my video camera, threatening to send my film back to his home church in America. Over the years I have had many dancers on my team who have really been able to praise God using dance. Interesting also that it has not always been girls; we have had some great male dancers as well.

THE POINT It's beautiful watching people praise God with dance as in today's verse: We all need to find a way to express our praise to God but, like singing, dancing may not be everyone's gift.

PRAYER *Lord, today I am going to praise Your name with dancing, but maybe not in public.*

11 DEC *'Praise be to the Lord, to God our Saviour, who daily bears our burdens.' Psalm 68:19*

KEY WORDS 'carrying burdens'

AT THE TIME of writing we rent a space on the first floor of a building that has no lift but lots of doors. Here we store all the PA equipment, Irene's boxes of seminar materials, and all my CDs, DVDs and books. Every time we set off to take seminars or a concert booking, Irene and I have to carry all these things down the stairs to the car and every time we arrive back, up they all go again. It's sometimes easier on our return as, hopefully, we have sold some books, so at least that box is a little lighter.

A short while ago I was carrying the PA system back up the stairs and felt something go in my back. Having heard many horror stories from my friends with back problems I was a little worried; if this turned out to be long-term, it could really affect my ministry. Praise the Lord, after a bit of prayer the aching only lasted a short while but it was a warning about lifting heavy things. Of course in days gone by I have never even thought about the effects on my back through lifting. When I was young and working on the farm I was very fit and healthy. The corn and animal food would arrive on large lorries in very heavy sacks. A friend and I would often have a competition to see who could bear the greatest burden of heavy sacks on our backs for the longest period of time. It was a crazy thing to do, but no one seemed to worry so much about back problems in those days. Nowadays, we still tend to carry spiritual burdens, although not through choice. We are burdened by tough times at work, problems in the home, and even, dare I say it, difficult times in church.

 THE POINT The good news is we need not walk around struggling with those great heavy burdens; the Lord says He is willing to take them from us so we can be free and released again.

 PRAYER *Lord, please today release me from any burdens that are weighing me down.*

12 DEC *'Come to me, all you who are weary and burdened, and I will give you rest.' Matthew 11:28*

 KEY WORD 'rest'

I HAVE COME to the conclusion that there is no such thing as a 'Christian' holiday. Some close friends very kindly let us use their cottage in the Cotswolds for a few days so that we could have a bit of a break from music and touring. Their house was situated right next door to the village primary school. As I was in the garden collecting some logs for the fire I could hear the children in the playground. God spoke to me and clearly told me that He wanted me to take an assembly there. Of course I tried to argue that I was having a break away from music and needed a rest. I even told God that they would never have heard of me in the school. In fact, in such a remote village, I wondered if they would have heard of Him! There was no way that they would let me, a perfect stranger, just walk in and take an assembly. God continued to tell me to do it. The next day, I obediently gave a note to the school secretary and, just as I had thought, she had never heard of me but promised to hand it to the head teacher. Within hours my phone rang and a delighted head teacher invited me to take a specially laid-on assembly and the whole school would attend. Well, the whole school did attend, all 59 of them, and I sang some songs and taught them about the Christian faith. It was amazing; both the teachers and children agreed that it was the best assembly that they had ever been to and the head teacher urged me to come back as soon as possible. Of course I spent the rest of the break signing autographs and chatting to the children over the garden wall. The moral of the story is this: a holiday may take us to a different location, but for those who rest in God and not just on a sun bed, our ministry continues!

 THE POINT Real rest comes by spending time with Jesus, not just 'getting away from it all'.

 PRAYER *Lord, today I realise that if I stay obedient to You, You will give me all the rest I need.*

13
DEC

'These are the men that David put in charge of the music in the house of the LORD *…' 1 Chronicles 6:31*

KEY WORD > 'musician'

I WAS INVITED to lead a musical event in the West Country. On previous visits I had used local musicians but decided for a change just to use CDs, DVDs and my acoustic guitar and give the musicians a break. It was a hard venue for my interactive participation songs as the seats were all fixed pews with little room to move around. Anyway, we had a good turnout of all ages and plenty of children who seemed to enjoy the event. A few months later I met the organiser's wife at a conference. She approached me with the greeting that everyone felt I had had an 'off' night on my last visit and was not nearly as good as I had been on previous visits. This came as a bit of a shock and I didn't really know how to respond. I suggested it may have been the cold, or the pews, but she insisted it was me who was 'off', which felt quite demoralising. I asked her if she could be more specific and she said it was the music. I did not use the local musicians. It was then I realised the motive behind her criticism. Her husband was one of the musicians and she was upset because I chose not to use him. In her opinion the evening was a disaster because I had not involved him. When I am invited to lead a musical event, I believe that I must be, under God's guidance, in charge of the music. King David loved music and it was a priority for him to put men in charge of the music in the house of the Lord to see it was done well. Nowadays, music still has quite a priority in many of our meetings. I always encourage both young and old to learn to play an instrument and don't give up when the rehearsals gets boring and other things seem more exciting.

THE POINT > **Once we have learned to play even simple tunes on an instrument, God can use that talent, and also the musician can find it really satisfying and relaxing.**

PRAYER > *Lord, I thank You today that music can help me to praise You.*

14 DEC

'Then put my cup, the silver one, in the mouth of the youngest one's sack …' Genesis 44:2

'changed'

MY FRIEND STEVE, who is an escapologist and magician, uses escapes and tricks to communicate the good news of Jesus to people. Now, he loves playing the odd practical joke, so I thought that I would play one on him. We were both sharing the stage in a large thousand-seater auditorium. He was going to do a trick that I had seen him do many times before. He would get a child onstage, ask them to remove a sock, then put that sock into a bag. He would then ask the audience if they believed that he could turn that one sock into a pair. After a lot of banter he would pull a plastic pear out of his bag. Just before his act, I changed the plastic pear in his bag for a battery. They both weighed about the same and I was sure that Steve would not notice the switch. Sure enough, the time came for the trick. He went through the routine, put his hand into the bag, and, with a roll of the drums, announced: 'Ladies and gentlemen, you all witnessed me put one sock into the bag, now here, as if by magic, I have a ...' but instead of saying 'pair' he said '… battery?' Then, in front of the whole audience, he shouted 'Ishmael, I'm going to get you.' He immediately started chasing me around the stage, much to everyone's delight. I don't know how many people knew that this was not 'staged', but it certainly raised a lot of laughter.

Steve was shocked to find a battery in his bag, but not half as shocked as young Benjamin was when he found Joseph's silver cup in his grain sack. This story had a very happy ending, though, as Joseph didn't seek revenge on his wicked brothers, but showed them great love and forgiveness.

THE POINT **Joseph knew that over the years his brothers had changed for the better. I wonder if those around us notice that we have changed in the past year and are gradually becoming more like Jesus.**

PRAYER *Lord, I pray today that people might see that my life is changing and becoming more like Yours as the years go by.*

15 DEC

'Their venom is like the venom of a snake ...' Psalm 58:4

KEY WORD 'venom'

KING DAVID DRAWS an analogy between the evil of the wicked and the poisonous venom of a snake. On one of our ministry trips to Arkansas, Irene and I were taking a short break, relaxing by a friend's pool. I noticed a small brown spider, so I thought, for a bit of fun, I would manoeuvre it under Irene's sun bed and make her jump. I knew she wasn't keen on spiders. OK, I know, I'm a terrible husband and you are wondering how Irene has managed to put up with me for all these years! Anyway, I flicked the spider with my foot and it ran off in the opposite direction. So Irene carried on undisturbed and completely oblivious of the spider. Later, we joined a church group to minister at a camp in the mountains. I suddenly felt ill with a raging fever and was sick. My head was thumping and I felt dreadful. My foot was hurting and swollen so much that I couldn't get my shoe on. One of the team recognised the symptoms and asked if I had encountered a small brown spider. I had to confess about the one I had tried to flick at Irene earlier. He examined my swollen foot and told me that I had been bitten by a very venomous spider called the 'brown recluse'. I was taken to the clinic but the doctor did nothing except tell me that the bite could affect the surrounding tissue and muscle, which was not the news I wanted to hear! Back at the church one of the church leaders, who had great faith, asked me to remove my sock and shoe. He spat on to my foot and prayed. I had never heard of spit being used before, except when Jesus healed the blind man. The great news was that God wonderfully healed me and I soon felt fine again.

THE POINT
Our verse tells us that wicked people can be venomous just like a snake, or spider. Although their poisonous words can bring damage and hurt to followers of Jesus, we must still pray for them; they are not beyond saving and Jesus still loves them.

PRAYER
Lord, help me today to pray for those people who seem full of poison.

16 DEC

'... where the Spirit of the Lord is, there is freedom.' 2 Corinthians 3:17

KEY WORD 'freedom'

WE WERE INVITED to participate in a family day that was being organised by a friend in Wells Cathedral. It was a beautiful hot sunny day and coachloads of children arrived from different parishes all having made banners which represented their local church. As everyone arrived we all met up in the Bishop's Palace Gardens where the organiser introduced me to the children. Then there was a programme of outdoor games where everyone joined in. After a while everyone divided up to take part in various workshops held all around the cathedral and grounds. The children were able to participate in everything from creative art to dance and flags. My sessions were on song writing and music. I was in a marquee outside and it was a great atmosphere teaching the children in the bright sunshine. At the end of the day we all met together inside the cathedral itself for a final time of praise. It was amazing to see everyone so happy and dancing around in such an historic building. I was so pleased to see the archdeacon join in, dressed in a very colourful clerical shirt which had been presented to him on a visit to Africa. The highlight for me, though, was when we sang the last song which was called 'Freedom', the same words as those in today's verse. Imagine seeing hundreds of children marching out of the cathedral waving banners and singing, 'Where the Spirit of the Lord is, there is freedom.' Awesome!

Long before I became a committed Christian I remember spending just a few hours in a very small prison cell for driving my car dangerously. It was horrible being trapped in a small room with no window and the door locked. Before we were Christians, the Bible tells us that we were like prisoners to sin and that Jesus died to free us from all our wrongdoing. By allowing the Holy Spirit to live inside us, we can live a life enjoying real freedom.

THE POINT Jesus died to set us free. We must not allow any person to put chains back on us again.

PRAYER *Lord, today I thank You that I have been freed from my sin and live in freedom to worship You.*

17 DEC

'All kinds of animals, birds, reptiles and creatures of the sea are being tamed and have been tamed by man,' James 3:7

 KEY WORD 'tamed'

AS A TEENAGER I owned a Ford Popular car. Now for those who cannot remember the days when all cars were sprayed black, this model really was one of the most boring-looking cars imaginable. Especially to a trendy sixties teenager like myself when the fashion was all kaftans, bells and beads. One thing I have never liked is boring. So, I decided to 'reinvent' my car with a little help from my friends. A spot of paint soon transformed my vehicle into a multicoloured psychedelic machine. Then we added little extras like Union Jack headlights, ultra-loud air horns, and a painted toilet seat on the front grill. Thus my car was a pure joy to behold. I proved this by getting stopped everywhere, either by intrigued passers-by or interrogating policemen. On one particular trip we visited Longleat Safari Park. I thought it was time to wake up those sleepy lions with our air horns because they looked more stuffed than real. Within minutes we were surrounded by a pride of vicious-looking Aslan types. These were rapidly followed by an even more frightening sight, a Land Rover full of rifle-toting game wardens pointing at us and/or the lions. After a little verbal exchange, which was about as colourful as my car, we were escorted towards the gate and ordered to leave. The wardens were very upset that we had upset their animals; we were even more upset that we had paid a lot of money just to see a jeep full of angry wardens. Today's Bible verse reminds us that most animals can be tamed to a certain degree. My little anecdote is a prime example of something more difficult to tame, that pink flappy thing inside our mouth. There have been many times when I have both dished out and been on the receiving end of a good tongue-lashing. I have hurt and been hurt and realise the pain it can cause.

 THE POINT **It's hard to tame the human tongue which is capable of inflicting more pain and hurt than the paws or jaws of a wild animal.**

 PRAYER *Lord, please help me today to think before I open my mouth; I do not want to hurt anyone with the words that I say.*

18 DEC

'He who believes in me will live, even though he dies;' John 11:25

KEY WORDS 'living after dying'

I WAS IN a very large hall faced with about 1,000 eight- to eleven-year-old children. I had spent quite a while teaching how important healing was in the Bible and had then given some personal testimony about healings that I had seen. I wanted to pave the way for the children so that they could contribute. I asked any who had seen or experienced healing to come to the microphone and tell us all about what they had seen. Many did come forward and shared some great stories of how God had healed people. Then a young boy took the microphone and started telling us about his grandfather and how he had been seriously ill with cancer. The excitement level was building up now in all of us; no one had seen someone healed from cancer, especially a grandfather. 'And how is your grandfather now?' I asked, expecting him to say that he was healed, but he answered that he had died. Everything went quiet; even I didn't know how to follow that. Then I noticed that the little boy was not sad, he really believed that Jesus had 'healed' his grandfather by letting him die and so had released him of the great pain that he was suffering. He also believed that his grandfather was in a far better place now, as he was living with Jesus.

Most of us have witnessed a hearse pass by. Through the windows we see the pall-bearers dressed in black, looking very sombre. In the back of the hearse the coffin contains the body of the person who has passed away. Often a coffin is draped and covered in beautiful flowers. Inside the car behind are the relatives and friends of the person who has died, again looking sombre and sad. Death is sad, but it's not all bad news. Jesus says that even though we die, those who believe in Him will live.

THE POINT **Death is the Christian's door into a new life and heaven where there will be no more pain and no more sadness.**

PRAYER *Lord, today I thank You that the grave is not the end for the Christian, it's just the beginning.*

19 DEC

'Enlarge the place of your tent, stretch your tent curtains wide, do not hold back …' Isaiah 54:2

KEY WORD 'tent'

IN MY 'ISHMAEL, the wild hairy man days' before I committed my life to following Jesus, a few friends and myself jumped into my multicoloured car and drove to the West Country. We'd heard of this very cheap potent drink called scrumpy and had decided to go to the place where it was produced to experience it at first hand. We purchased a few flagons then merrily quaffed the lethal brew. It tasted dreadful, like salt water, but in no time the taste didn't seem to matter as we were happily singing away. Although the drink-driving laws were not strictly enforced in those days, I knew I was unfit to drive. So we just drove a short distance down a country lane in the dark before we rigged up our tent and put our heads down. We were wakened early by an alarm clock and I asked one of my friends to switch it off. After looking around the tent he remembered he had not brought one; the ringing was coming from outside. Gingerly we looked out and realised that we had pitched our tent in someone's driveway. The guy ropes were tied at one end to my headlights and at the other to the gatepost of a house. The alarm was coming from the bedroom window of the owner just a few feet away from the tent. I have never seen a tent dismantled and a car move off so quickly. Strong stuff that scrumpy, and I don't recommend it!

In today's verse we find Isaiah prophesying that good times were in store in future. He uses the analogy of the tent to illustrate this. After my 'wild years', we took our family on many camping holidays. It was really the only holiday that we could afford and it was always great fun. If you think about it, though, a tent takes up a tiny space of ground. Five of us would eat and sleep in an area not much bigger than our car.

THE POINT God promises us great things if we follow Him, so we, too, better get ready to expand our tent area for all the good things that He has prepared for us.

PRAYER *Lord, today I want to be prepared for all the great things that You have got lined up for me.*

20 DEC *'No-one has ever seen God …' 1 John 4:12*

KEY WORD 'see'

WITH OUR FRIENDS Jeff and Kay Lucas we booked to stay in what sounded an idyllic hotel on the Welsh border. We envisaged spending the weekend together taking lots of beautiful country walks, then relaxing in luxury in front of a roaring log fire. When we arrived at our destination we found a dilapidated, large, creepy country house which resembled something akin to the one in the TV series *The Munsters*. Jeff and I decided that we would ask to check out the rooms first. The receptionist was very helpful and had no problem handing us the keys. Meanwhile Irene and Kay waited in reception. We ascended the grand staircase and noticed that some of the bedrooms were decorated in original 1960s style. Eventually, we came to a series of corridors that were hopefully going to lead to our room. Then it happened. One of the fire doors closed and we were stranded in this long maze of corridors in the pitch black. We couldn't see a thing and were fumbling around trying to find a light or a door. By now of course we were in hysterics, falling over each other and totally lost. About 15 minutes later we rejoined the ladies, still laughing our heads off. They asked where on earth we had been. We explained that we had been stuck in a maze of corridors in total darkness. We then told them that when we did eventually manage to find our allocated rooms, like all the other rooms they were dreadful. So, needless to say, we made our apologies and beat a hasty retreat.

There are people who say that they cannot believe in God because they cannot see Him. They say it's impossible to believe in something you cannot see. I wonder if they believe in electricity? They can't see it, but every time they switch it on, they expect to see a bulb light up. True, we can't see God, but we can see His work in His wonderful creation. Look at the sea, the stars, the flowers, animals, birds and a newborn baby.

THE POINT **Looking at His wonderful creation, I find it's harder not to believe in God than it is to believe Him.**

PRAYER *Lord, today I can't see You, but I can see Your beauty in the things You have created.*

21 DEC

'Then Manoah prayed to the LORD, "O Lord, I beg you, let the man of God you sent to us come again to teach us how to bring up the boy who is to be born."' Judges 13:8

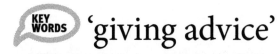

KEY WORDS 'giving advice'

I WAS PLAYING at a family musical event on a fairly high stage that had steps up the front. The stage itself was safe but the steps were dangerously steep and I was frightened that little children could get hurt if they started playing on them. I made an announcement and asked all the parents to please keep their children off the steps. Halfway through the first song a small child came rushing to the front and started playing on the steps. When the song finished I announced once again, please could a parent take the child down from the steps because I was frightened that she would fall off and hurt herself. A mother came and did so. From then on, during nearly every song, the child ran forward and started climbing the steps with sometimes the parent following and other times not. I was watching the child's face and could see she was deliberately rebelling against her mother's instructions and the mother didn't know what to do about it. At the end of the evening someone told me that the child had special needs and that accounted for the behaviour problem. I disagreed; looking at the defiance on the little one's face I felt she needed to be disciplined. It frightens me to think how that child will turn out when she gets older if someone doesn't give advice and help to the mother.

Manoah was Samson's father and he had been given specific instructions on how God wanted his child to be raised. Manoah, like most fathers, wanted to get it right and wanted help on how to do the job properly. Whatever anyone says, bringing up children in the way of God is no easy task. I have discovered that, as parents, we do our best, but when we get stuck, it's no shame to get advice from other godly parents who may be older than us and whose children have grown up.

 THE POINT — **None of us have all the answers; that is why the family of God needs to listen to advice from others.**

 PRAYER — *Lord, today help me to be able to advise, and also to listen to advice from others.*

22 DEC

'Thus the saying "One sows and another reaps" is true.' John 4:37

KEY WORD: 'reap'

NOWADAYS FARMING IS very different to when I was a farm labourer back in 1964. Sowing and reaping are now accomplished through amazing machines and usually only a skilled tractor driver is needed for both tasks. Back in 1964 winters were much colder than they are today which made those tasks worse. One of the first jobs I was given when I arrived on the farm at the age of 15½ was 'mangelwurzel' harvesting. Before arriving at the farm I thought mangelwurzels were people who lived in the country, not a crop to be harvested. I discovered that the mangel was similar to a large swede and that it originates from the beet crop. It was used to feed cattle over the winter months. In those days sowing was easily achieved by tractor but reaping was dreadful. Every morning we would venture out into the mangel field in the freezing cold, pull these things out of the ground, and then with a sharp machete cut off the green tops and throw the root on to a trailer. The worst thing was that the mangel was still covered in frost and it was impossible to pull it out of the ground wearing gloves. By the time the trailer was full, my back was breaking and my fingers were frostbitten and bleeding. I can understand why the mangel has become extinct on the British farm!

I am sure that I have said this before, but I think that I have one of the most enjoyable ministries imaginable. Although it's not always the easiest, I do praise God that I can do what I do. Every week I sing songs and share the good news of Jesus with all ages. And every week I find people who want to change and decide to follow Jesus. I have to say that's a lot more rewarding than reaping mangels! But I also appreciate the fact that, before I arrive on the scene, there are church leaders, parents, children's workers, friends, etc. who have done all the hard work, week in, week out, sowing the Word of God faithfully into people's lives.

THE POINT **There would be nothing for me to reap, if sowers had not faithfully sowed beforehand.**

PRAYER *Lord, today I thank You for both sowers and reapers.*

23 DEC *'There are different kinds of gifts, but the same Spirit.' 1 Corinthians 12:4*

'special gifts'

WHEN I BUY Christmas presents for people I like to surprise them. Many Christmases ago I really did surprise Irene! Just for a change I decided to buy her some new clothes. This was something that I had rarely done before. I discreetly asked her what size she was and then off I went to search in the ladies department store. Now this was a new experience for me and not one that I was to enjoy very much. I had seen other poor husbands being dragged around these shops by their wives, but Irene had never demanded such a torture for me. However, it was a challenge for a loving husband, and I was determined, despite my embarrassment, to put myself out and see it through. Finally, I found some items I thought she would like and the good news was that there was a sale of two items for one! Once home I carefully wrapped up the clothes and put them under the Christmas tree, hoping that Irene's taste would be similar to mine. Christmas morning came and all the family sat around the tree as I handed out the presents. Then I handed Irene her first article of clothing and waited with baited breath to see her reaction. As she opened it her face dropped. What was wrong, was it the colour or the design? No. The problem was that I had misheard her when she told me her size and all the garments I had bought for her were eight sizes too big! Needless to say these were not the best gifts she received that year, and from then on I thought I would forget clothes and resort back to the safety of flowers and a good old-fashioned box of chocolates!

In 1 Corinthians 12:8–10, we have Paul's list of the gifts of the Holy Spirit. These are supernatural presents that God gives to those who would both like them and need them. The great news is that these gifts are given to all ages and to both sexes! They are not just for church leaders.

THE POINT **These special gifts do not make us more spiritual, but they do show those around us that the supernatural power of Jesus is still at work today.**

PRAYER *Lord, today I want to thank You for all Your supernatural gifts.*

24 DEC *'But the fruit of the Spirit is love …' Galatians 5:22*

KEY WORDS 'special fruit'

PLAYING IN BANDS like Ishmael United and Rev Counta and the Speedoze were some of the hardest years of my life. As a band we were too Christian to be accepted by the secular world and too secular to be accepted by the Christian world. This dilemma caused tension among band members. Pete our drummer sometimes arrived irritable at a gig and kicked his drum cases all over the stage. Laurie our bass player sometimes arrived hurt as cutting remarks had been made on the journey, and being the most sensitive member in the band, he would be deeply affected by these comments. Dave our guitarist would sometimes arrive at a gig quite cynical and critical. I would arrive ready to argue with both the organisers and the band. On one occasion Dave and I had an argument over drumsticks. I had wound him up so much that he grabbed me and started thumping me against the side of the van. And this was with an organiser watching! On reflection, very little of the fruit of the spirit could be seen in our personal lives, even though I was preaching about the love of Jesus over a microphone to vast audiences. The good news is that today all of the members of both bands have a great love and respect for each other. Whenever we meet up it's laughs all round as we reflect on the 'war stories' from the old band days.

But the fruit of the Spirit is not just love. It's also joy, peace, patience, kindness, goodness, faithfulness, gentleness and self-control. Try to imagine that we are like fruit trees. When we first began to follow Jesus our branches were very bare, but the more we get to know and become like Jesus the more His wonderful fruit mentioned above begins to both grow and show in our lives.

THE POINT **Some Christians become very unhappy because they do not become perfect instantly. Fruit always takes time to grow, and some fruit takes longer than others, but one thing is guaranteed, the closer we walk with Jesus, the nicer people we will be.**

PRAYER *Lord, I pray that others may see the fruit of the Spirit in my life today.*

25 DEC *'She will give birth to a son, and you are to give him the name Jesus …' Matthew 1:21*

KEY WORD 'Christmas'

ON 25 JANUARY Scottish people celebrate the birth of Robert Burns by piping in the haggis. The haggis is carried on a silver platter with a piper leading the way, followed by the chef. Many years ago, two close friends of ours, Mike and Katey, decided to join us for our Christmas lunch. They had a huge oven so they offered to cook the turkey. We agreed to sort out the rest and then we would all eat at our house. As we were all a little crazy, we decided to start our own tradition of piping in the Christmas turkey. After the Christmas morning service we went to their home to collect the cooked turkey. We dressed in appropriate clothes and Mike even found a kilt to wear to make the occasion even more authentic. I brought along a ghetto blaster and my wheelbarrow, which we decorated with Christmas paper and tinsel. The turkey was carefully placed on a silver platter, then put into the wheelbarrow. We formed a straight line with the ghetto blaster blasting out carols, and the chef led the march to our house a few doors away. It must have looked rather strange; a group of oddly dressed people pushing a turkey in a wheelbarrow while carol singing. But all new traditions I guess must seem rather odd in their infancy, to the uninitiated. Why did we do it? I have no idea. Sadly, the tradition of 'piping the turkey' never caught on, but we did have fun, and so did all our neighbours watching us.

Joseph was a good man and probably quite a lot older than Mary. They had been betrothed for some time. All was going well and then suddenly he discovered that she was pregnant, and he knew the baby was not his. Soon afterwards, an angel appeared to him in a dream telling him not to worry as God was the baby's Father and that he should call the baby Jesus, because He would save the people from their sins.

Joseph did all that the angel had told him to. He must really have been a very obedient man. I guess that's why God chose him.

Lord, today, like Joseph, help me to be obedient and to do the things You ask me to do.

26 DEC

'I was pushed back and about to fall, but the LORD helped me.' Psalm 118:13

KEY WORD **'pushed'**

I WAS INVITED to attend a national church leaders' conference. As usual, everyone seemed very excited about attending except me! Now don't get me wrong, I enjoy both fellowship and teaching but I don't like being cooped up inside when the sun is shining outside. I think, weather permitting, we should follow Jesus' example and whenever possible hold our meetings in the open air. When coffee time eventually arrived, there came the chance for any who were not interested in debating the contents of the last meeting to escape into the fresh air. One of my friends joined me and he was feeling as silly as I was. It was time to have some fun. Not too far away from the main door of the conference centre was a long, low wall. I jumped up on to it and told my friend to join me. I suggested a game where we would see who could be the first one to knock the other off the wall just by using our shoulders. Now what I hadn't counted on was that my friend was quite a lot bigger and heavier than I was, so he might have had a slight advantage. Well, the battle began and, for a while, both of us managed to keep our balance. By now some of the bemused delegates were watching us in between discussing deep theological matters. Then I must have had a momentary lapse of concentration because my friend charged at me and I went flying off the wall and crashing to the ground. I didn't forget that game for a very long time because when I fell from the wall I cracked a few ribs and the pain was an ever-present reminder. We have all at times been 'spiritually' pushed off the wall; all it takes is someone to say an unkind word to us and to put us down.

Let's never forget that we may often be pushed back, but the Lord is always there to catch us and to help us to stand up again.

Lord, today help me to realise that every time I am unfairly pushed and about to fall, You are ready to catch me so the hurt need not last.

27 DEC *'I can do everything through him who gives me strength.' Philippians 4:13*

'I can do everything'

EDUCATION PLUS IS the Christian charity working with very poor children in Costa Rica. There, education is free but to attend lessons the children must have a school uniform, shoes, books, etc. Education Plus encourages people to sponsor children and so allow them to have both education and a future. Irene and I became patrons of this valuable work and were invited to visit them and see what they were doing first hand. Keith, who was leading the project, gave us a few tips before we started walking around the shanty towns and one of them was not to drink anything. On our travels a child invited us into his hut to meet his mother. As we entered the hut and sat down, his mother kindly offered me a red-coloured drink. I had no idea what it was and I could see Keith shaking his head. This lady who had absolutely nothing was offering me something out the kindness of her heart. I could not refuse and gulped down this strange-tasting liquid. I was praying that I would not get an upset stomach because the toilet consisted of a hole in the ground and I feared I might catch something even worse if I used it, but of course I was fine. Drinking some unknown liquid in a shanty town was not something I would have chosen to do, but God gave both me and my stomach the strength to do what was right.

Today's verse by itself sounds great, but it follows on from Paul's exclamation that he had known what it was like to be in need, and also to have plenty. He'd known what it was like to be well fed and also hungry. This means that there may be times when we are hungry and in need, and that's not always a sign that we are out of the will of God. Paul continues that only when we are content in all situations will we be able to do everything through God's strength.

We must be as happy and content when we are hungry or in need as we are when we are well fed and have plenty. That's a challenge!

Lord, today I know that nothing is impossible with You here to help me.

'So Lot chose for himself the whole plain of the Jordan and set out towards the east.' Genesis 13:11

KEY WORD 'best'

WHEN I WAS young I decided I wanted to join the Scouts because a lot of my school friends were Sea Scouts. I'll be honest with you, I was never a good Sea Scout, I never even managed to achieve my first-class badge. Our scoutmaster decided that the troop would go away camping for a week in the New Forest and I was really excited about this. On arrival we looked around the forest to find the best place to pitch our tents; next to the picturesque river seemed the ideal spot. Once we were all set up it started to rain. The scoutmaster decided that as there was little that we could do in the wet forest that night, we should drive into Southampton and spend the night at the movies. This seemed like a brilliant idea. However, while we were in the warm cinema enjoying our film, unknown to us the gentle rain had turned into a raging torrential storm! When we left the cinema and got back into our vehicles water was everywhere and when we tried to get back to our campsite we discovered that the river had flooded and washed all our tents and belongings downstream. Fortunately a kind vicar allowed us to sleep in his parish church. I found that very cold and creepy. It's strange, beside the river looked the best place to camp but it worked out to be the worst possible place in the whole forest.

Travelling together was not working for friends Abraham and Lot. There just wasn't enough grass for their enormous flocks and herds. Abraham didn't want to lose his friendship with Lot, so gave him first choice of the land. Lot saw the best land was towards the east and chose that. The problem was, while Lot chose what looked good, he also chose to head towards Sodom and Gomorrah, the most wicked places on earth.

THE POINT **What's best is not always what looks the best. Best is knowing God's heart and living our lives according to His plans.**

PRAYER *Lord, today help me to know the difference between what looks good to me, and what is best to You.*

29 DEC

'For I am convinced that neither death nor life …
will be able to separate us from the love of God that
is in Christ Jesus our Lord.' Romans 8:38–39

KEY WORD ‘loneliness’

BUT IT'S NOT just 'death nor life', the verse continues, it's 'neither angels nor demons, neither the present nor the future, nor any powers, neither height nor depth, nor anything else in all creation'. I think that must just about cover everything. As I have mentioned elsewhere, when I was 15, I left home to pursue a farming career in a town called Petworth. Although it was not many miles away from my family home, it seemed like the other end of the world to me. I have also explained elsewhere that I was raised in a Christian community, where I was surrounded by Christian people day and night. This was going to be a new experience for me, living in a town where I didn't know anyone and living with a family that would not claim to be Christian. I was very frightened of this new life before me. I didn't share my fear with my parents because I felt that I was now a man and had to learn to stand on my own two feet. When people see me now they cannot imagine a shy quiet person, but in those days I was just that. For many months I would spend every night shut in my bedroom. I was far too nervous to go downstairs and sit with the family in the lounge. I didn't really feel that they would want me with them. I had never known loneliness like this before. I was away from the people I loved most and away from the ones who loved me. Of course now I realise that God was with me and would help me, but even with the Christian upbringing that I had experienced, I cannot remember anyone teaching me how I could find God in such a lonely situation.

THE POINT Let's remember today's verse when we are feeling alone and thinking that nobody cares or loves us. Nothing and no one can ever separate us from God's love. You'd think that the whole world would want to follow Christ just by reading this verse, wouldn't you?

PRAYER *Lord, today I thank You that I need never feel lonely and realise that nothing could stop You loving me.*

30 DEC *'Children obey your parents in the Lord, for this is right.' Ephesians 6:1*

KEY WORDS 'children obey'

MANY YEARS AGO Irene and I took our three young children for a holiday on the Isle of Wight. The two boys had been surprisingly good so I took them to a local toy shop and allowed them to choose the toy of their choice, within a certain price range of course! After searching every shelf in the shop they both decided to buy water pistols and as it was a nice hot summer's day, I agreed to this, knowing that they would have a lot fun squirting water at each other. I did warn them that they were not allowed to use them in the apartment where we were staying, they must just play with them outside. They were having great fun with their new toys in the garden but then they entered the house and disobeyed me. Once they had re-filled their water pistols they suddenly started squirting each other in the lounge. Now I rarely lose my temper, but for some reason or other at this moment I did. I was very angry with them both, ran over to them, and grabbed both the pistols from them. I threw the offending pistols outside smashing them on to the concrete path. I will always regret doing this and still feel ashamed of myself today. Disciplining children is very important but I wonder how a child observes a parent who is not able to control their temper. It never happened again so hopefully I did learn my lesson and became a slightly better example to my children.

God knows that no parent is perfect. All parents sometimes make the wrong decisions, all parents sometimes say the wrong things, and all parents at some time or other are really bad examples and role models. But still, even after saying all this, the Bible does say that children should obey their parents.

THE POINT Let's never forget though, that like husband and wife, parenting is all about a relationship with our children. I believe the more that parents give real love, respect and attention to their children the more obedience they will get in return.

 PRAYER *Lord, today help parents to love their children more, and for children to be more obedient to their parents.*

31 DEC

'He walked right through the crowd and went on his way.' Luke 4:30

'near death experience'

VACCINATING CHICKENS AGAINST infectious bronchitis and fowl pest was not a very pleasant vocation. But the upside was, I travelled with a team and we always had fun – well, usually. Very early one winter's morning we loaded the Land Rover with vaccine and overalls. It was very cold and I was wearing a leather flying jacket with a high collar and wool lining. As we drove off in the dark I decided to have a sleep in the back. We had only been travelling for about 30 minutes when I heard a scream as the Land Rover hit a patch of black ice and went totally out of control. The next thing I knew was that our vehicle had left the road and was rolling over. It ended upside down in someone's front garden but I was not in it. As it rolled the back door burst open and I was thrown out on to the mud. We were all very shaken but miraculously no one was seriously injured. As we waited for the ambulance to arrive I suddenly realised that the collar of my flying jacket was missing. Then I saw it hanging on the rear door of the Land Rover; it had been torn clean off. I realised that I had been a fraction of an inch from death. If I had not been wearing that jacket that collar would have been my neck.

Jesus experienced some 'near death experiences'. He was preaching in His hometown of Nazareth, surrounded by supposedly old friends and neighbours, probably some whom He had known throughout His childhood. Unfortunately, they didn't enjoy Jesus' preaching. In fact, they detested both Him and what He said so much that they tried to kill Him by threatening to throw Him off a cliff. No chance. No one was going to take Jesus' life from Him; only when the time was right, would He be given over to be crucified.

God has a plan and a set time for all of us to be on this earth. He was not going to let me die in a Land Rover accident at the age of 19 when He had other things for me later on in life.

Thank You, Lord, that both my birth and death are in Your hands.

Ish is a one-off! His spiritual journey has been larger than life, which is why he is such a hit with children and young people. This book is full of stories about people Ish has met; some are serious, some hilarious, but all appear in these pages for one purpose: to bring the Bible to life, and to help us in *our* daily lives to learn more about the good news of Jesus.

Ish now has become a Deacon in the Church of England, based at Chichester Cathedral, where he and Irene worship. As Ish would say, 'Who'd have thought it!' But he would add, 'Thanks be to God,' and so do I for this gem of a book.

Nicholas Frayling
Dean of Chichester

....

To have Ish as a friend is to learn to play. The man loves to turn life into a game. But his game playing has a serious side. Ish is someone who has been playing hide and seek with truth and reality for as long as I've known him. Unwilling to just download what everyone else says about God and make it his own, he is someone who has been hunting for genuine spirituality all his life. And that means that he's been willing to change, and even admit that he's got it wrong at times. He's taken some steps that even his closest friends would never have anticipated. As one loved by hundreds of thousands of children, Ish exemplifies the heart of a child – still ready to embrace wonder, still open to new ideas (or old ideas overlooked) and still wearing a face that slips most naturally into a smile. Life is still an adventure, a lark in the park with God who, according to Dallas Willard, is always at play throughout the earth. The fun continues.

I'm privileged to call him friend, and play along whenever I can.

Jeff Lucas

NATIONAL DISTRIBUTORS

UK: (and countries not listed below)
CWR, Waverley Abbey House, Waverley Lane, Farnham, Surrey GU9 8EP.
Tel: (01252) 784700 Outside UK (44) 1252 784700

AUSTRALIA: CMC Australasia, PO Box 519, Belmont, Victoria 3216.
Tel: (03) 5241 3288 Fax: (03) 5241 3290

CANADA: Cook Communications Ministries, PO Box 98, 55 Woodslee Avenue,
Paris, Ontario N3L 3E5. Tel: 1800 263 2664

GHANA: Challenge Enterprises of Ghana, PO Box 5723, Accra.
Tel: (021) 222437/223249 Fax: (021) 226227

HONG KONG: Cross Communications Ltd, 1/F, 562A Nathan Road, Kowloon.
Tel: 2780 1188 Fax: 2770 6229

INDIA: Crystal Communications, 10-3-18/4/1, East Marredpalli, Secunderabad
– 500026, Andhra Pradesh. Tel/Fax: (040) 27737145

KENYA: Keswick Books and Gifts Ltd, PO Box 10242, Nairobi.
Tel: (02) 331692/226047 Fax: (02) 728557

MALAYSIA: Salvation Book Centre (M) Sdn Bhd, 23 Jalan SS 2/64,
47300 Petaling Jaya, Selangor.
Tel: (03) 78766411/78766797 Fax: (03) 78757066/78756360

NEW ZEALAND: CMC Australasia, PO Box 303298, North Harbour,
Auckland 0751. Tel: 0800 449 408 Fax: 0800 449 049

NIGERIA: FBFM, Helen Baugh House, 96 St Finbarr's College Road,
Akoka, Lagos. Tel: (01) 7747429/4700218/825775/827264

PHILIPPINES: OMF Literature Inc, 776 Boni Avenue, Mandaluyong City.
Tel: (02) 531 2183 Fax: (02) 531 1960

SINGAPORE: Alby Commercial Enterprises Pte Ltd, 95 Kallang Avenue #04-00,
AIS Industrial Building, 339420. Tel: (65) 629 27238 Fax: (65) 629 27235

SOUTH AFRICA: Struik Christian Books, 80 MacKenzie Street, PO Box 1144,
Cape Town 8000. Tel: (021) 462 4360 Fax: (021) 461 3612

SRI LANKA: Christombu Publications (Pvt) Ltd, Bartleet House, 65 Braybrooke
Place, Colombo 2. Tel: (9411) 2421073/2447665

TANZANIA: CLC Christian Book Centre, PO Box 1384, Mkwepu Street,
Dar es Salaam. Tel/Fax: (022) 2119439

USA: Cook Communications Ministries, PO Box 98, 55 Woodslee Avenue, Paris,
Ontario N3L 3E5, Canada. Tel: 1800 263 2664

ZIMBABWE: Word of Life Books (Pvt) Ltd, Christian Media Centre, 8 Aberdeen
Road, Avondale, PO Box A480 Avondale, Harare.
Tel: (04) 333355 or 091301188

For email addresses, visit the CWR website: www.cwr.org.uk
CWR is a Registered Charity – Number 294387
CWR is a Limited Company registered in England – Registration Number
1990308

Day and Residential Courses
Counselling Training
Leadership Development
Biblical Study Courses
Regional Seminars
Ministry to Women
Daily Devotionals
Books and Videos
Conference Centre

Trusted all Over the World

CWR HAS GAINED A WORLDWIDE reputation as a centre of excellence for Bible-based training and resources. From our headquarters at Waverley Abbey House, Farnham, England, we have been serving God's people for over 40 years with a vision to help apply God's Word to everyday life and relationships. The daily devotional *Every Day with Jesus* is read by nearly a million readers an issue in more than 150 countries, and our unique courses in biblical studies and pastoral care are respected all over the world. Waverley Abbey House provides a conference centre in a tranquil setting.

For free brochures on our seminars and courses, conference facilities, or a catalogue of CWR resources, please contact us at the following address.
CWR, Waverley Abbey House, Waverley Lane, Farnham, Surrey GU9 8EP, UK

Telephone: +44 (0)1252 784700
Email: mail@cwr.org.uk
Website: www.cwr.org.uk

CWR   **Applying God's Word**
to everyday life and relationships

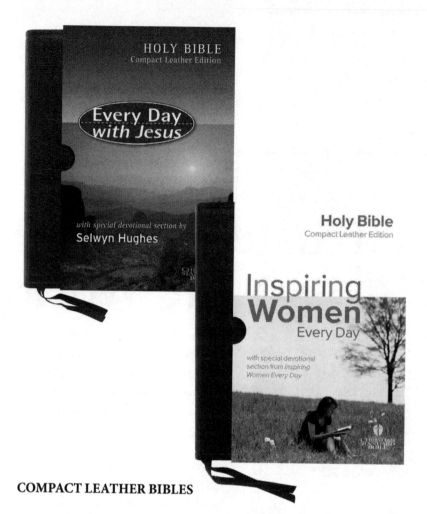

COMPACT LEATHER BIBLES

If you want a Bible to carry with you at all times, one of these would be ideal. They are Holman Christian Standard versions in bonded leather, gilt-edged with two ribbon markers and the words of Jesus in red, presented in a protective slipcase.

The *Every Day with Jesus Compact Bible* comes with an additional 30-day devotional section by Selwyn Hughes; while the *Inspiring Women Every Day Compact Bible* has a devotional section focusing on 'Daughters of the King'.

[EDWJ] ISBN: 978-1-85345-400-4
[IWED] ISBN: 978-1-85345-401-1
£17.99 each
Prices correct at time of printing